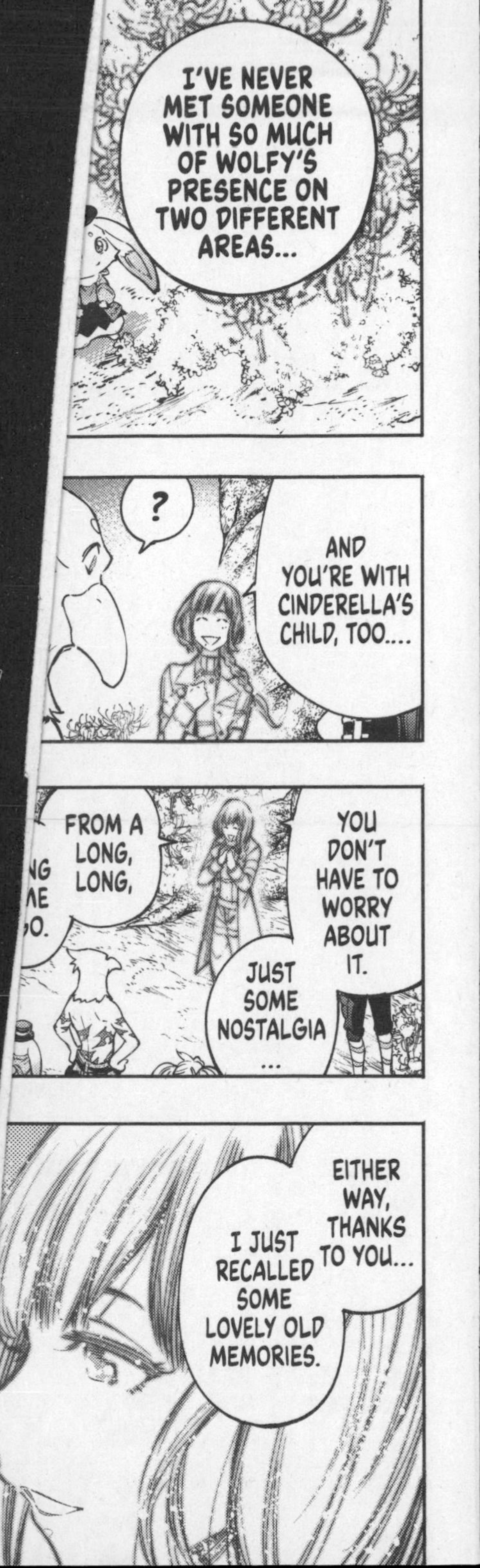

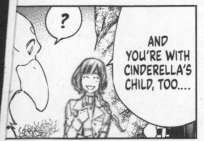

I'VE NEVER MET SOMEONE WITH SO MUCH OF WOLFY'S PRESENCE ON TWO DIFFERENT AREAS...
?
AND YOU'RE WITH CINDERELLA'S CHILD, TOO....
YOU DON'T HAVE TO WORRY ABOUT IT.
FROM A LONG, LONG,
JUST SOME NOSTALGIA ...
EITHER WAY, THANKS TO YOU...
I JUST RECALLED SOME LOVELY OLD MEMORIES.

SHANGRI-LA FRONTIER

4

KATARINA

RYOSUKE FUJI

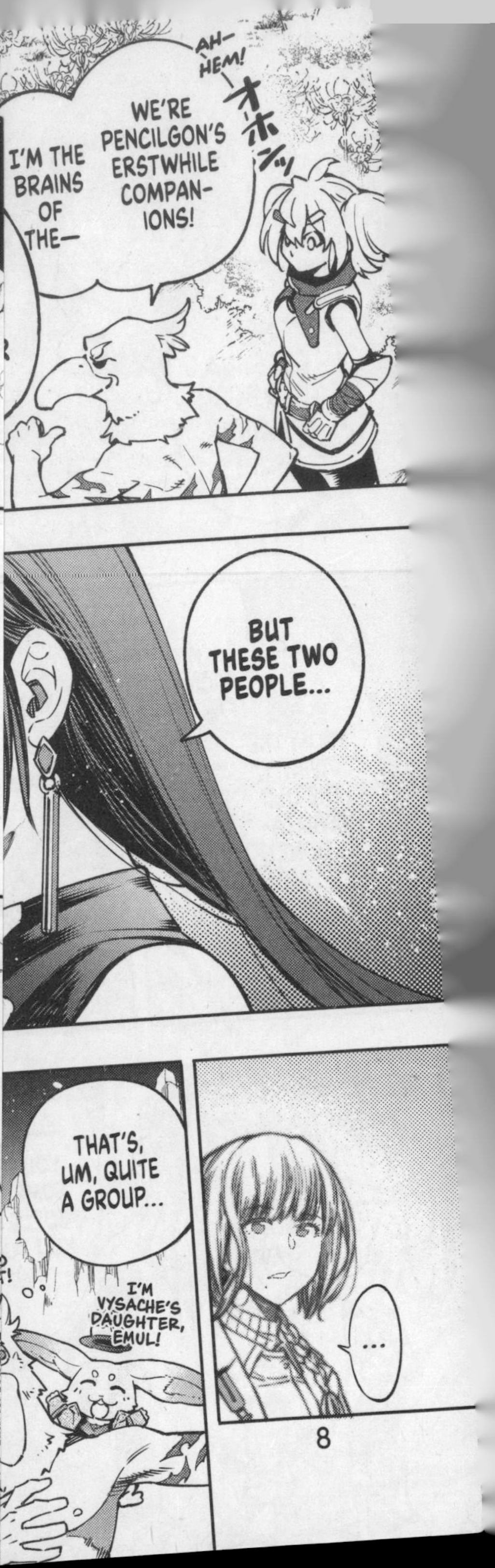
AH-HEM!
オーホンッ
WE'RE PENCILGON'S ERSTWHILE COMPAN-IONS!
I'M THE BRAINS OF THE—
BUT THESE TWO PEOPLE...
...
THAT'S, UM, QUITE A GROUP...
I'M VYSACHE'S DAUGHTER, EMUL!

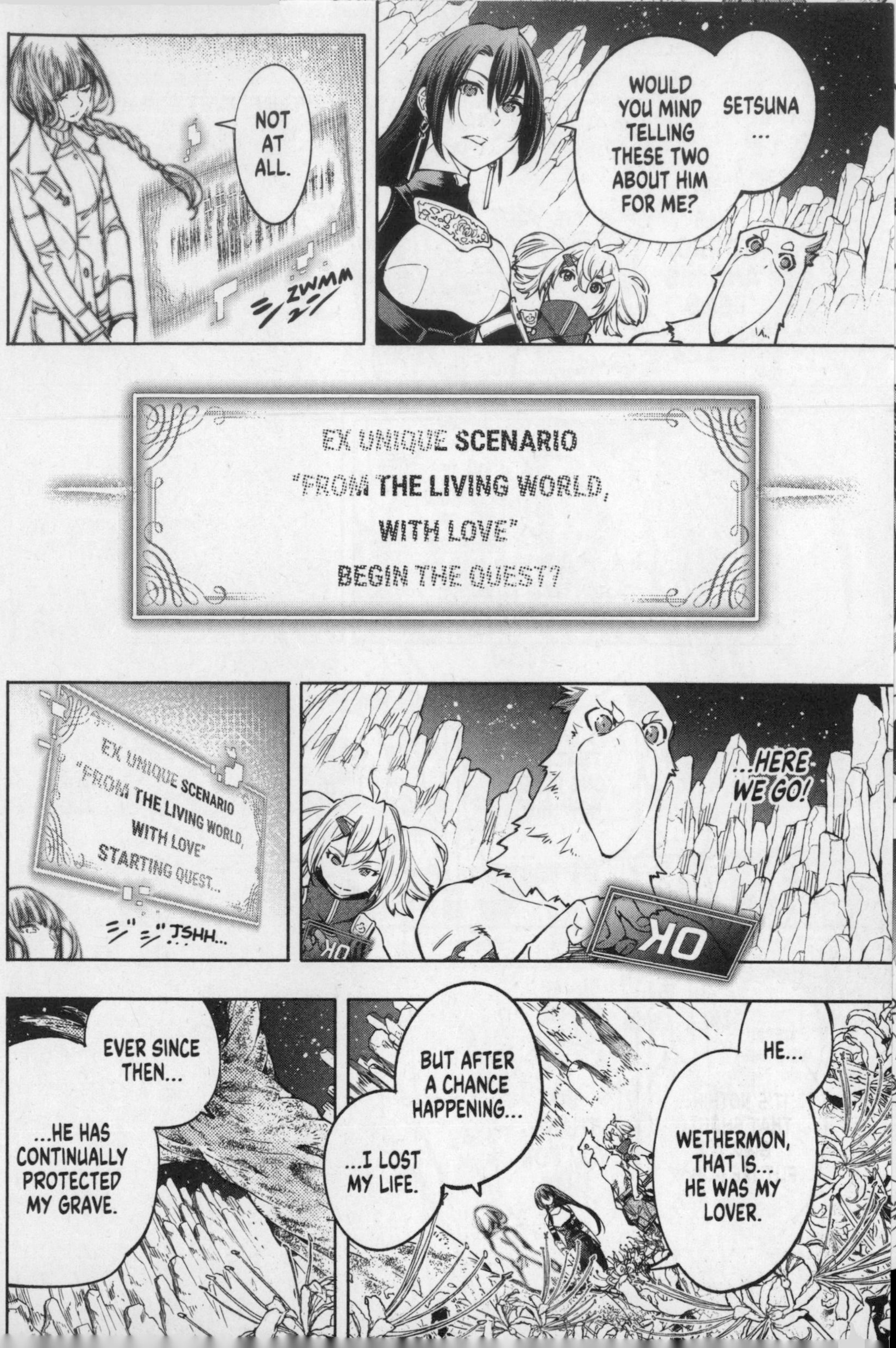
SETSUNA ...
WOULD YOU MIND TELLING THESE TWO ABOUT HIM FOR ME?
NOT AT ALL.
ZWMM
EX UNIQUE SCENARIO
"FROM THE LIVING WORLD,
WITH LOVE"
BEGIN THE QUEST?
...HERE WE GO!
OK
EX UNIQUE SCENARIO
"FROM THE LIVING WORLD,
WITH LOVE"
STARTING QUEST...
JSHH...
HE...
WETHERMON, THAT IS... HE WAS MY LOVER.
BUT AFTER A CHANCE HAPPENING...
...I LOST MY LIFE.
EVER SINCE THEN...
...HE HAS CONTINUALLY PROTECTED MY GRAVE.

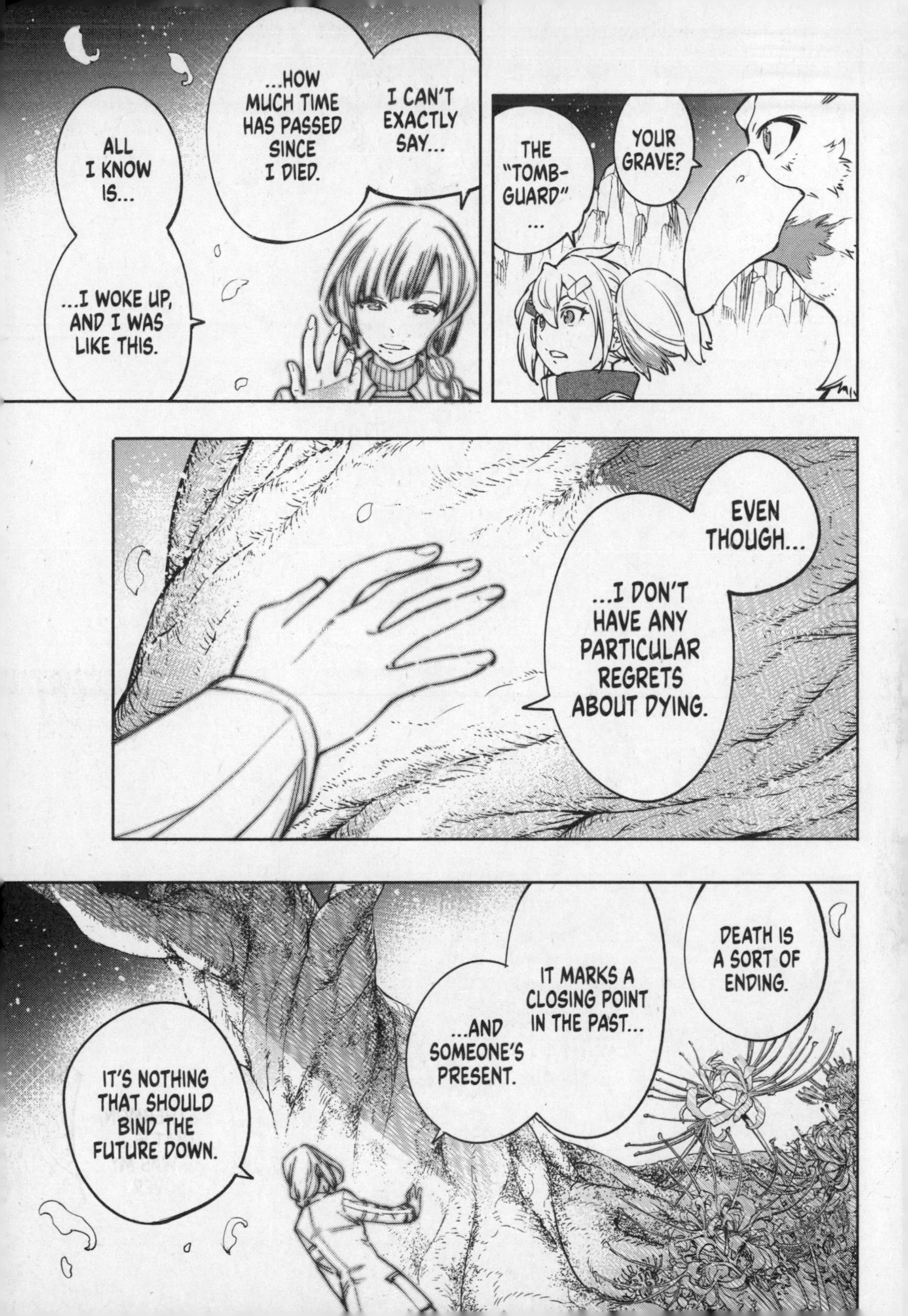
YOUR GRAVE?
THE "TOMB-GUARD"...
I CAN'T EXACTLY SAY...
...HOW MUCH TIME HAS PASSED SINCE I DIED.
ALL I KNOW IS...
...I WOKE UP, AND I WAS LIKE THIS.
EVEN THOUGH...
...I DON'T HAVE ANY PARTICULAR REGRETS ABOUT DYING.
DEATH IS A SORT OF ENDING.
IT MARKS A CLOSING POINT IN THE PAST...
...AND SOMEONE'S PRESENT.
IT'S NOTHING THAT SHOULD BIND THE FUTURE DOWN.

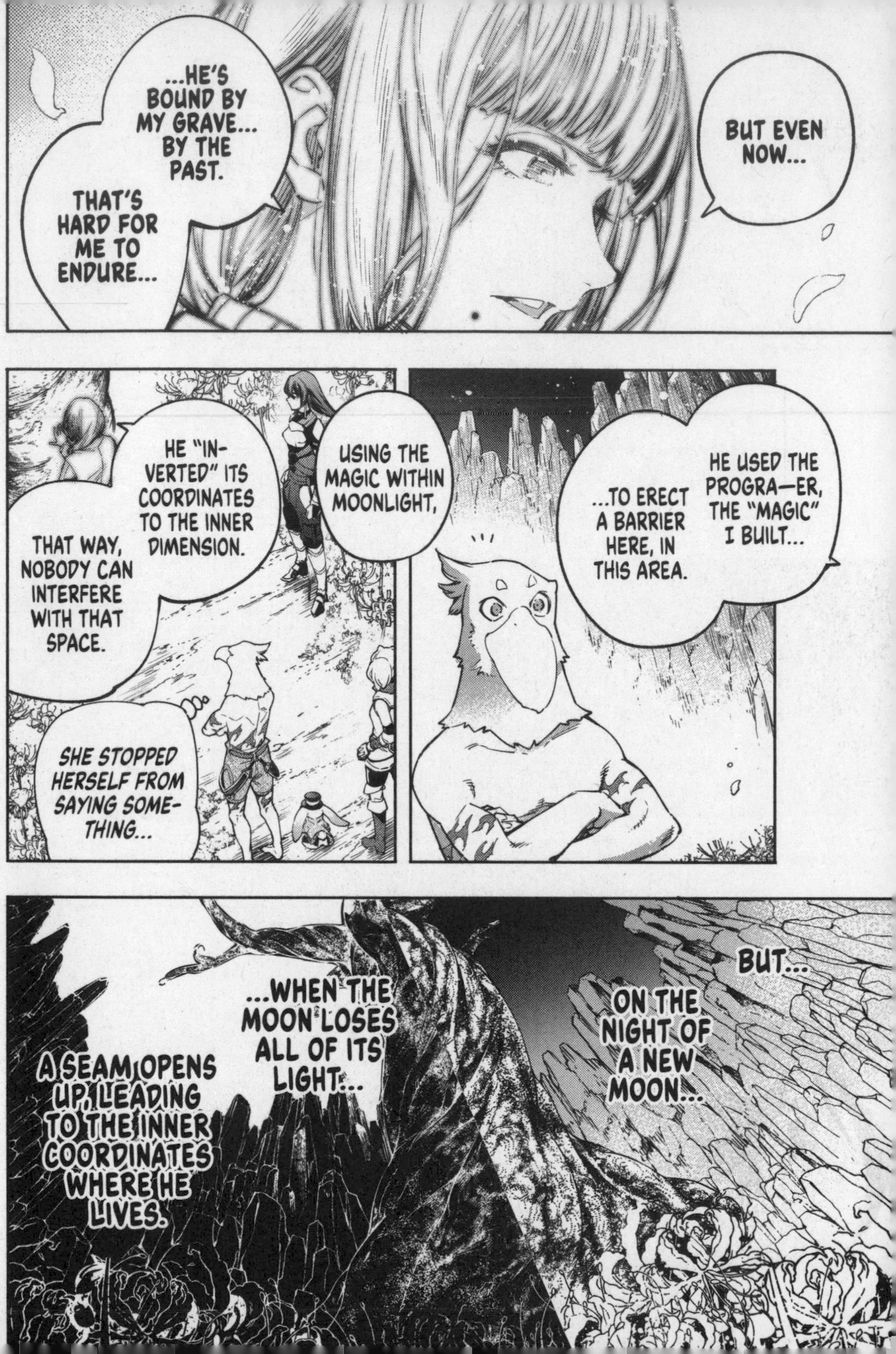
BUT EVEN NOW...
...HE'S BOUND BY MY GRAVE... BY THE PAST.
THAT'S HARD FOR ME TO ENDURE...
HE USED THE PROGRA—ER, THE "MAGIC" I BUILT...
...TO ERECT A BARRIER HERE, IN THIS AREA.
USING THE MAGIC WITHIN MOONLIGHT,
HE "INVERTED" ITS COORDINATES TO THE INNER DIMENSION.
THAT WAY, NOBODY CAN INTERFERE WITH THAT SPACE.
SHE STOPPED HERSELF FROM SAYING SOMETHING...
BUT...
ON THE NIGHT OF A NEW MOON...
...WHEN THE MOON LOSES ALL OF ITS LIGHT...
A SEAM OPENS UP, LEADING TO THE INNER COORDINATES WHERE HE LIVES.

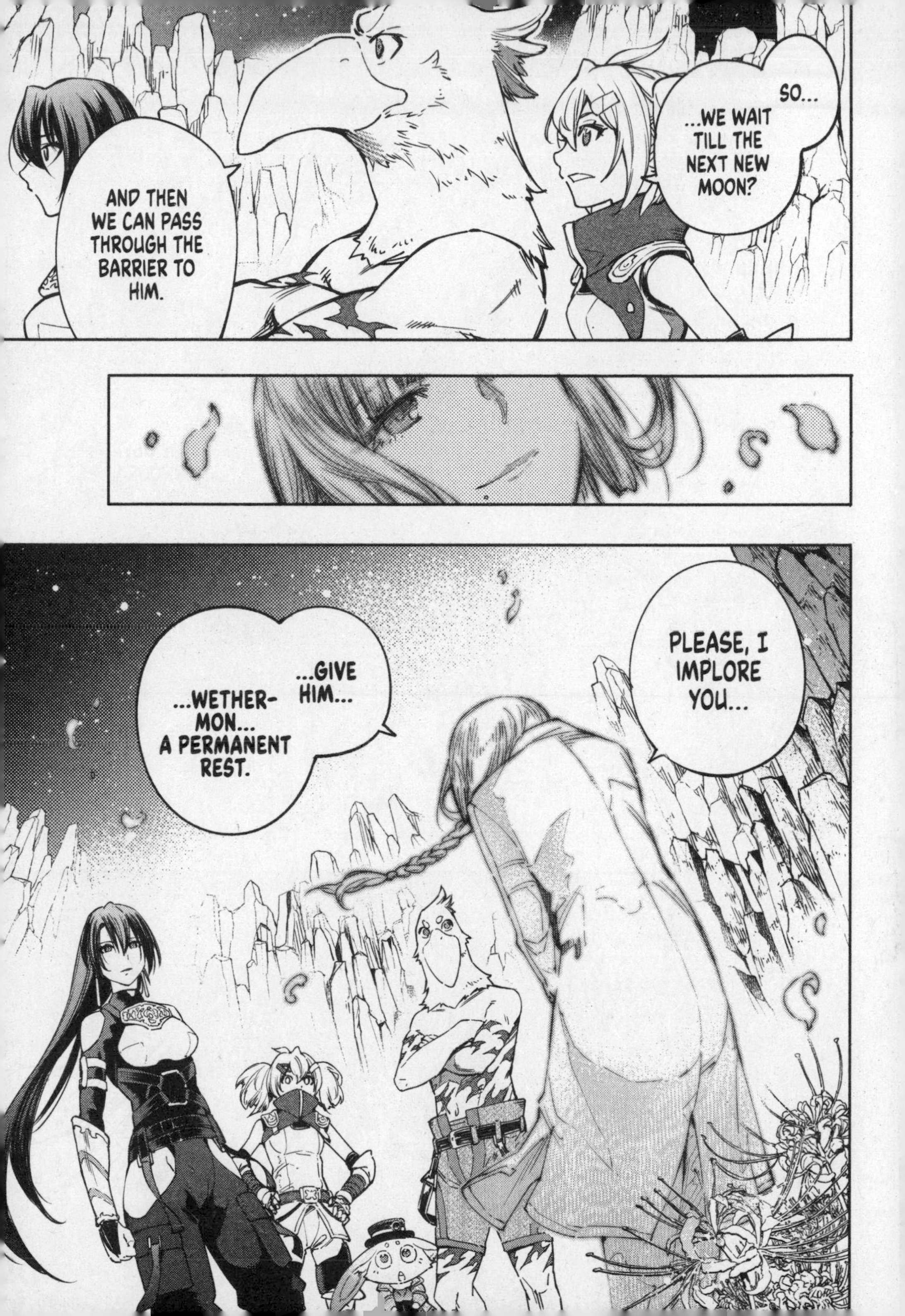
SO... ...WE WAIT TILL THE NEXT NEW MOON?
AND THEN WE CAN PASS THROUGH THE BARRIER TO HIM.
PLEASE, I IMPLORE YOU...
...GIVE HIM...
...WETHER-MON... A PERMANENT REST.

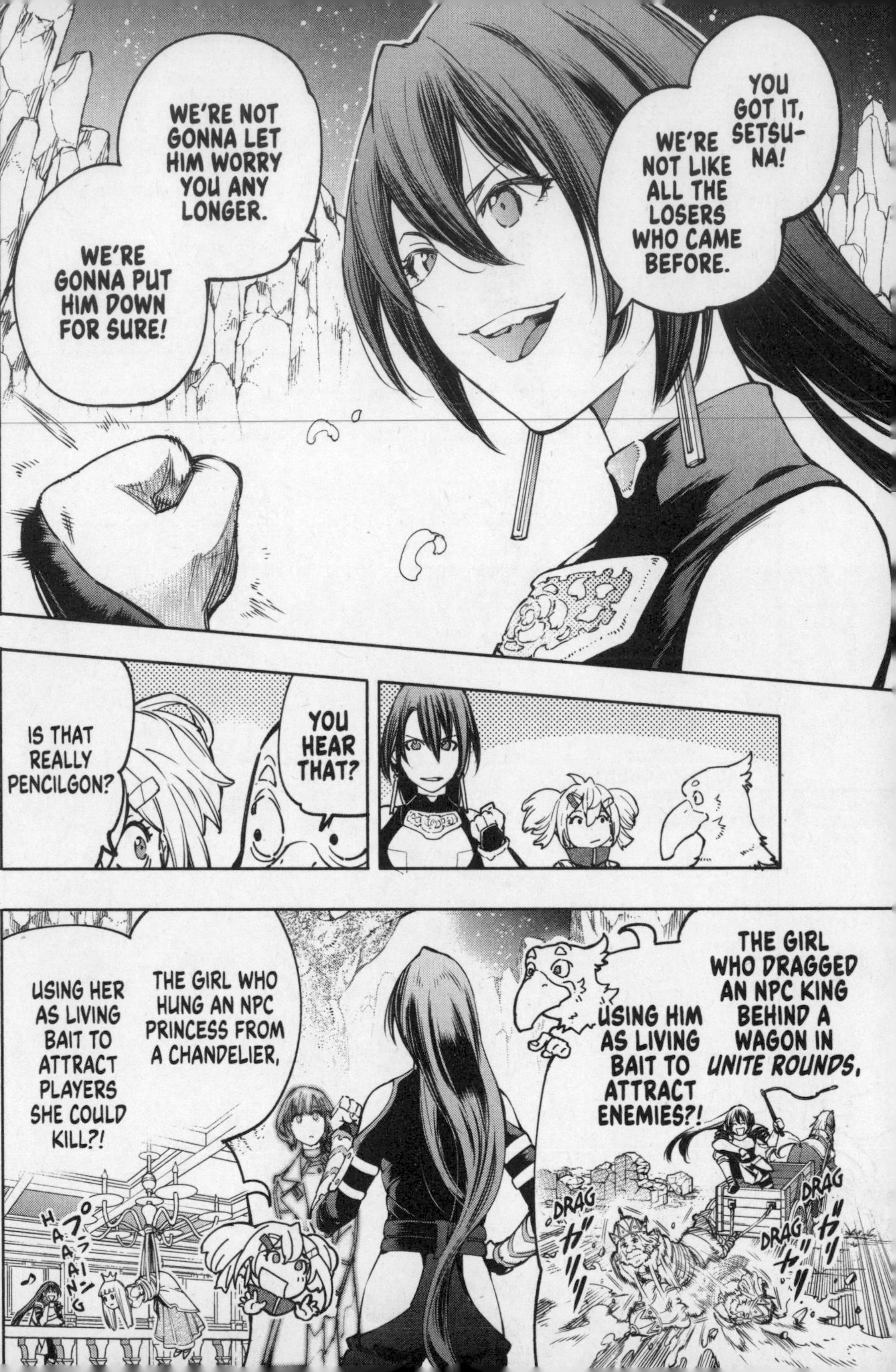
YOU GOT IT, SETSUNA!
WE'RE NOT LIKE ALL THE LOSERS WHO CAME BEFORE.
WE'RE NOT GONNA LET HIM WORRY YOU ANY LONGER.
WE'RE GONNA PUT HIM DOWN FOR SURE!
YOU HEAR THAT?
IS THAT REALLY PENCILGON?
THE GIRL WHO DRAGGED AN NPC KING BEHIND A WAGON IN *UNITE ROUNDS*,
USING HIM AS LIVING BAIT TO ATTRACT ENEMIES?!
DRAG
DRAG
DRAG
THE GIRL WHO HUNG AN NPC PRINCESS FROM A CHANDELIER,
USING HER AS LIVING BAIT TO ATTRACT PLAYERS SHE COULD KILL?!

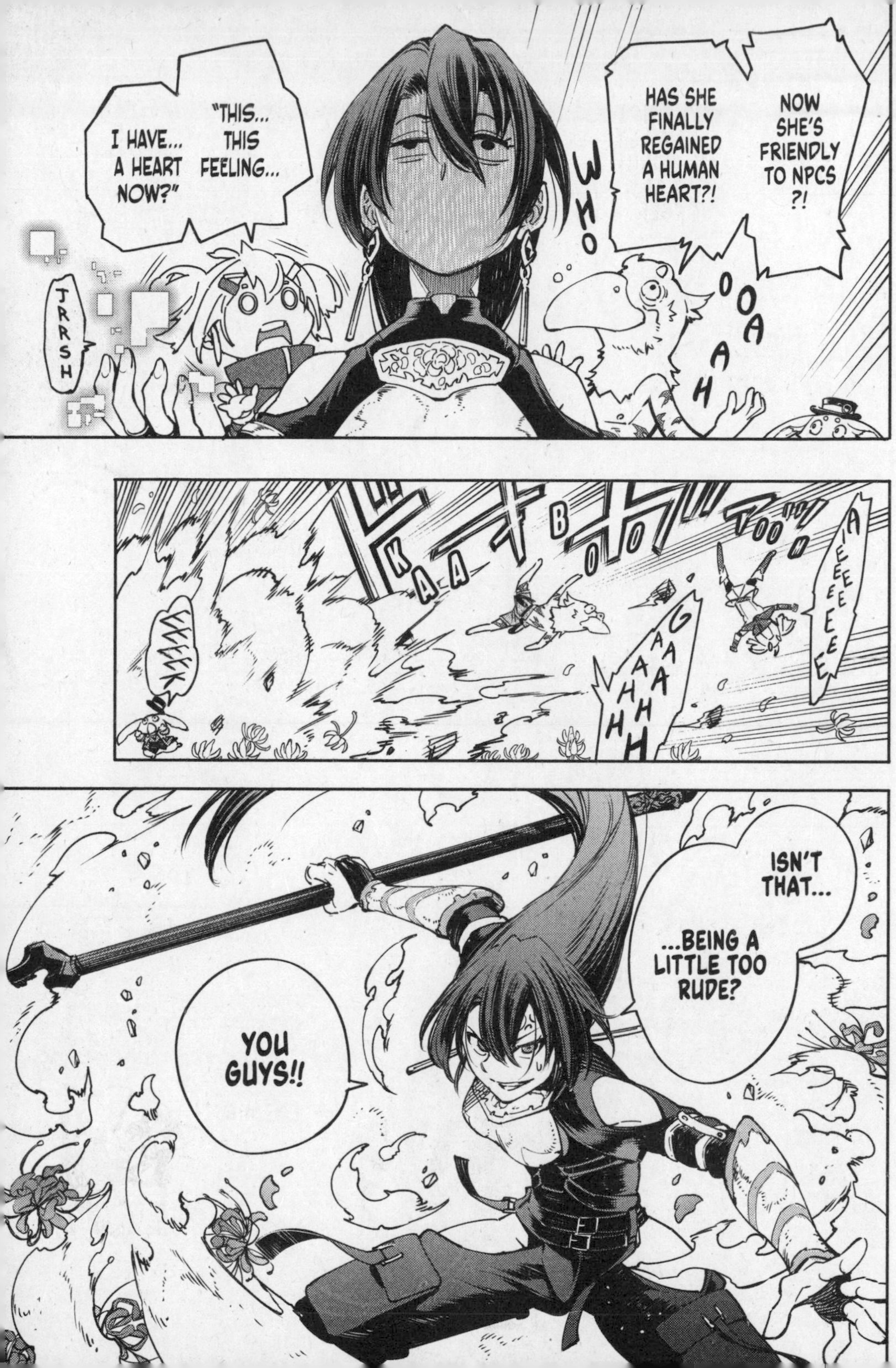
NOW SHE'S FRIENDLY TO NPCS?!
HAS SHE FINALLY REGAINED A HUMAN HEART?!
WHOOOAAH
"THIS... THIS FEELING...
I HAVE... A HEART NOW?"
JRRSH
AIEEEEEEEE
TOOM
GAAAAAHHHH
KAABOOO
EEEEEK
ISN'T THAT...
...BEING A LITTLE TOO RUDE?
YOU GUYS!!

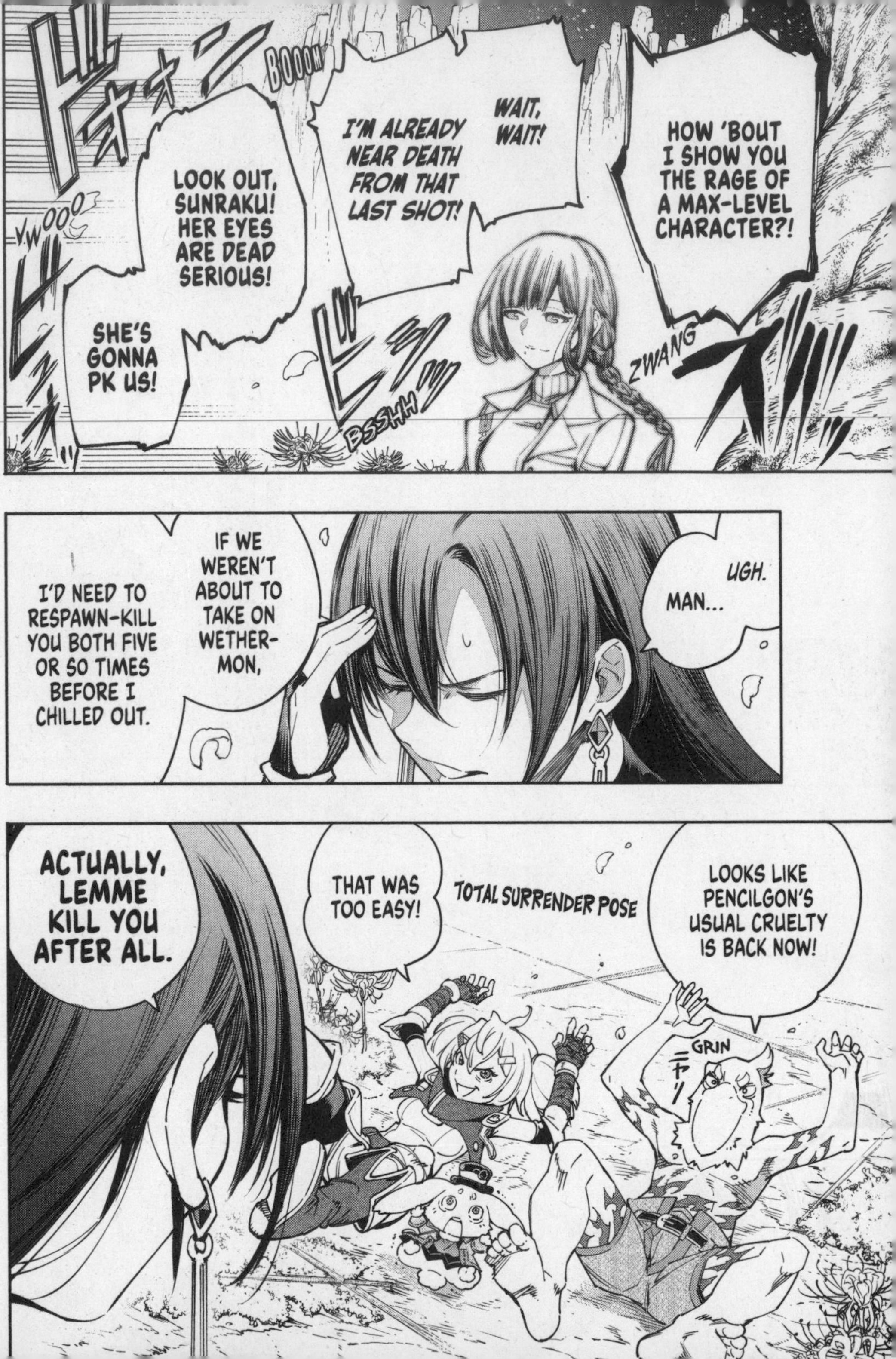
HOW 'BOUT I SHOW YOU THE RAGE OF A MAX-LEVEL CHARACTER?!
ZWANG
WAIT, WAIT!
I'M ALREADY NEAR DEATH FROM THAT LAST SHOT!
BSSHH
BOOOM
LOOK OUT, SUNRAKU! HER EYES ARE DEAD SERIOUS!
SHE'S GONNA PK US!
VWOOO
UGH. MAN...
IF WE WEREN'T ABOUT TO TAKE ON WETHERMON,
I'D NEED TO RESPAWN-KILL YOU BOTH FIVE OR SO TIMES BEFORE I CHILLED OUT.
LOOKS LIKE PENCILGON'S USUAL CRUELTY IS BACK NOW!
GRIN
ニヤリ
TOTAL SURRENDER POSE
THAT WAS TOO EASY!
ACTUALLY, LEMME KILL YOU AFTER ALL.

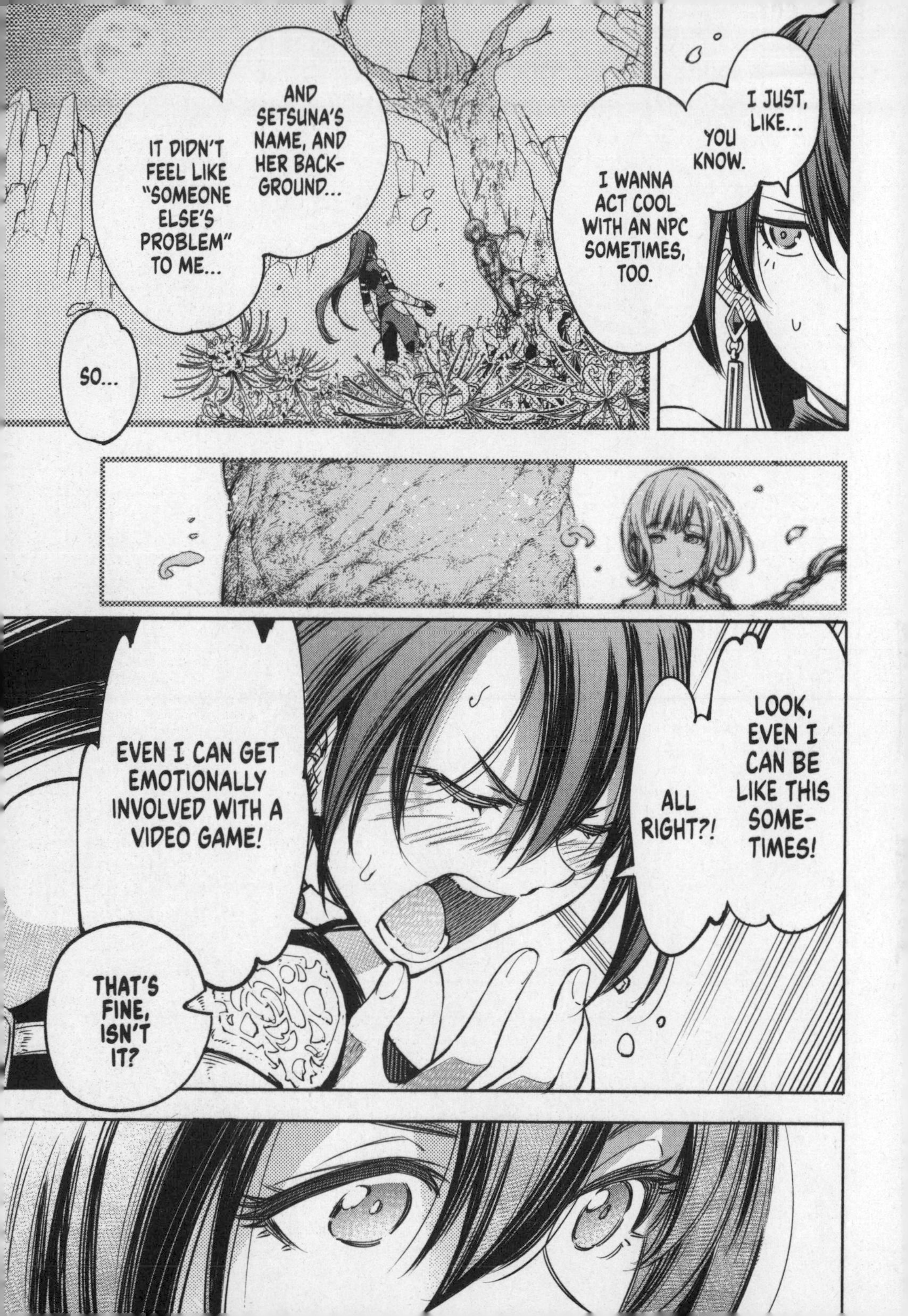
I JUST, LIKE...
YOU KNOW.
I WANNA ACT COOL WITH AN NPC SOMETIMES, TOO.
AND SETSUNA'S NAME, AND HER BACK-GROUND...
IT DIDN'T FEEL LIKE "SOMEONE ELSE'S PROBLEM" TO ME...
SO...
LOOK, EVEN I CAN BE LIKE THIS SOME-TIMES!
ALL RIGHT?!
EVEN I CAN GET EMOTIONALLY INVOLVED WITH A VIDEO GAME!
THAT'S FINE, ISN'T IT?

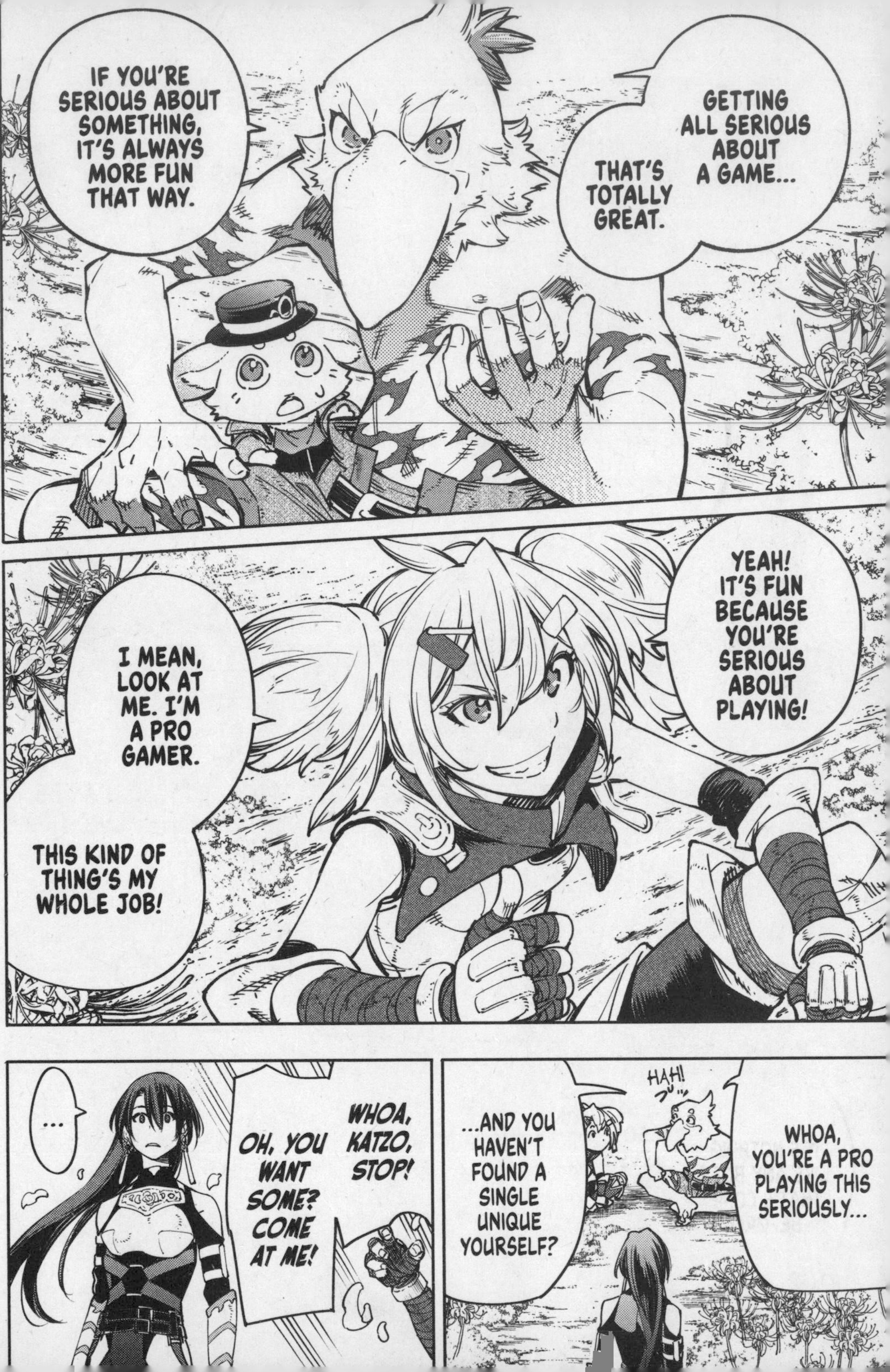
GETTING ALL SERIOUS ABOUT A GAME...
THAT'S TOTALLY GREAT.
IF YOU'RE SERIOUS ABOUT SOMETHING, IT'S ALWAYS MORE FUN THAT WAY.
YEAH! IT'S FUN BECAUSE YOU'RE SERIOUS ABOUT PLAYING!
I MEAN, LOOK AT ME. I'M A PRO GAMER.
THIS KIND OF THING'S MY WHOLE JOB!
WHOA, YOU'RE A PRO PLAYING THIS SERIOUSLY...
HAH!
...AND YOU HAVEN'T FOUND A SINGLE UNIQUE YOURSELF?
WHOA, KATZO, STOP!
OH, YOU WANT SOME? COME AT ME!
...

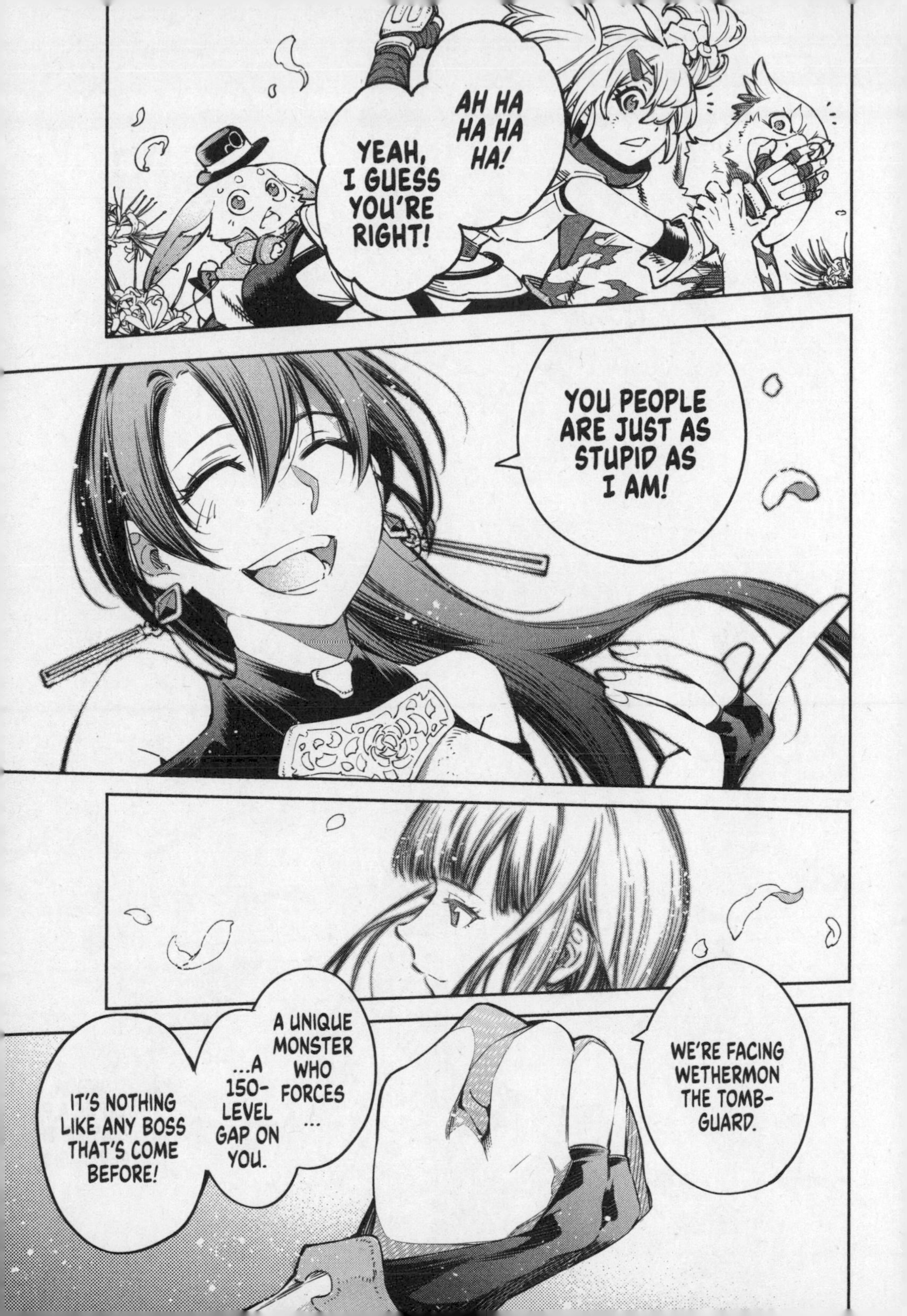
AH HA HA HA HA!
YEAH, I GUESS YOU'RE RIGHT!
YOU PEOPLE ARE JUST AS STUPID AS I AM!
WE'RE FACING WETHERMON THE TOMB-GUARD.
A UNIQUE MONSTER WHO FORCES ...
...A 150-LEVEL GAP ON YOU.
IT'S NOTHING LIKE ANY BOSS THAT'S COME BEFORE!

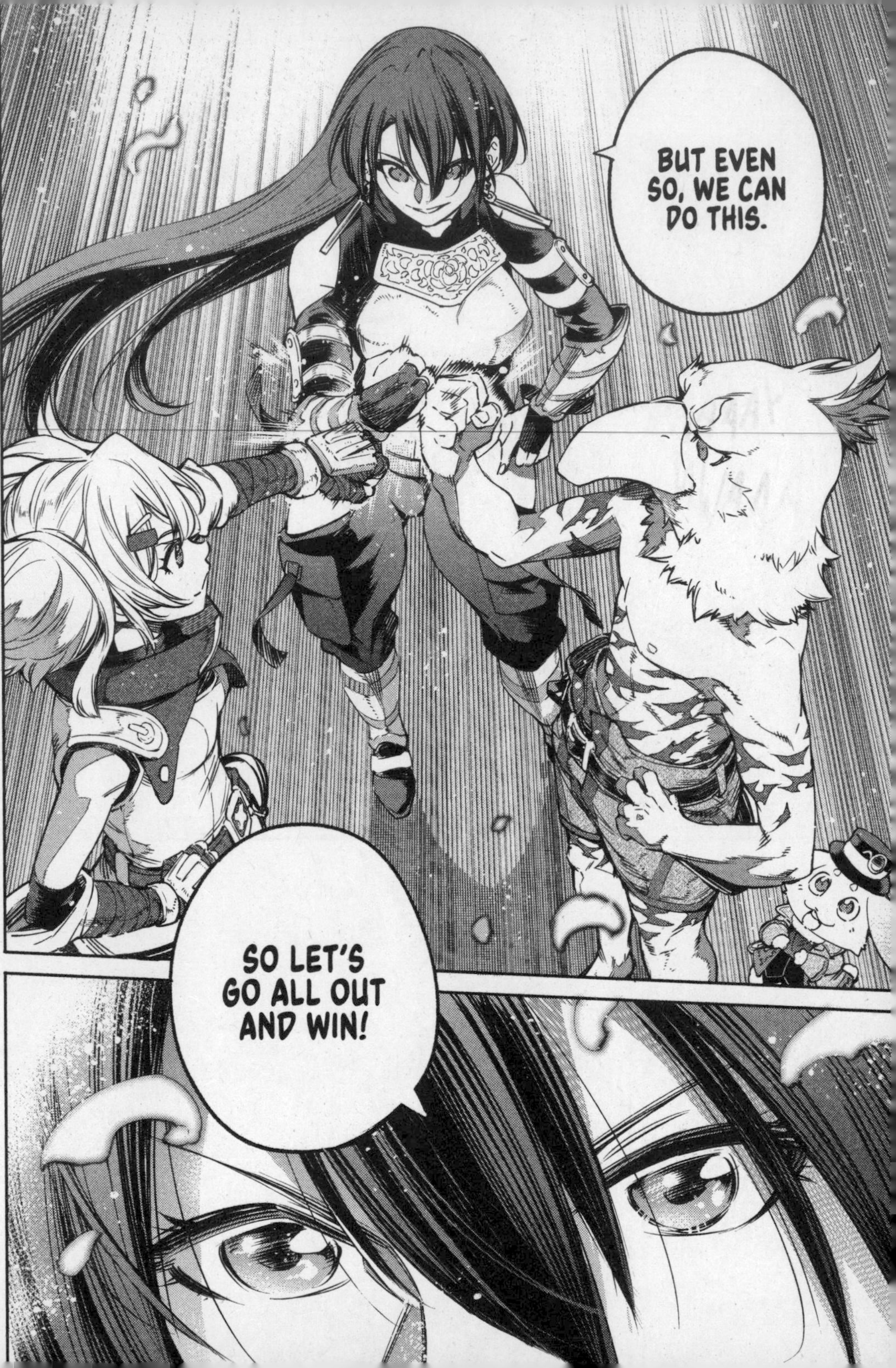
BUT EVEN SO, WE CAN DO THIS.
SO LET'S GO ALL OUT AND WIN!

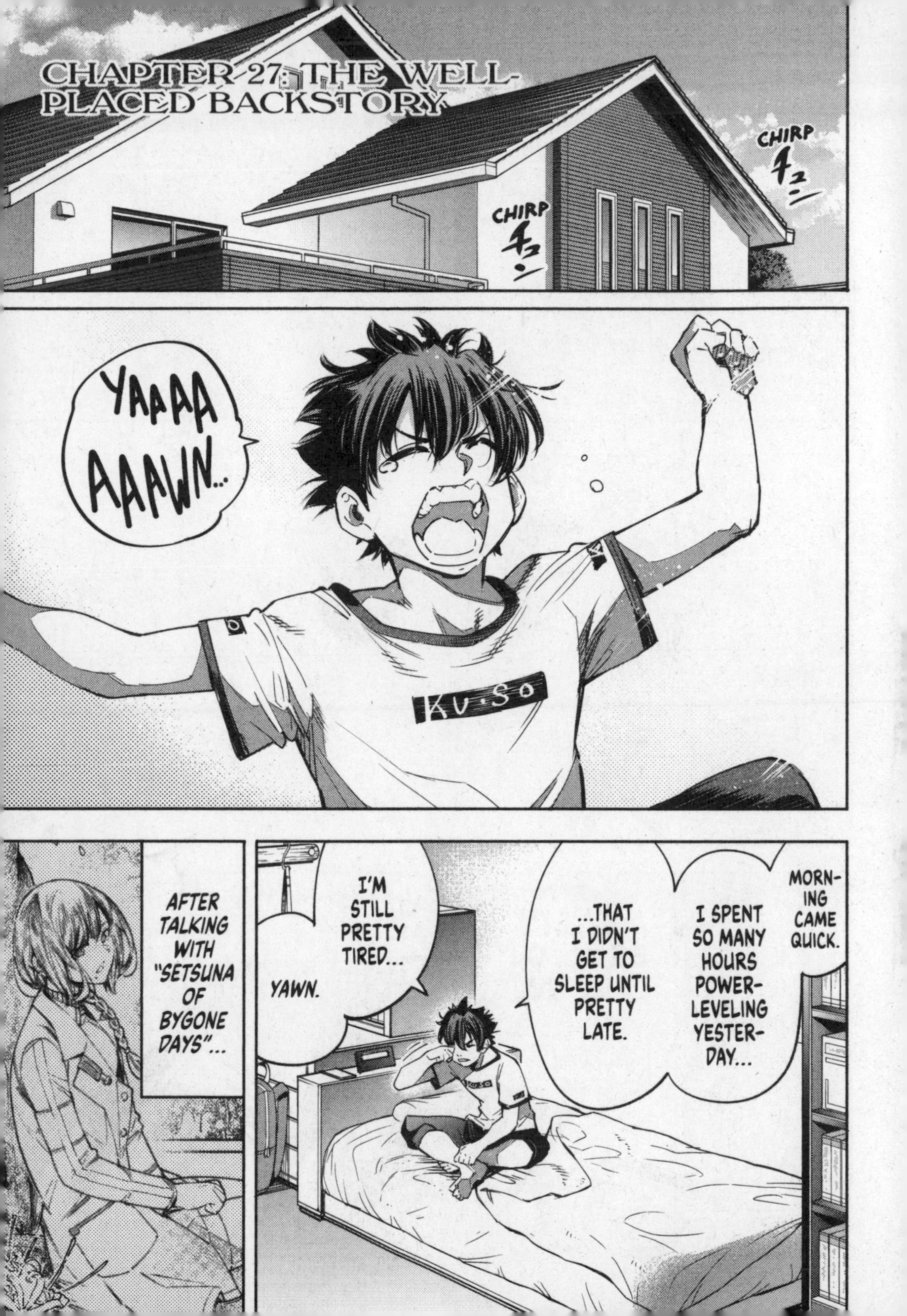
CHAPTER 27: THE WELL-PLACED BACKSTORY
CHIRP
CHIRP
YAAAA AAAWN...
MORNING CAME QUICK.
I SPENT SO MANY HOURS POWER-LEVELING YESTERDAY...
...THAT I DIDN'T GET TO SLEEP UNTIL PRETTY LATE.
I'M STILL PRETTY TIRED...
YAWN.
KU·SO
AFTER TALKING WITH "SETSUNA OF BYGONE DAYS"...

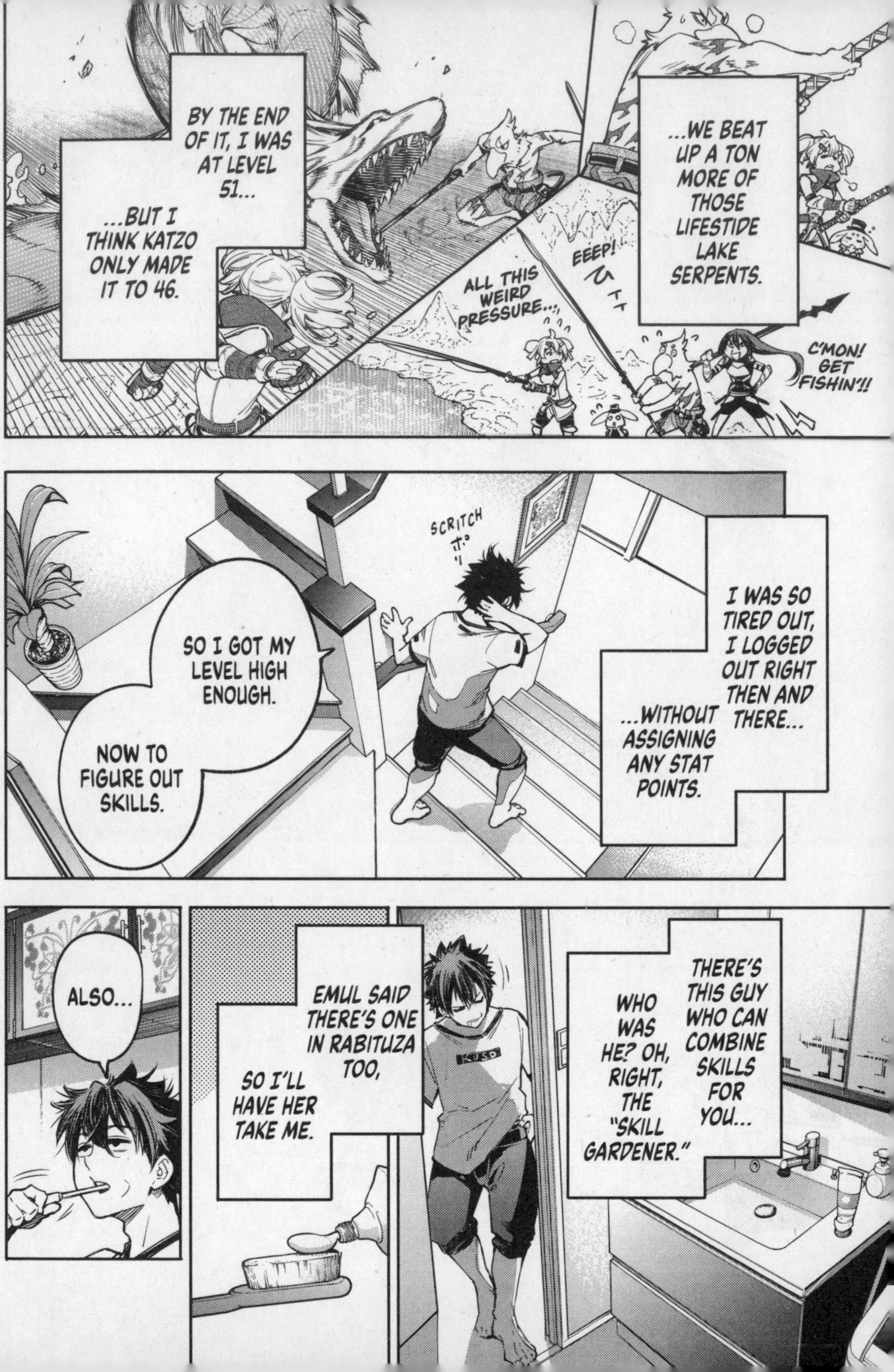
...WE BEAT UP A TON MORE OF THOSE LIFESTIDE LAKE SERPENTS.
C'MON! GET FISHIN'!!
EEEP!
ALL THIS WEIRD PRESSURE...
BY THE END OF IT, I WAS AT LEVEL 51...
...BUT I THINK KATZO ONLY MADE IT TO 46.
I WAS SO TIRED OUT, I LOGGED OUT RIGHT THEN AND THERE...
...WITHOUT ASSIGNING ANY STAT POINTS.
SCRITCH
SO I GOT MY LEVEL HIGH ENOUGH.
NOW TO FIGURE OUT SKILLS.
THERE'S THIS GUY WHO CAN COMBINE SKILLS FOR YOU...
WHO WAS HE? OH, RIGHT, THE "SKILL GARDENER."
EMUL SAID THERE'S ONE IN RABITUZA TOO,
SO I'LL HAVE HER TAKE ME.
ALSO...

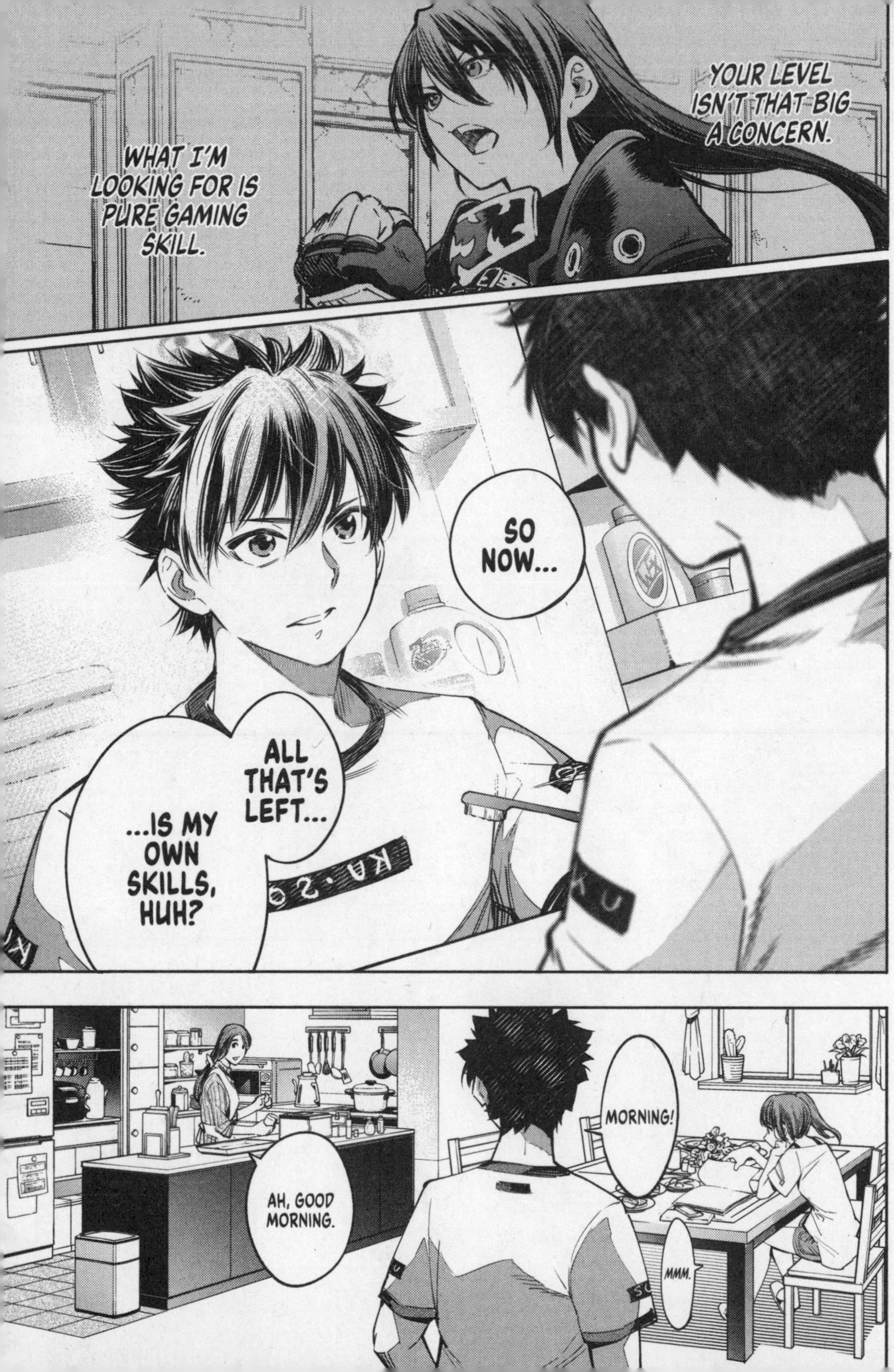
YOUR LEVEL ISN'T THAT BIG A CONCERN.
WHAT I'M LOOKING FOR IS PURE GAMING SKILL.
SO NOW...
ALL THAT'S LEFT...
...IS MY OWN SKILLS, HUH?
MORNING!
AH, GOOD MORNING.
MMM.

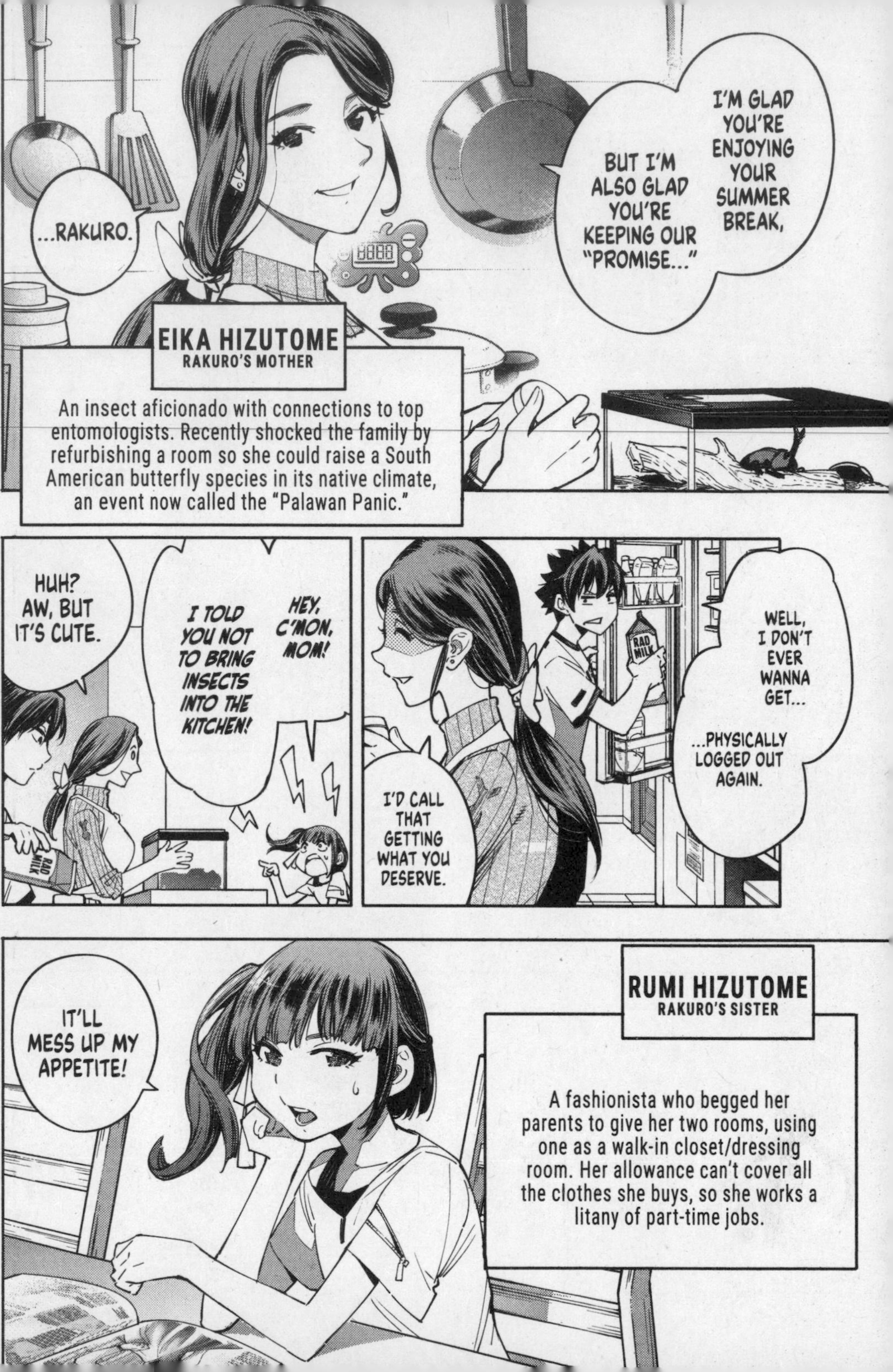
I'M GLAD YOU'RE ENJOYING YOUR SUMMER BREAK,
BUT I'M ALSO GLAD YOU'RE KEEPING OUR "PROMISE..."
...RAKURO.
EIKA HIZUTOME
RAKURO'S MOTHER
An insect aficionado with connections to top entomologists. Recently shocked the family by refurbishing a room so she could raise a South American butterfly species in its native climate, an event now called the "Palawan Panic."
WELL, I DON'T EVER WANNA GET...
...PHYSICALLY LOGGED OUT AGAIN.
RAD MILK
I'D CALL THAT GETTING WHAT YOU DESERVE.
HEY, C'MON, MOM!
I TOLD YOU NOT TO BRING INSECTS INTO THE KITCHEN!
HUH? AW, BUT IT'S CUTE.
RAD MILK
RUMI HIZUTOME
RAKURO'S SISTER
A fashionista who begged her parents to give her two rooms, using one as a walk-in closet/dressing room. Her allowance can't cover all the clothes she buys, so she works a litany of part-time jobs.
IT'LL MESS UP MY APPETITE!

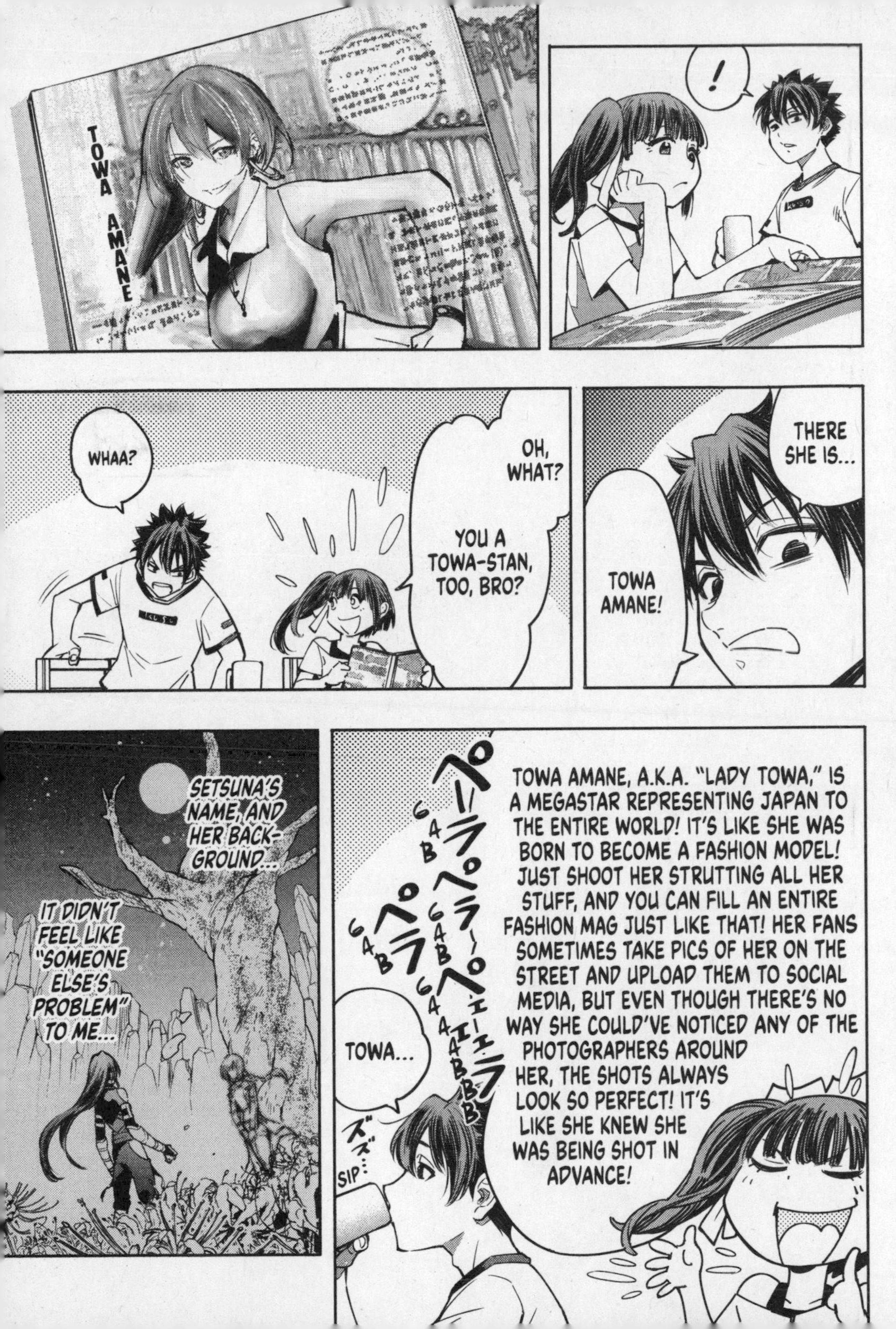
!
TOWA AMANE
THERE SHE IS...
TOWA AMANE!
OH, WHAT?
YOU A TOWA-STAN, TOO, BRO?
WHAA?
TOWA AMANE, A.K.A. "LADY TOWA," IS A MEGASTAR REPRESENTING JAPAN TO THE ENTIRE WORLD! IT'S LIKE SHE WAS BORN TO BECOME A FASHION MODEL! JUST SHOOT HER STRUTTING ALL HER STUFF, AND YOU CAN FILL AN ENTIRE FASHION MAG JUST LIKE THAT! HER FANS SOMETIMES TAKE PICS OF HER ON THE STREET AND UPLOAD THEM TO SOCIAL MEDIA, BUT EVEN THOUGH THERE'S NO WAY SHE COULD'VE NOTICED ANY OF THE PHOTOGRAPHERS AROUND HER, THE SHOTS ALWAYS LOOK SO PERFECT! IT'S LIKE SHE KNEW SHE WAS BEING SHOT IN ADVANCE!
TOWA...
ズズ… SIP
SETSUNA'S NAME, AND HER BACK-GROUND...
IT DIDN'T FEEL LIKE "SOMEONE ELSE'S PROBLEM" TO ME...

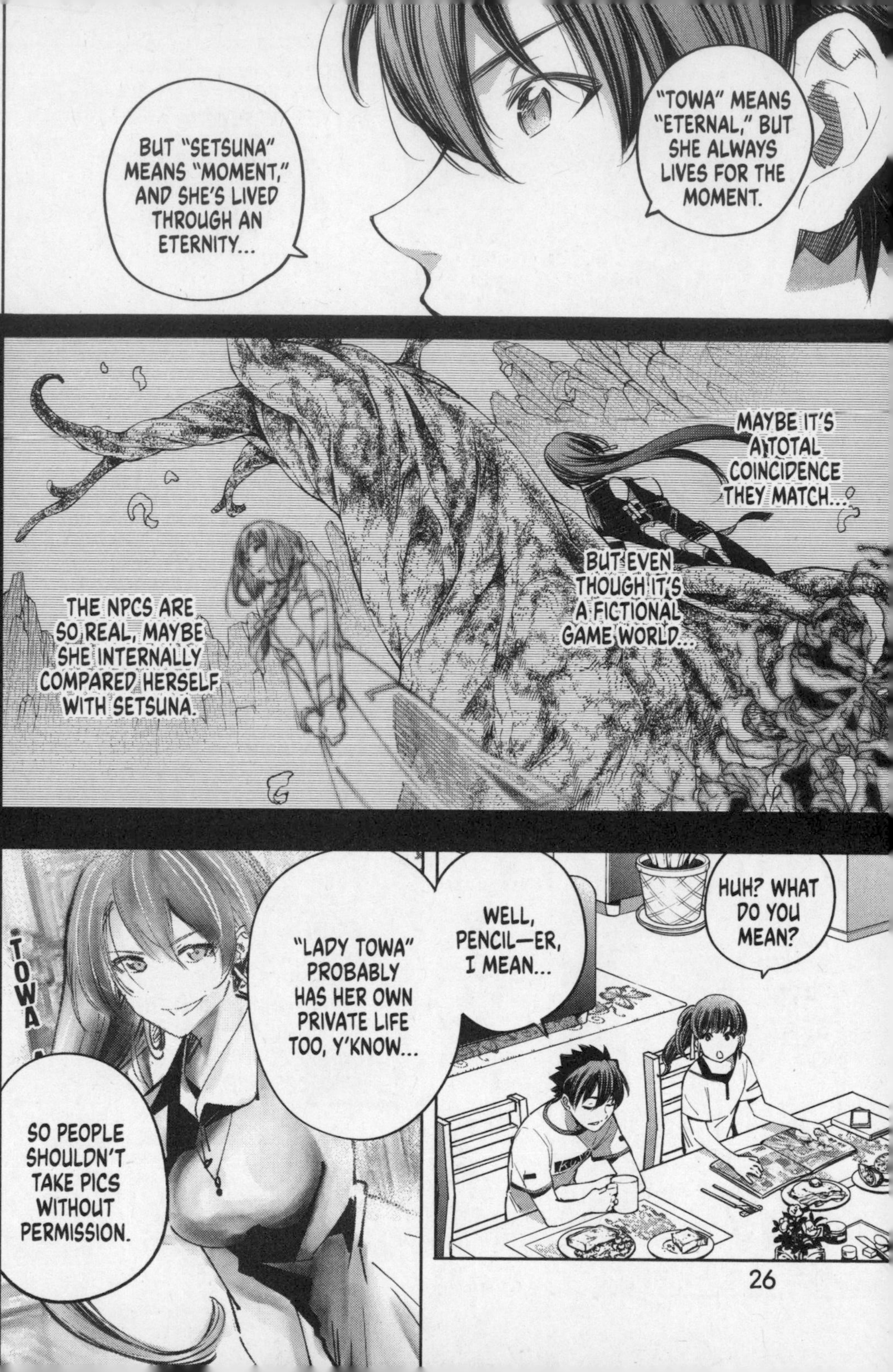
"TOWA" MEANS "ETERNAL," BUT SHE ALWAYS LIVES FOR THE MOMENT.
BUT "SETSUNA" MEANS "MOMENT," AND SHE'S LIVED THROUGH AN ETERNITY...
MAYBE IT'S A TOTAL COINCIDENCE THEY MATCH...
BUT EVEN THOUGH IT'S A FICTIONAL GAME WORLD...
THE NPCS ARE SO REAL, MAYBE SHE INTERNALLY COMPARED HERSELF WITH SETSUNA.
HUH? WHAT DO YOU MEAN?
WELL, PENCIL—ER, I MEAN...
"LADY TOWA" PROBABLY HAS HER OWN PRIVATE LIFE TOO, Y'KNOW...
SO PEOPLE SHOULDN'T TAKE PICS WITHOUT PERMISSION.

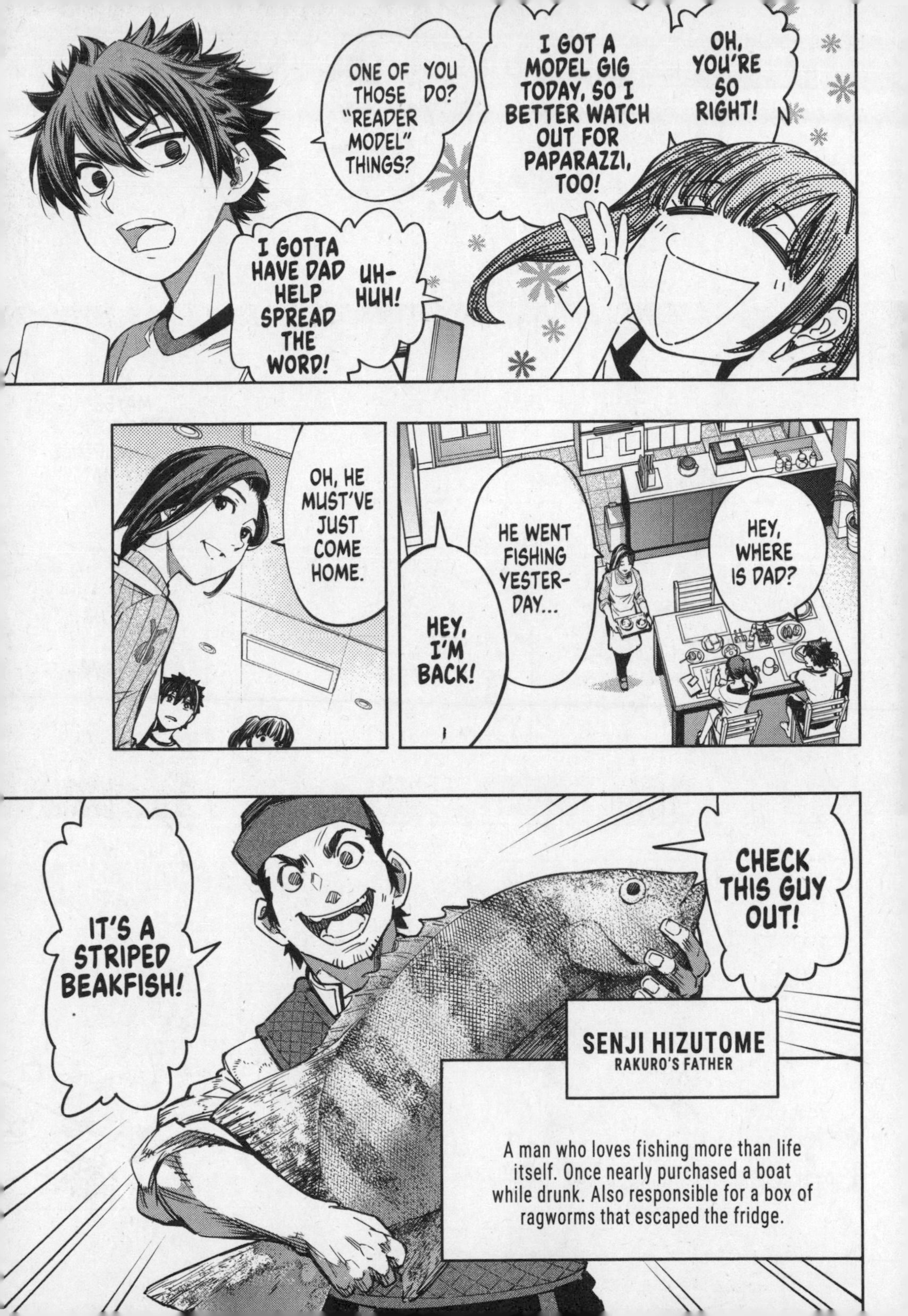
OH, YOU'RE SO RIGHT!
I GOT A MODEL GIG TODAY, SO I BETTER WATCH OUT FOR PAPARAZZI, TOO!
YOU DO? ONE OF THOSE "READER MODEL" THINGS?
UH-HUH!
I GOTTA HAVE DAD HELP SPREAD THE WORD!
HEY, WHERE IS DAD?
HE WENT FISHING YESTER-DAY...
HEY, I'M BACK!
OH, HE MUST'VE JUST COME HOME.
CHECK THIS GUY OUT!
IT'S A STRIPED BEAKFISH!
SENJI HIZUTOME
RAKURO'S FATHER
A man who loves fishing more than life itself. Once nearly purchased a boat while drunk. Also responsible for a box of ragworms that escaped the fridge.

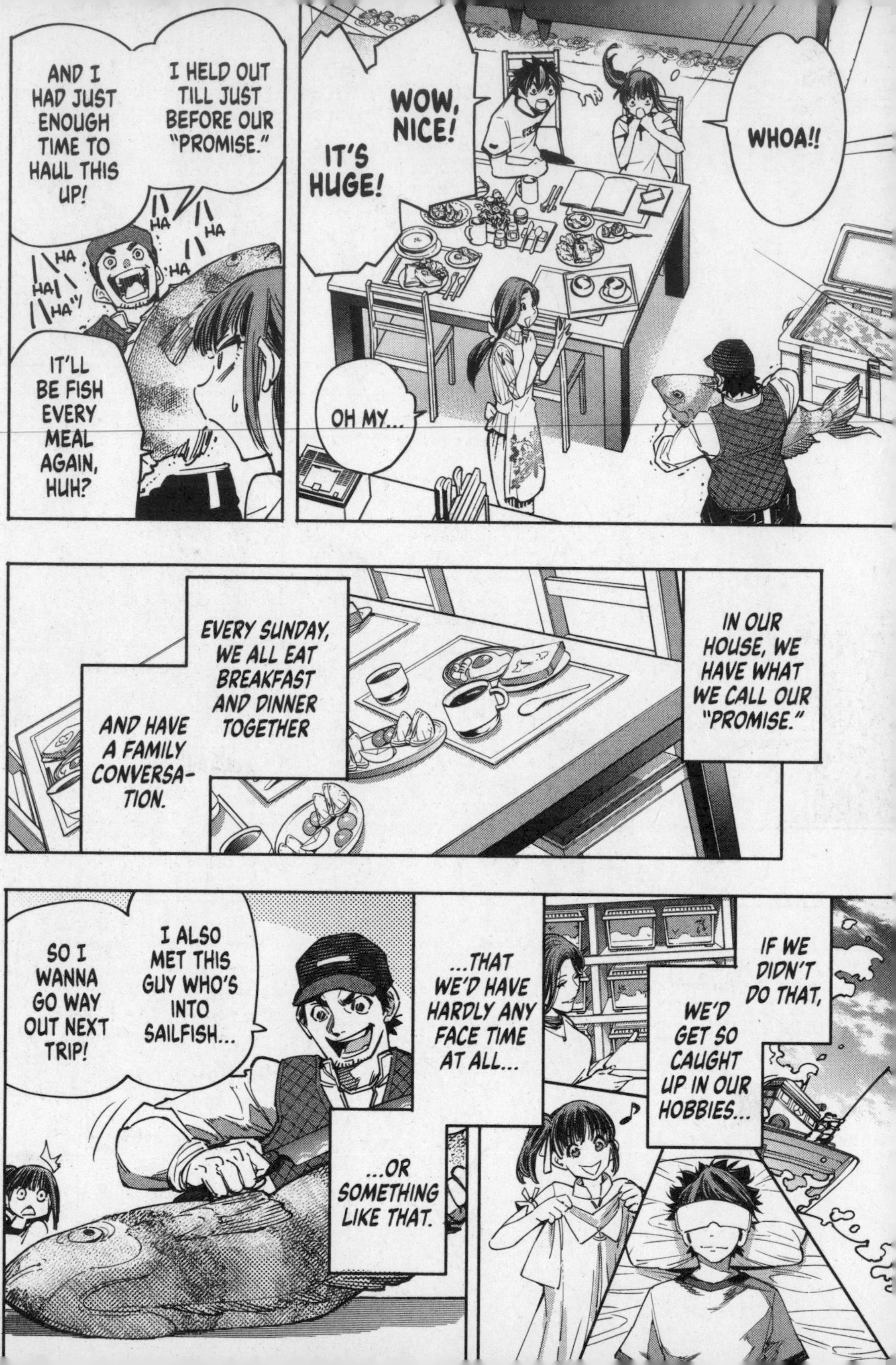
WHOA!!
WOW, NICE!
IT'S HUGE!
OH MY...
I HELD OUT TILL JUST BEFORE OUR "PROMISE."
AND I HAD JUST ENOUGH TIME TO HAUL THIS UP!
HA HA HA HA HA HA HA
IT'LL BE FISH EVERY MEAL AGAIN, HUH?
IN OUR HOUSE, WE HAVE WHAT WE CALL OUR "PROMISE."
EVERY SUNDAY, WE ALL EAT BREAKFAST AND DINNER TOGETHER
AND HAVE A FAMILY CONVERSA-TION.
IF WE DIDN'T DO THAT,
WE'D GET SO CAUGHT UP IN OUR HOBBIES...
...THAT WE'D HAVE HARDLY ANY FACE TIME AT ALL...
I ALSO MET THIS GUY WHO'S INTO SAILFISH...
SO I WANNA GO WAY OUT NEXT TRIP!
...OR SOMETHING LIKE THAT.

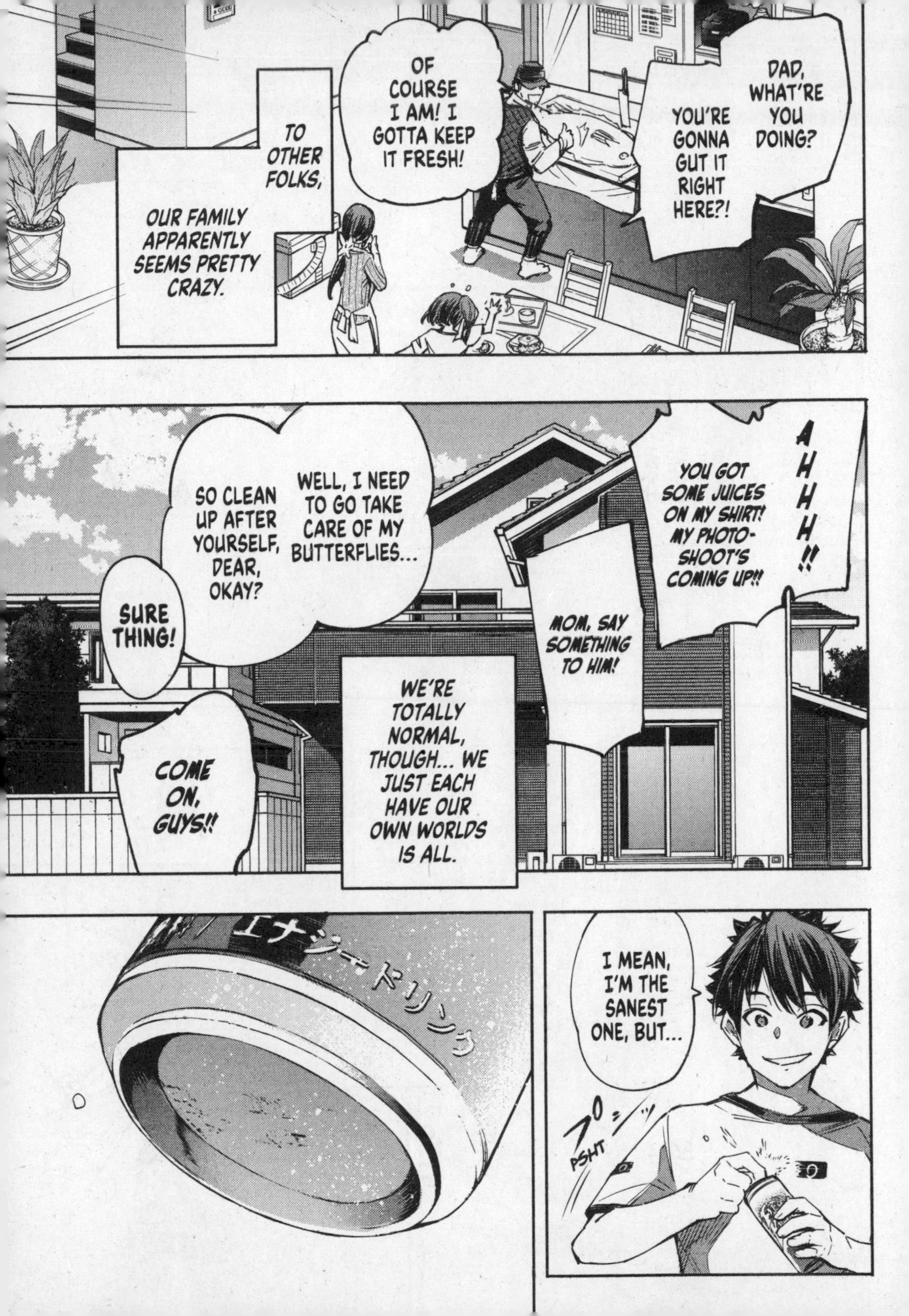
DAD, WHAT'RE YOU DOING?
YOU'RE GONNA GUT IT RIGHT HERE?!
OF COURSE I AM! I GOTTA KEEP IT FRESH!
TO OTHER FOLKS,
OUR FAMILY APPARENTLY SEEMS PRETTY CRAZY.
AHHH!!
YOU GOT SOME JUICES ON MY SHIRT! MY PHOTO-SHOOT'S COMING UP!!
MOM, SAY SOMETHING TO HIM!
WELL, I NEED TO GO TAKE CARE OF MY BUTTERFLIES...
SO CLEAN UP AFTER YOURSELF, DEAR, OKAY?
SURE THING!
WE'RE TOTALLY NORMAL, THOUGH... WE JUST EACH HAVE OUR OWN WORLDS IS ALL.
COME ON, GUYS!!
I MEAN, I'M THE SANEST ONE, BUT...
PSHT

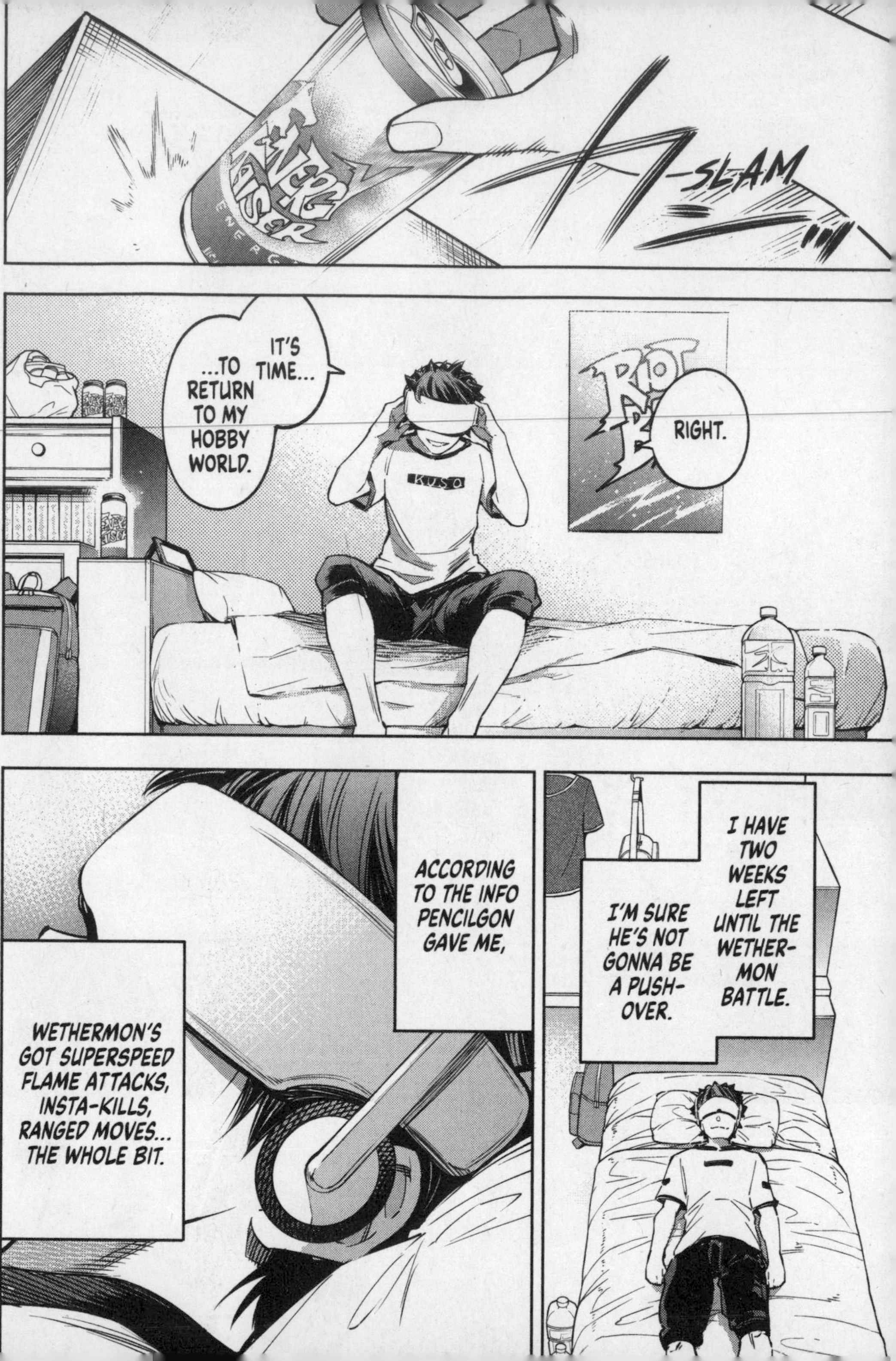
SLAM
RIGHT.
IT'S TIME... ...TO RETURN TO MY HOBBY WORLD.
KUSO
I HAVE TWO WEEKS LEFT UNTIL THE WETHER-MON BATTLE.
I'M SURE HE'S NOT GONNA BE A PUSH-OVER.
ACCORDING TO THE INFO PENCILGON GAVE ME,
WETHERMON'S GOT SUPERSPEED FLAME ATTACKS, INSTA-KILLS, RANGED MOVES... THE WHOLE BIT.

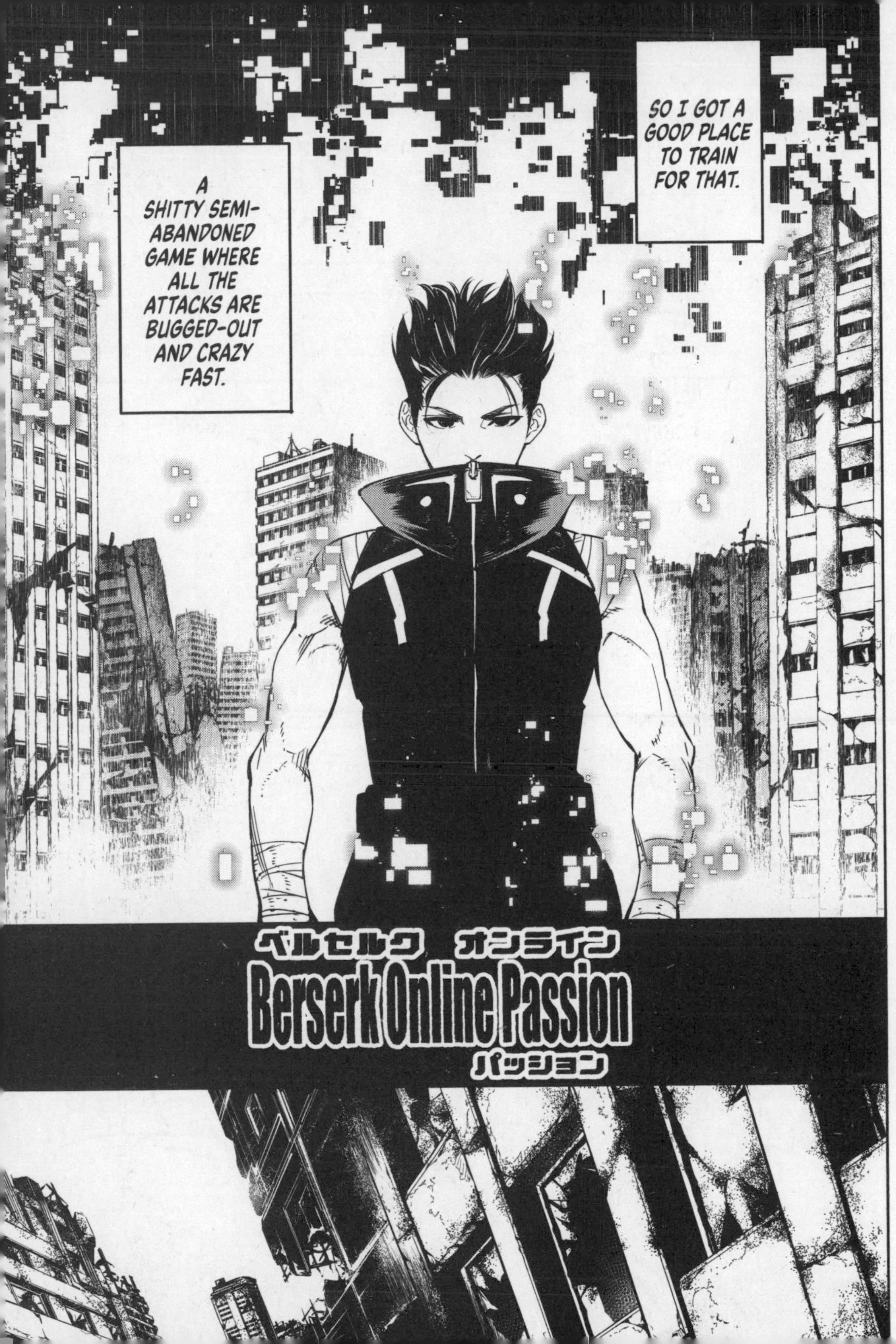
SO I GOT A GOOD PLACE TO TRAIN FOR THAT.
A SHITTY SEMI-ABANDONED GAME WHERE ALL THE ATTACKS ARE BUGGED-OUT AND CRAZY FAST.
ベルセルク オンライン
Berserk Online Passion
パッション

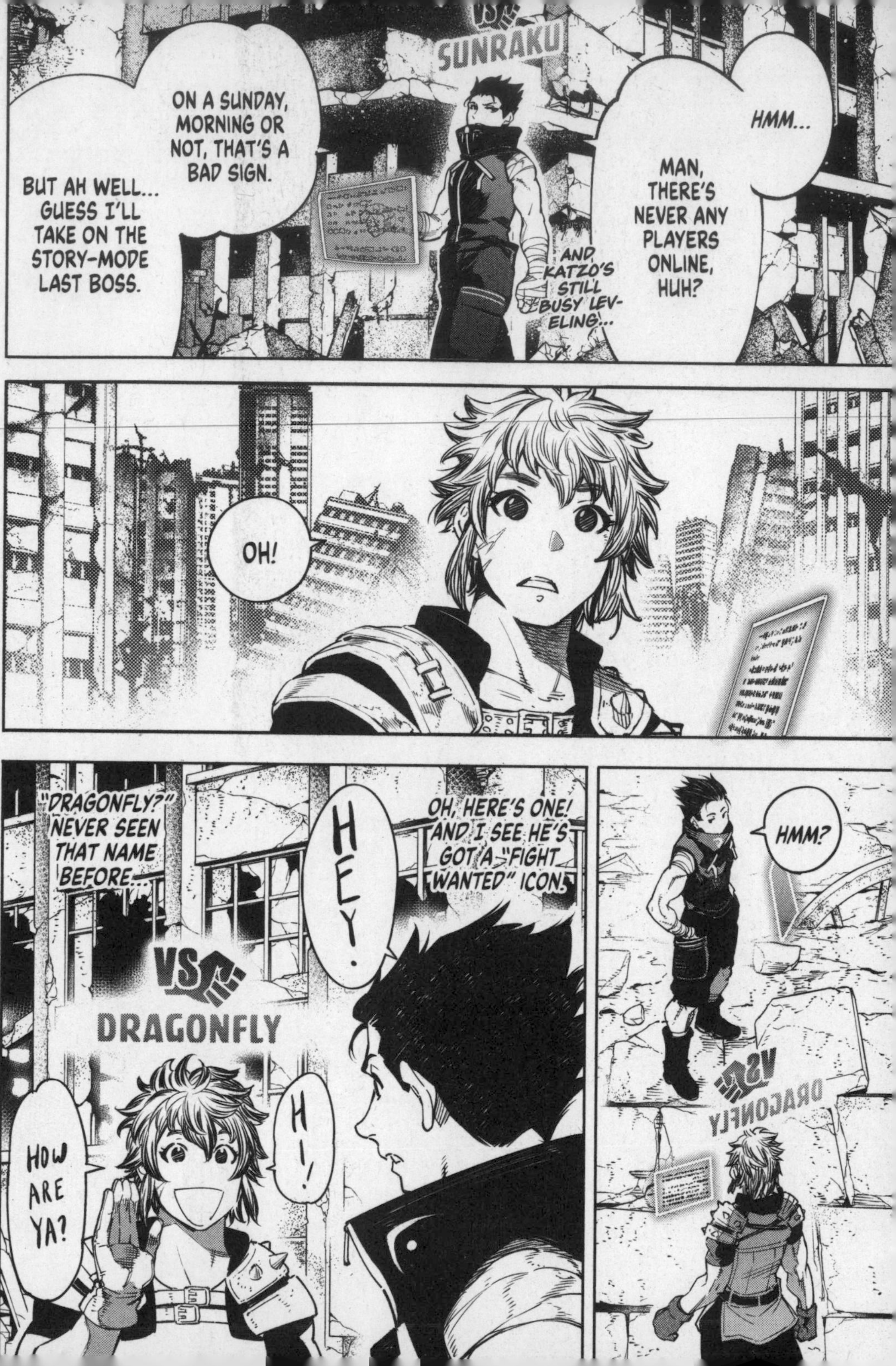
HMM...
MAN, THERE'S NEVER ANY PLAYERS ONLINE, HUH?
AND, KATZO'S STILL BUSY LEVELING...
VS SUNRAKU
ON A SUNDAY, MORNING OR NOT, THAT'S A BAD SIGN.
BUT AH WELL... GUESS I'LL TAKE ON THE STORY-MODE LAST BOSS.
OH!
HMM?
OH, HERE'S ONE! AND I SEE HE'S GOT A "FIGHT WANTED" ICON.
HEY!
"DRAGONFLY?" NEVER SEEN THAT NAME BEFORE...
VS DRAGONFLY
HI!
HOW ARE YA?

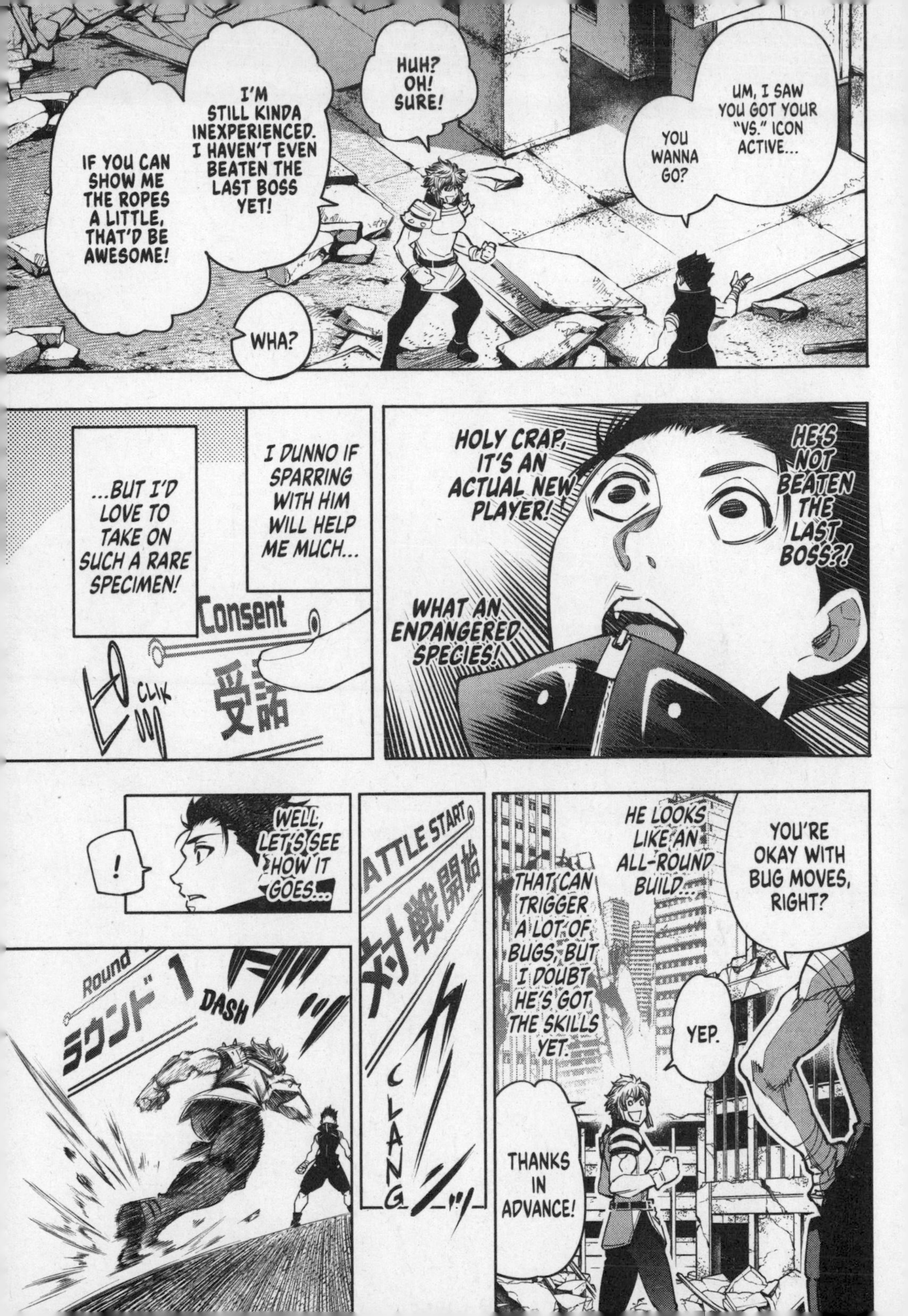
UM, I SAW YOU GOT YOUR "VS." ICON ACTIVE...
YOU WANNA GO?
HUH? OH! SURE!
I'M STILL KINDA INEXPERIENCED. I HAVEN'T EVEN BEATEN THE LAST BOSS YET!
IF YOU CAN SHOW ME THE ROPES A LITTLE, THAT'D BE AWESOME!
WHA?
HE'S NOT BEATEN THE LAST BOSS?!
HOLY CRAP, IT'S AN ACTUAL NEW PLAYER!
WHAT AN ENDANGERED SPECIES!
I DUNNO IF SPARRING WITH HIM WILL HELP ME MUCH...
...BUT I'D LOVE TO TAKE ON SUCH A RARE SPECIMEN!
Consent
受諾
CLIK
YOU'RE OKAY WITH BUG MOVES, RIGHT?
HE LOOKS LIKE AN ALL-ROUND BUILD...
THAT CAN TRIGGER A LOT OF BUGS, BUT I DOUBT HE'S GOT THE SKILLS YET.
YEP.
THANKS IN ADVANCE!
ATTLE START
対戦開始
CLANG
WELL, LET'S SEE HOW IT GOES...
!
Round
ラウンド 1
DASH

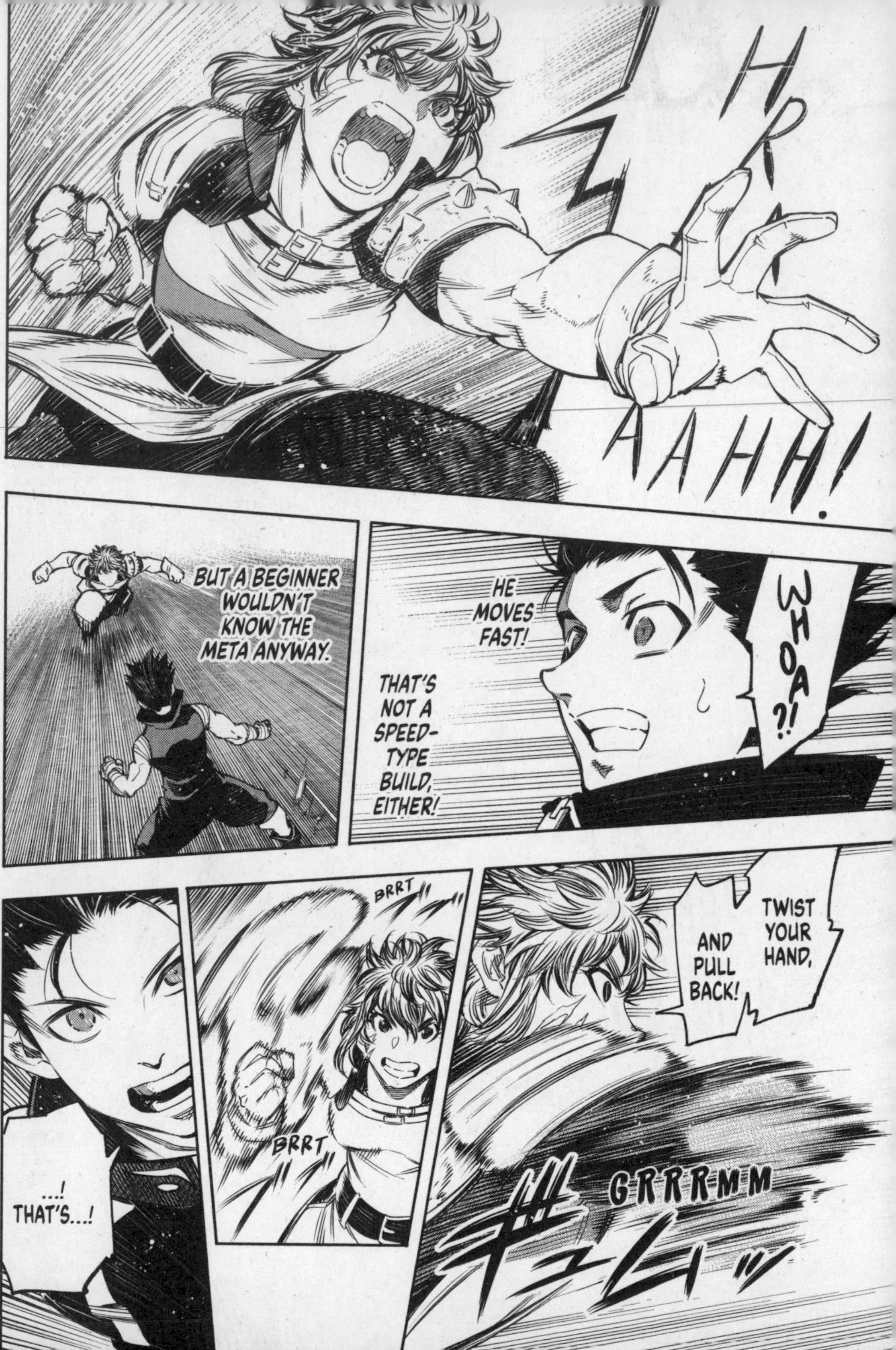
HRA
AAHH!
WHOA?!
HE MOVES FAST!
THAT'S NOT A SPEED-TYPE BUILD, EITHER!
BUT A BEGINNER WOULDN'T KNOW THE META ANYWAY.
TWIST YOUR HAND,
AND PULL BACK!
GRRRMM
ギュムッ
BRRT
BRRT
...! THAT'S...!

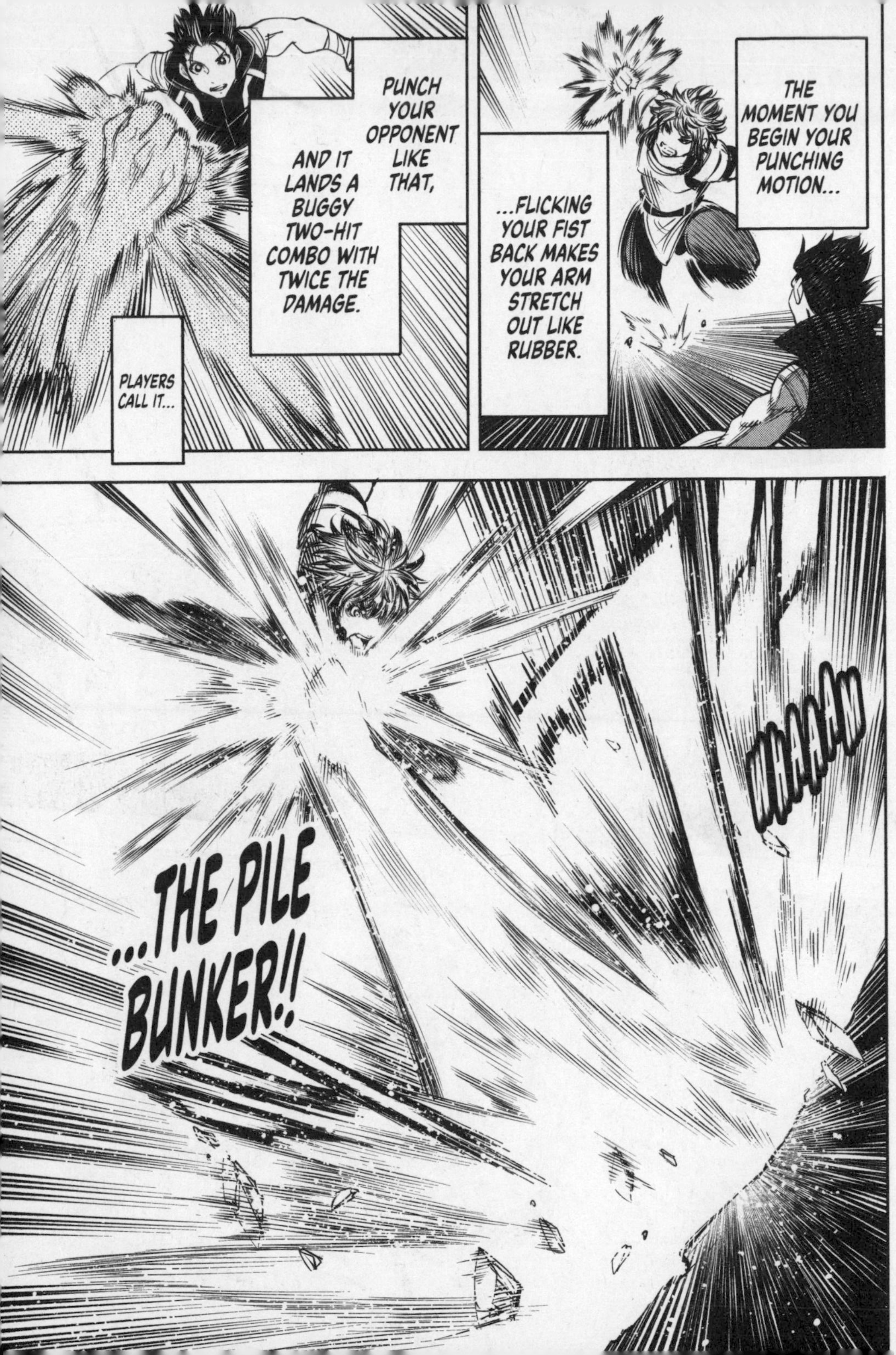
THE MOMENT YOU BEGIN YOUR PUNCHING MOTION...
...FLICKING YOUR FIST BACK MAKES YOUR ARM STRETCH OUT LIKE RUBBER.
PUNCH YOUR OPPONENT LIKE THAT,
AND IT LANDS A BUGGY TWO-HIT COMBO WITH TWICE THE DAMAGE.
PLAYERS CALL IT...
WHAAAM
...THE PILE BUNKER!!

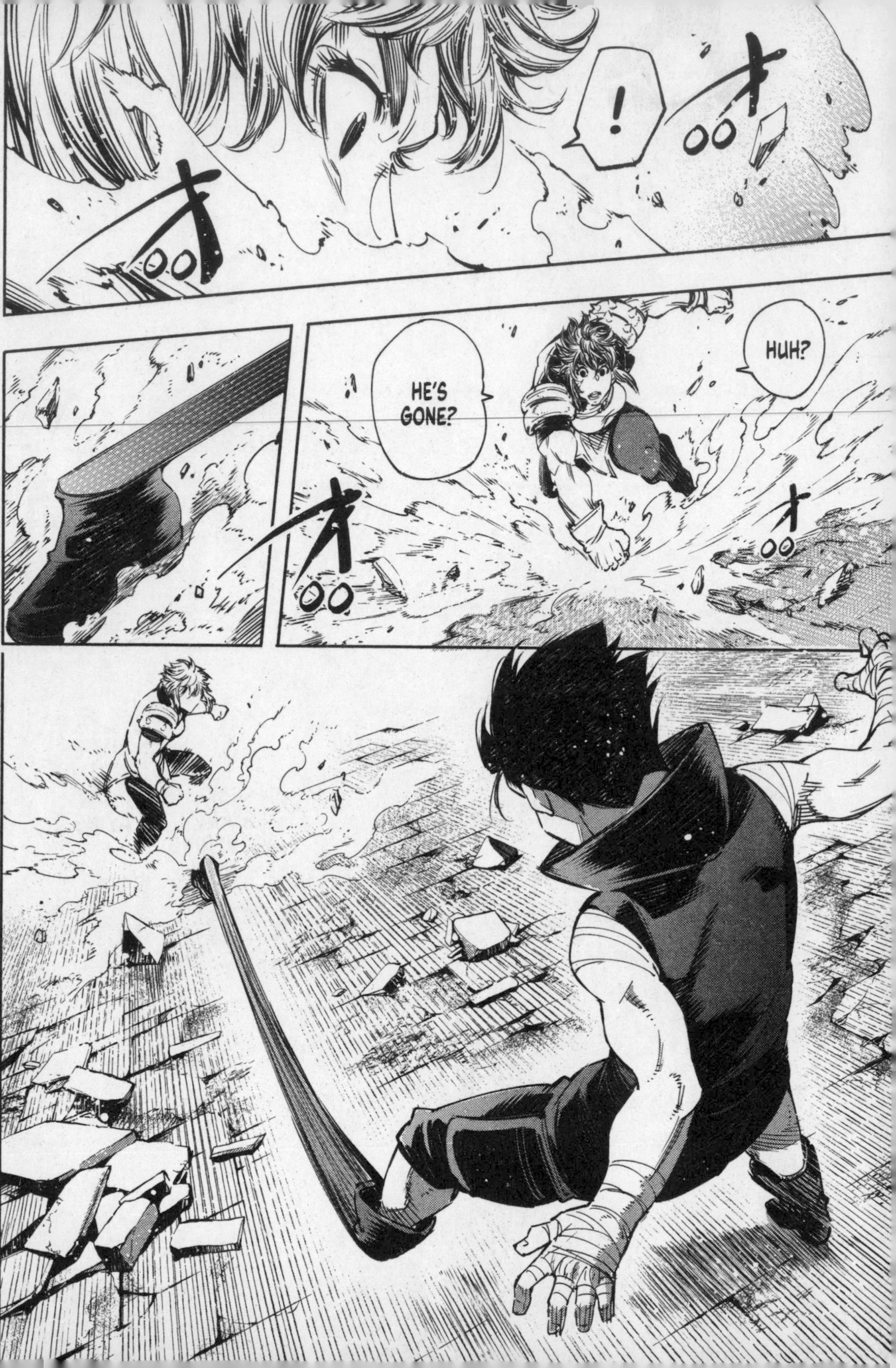
!
HUH?
HE'S GONE?

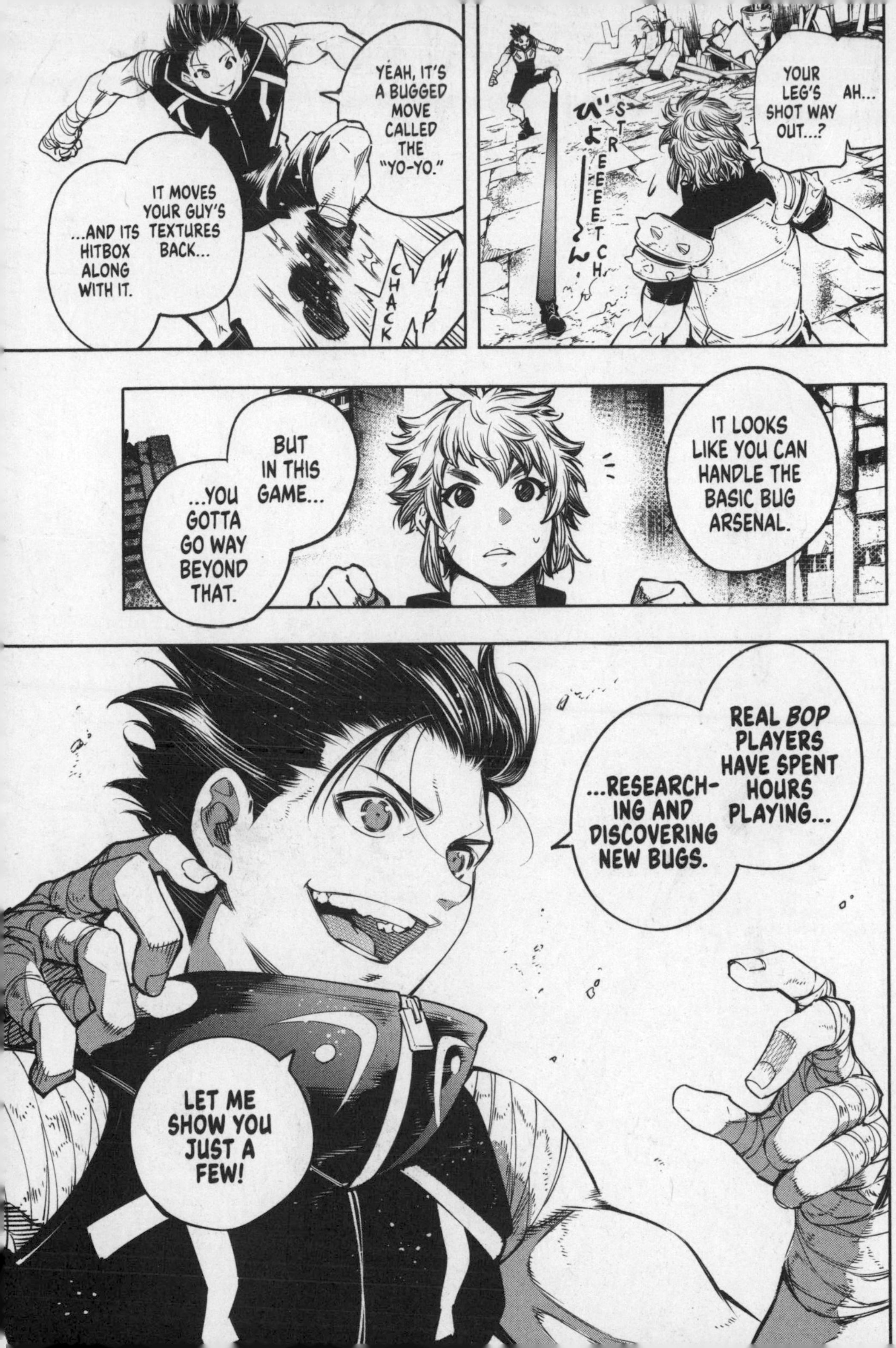
AH...
YOUR LEG'S SHOT WAY OUT...?
STREEEETCH
びよ~~ん
YEAH, IT'S A BUGGED MOVE CALLED THE "YO-YO."
IT MOVES YOUR GUY'S TEXTURES BACK...
...AND ITS HITBOX ALONG WITH IT.
WHIP
CHACK
IT LOOKS LIKE YOU CAN HANDLE THE BASIC BUG ARSENAL.
BUT IN THIS GAME...
...YOU GOTTA GO WAY BEYOND THAT.
REAL *BOP* PLAYERS HAVE SPENT HOURS PLAYING...
...RESEARCHING AND DISCOVERING NEW BUGS.
LET ME SHOW YOU JUST A FEW!

READ TO LEARN MORE ABOUT THE SLF WORLD!

SHANGRI-LA FRONTIER STRATEGY FORUM

VOL. 15

LET SLF MASTER REI-CHAN TAKE YOU THROUGH THE WORLD!

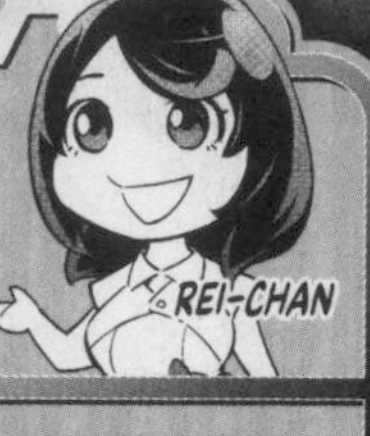
REI-CHAN

BONUS COVERAGE!

UNCOVERING THE REAL WORLD BEHIND SLF!

SHANGRI-LA FRONTIER HAS OVER 30 MILLION ACCOUNTS. WHAT'S IT LIKE IN THE REAL WORLD THAT SUNRAKU AND HIS COHORTS LIVE IN AS THEY CHALLENGE THIS GOD-TIER TITLE? HERE ARE THREE SNIPPETS!

1: A NEAR FUTURE WITH "FULL-DIVE" V.R. GAMES!

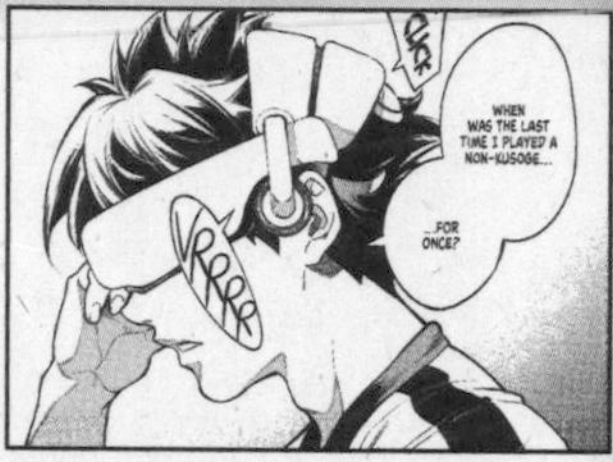
CLICK
WHEN WAS THE LAST TIME I PLAYED A NON-KUSOGE...
...FOR ONCE?
VRRRRR

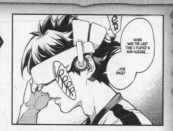

FULL-DIVE TECH WAS ESTABLISHED AROUND SIX YEARS AGO, AND THESE DAYS, FULL-DIVE VR GAMES ARE MAINSTREAM. GAMES RUNNING ON MONITORS ARE RETRO STUFF NOW! WHILE DAILY LIFE ISN'T TOO DIFFERENT, WE'RE SEEING INNOVATIVE TECH IN MANY AREAS.

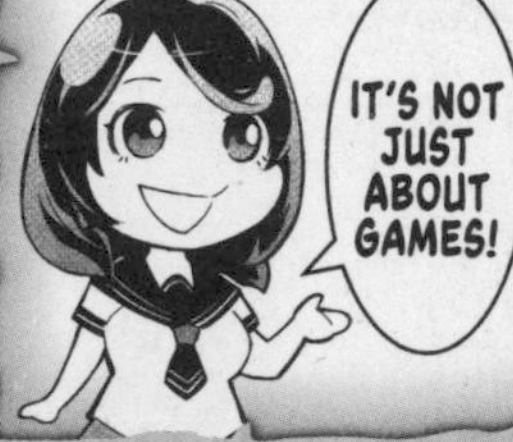
IT'S NOT JUST ABOUT GAMES!

MEDICINE: MEDICAL TECH IS ADVANCING IN TWO AREAS: (1) ORGANIC SUPPORT FOR BODILY SYSTEMS, SUCH AS LIMITED CLONING, AND (2) MECHANICAL SUPPORT FOR MISSING PARTS, LIKE ARTIFICIAL LIMBS. FULL-DIVE TECH IS ALSO USED FOR REHAB. IT SHOWS BACKGROUND SCENERY FOR REHAB PURPOSES.

INDUSTRY: ROBOTS HANDLE THE MAJORITY OF LABOR. WITH ADVANCES IN TECH, IT'S BECOME FEASIBLE TO LITERALLY BUILD NEW LAND—A GIANT FLOATING ISLAND CALLED A "MEGAFLOAT," WHICH HOUSES THE NEW TOKYO INTERNATIONAL EXHIBITION ISLAND.

2: PRO GAMERS HIT IT BIG!

ESPORTS ARE AN ESTABLISHED THING, WITH PRO GAMERS AS POPULAR AS FOOTBALL STARS! WORLD CUP-STYLE TOURNAMENTS BETWEEN NATIONS ARE HELD, WITH THE US, GERMANY, AND SOUTH KOREA SEEN AS THE BIG THREE (EACH PROVIDING PLAYERS WITH GOVERNMENT SUPPORT).

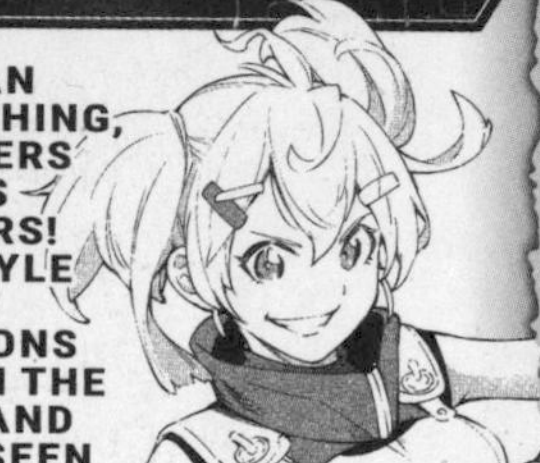

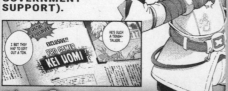

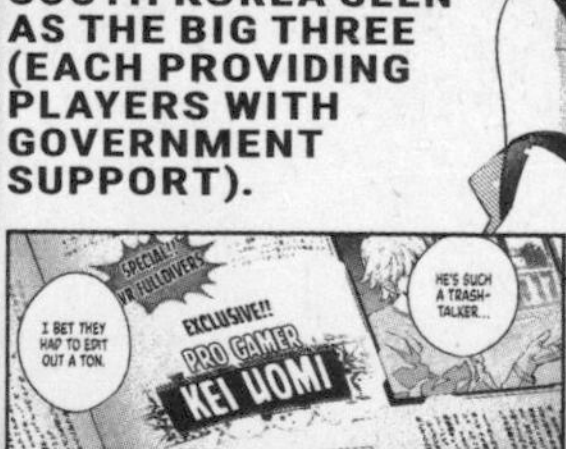
HE'S SUCH A TRASH-TALKER...
SPECIAL!! VR FULLDIVERS
EXCLUSIVE!!
PRO GAMER
KEI UOMI
I BET THEY HAD TO EDIT OUT A TON.

3: NEW JOB DIVERSITY!

INNOVATIVE NEW TECH HAS ALLOWED AI AND ROBOTS TO HANDLE A HEFTY CHUNK OF WORK. BUT MANY PEOPLE STILL WORK IN THE SERVICE INDUSTRY, WHERE A LARGE CONSUMER BASE STILL DEMANDS TO WORK WITH HUMAN BEINGS.

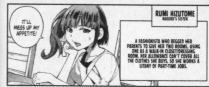

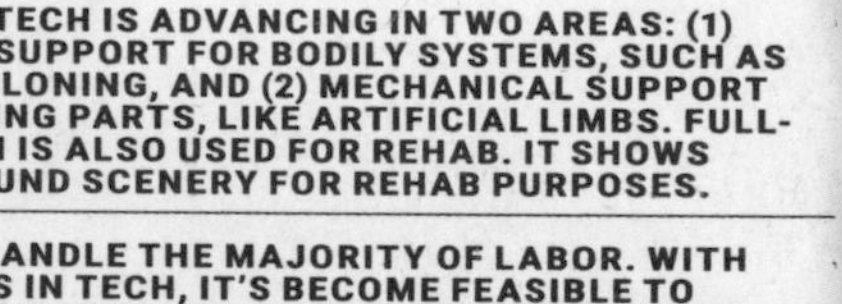
RUMI HIZUTOME
RAKURO'S SISTER
A FASHIONISTA WHO BEGGED HER PARENTS TO GIVE HER TWO ROOMS, USING ONE AS A WALK-IN CLOSET/DRESSING ROOM. HER ALLOWANCE CAN'T COVER ALL THE CLOTHES SHE BUYS, SO SHE WORKS A LITANY OF PART-TIME JOBS.
IT'LL MESS UP MY APPETITE!

IN THIS AGING SOCIETY, FEWER PEOPLE ARE ABLE TO WORK. AS A RESULT, THE MINIMUM WORKING AGE HAS BEEN LOWERED FOR PART-TIME JOBS, GIVING EVEN MIDDLE-SCHOOLERS ACCESS TO THEM! THAT'S WHY RAKURO'S SISTER, RUMI, IS SO BUSY WITH WORK!

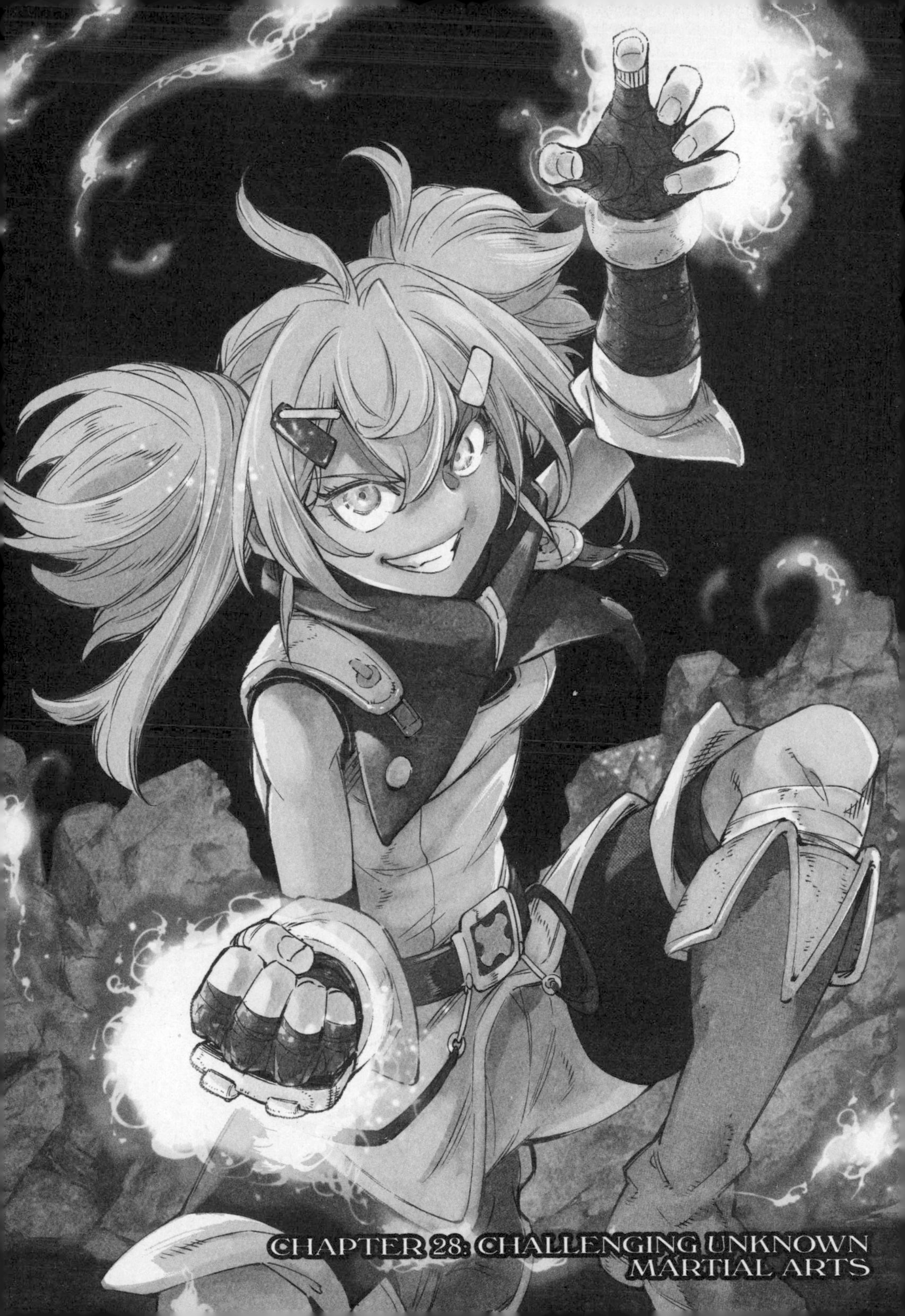

CHAPTER 28: CHALLENGING UNKNOWN MARTIAL ARTS

SHANGRI-LA
FRONTIER

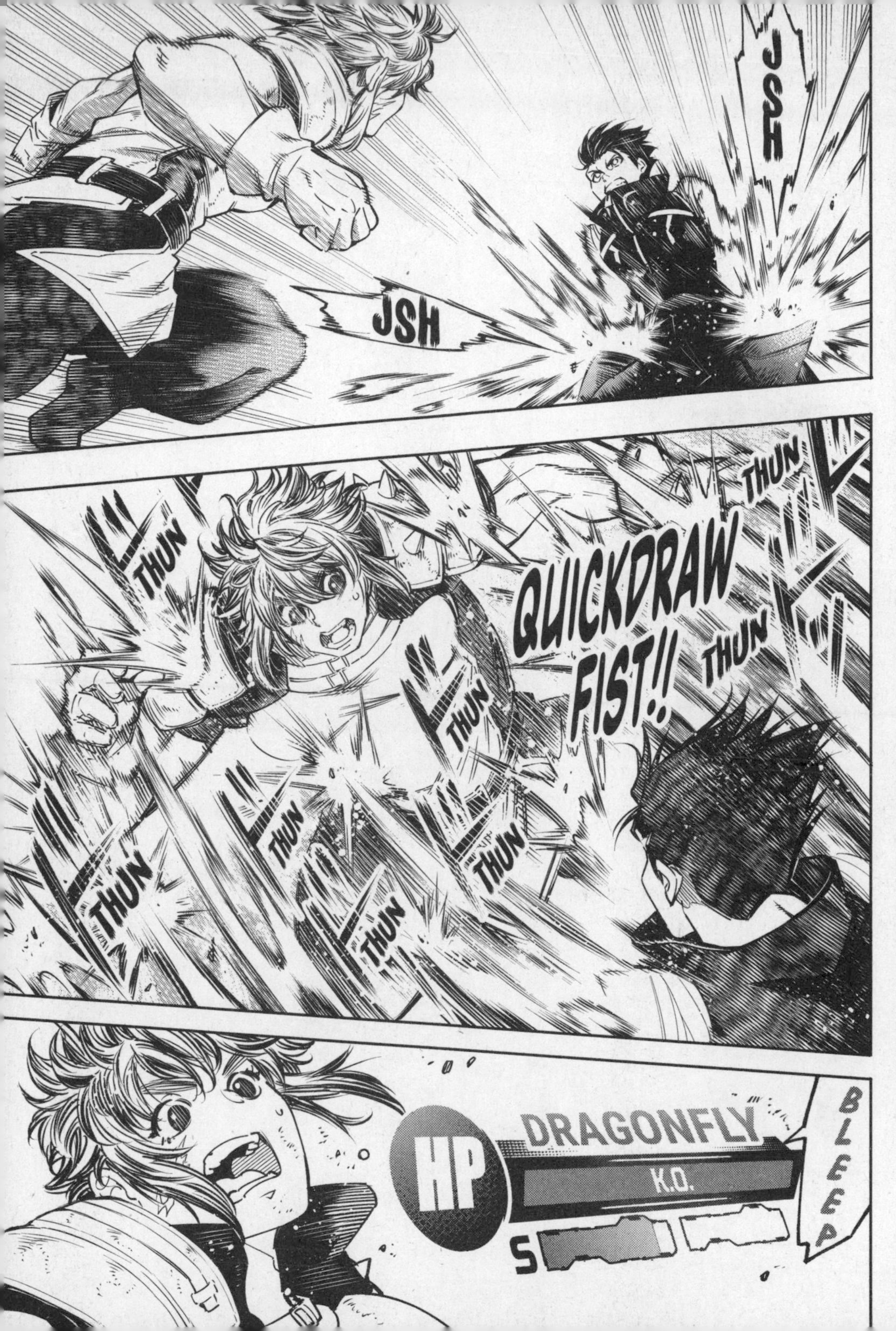
JSH
JSH
THUN
THUN
QUICKDRAW FIST!!
THUN
THUN
THUN
THUN
THUN
THUN
THUN
HP
DRAGONFLY
K.O.
S
BLEEP

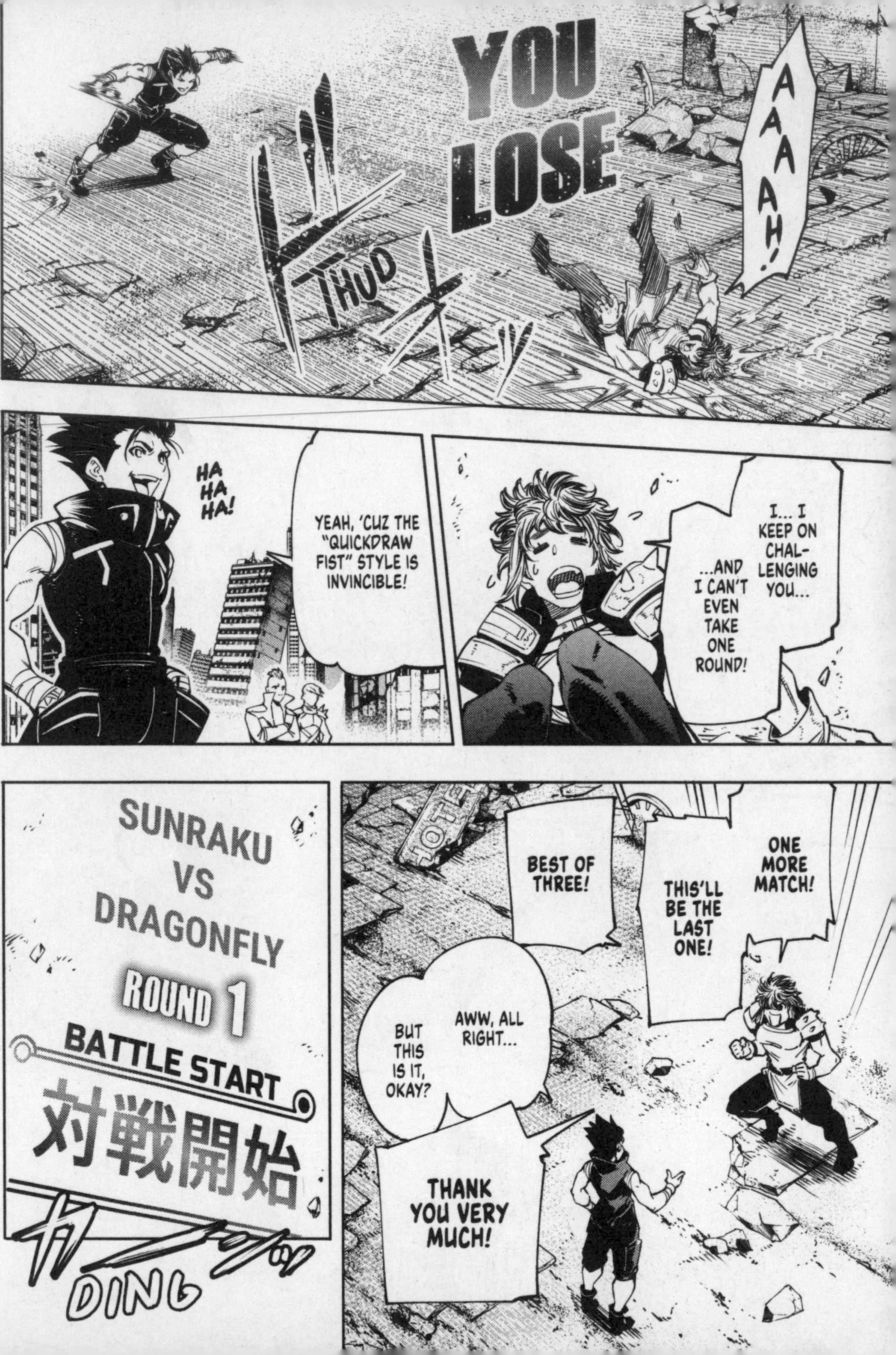
AAAAH!
YOU LOSE
THUD
I... I KEEP ON CHALLENGING YOU...
...AND I CAN'T EVEN TAKE ONE ROUND!
YEAH, 'CUZ THE "QUICKDRAW FIST" STYLE IS INVINCIBLE!
HA HA HA!
ONE MORE MATCH!
THIS'LL BE THE LAST ONE!
BEST OF THREE!
AWW, ALL RIGHT...
BUT THIS IS IT, OKAY?
THANK YOU VERY MUCH!
SUNRAKU VS DRAGONFLY
ROUND 1
BATTLE START
対戦開始
DING

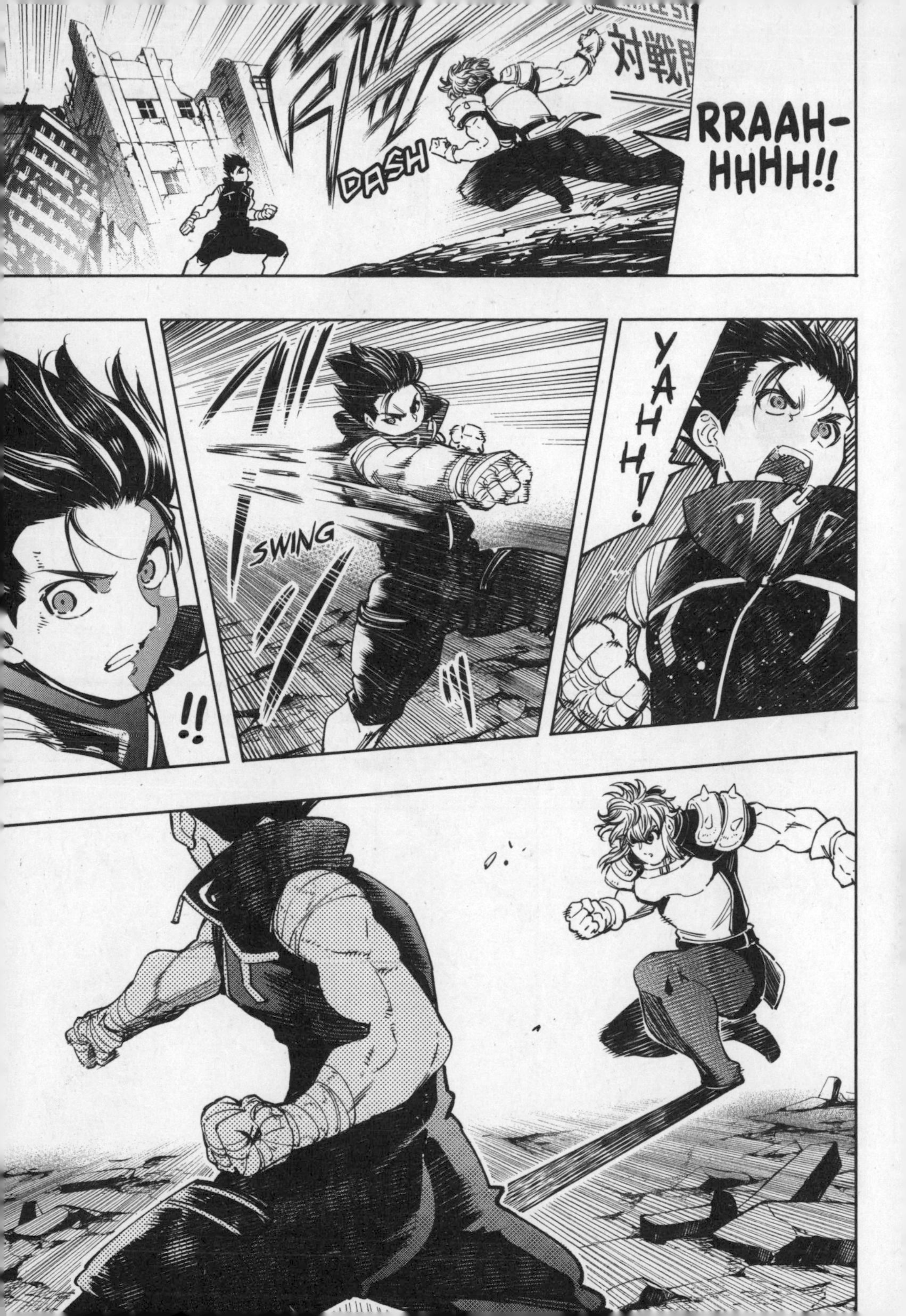
RRAAH-HHHH!!
DASH
YAHHH!
SWING
!!

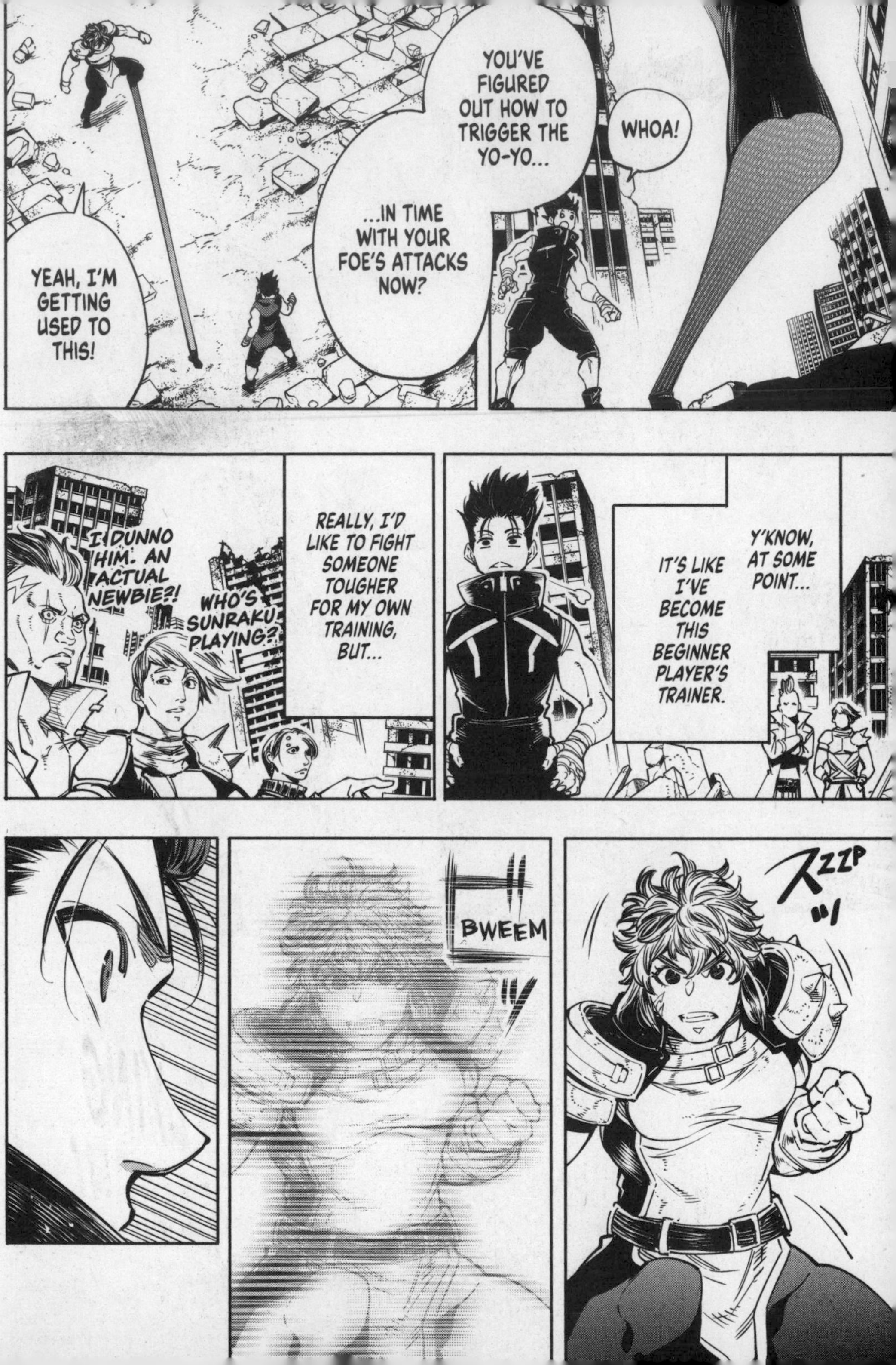
WHOA!
YOU'VE FIGURED OUT HOW TO TRIGGER THE YO-YO...
...IN TIME WITH YOUR FOE'S ATTACKS NOW?
YEAH, I'M GETTING USED TO THIS!
Y'KNOW, AT SOME POINT...
IT'S LIKE I'VE BECOME THIS BEGINNER PLAYER'S TRAINER.
REALLY, I'D LIKE TO FIGHT SOMEONE TOUGHER FOR MY OWN TRAINING, BUT...
WHO'S SUNRAKU PLAYING?
I DUNNO HIM. AN ACTUAL NEWBIE?!
SZZP
BWEEM

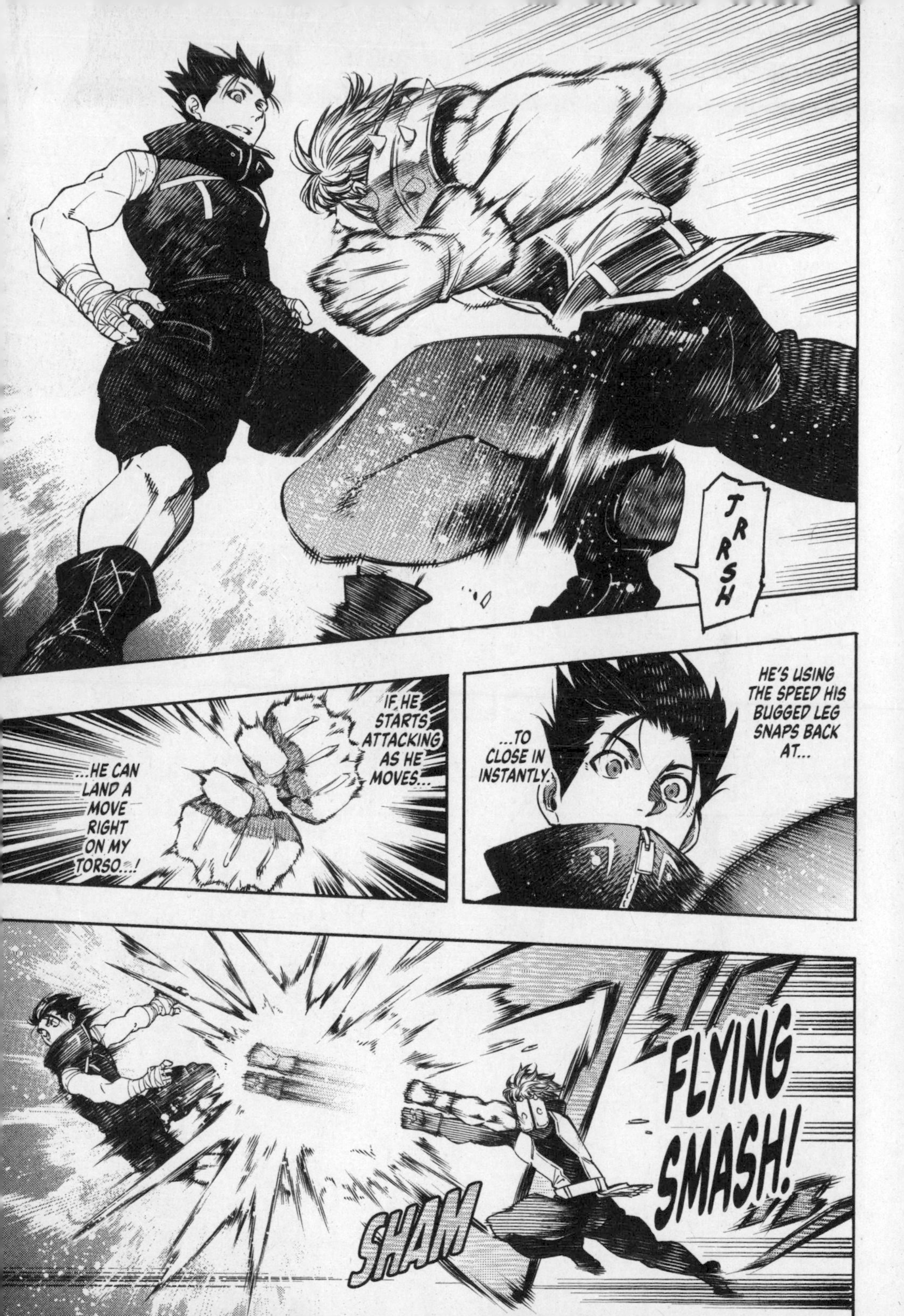
JRRSH
HE'S USING THE SPEED HIS BUGGED LEG SNAPS BACK AT...
...TO CLOSE IN INSTANTLY.
IF HE STARTS ATTACKING AS HE MOVES...
...HE CAN LAND A MOVE RIGHT ON MY TORSO...!
FLYING SMASH!
SHAM

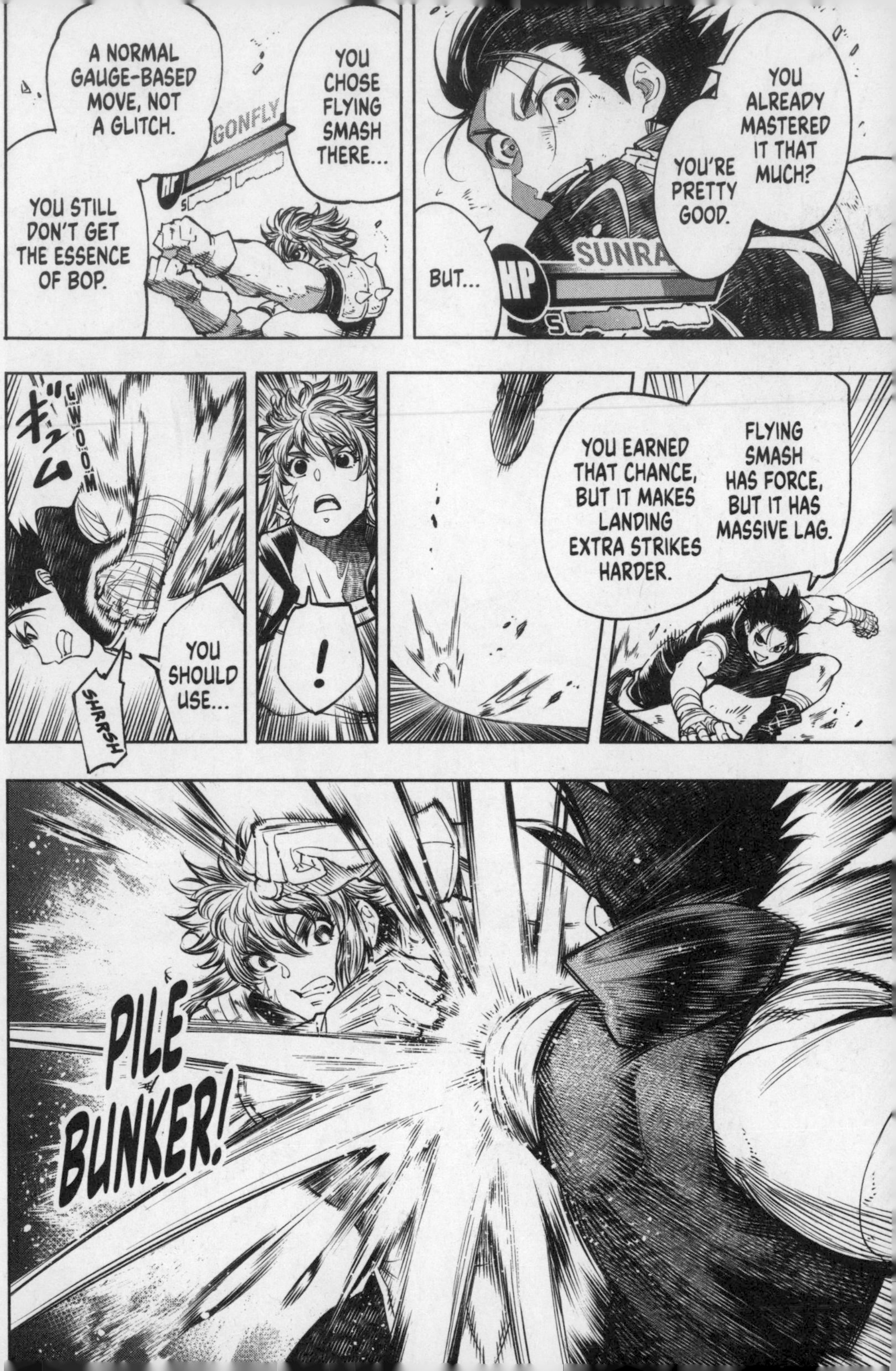
YOU ALREADY MASTERED IT THAT MUCH?
YOU'RE PRETTY GOOD.
SUNRA
HP
S
BUT...
YOU CHOSE FLYING SMASH THERE...
A NORMAL GAUGE-BASED MOVE, NOT A GLITCH.
GONFLY
HP
S
YOU STILL DON'T GET THE ESSENCE OF BOP.
FLYING SMASH HAS FORCE, BUT IT HAS MASSIVE LAG.
YOU EARNED THAT CHANCE, BUT IT MAKES LANDING EXTRA STRIKES HARDER.
!
ギュム
GWOOOM
YOU SHOULD USE...
SHRRSH
PILE BUNKER!

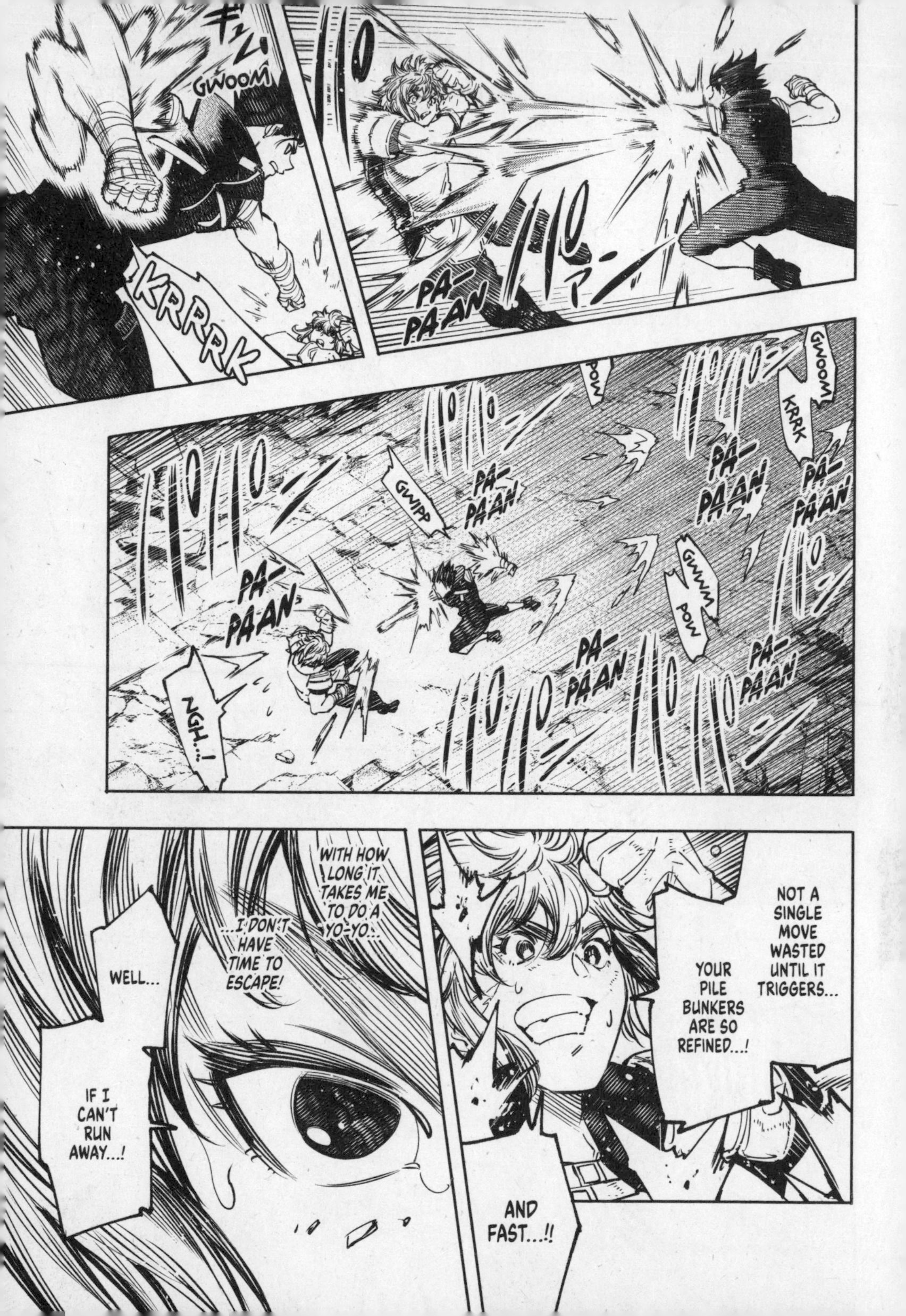
PA-PAAN
GWOOM
KRRRRK
GWOOM
KRRK
PA-PAAN
PA-PAAN
POW
GWWM POW
PA-PAAN
GWIPP
PA-PAAN
PA-PAAN
PA-PAAN
NGH...!
NOT A SINGLE MOVE WASTED UNTIL IT TRIGGERS...
YOUR PILE BUNKERS ARE SO REFINED...!
AND FAST...!!
WITH HOW LONG IT TAKES ME TO DO A YO-YO...
...I DON'T HAVE TIME TO ESCAPE!
WELL...
IF I CAN'T RUN AWAY...!

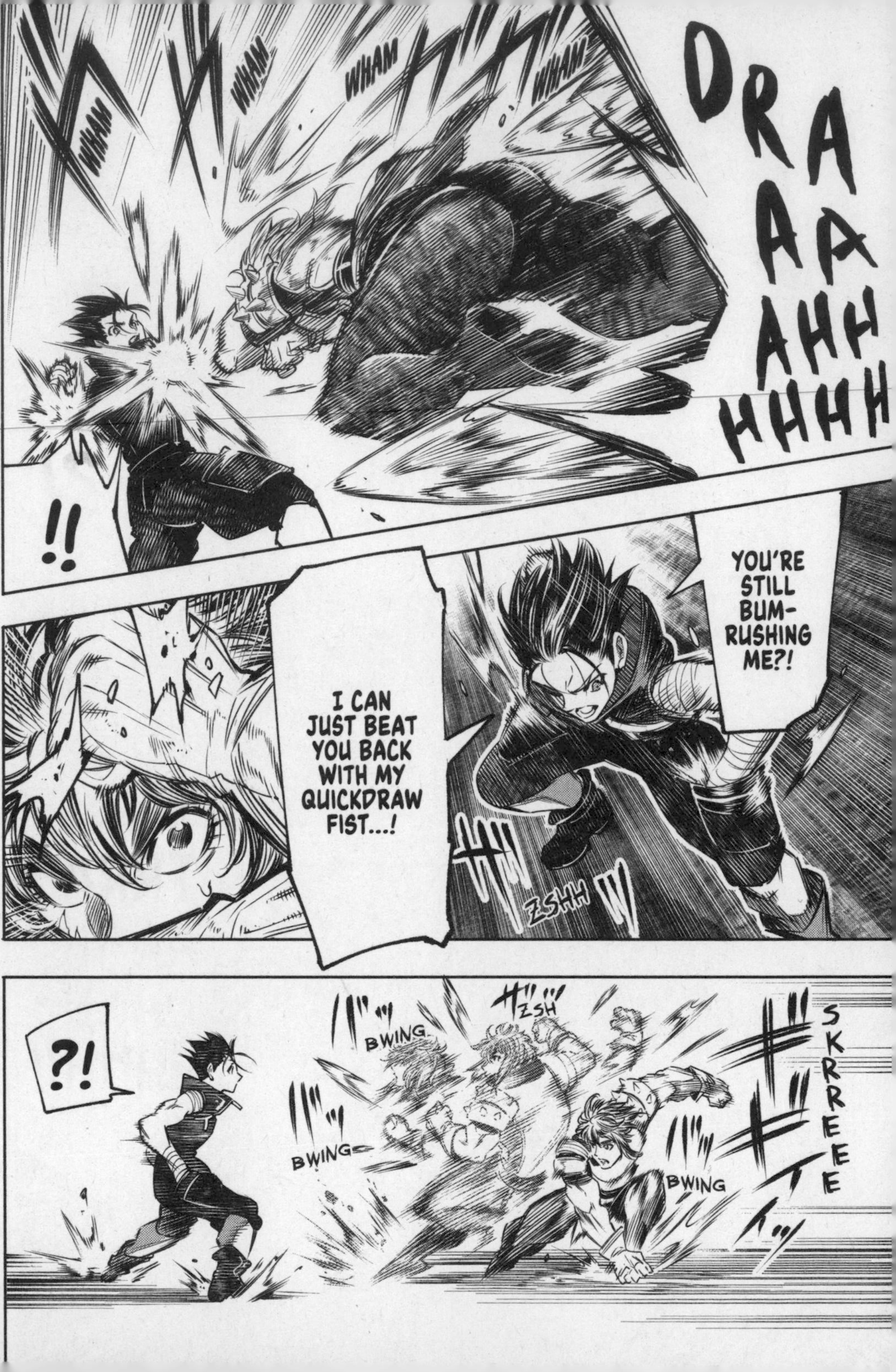
DRAAAAAHHHHHH
WHAM
WHAM
WHAM
WHAM
!!
YOU'RE STILL BUM-RUSHING ME?!
I CAN JUST BEAT YOU BACK WITH MY QUICKDRAW FIST...!
ZSHH
SKREEEE
ZSH
BWING
BWING
BWING
?!

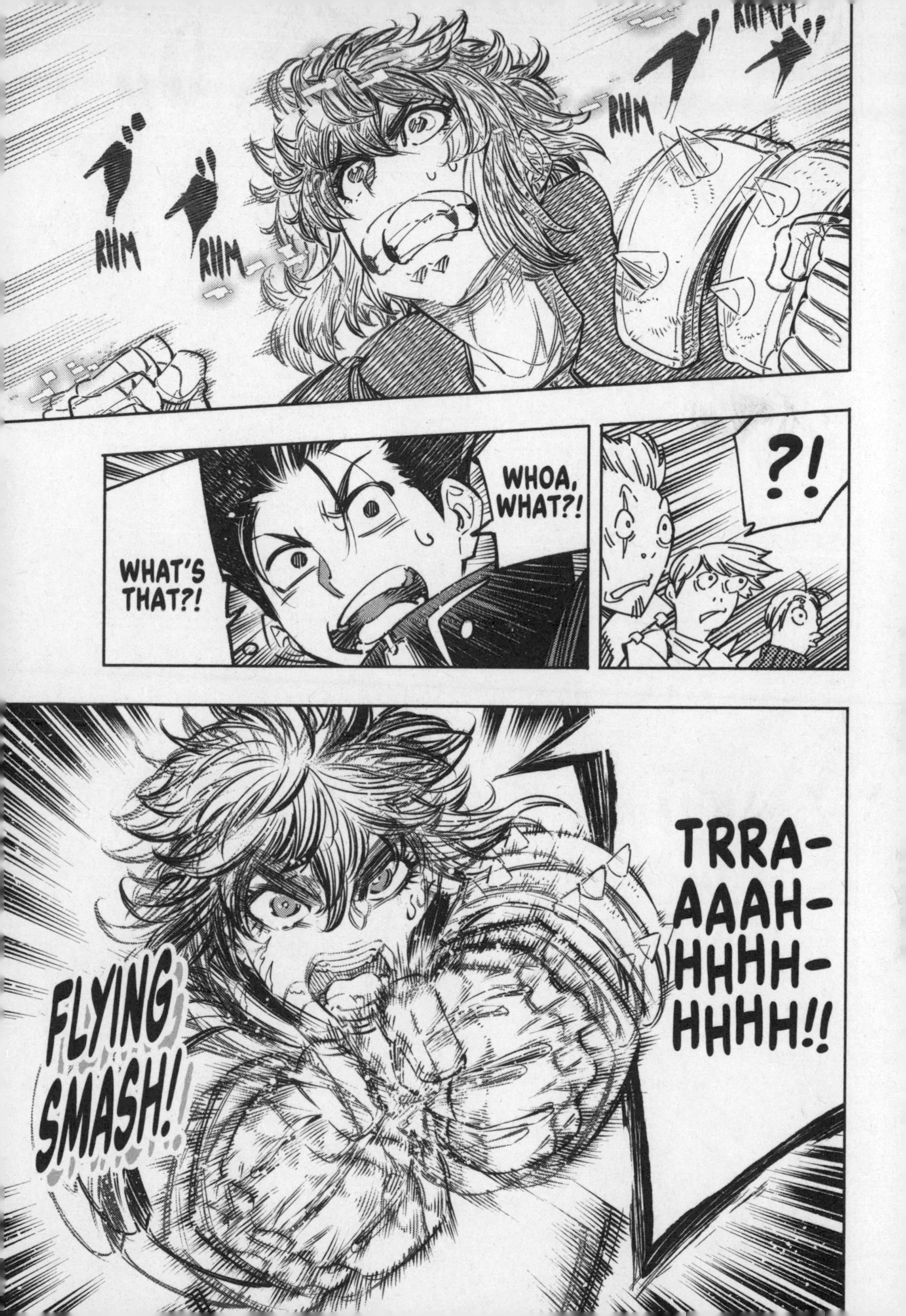
RHM
RHM
RHM
?!
WHOA, WHAT?!
WHAT'S THAT?!
TRRA-AAAH-HHHH-HHHH!!
FLYING SMASH!

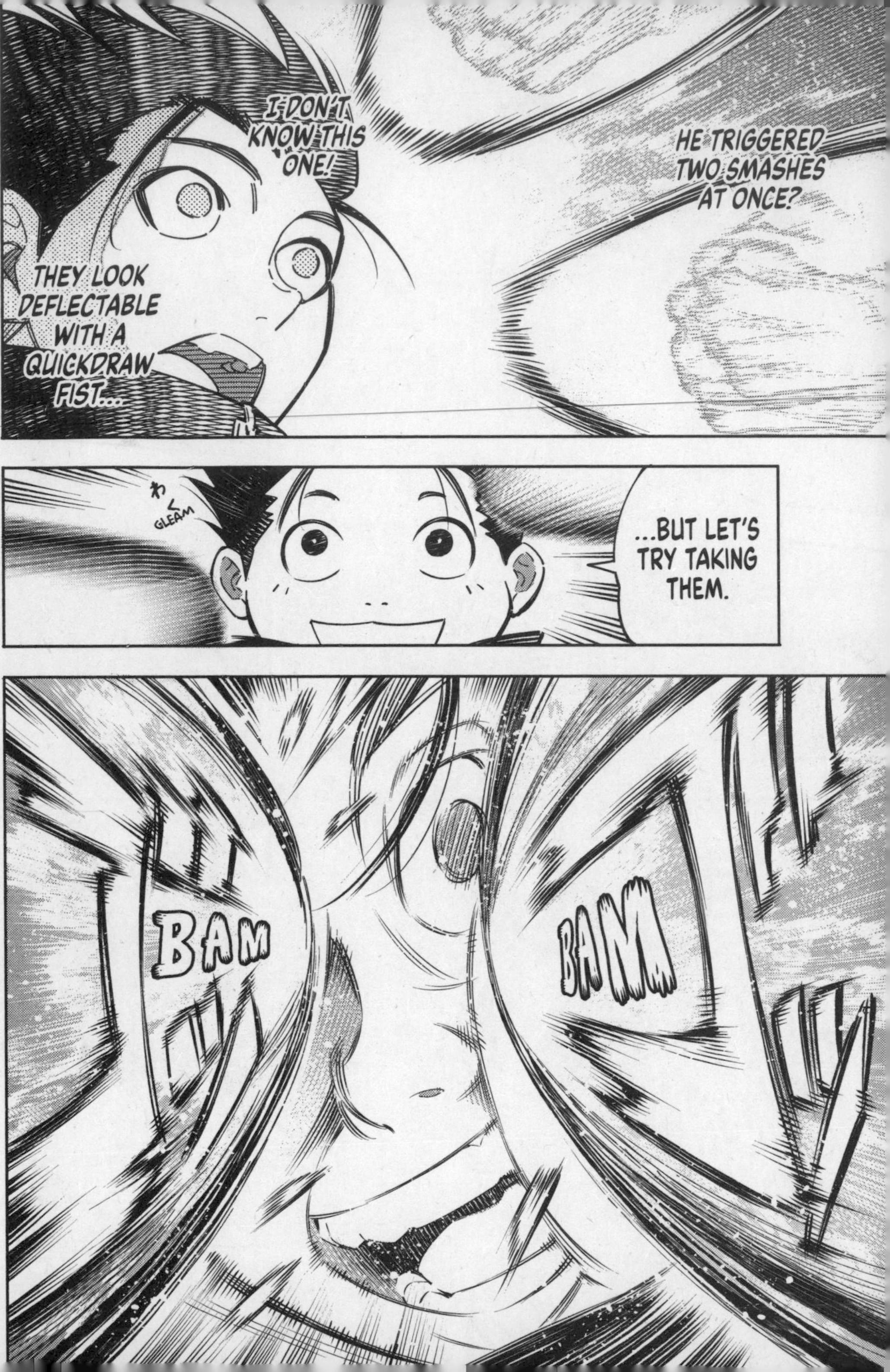
HE TRIGGERED TWO SMASHES AT ONCE?
I DON'T KNOW THIS ONE!
THEY LOOK DEFLECTABLE WITH A QUICKDRAW FIST...
...BUT LET'S TRY TAKING THEM.
わく
GLEAM
BAM
BAM

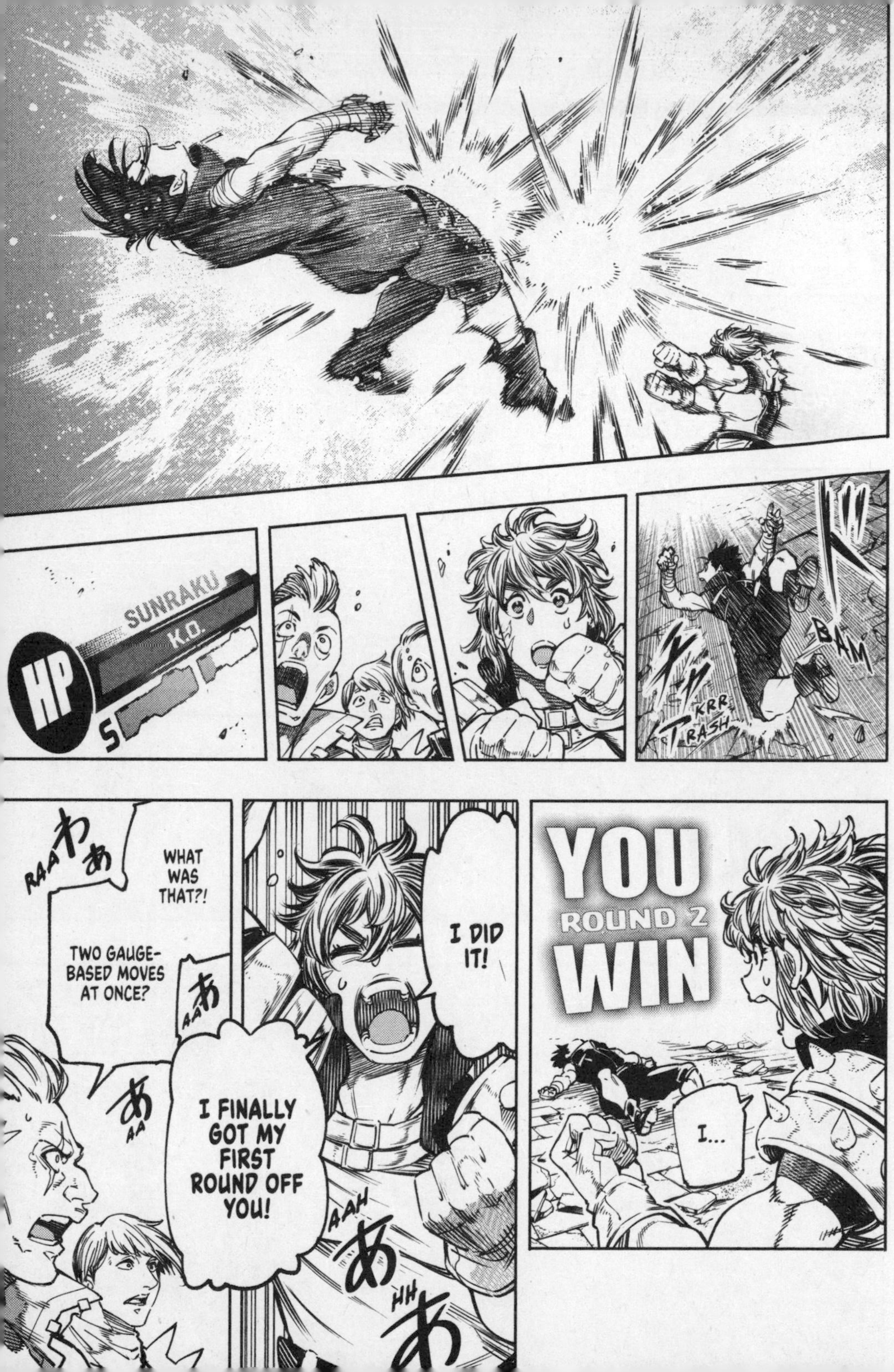
BAM
KRR
RASH
HP
SUNRAKU
K.O.
S
YOU
ROUND 2
WIN
I...
I DID IT!
I FINALLY GOT MY FIRST ROUND OFF YOU!
AAH あ HH あ
RAA わ あ
WHAT WAS THAT?!
TWO GAUGE-BASED MOVES AT ONCE?
AA あ
あ AA

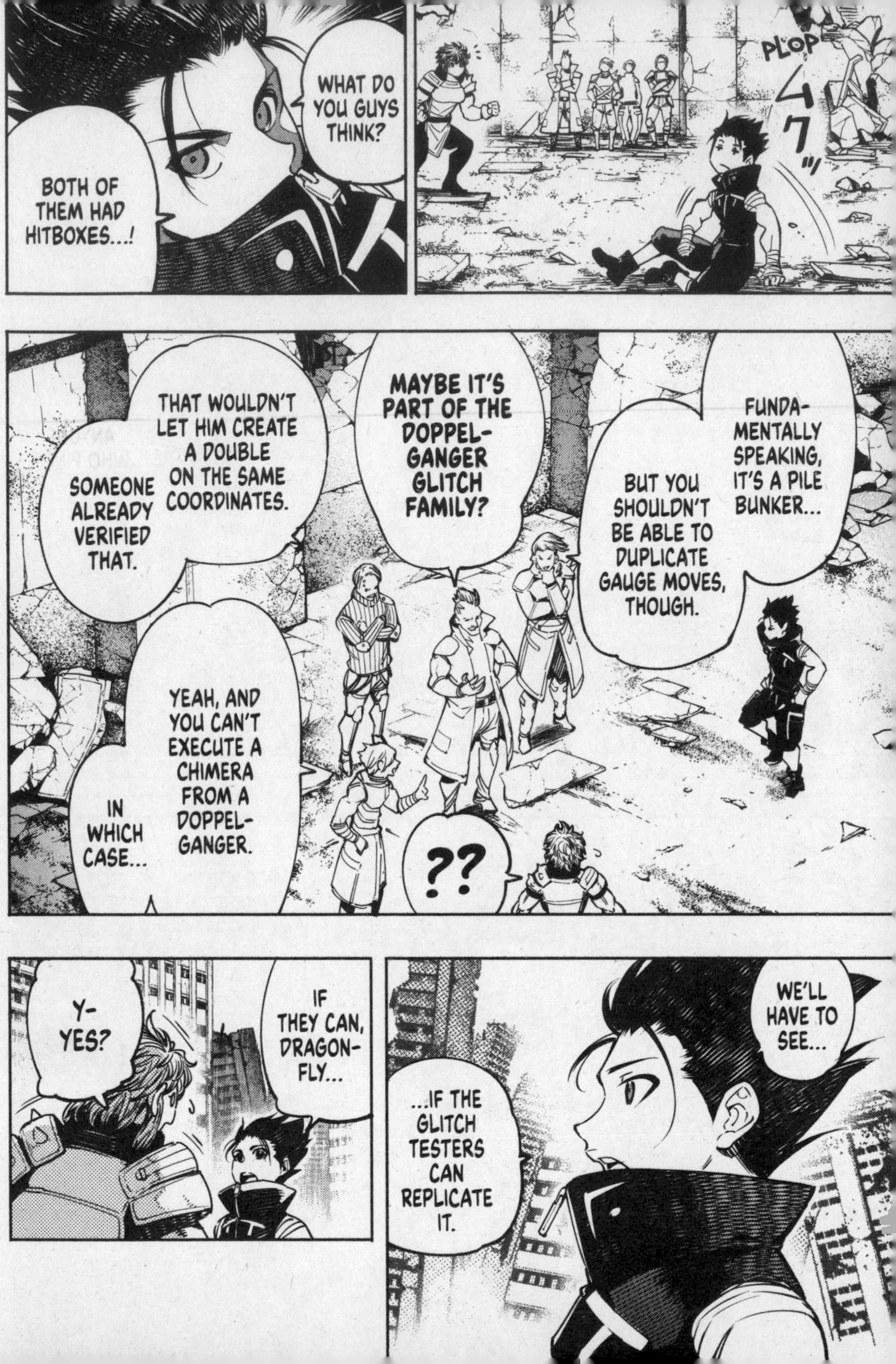
PLOP
ムクッ
WHAT DO YOU GUYS THINK?
BOTH OF THEM HAD HITBOXES...!
FUNDAMENTALLY SPEAKING, IT'S A PILE BUNKER...
BUT YOU SHOULDN'T BE ABLE TO DUPLICATE GAUGE MOVES, THOUGH.
MAYBE IT'S PART OF THE DOPPELGANGER GLITCH FAMILY?
THAT WOULDN'T LET HIM CREATE A DOUBLE ON THE SAME COORDINATES.
SOMEONE ALREADY VERIFIED THAT.
??
YEAH, AND YOU CAN'T EXECUTE A CHIMERA FROM A DOPPELGANGER.
IN WHICH CASE...
WE'LL HAVE TO SEE...
...IF THE GLITCH TESTERS CAN REPLICATE IT.
IF THEY CAN, DRAGONFLY...
Y-YES?

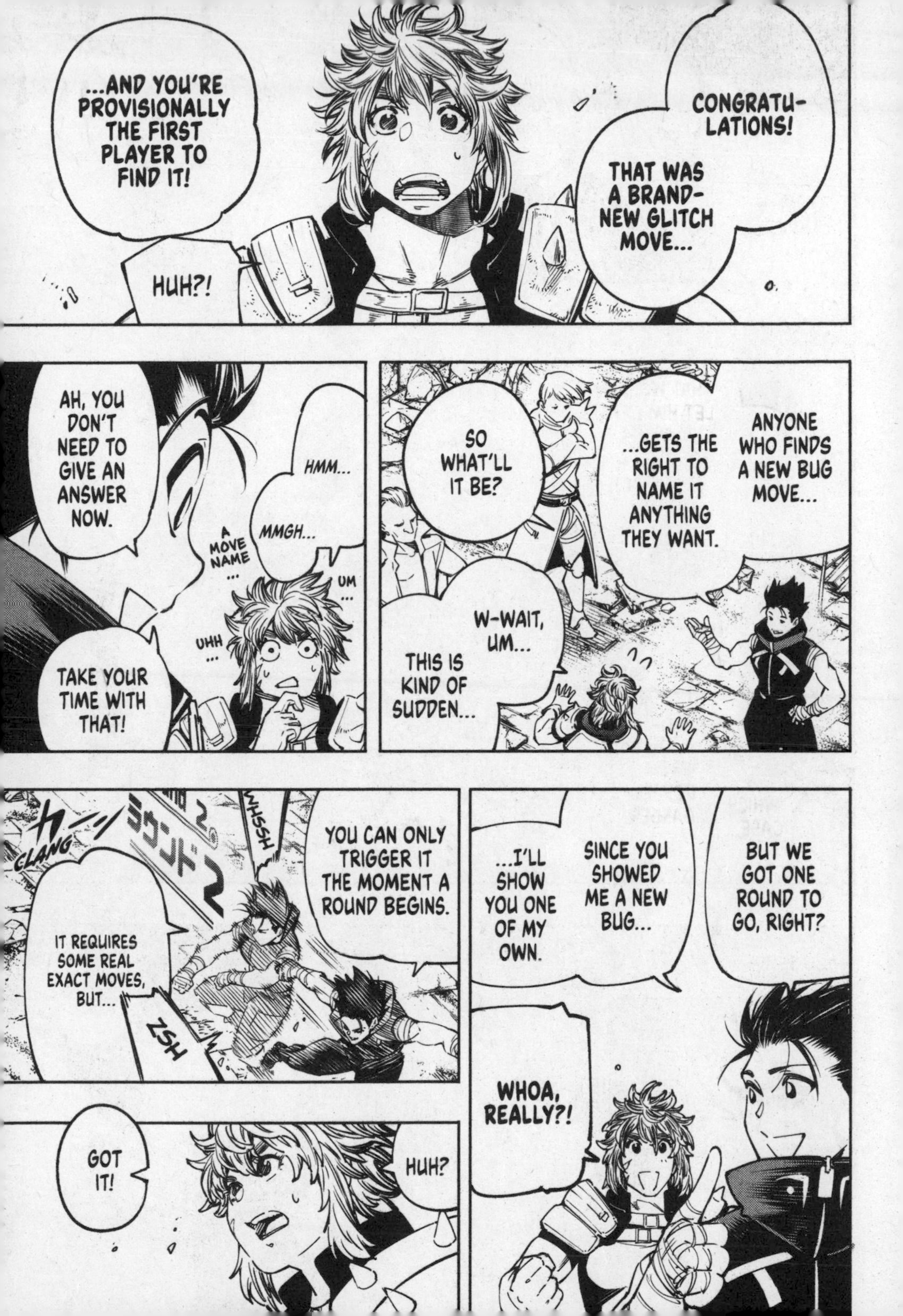
CONGRATULATIONS!
THAT WAS A BRAND-NEW GLITCH MOVE...
...AND YOU'RE PROVISIONALLY THE FIRST PLAYER TO FIND IT!
HUH?!
ANYONE WHO FINDS A NEW BUG MOVE...
...GETS THE RIGHT TO NAME IT ANYTHING THEY WANT.
SO WHAT'LL IT BE?
W-WAIT, UM...
THIS IS KIND OF SUDDEN...
HMM...
MMGH...
AH, YOU DON'T NEED TO GIVE AN ANSWER NOW.
A MOVE NAME ...
UM ...
UHH ...
TAKE YOUR TIME WITH THAT!
BUT WE GOT ONE ROUND TO GO, RIGHT?
SINCE YOU SHOWED ME A NEW BUG...
...I'LL SHOW YOU ONE OF MY OWN.
WHOA, REALLY?!
YOU CAN ONLY TRIGGER IT THE MOMENT A ROUND BEGINS.
WHSSH
CLANG
IT REQUIRES SOME REAL EXACT MOVES, BUT...
ZSH
HUH?
GOT IT!

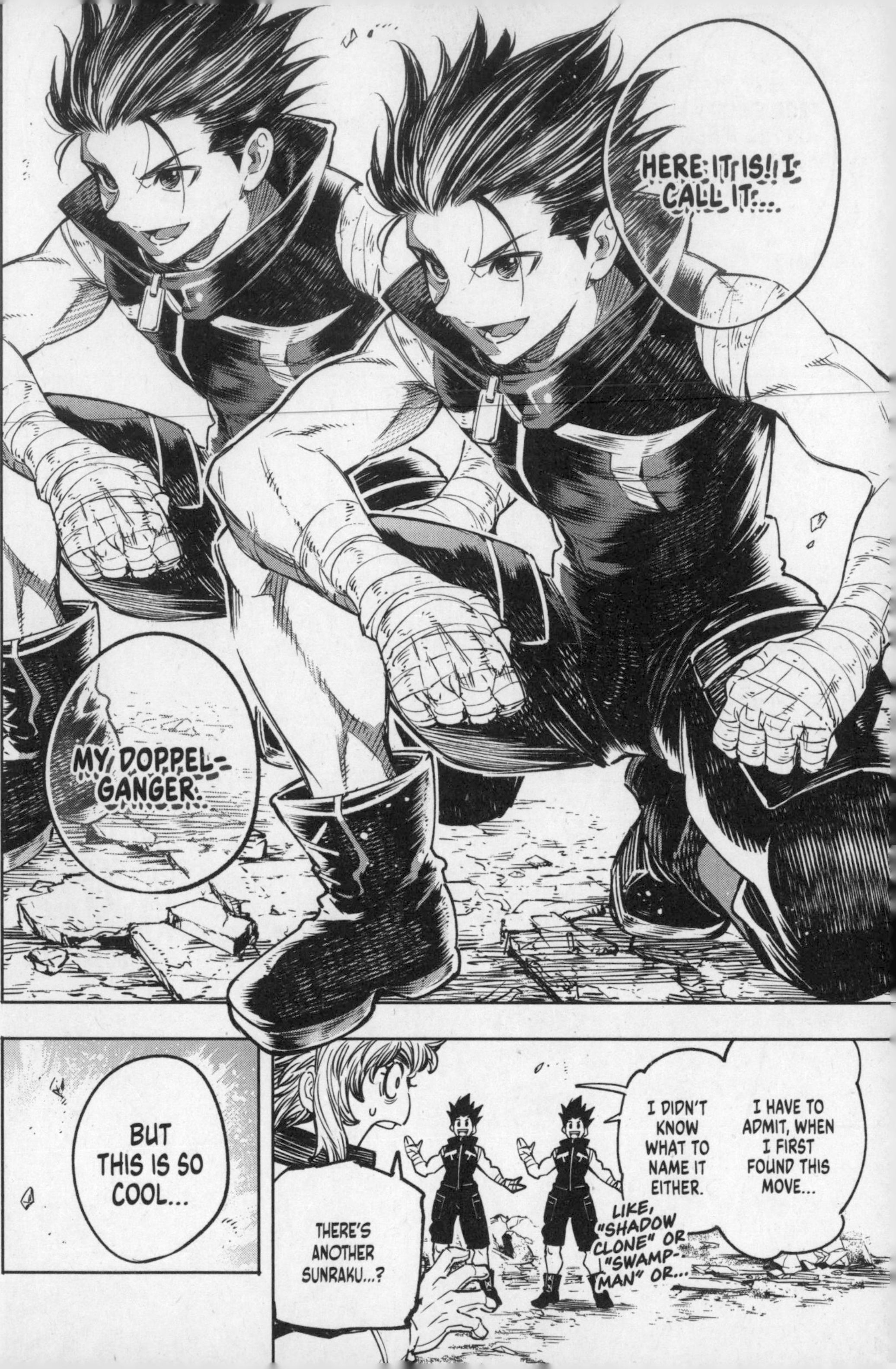
HERE IT IS!! I CALL IT...
MY DOPPEL-GANGER.
I HAVE TO ADMIT, WHEN I FIRST FOUND THIS MOVE...
I DIDN'T KNOW WHAT TO NAME IT EITHER.
LIKE, "SHADOW CLONE" OR "SWAMP-MAN" OR...
THERE'S ANOTHER SUNRAKU...?
BUT THIS IS SO COOL...

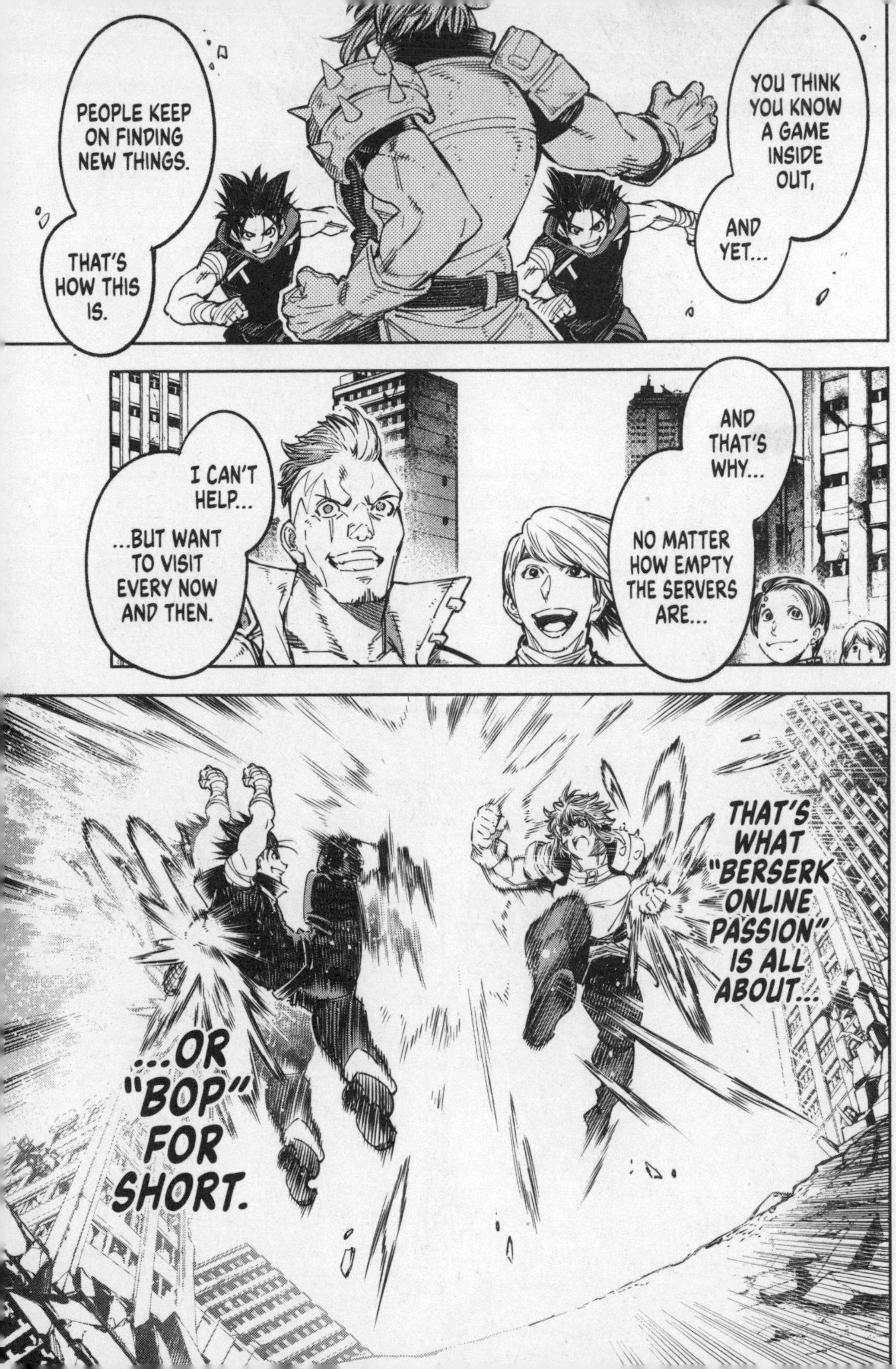
YOU THINK YOU KNOW A GAME INSIDE OUT,
AND YET...
PEOPLE KEEP ON FINDING NEW THINGS.
THAT'S HOW THIS IS.
AND THAT'S WHY...
NO MATTER HOW EMPTY THE SERVERS ARE...
I CAN'T HELP...
...BUT WANT TO VISIT EVERY NOW AND THEN.
THAT'S WHAT "BERSERK ONLINE PASSION" IS ALL ABOUT...
...OR "BOP" FOR SHORT.

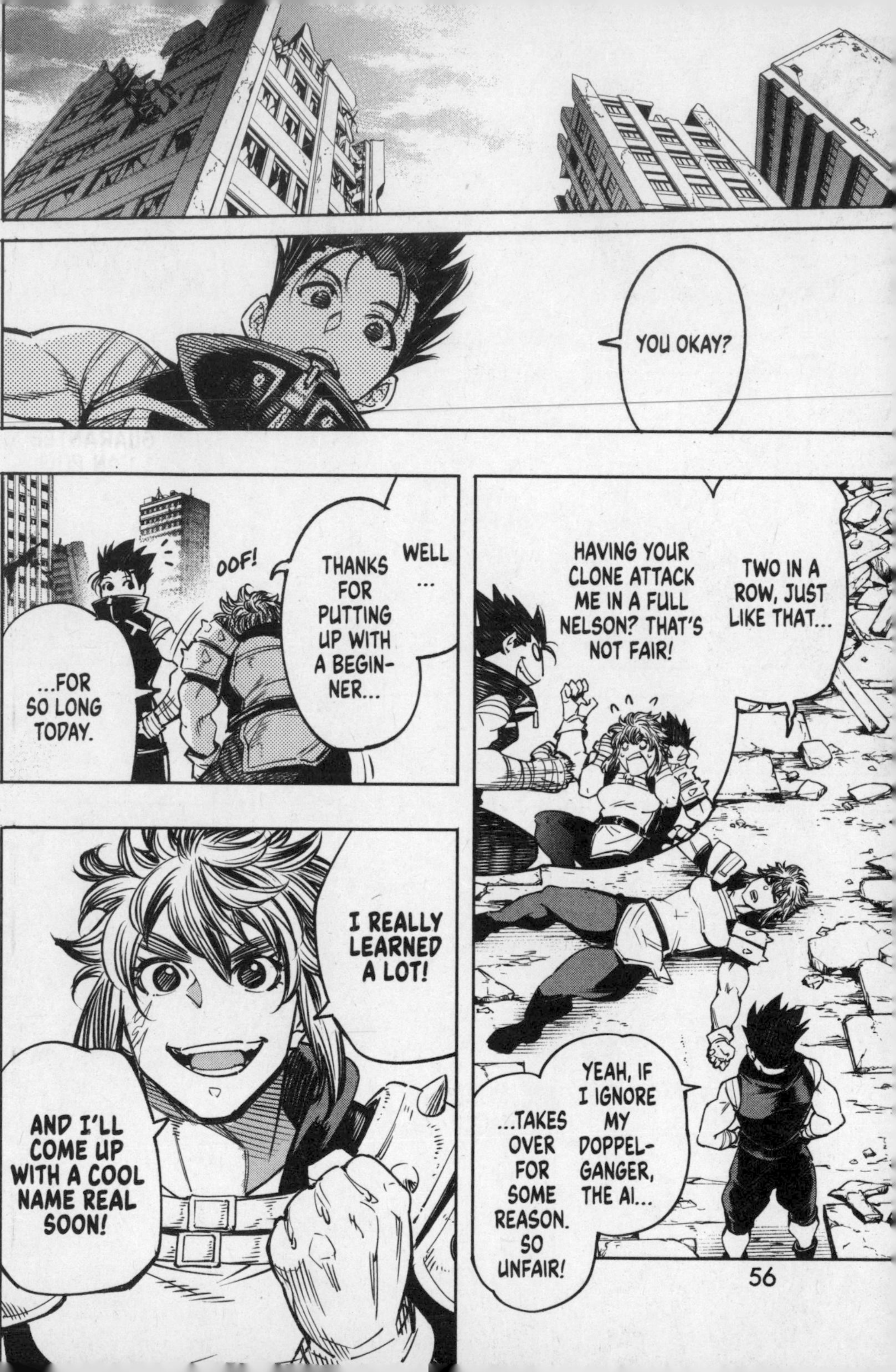
YOU OKAY?
TWO IN A ROW, JUST LIKE THAT...
HAVING YOUR CLONE ATTACK ME IN A FULL NELSON? THAT'S NOT FAIR!
YEAH, IF I IGNORE MY DOPPEL-GANGER, THE AI...
...TAKES OVER FOR SOME REASON. SO UNFAIR!
WELL ...
THANKS FOR PUTTING UP WITH A BEGIN-NER...
OOF!
...FOR SO LONG TODAY.
I REALLY LEARNED A LOT!
AND I'LL COME UP WITH A COOL NAME REAL SOON!

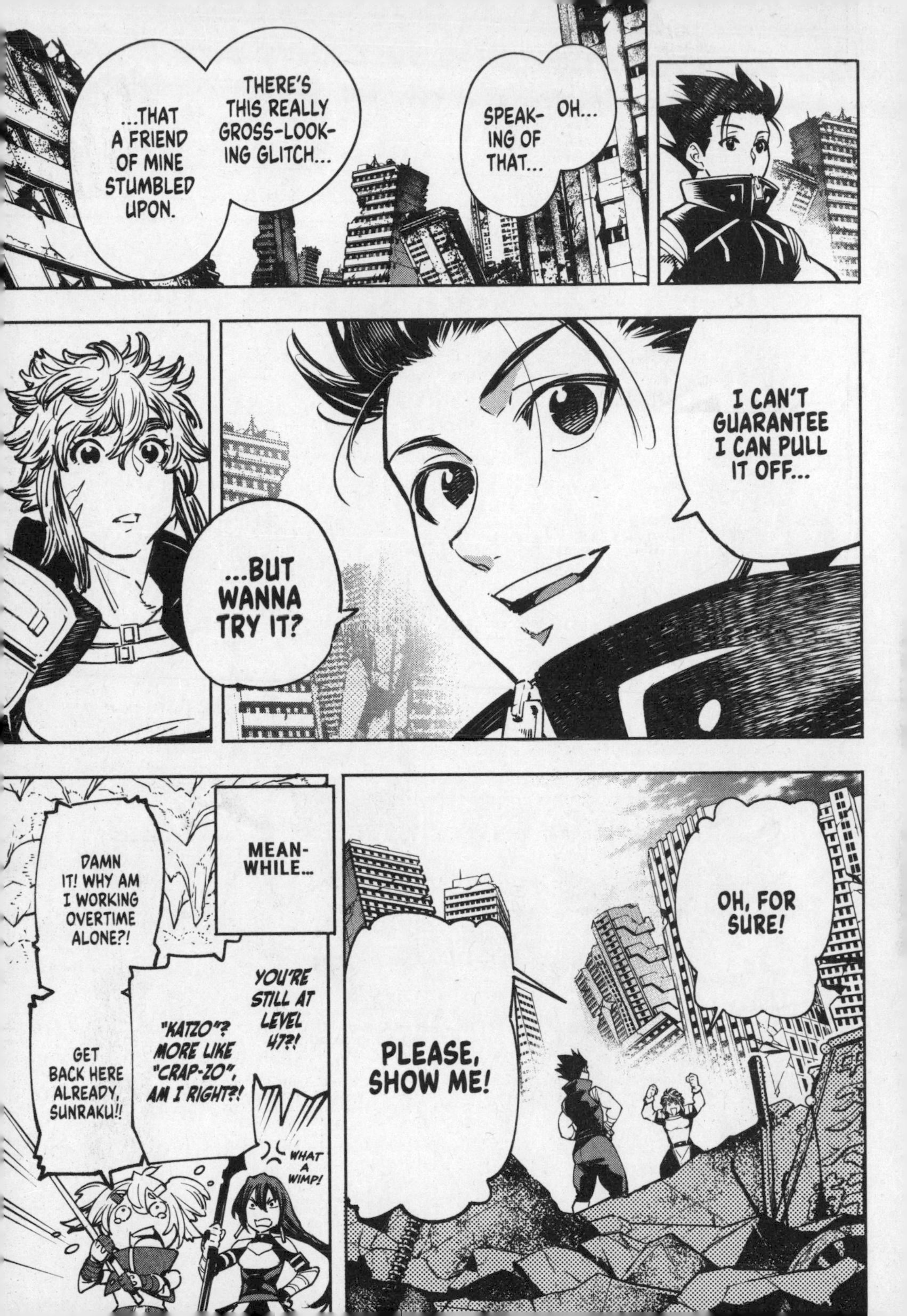
OH...
SPEAK-ING OF THAT...
THERE'S THIS REALLY GROSS-LOOK-ING GLITCH...
...THAT A FRIEND OF MINE STUMBLED UPON.
I CAN'T GUARANTEE I CAN PULL IT OFF...
...BUT WANNA TRY IT?
OH, FOR SURE!
PLEASE, SHOW ME!
MEAN-WHILE...
DAMN IT! WHY AM I WORKING OVERTIME ALONE?!
YOU'RE STILL AT LEVEL 47?!
"KATZO"? MORE LIKE "CRAP-ZO", AM I RIGHT?!
GET BACK HERE ALREADY, SUNRAKU!!
WHAT A WIMP!

READ TO LEARN MORE ABOUT THE WORLD OF SLF!

SHANGRI-LA FRONTIER STRATEGY FORUM

VOL. 16

LET SLF MASTER REI-CHAN TAKE YOU THROUGH THE WORLD!

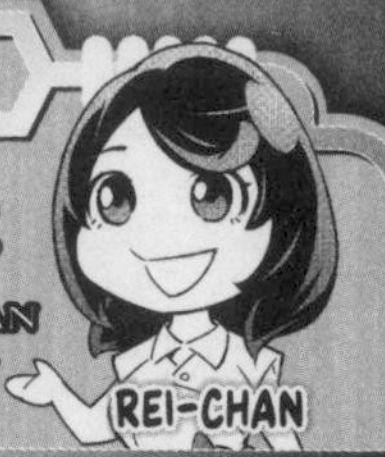
REI-CHAN

Looking at Sunraku's Fave Crap Games!!

LET'S EXAMINE SUNRAKU FROM THE BUGGY FIGHTER BERSERK ONLINE PASSION (BOP)!

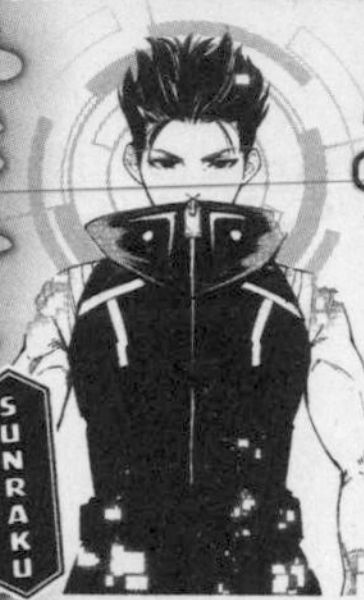
SUNRAKU

Style: Quickdraw Fist

Q: WHAT IS QUICKDRAW FIST?

A: IN BOP, THIS IS A COUNTER-BASED BATTLE STYLE GEARED AGAINST GLITCHED-OUT MOVES, STRIKING FOES JUST BEFORE THEY ATTACK TO CANCEL OUT THE ATTACK. NOT EVEN SUNRAKU HAS MASTERED IT, AND A MASTER OF THE CRAFT COULD BEAT HIM WITH ONE HAND...APPARENTLY.

GLITCH **QUICKDRAW FIST**

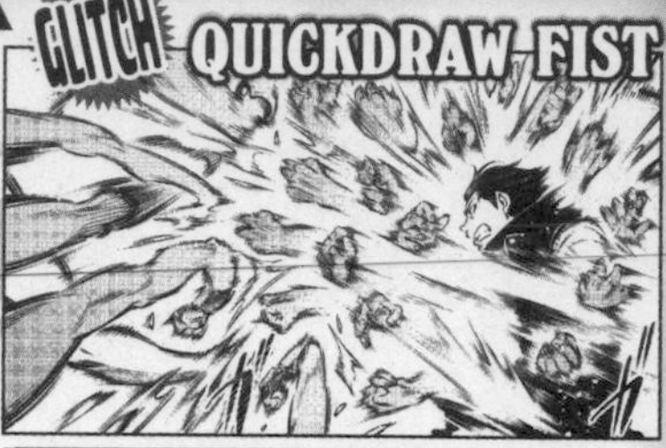

A RARE MOVE FOR THIS STYLE, USING THE "HANDS OUT OF POCKETS" MOTION TO UNLEASH A FLURRY OF HIGH-SPEED FISTS. THERE'S ALSO QUATTRO AGONY, AIMED AT FOES' PRESSURE POINTS, AND DELAYED QUICKDRAW FIST, LAUNCHED IN ANTICIPATION OF THE ENEMY'S MOVES.

HERE'S SOME OTHER GLITCH MOVES!

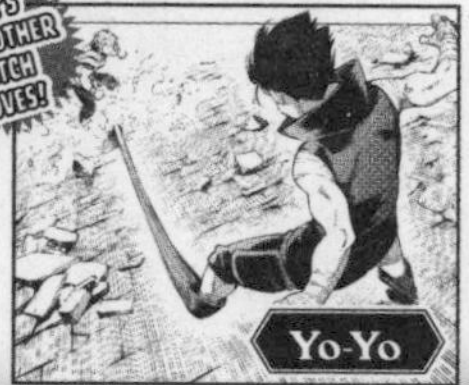

Yo-Yo

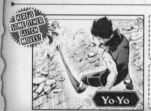

EFFECT WARP AWAY FROM YOUR LEFT FOOT TO EVADE FOR THREE SECONDS.

MOVE JUMP WITH YOUR RIGHT FOOT, BUT KEEP YOUR LEFT FOOT FIRM.

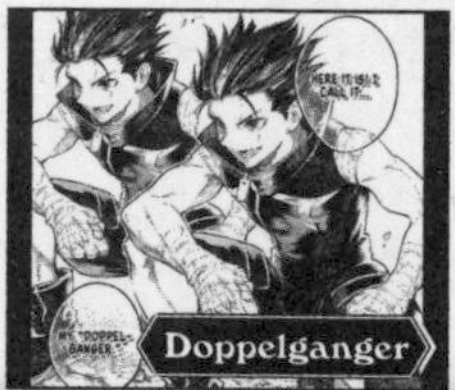

Doppelganger

EFFECT MAKES A CLONE. CANNOT PLACE ON YOUR SAME COORDINATES.

MOVE START A GAUGE ATTACK TO OPEN, THEN DODGE JUST BEFORE IT LAUNCHES.

BONUS *This Game Traumatized Sunraku!!*

Love Clock

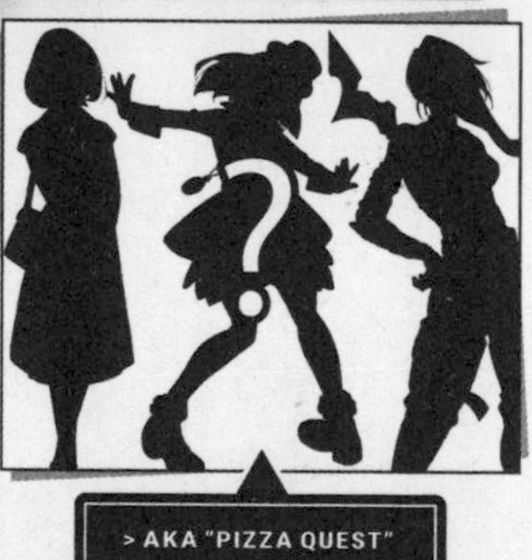

> AKA "PIZZA QUEST"

GENRE: DATING SIM

THIS IS CRAP! **Fiendish Girl Stat Management!**

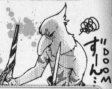

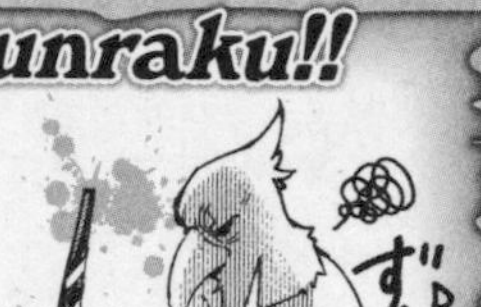
DOOOM

IN THIS DATING SIM, YOU'VE GOT TWELVE GIRLS TO TRY TO WOO...BUT MESS UP THE CHOICES OR TIMING, AND YOU'LL GET A BAD ENDING WHERE THEY ALL GO STUDY ABROAD IN ITALY TO LEARN HOW TO MAKE PIZZA!

MISS AN EVENT BY .1 SECONDS, AND THAT TRIGGERS A DOMINO EFFECT WITH ALL THE GIRLS, SO PLAYERS MUST TIME WHEN THEY TALK TO THE HEROINES ON THE MILLISECOND LEVEL.

BUT! SUNRAKU USED THIS GAME TO MASTER SKILLS LIKE INSTANT CHART MANAGEMENT, SITUATIONAL AWARENESS, AND BEST-CASE CALCULATION!

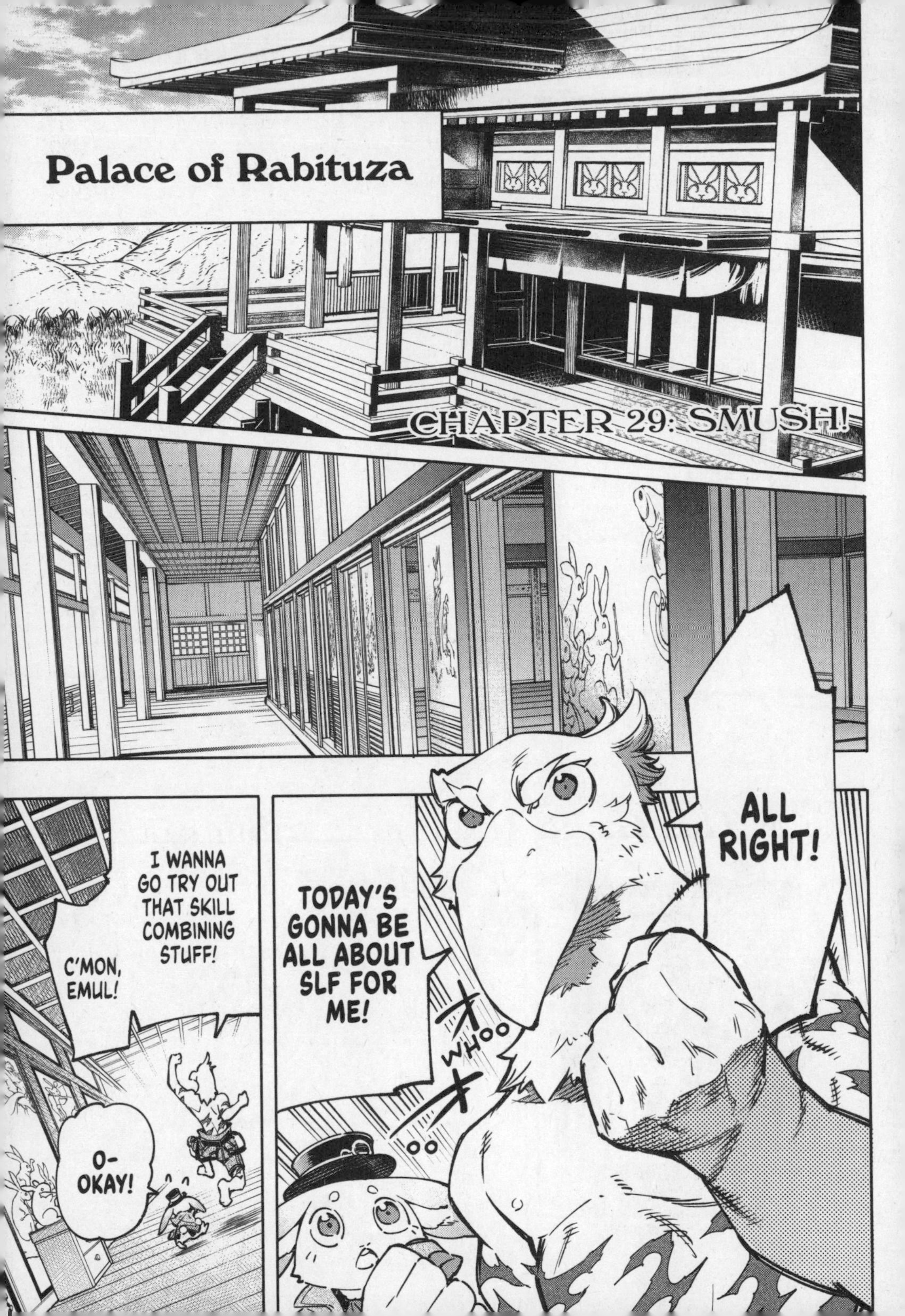
Palace of Rabituza
CHAPTER 29: SMUSH!
ALL RIGHT!
TODAY'S GONNA BE ALL ABOUT SLF FOR ME!
WHOO
...
I WANNA GO TRY OUT THAT SKILL COMBINING STUFF!
C'MON, EMUL!
O-OKAY!

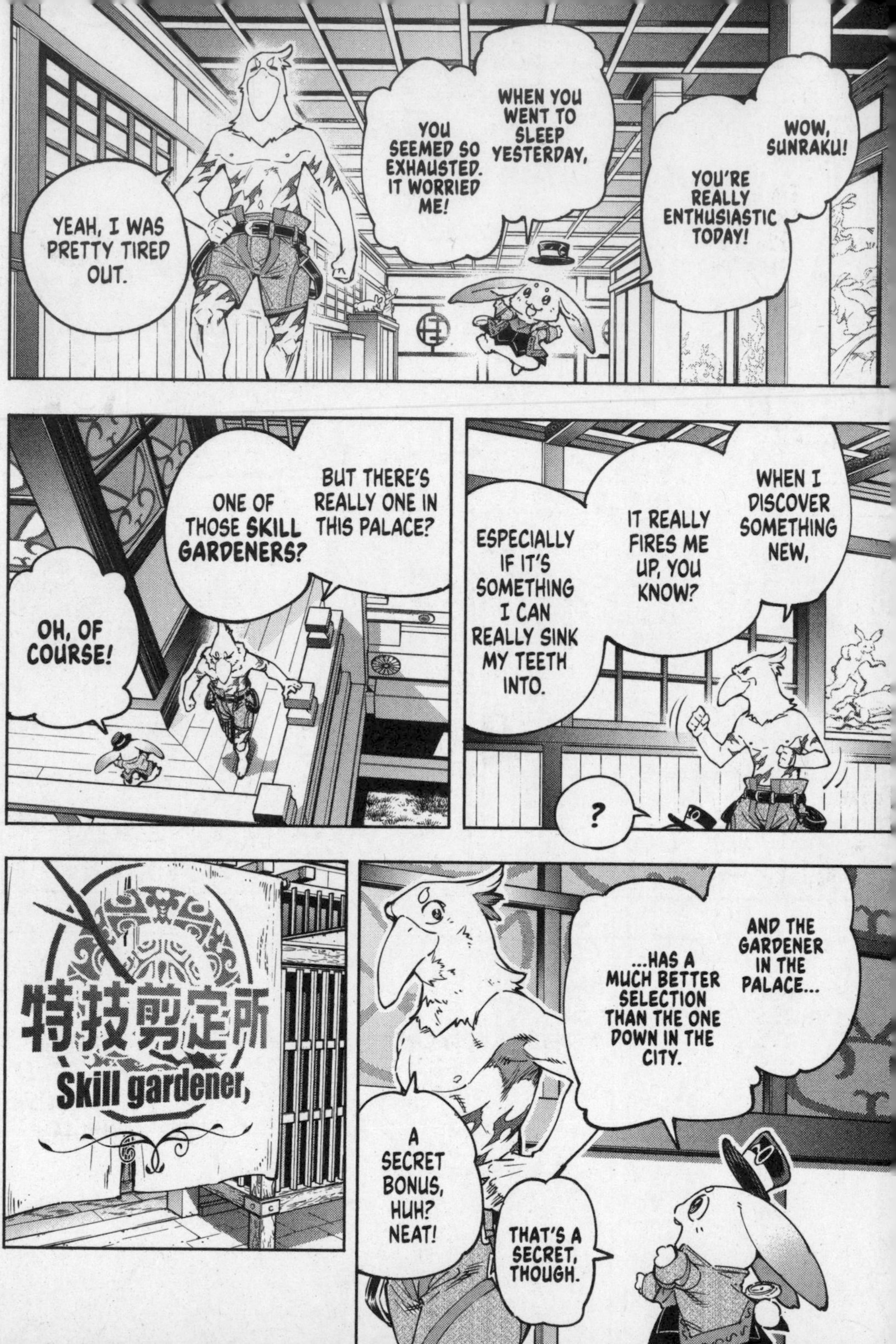
WOW, SUNRAKU!
YOU'RE REALLY ENTHUSIASTIC TODAY!
WHEN YOU WENT TO SLEEP YESTERDAY,
YOU SEEMED SO EXHAUSTED. IT WORRIED ME!
YEAH, I WAS PRETTY TIRED OUT.
WHEN I DISCOVER SOMETHING NEW,
IT REALLY FIRES ME UP, YOU KNOW?
ESPECIALLY IF IT'S SOMETHING I CAN REALLY SINK MY TEETH INTO.
?
BUT THERE'S REALLY ONE IN THIS PALACE?
ONE OF THOSE SKILL GARDENERS?
OH, OF COURSE!
AND THE GARDENER IN THE PALACE...
...HAS A MUCH BETTER SELECTION THAN THE ONE DOWN IN THE CITY.
THAT'S A SECRET, THOUGH.
A SECRET BONUS, HUH? NEAT!
特技剪定所
Skill gardener,

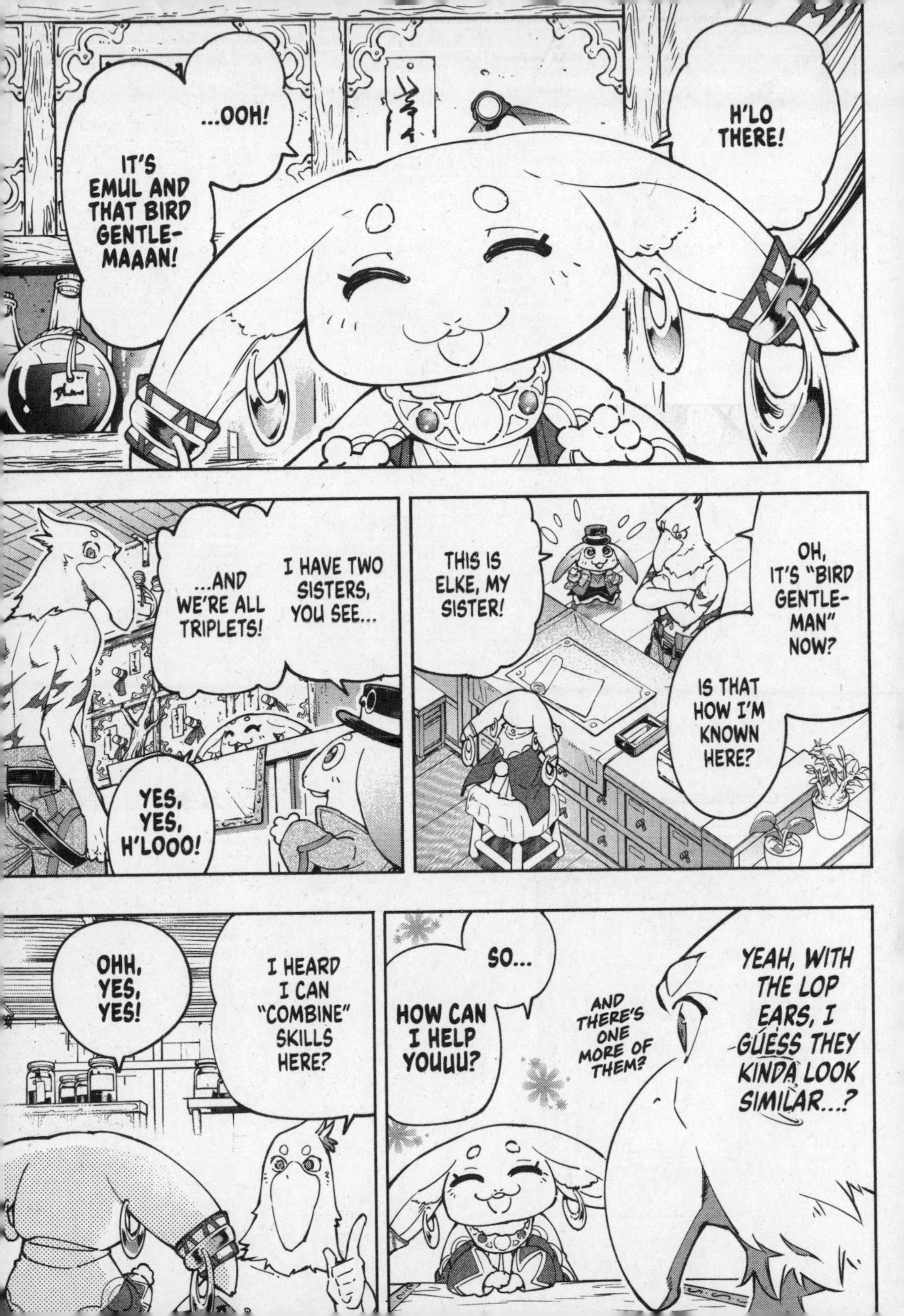
H'LO THERE!
...OOH! IT'S EMUL AND THAT BIRD GENTLE-MAAAN!
THIS IS ELKE, MY SISTER!
OH, IT'S "BIRD GENTLE-MAN" NOW?
IS THAT HOW I'M KNOWN HERE?
I HAVE TWO SISTERS, YOU SEE...
...AND WE'RE ALL TRIPLETS!
YES, YES, H'LOOO!
YEAH, WITH THE LOP EARS, I GUESS THEY KINDA LOOK SIMILAR...?
AND THERE'S ONE MORE OF THEM?
SO...
HOW CAN I HELP YOUUU?
I HEARD I CAN "COMBINE" SKILLS HERE?
OHH, YES, YES!

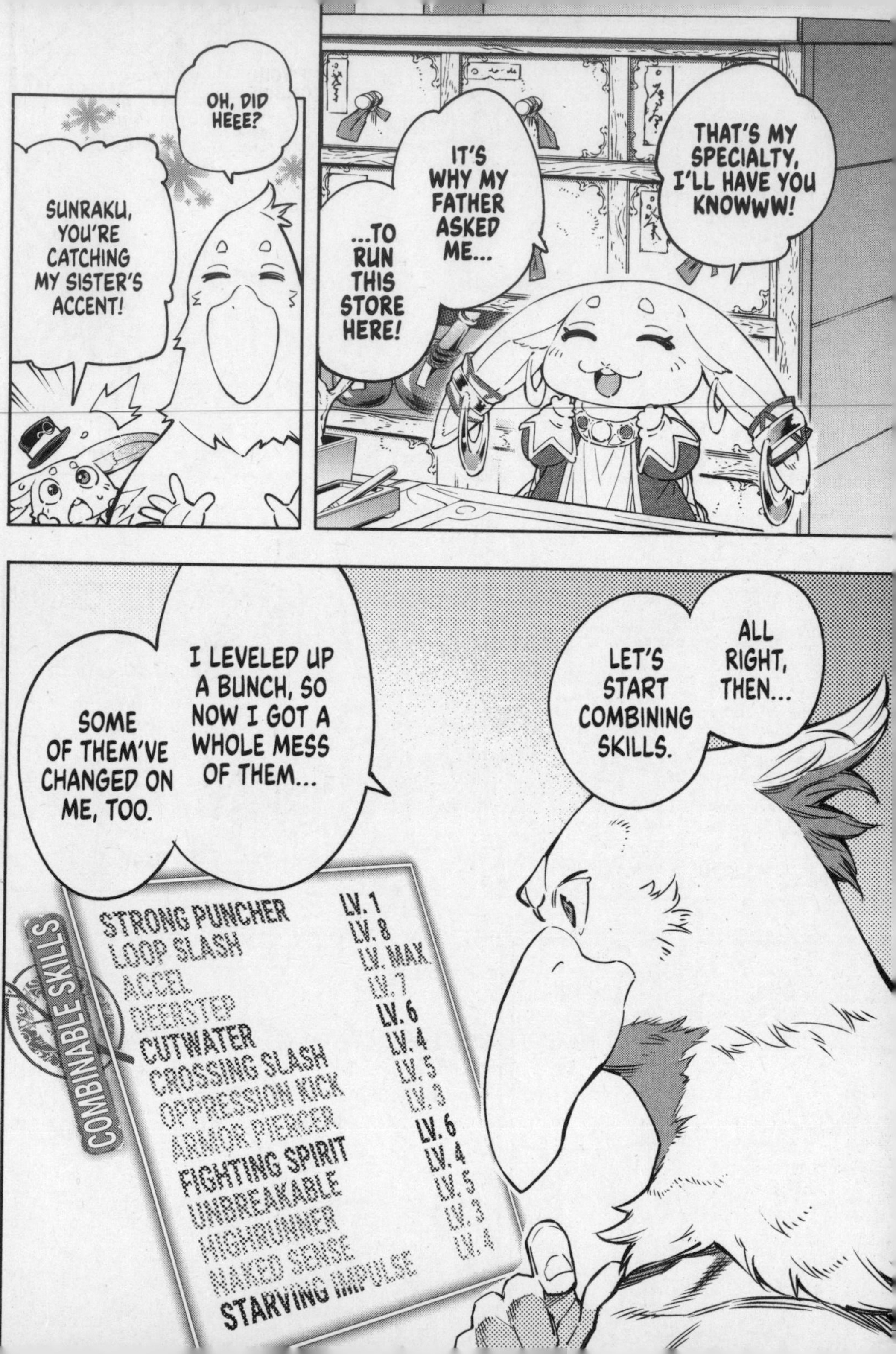
THAT'S MY SPECIALTY, I'LL HAVE YOU KNOWWW!
IT'S WHY MY FATHER ASKED ME...
...TO RUN THIS STORE HERE!
OH, DID HEEE?
SUNRAKU, YOU'RE CATCHING MY SISTER'S ACCENT!
ALL RIGHT, THEN...
LET'S START COMBINING SKILLS.
I LEVELED UP A BUNCH, SO NOW I GOT A WHOLE MESS OF THEM...
SOME OF THEM'VE CHANGED ON ME, TOO.
COMBINABLE SKILLS
STRONG PUNCHER LV. 1
LOOP SLASH LV. 8
ACCEL LV. MAX.
DEERSTEP LV. 7
CUTWATER LV. 6
CROSSING SLASH LV. 4
OPPRESSION KICK LV. 5
ARMOR PIERCER LV. 3
FIGHTING SPIRIT LV. 6
UNBREAKABLE LV. 4
HIGHRUNNER LV. 5
NAKED SENSE LV. 3
STARVING IMPULSE LV. 4

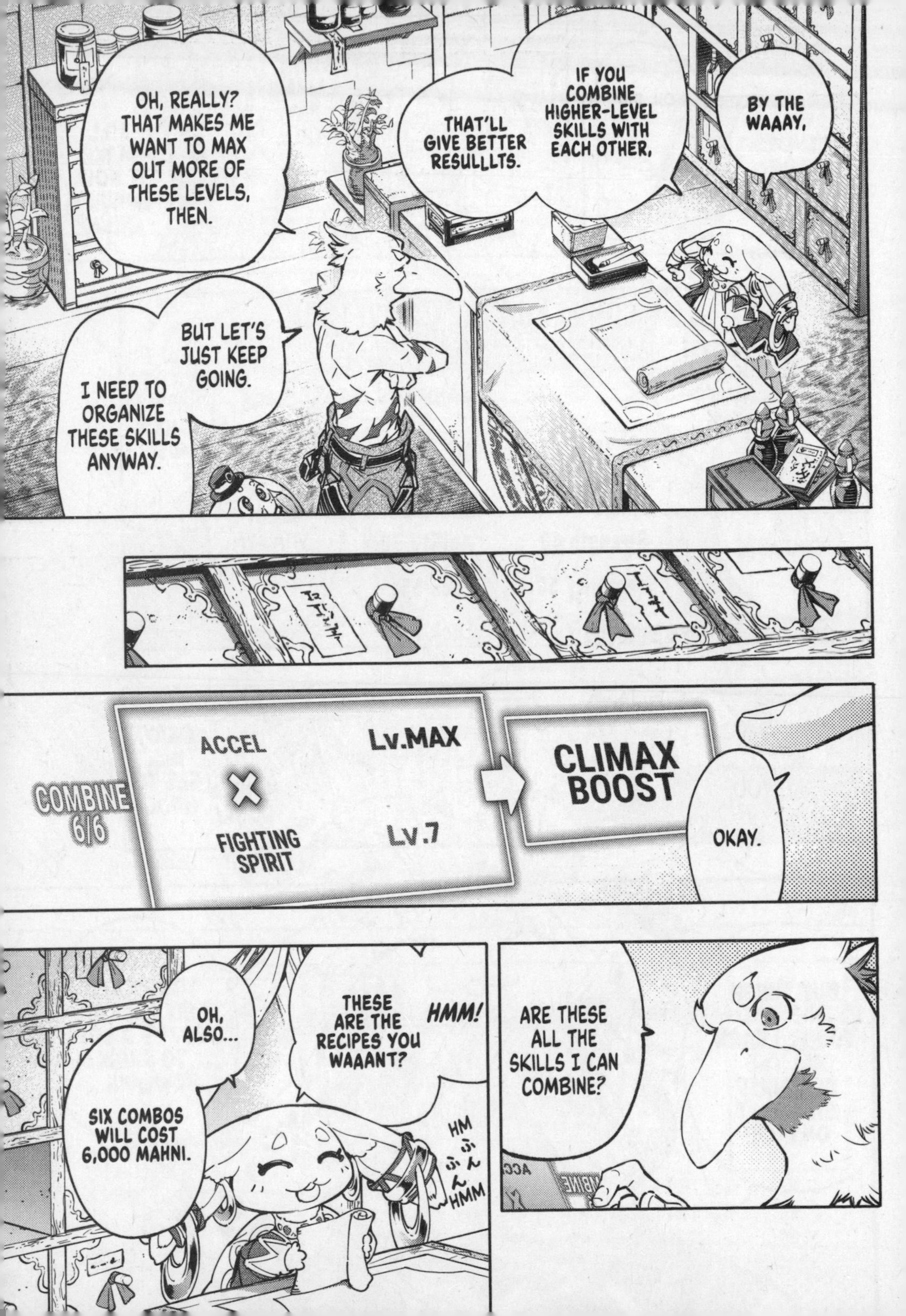
BY THE WAAAY,
IF YOU COMBINE HIGHER-LEVEL SKILLS WITH EACH OTHER,
THAT'LL GIVE BETTER RESULLLTS.
OH, REALLY? THAT MAKES ME WANT TO MAX OUT MORE OF THESE LEVELS, THEN.
BUT LET'S JUST KEEP GOING.
I NEED TO ORGANIZE THESE SKILLS ANYWAY.
OKAY.
COMBINE 6/6
ACCEL Lv.MAX
FIGHTING SPIRIT Lv.7
CLIMAX BOOST
ARE THESE ALL THE SKILLS I CAN COMBINE?
HMM!
THESE ARE THE RECIPES YOU WAAANT?
OH, ALSO...
SIX COMBOS WILL COST 6,000 MAHNI.
HM ふん ふん HMM

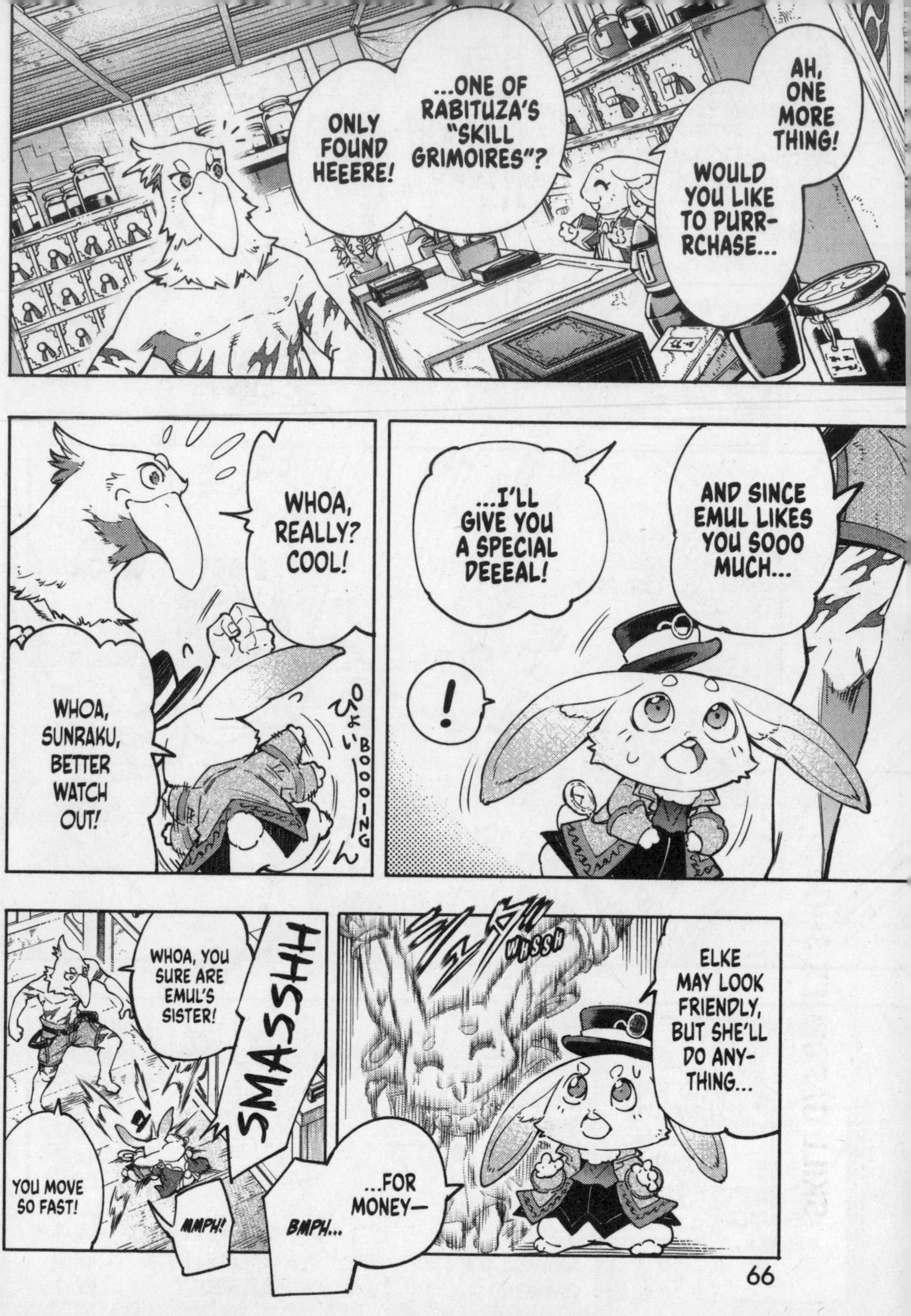
AH, ONE MORE THING!
WOULD YOU LIKE TO PURR-RCHASE...
...ONE OF RABITUZA'S "SKILL GRIMOIRES"?
ONLY FOUND HEEERE!
AND SINCE EMUL LIKES YOU SOOO MUCH...
...I'LL GIVE YOU A SPECIAL DEEEAL!
!
WHOA, REALLY? COOL!
ぴょいーん
BOOOOING
WHOA, SUNRAKU, BETTER WATCH OUT!
WHSSH
ELKE MAY LOOK FRIENDLY, BUT SHE'LL DO ANY-THING...
...FOR MONEY—
BMPH...
SMASSHH
WHOA, YOU SURE ARE EMUL'S SISTER!
YOU MOVE SO FAST!
MMPH!

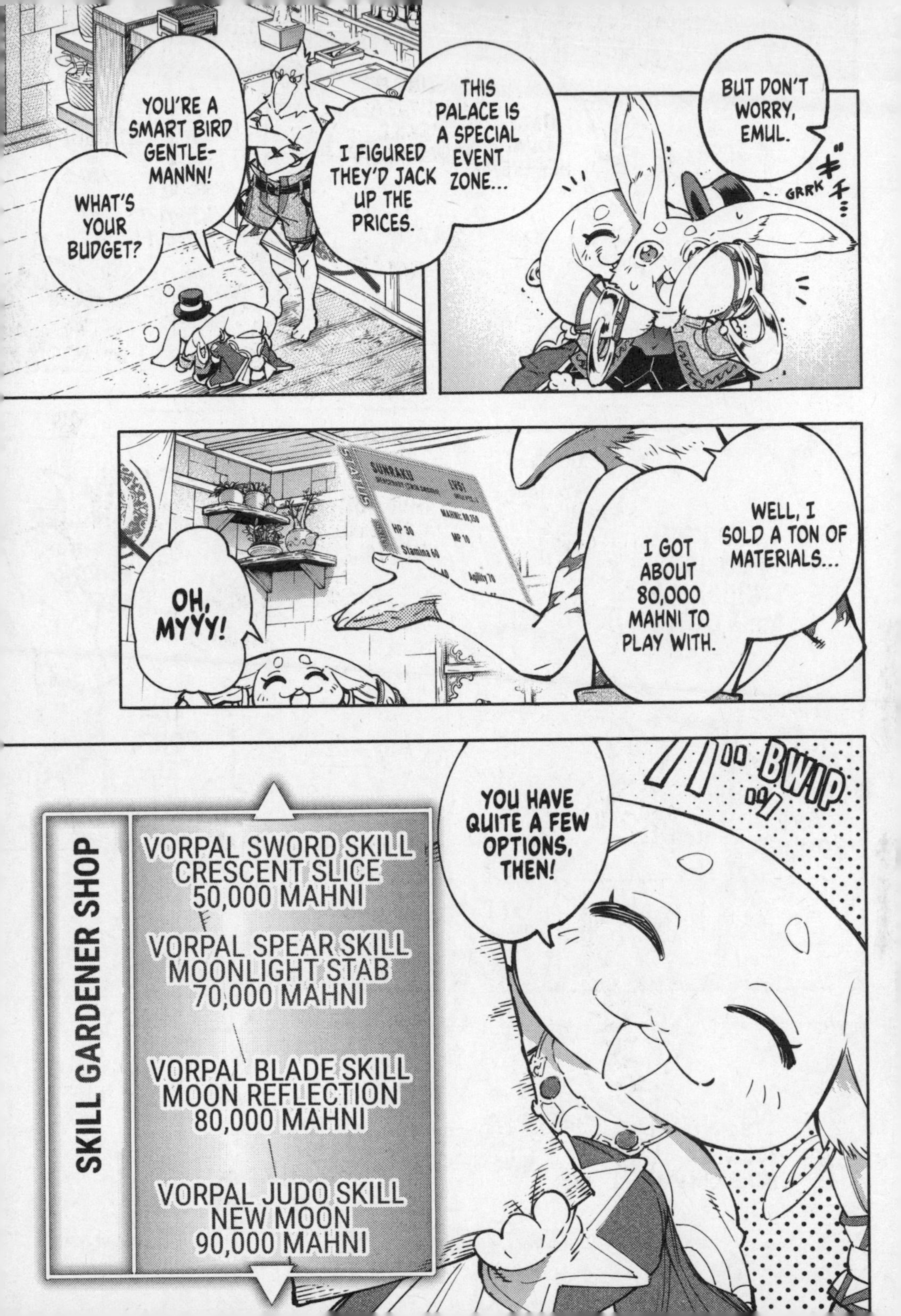

BUT DON'T WORRY, EMUL.
GRRK
THIS PALACE IS A SPECIAL EVENT ZONE...
I FIGURED THEY'D JACK UP THE PRICES.
YOU'RE A SMART BIRD GENTLE-MANNN!
WHAT'S YOUR BUDGET?
WELL, I SOLD A TON OF MATERIALS...
I GOT ABOUT 80,000 MAHNI TO PLAY WITH.
STATUS
SUNRAKU
HP 30
MP 10
Stamina 60
Agility 70
OH, MYYY!
BWIP
YOU HAVE QUITE A FEW OPTIONS, THEN!
SKILL GARDENER SHOP
VORPAL SWORD SKILL
CRESCENT SLICE
50,000 MAHNI
VORPAL SPEAR SKILL
MOONLIGHT STAB
70,000 MAHNI
VORPAL BLADE SKILL
MOON REFLECTION
80,000 MAHNI
VORPAL JUDO SKILL
NEW MOON
90,000 MAHNI

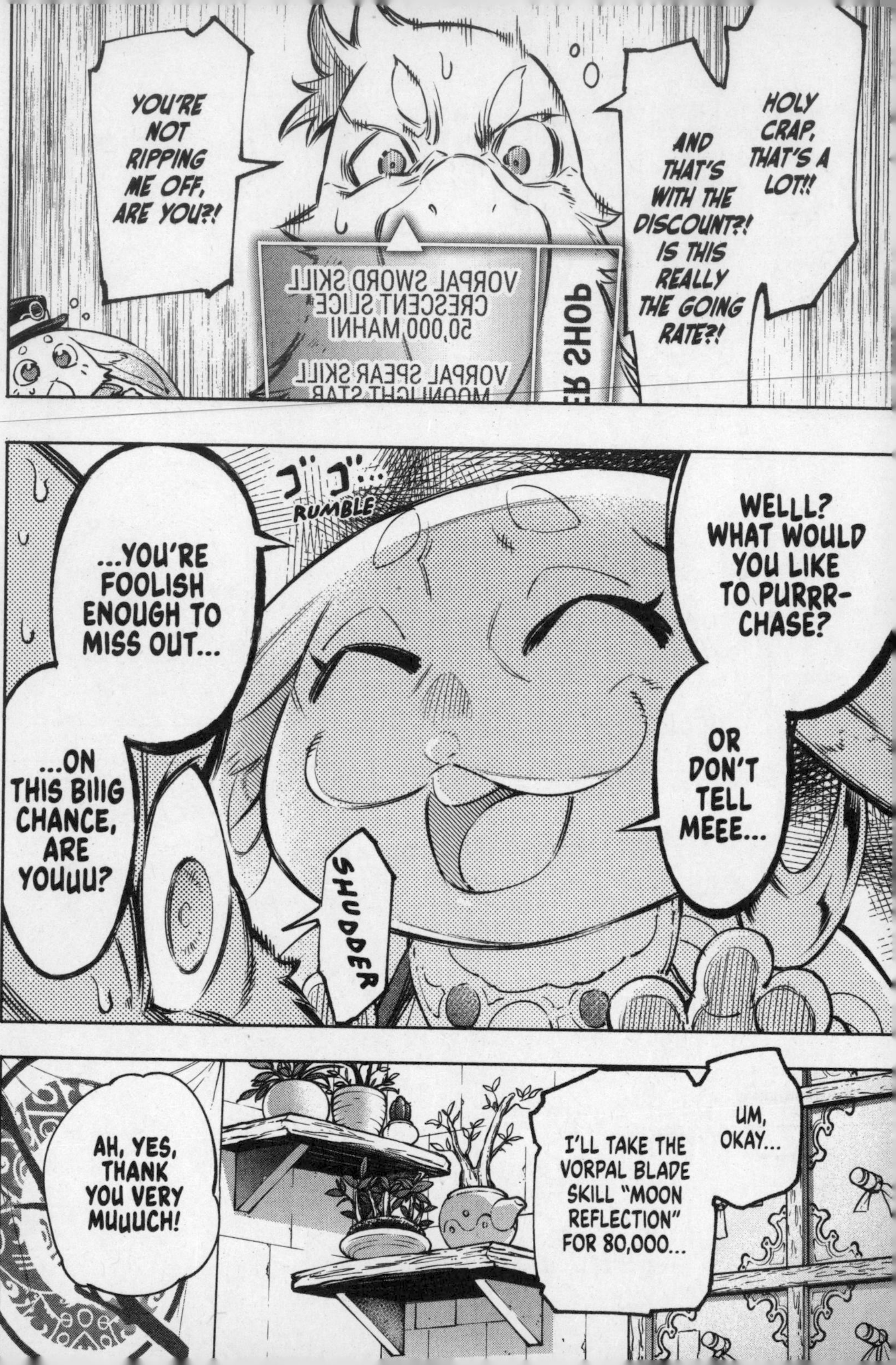
HOLY CRAP, THAT'S A LOT!!
AND THAT'S WITH THE DISCOUNT?! IS THIS REALLY THE GOING RATE?!
VORPAL SWORD SKILL
CRESCENT SLICE
50,000 MAHNI
VORPAL SPEAR SKILL
YOU'RE NOT RIPPING ME OFF, ARE YOU?!
WELLL? WHAT WOULD YOU LIKE TO PURRR-CHASE?
OR DON'T TELL MEEE...
ゴゴ...
RUMBLE
SHUDDER
...YOU'RE FOOLISH ENOUGH TO MISS OUT...
...ON THIS BIIIG CHANCE, ARE YOUUU?
UM, OKAY...
I'LL TAKE THE VORPAL BLADE SKILL "MOON REFLECTION" FOR 80,000...
AH, YES, THANK YOU VERY MUUUCH!

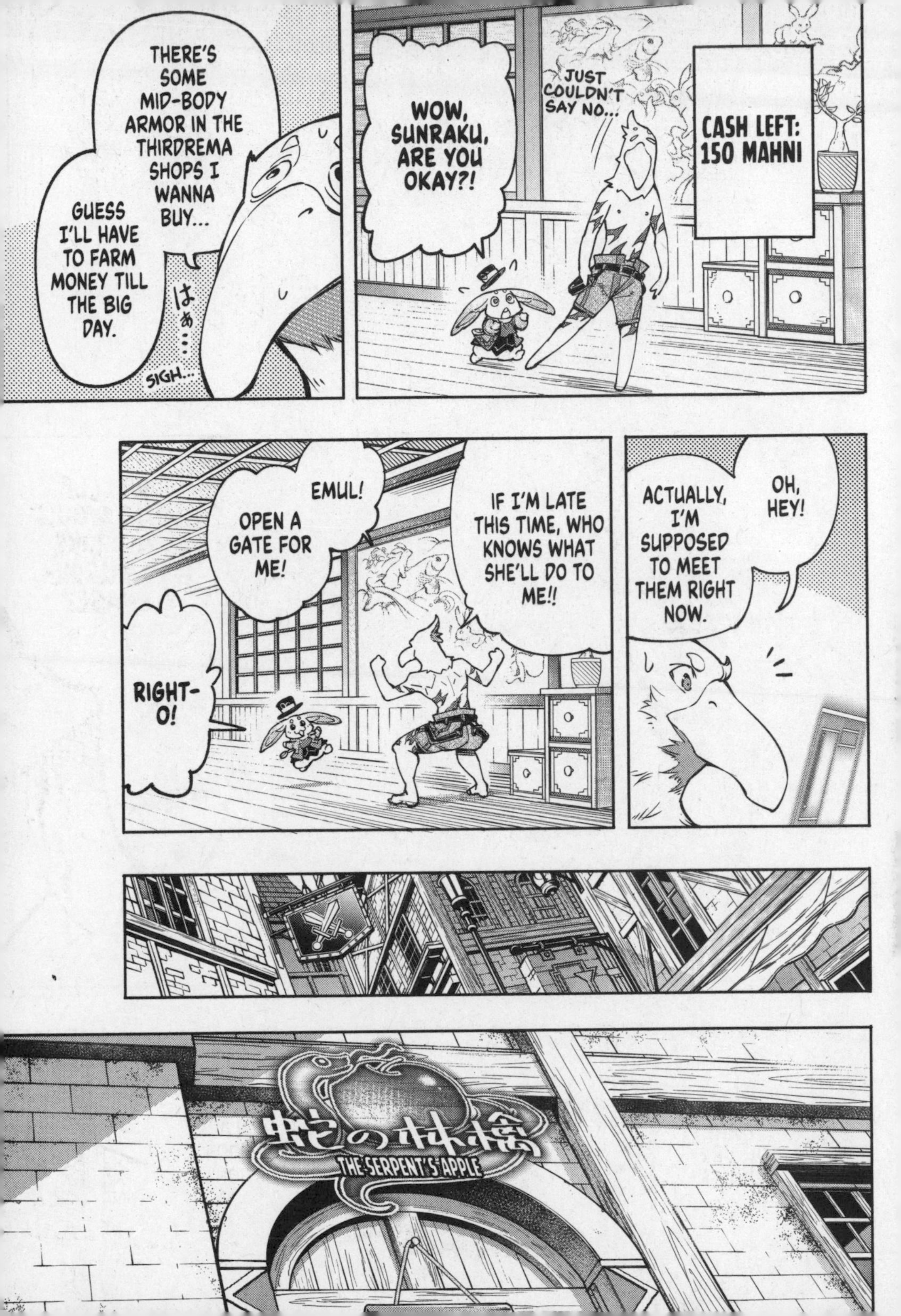
CASH LEFT: 150 MAHNI
JUST COULDN'T SAY NO...
WOW, SUNRAKU, ARE YOU OKAY?!
THERE'S SOME MID-BODY ARMOR IN THE THIRDREMA SHOPS I WANNA BUY...
GUESS I'LL HAVE TO FARM MONEY TILL THE BIG DAY.
はぁ…
SIGH...
OH, HEY!
ACTUALLY, I'M SUPPOSED TO MEET THEM RIGHT NOW.
IF I'M LATE THIS TIME, WHO KNOWS WHAT SHE'LL DO TO ME!!
EMUL!
OPEN A GATE FOR ME!
RIGHT-O!
THE SERPENT'S APPLE

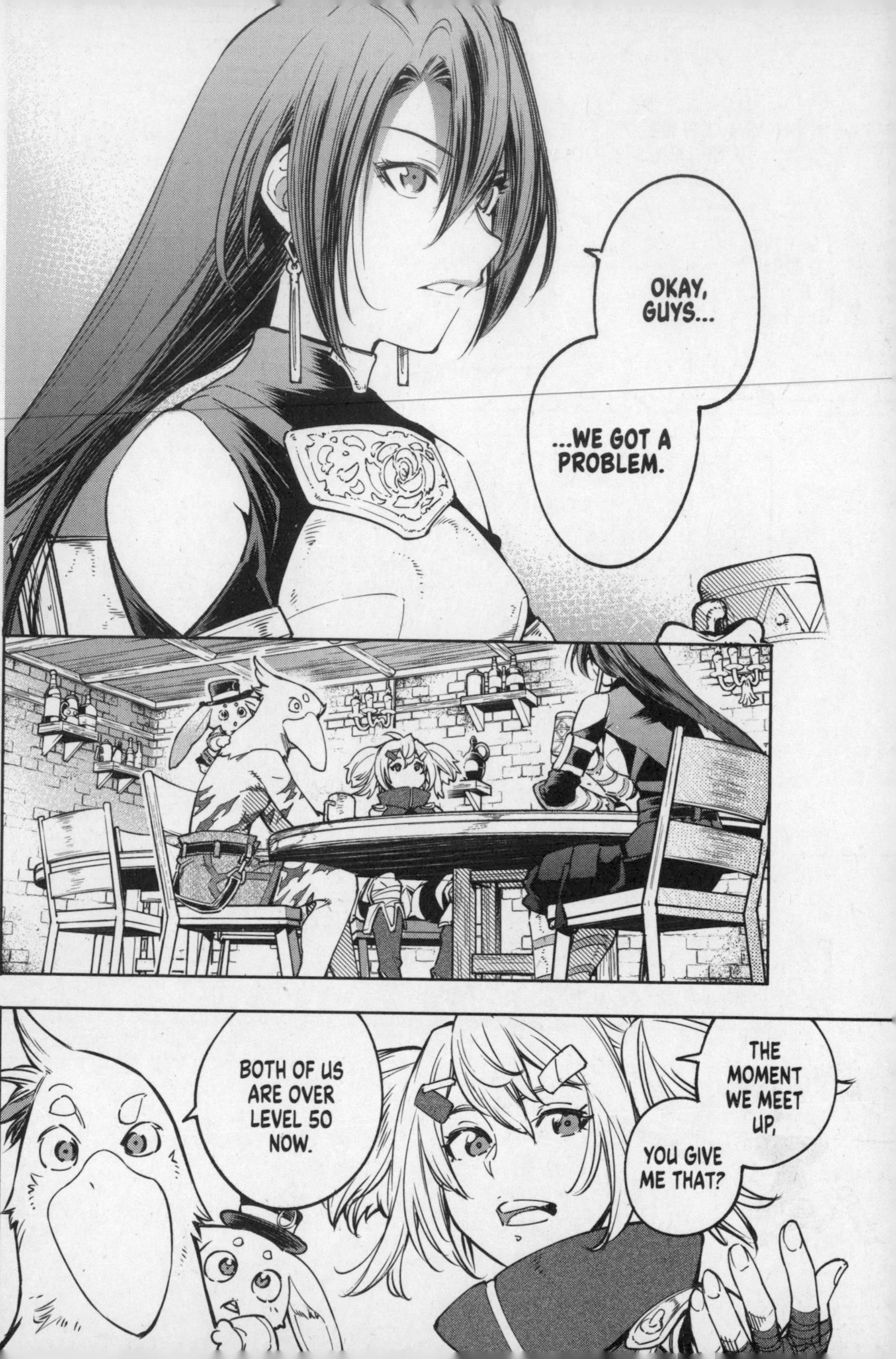
OKAY, GUYS...
...WE GOT A PROBLEM.
THE MOMENT WE MEET UP,
YOU GIVE ME THAT?
BOTH OF US ARE OVER LEVEL 50 NOW.

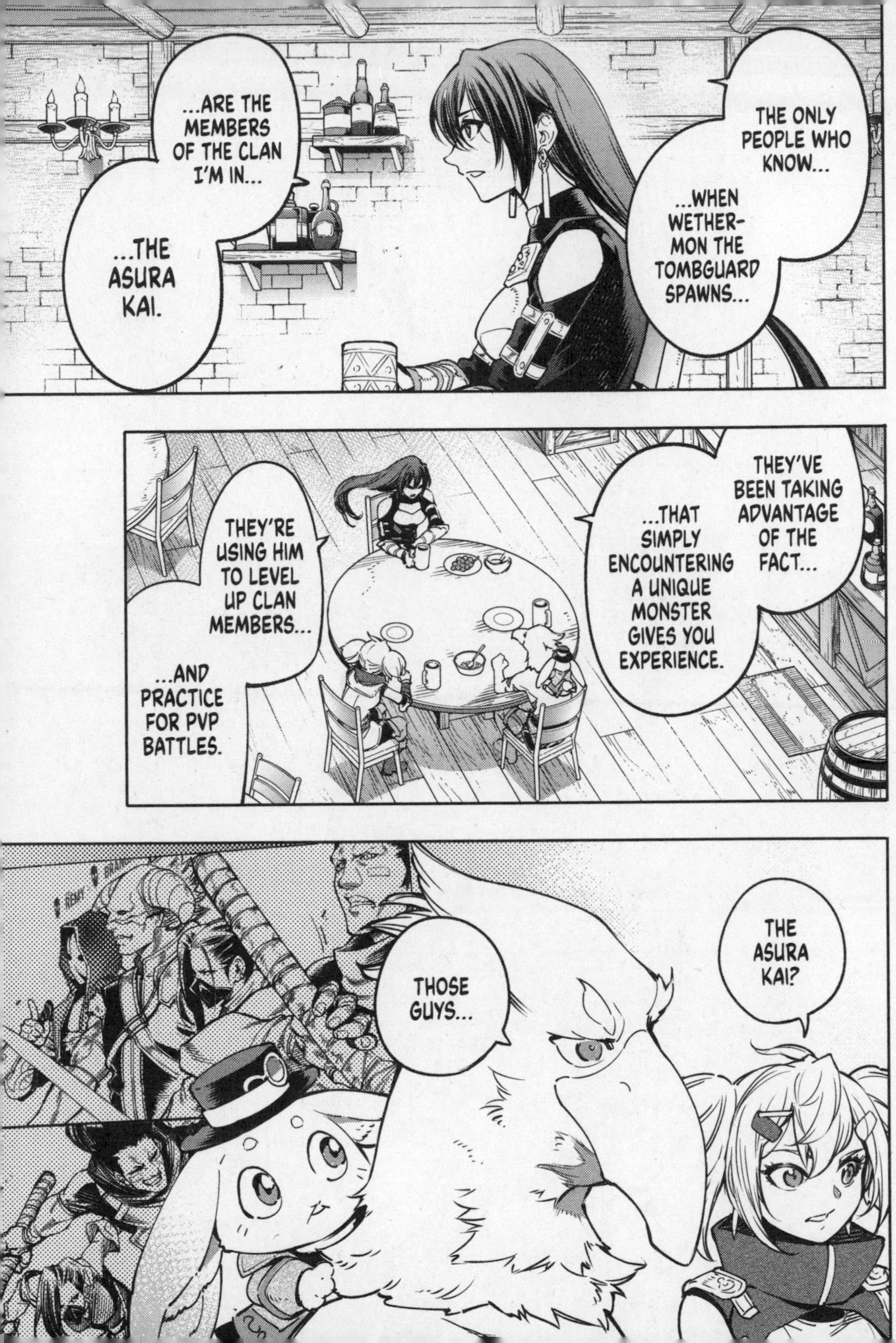
THE ONLY PEOPLE WHO KNOW...
...WHEN WETHER-MON THE TOMBGUARD SPAWNS...
...ARE THE MEMBERS OF THE CLAN I'M IN...
...THE ASURA KAI.
THEY'VE BEEN TAKING ADVANTAGE OF THE FACT...
...THAT SIMPLY ENCOUNTERING A UNIQUE MONSTER GIVES YOU EXPERIENCE.
THEY'RE USING HIM TO LEVEL UP CLAN MEMBERS...
...AND PRACTICE FOR PVP BATTLES.
THE ASURA KAI?
THOSE GUYS...

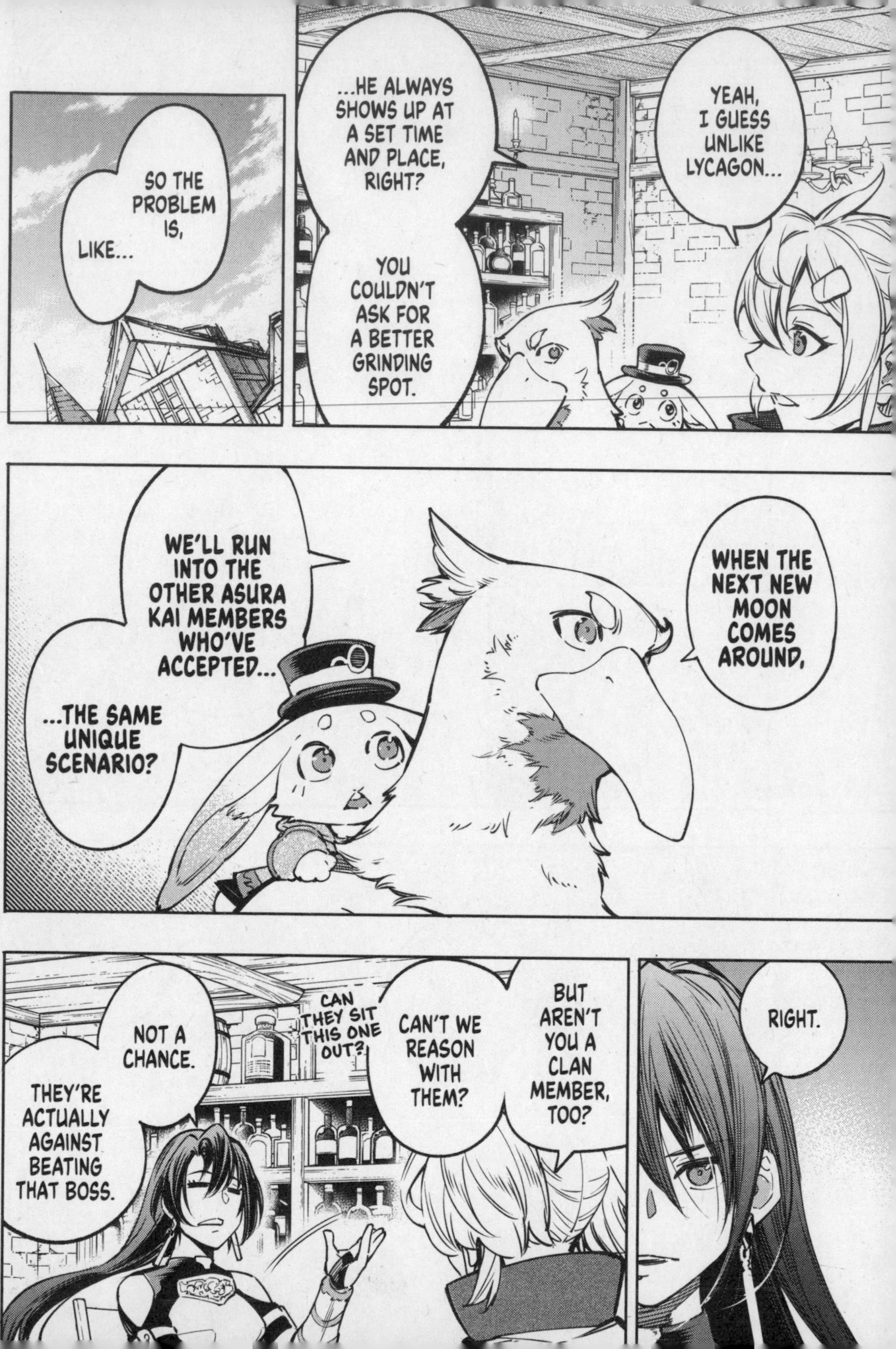
YEAH, I GUESS UNLIKE LYCAGON...
...HE ALWAYS SHOWS UP AT A SET TIME AND PLACE, RIGHT?
YOU COULDN'T ASK FOR A BETTER GRINDING SPOT.
SO THE PROBLEM IS, LIKE...
WHEN THE NEXT NEW MOON COMES AROUND,
WE'LL RUN INTO THE OTHER ASURA KAI MEMBERS WHO'VE ACCEPTED...
...THE SAME UNIQUE SCENARIO?
RIGHT.
BUT AREN'T YOU A CLAN MEMBER, TOO?
CAN'T WE REASON WITH THEM?
CAN THEY SIT THIS ONE OUT?
NOT A CHANCE.
THEY'RE ACTUALLY AGAINST BEATING THAT BOSS.

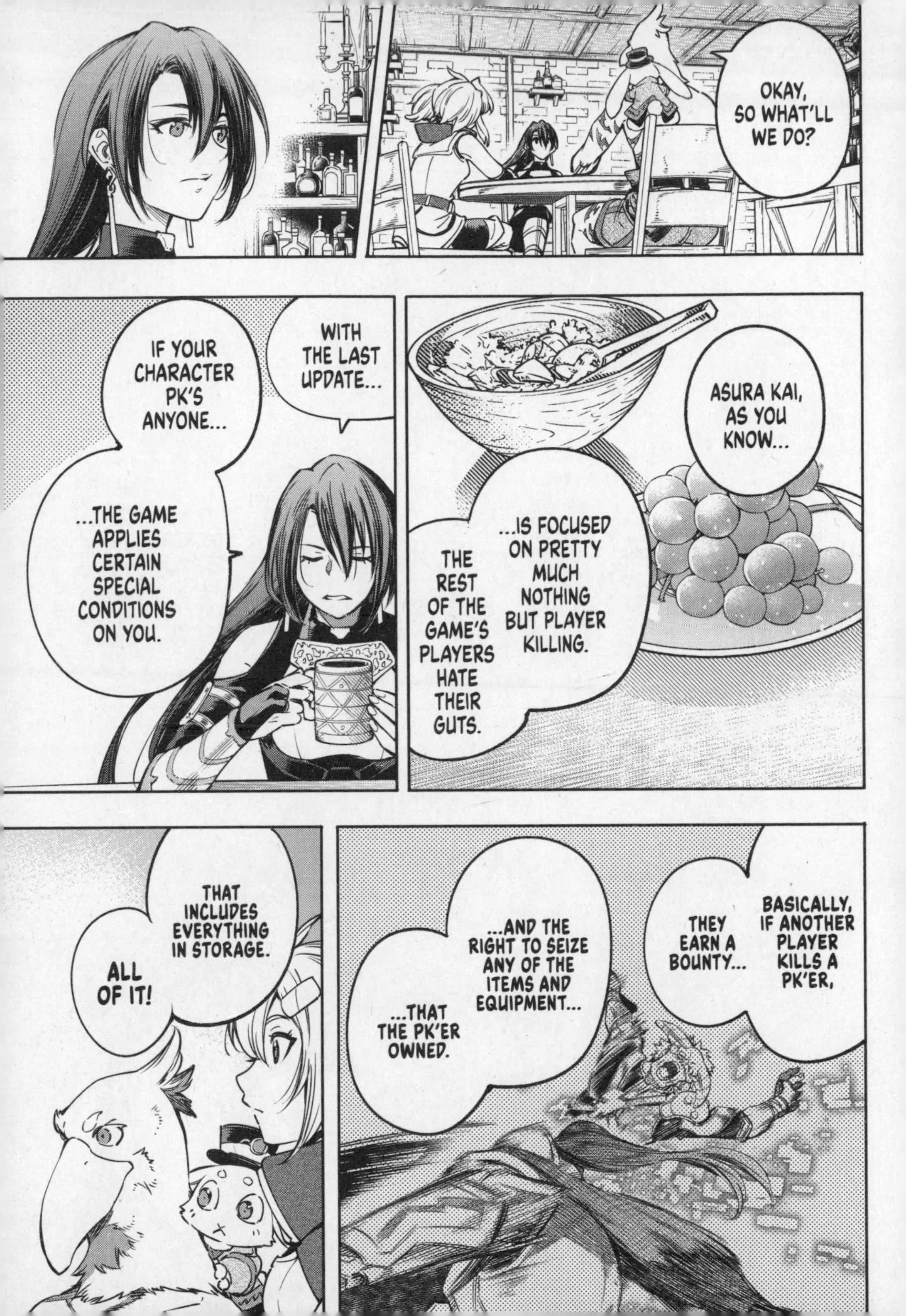
OKAY, SO WHAT'LL WE DO?
ASURA KAI, AS YOU KNOW...
...IS FOCUSED ON PRETTY MUCH NOTHING BUT PLAYER KILLING.
THE REST OF THE GAME'S PLAYERS HATE THEIR GUTS.
WITH THE LAST UPDATE...
IF YOUR CHARACTER PK'S ANYONE...
...THE GAME APPLIES CERTAIN SPECIAL CONDITIONS ON YOU.
BASICALLY, IF ANOTHER PLAYER KILLS A PK'ER,
THEY EARN A BOUNTY...
...AND THE RIGHT TO SEIZE ANY OF THE ITEMS AND EQUIPMENT...
...THAT THE PK'ER OWNED.
THAT INCLUDES EVERYTHING IN STORAGE.
ALL OF IT!

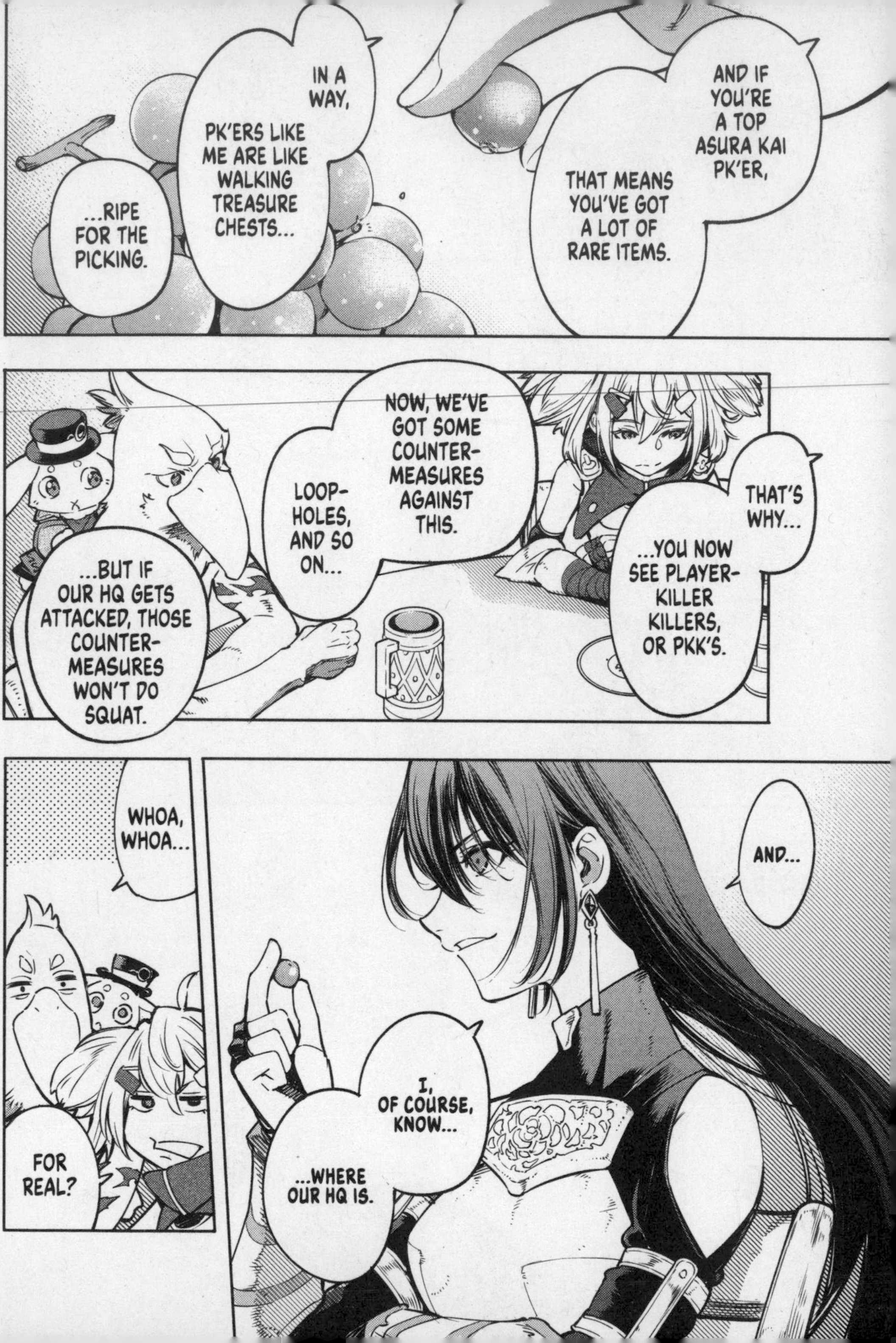
AND IF YOU'RE A TOP ASURA KAI PK'ER,
THAT MEANS YOU'VE GOT A LOT OF RARE ITEMS.
IN A WAY,
PK'ERS LIKE ME ARE LIKE WALKING TREASURE CHESTS...
...RIPE FOR THE PICKING.
THAT'S WHY...
...YOU NOW SEE PLAYER-KILLER KILLERS, OR PKK'S.
NOW, WE'VE GOT SOME COUNTER-MEASURES AGAINST THIS.
LOOP-HOLES, AND SO ON...
...BUT IF OUR HQ GETS ATTACKED, THOSE COUNTER-MEASURES WON'T DO SQUAT.
AND...
I, OF COURSE, KNOW...
...WHERE OUR HQ IS.
WHOA, WHOA...
FOR REAL?

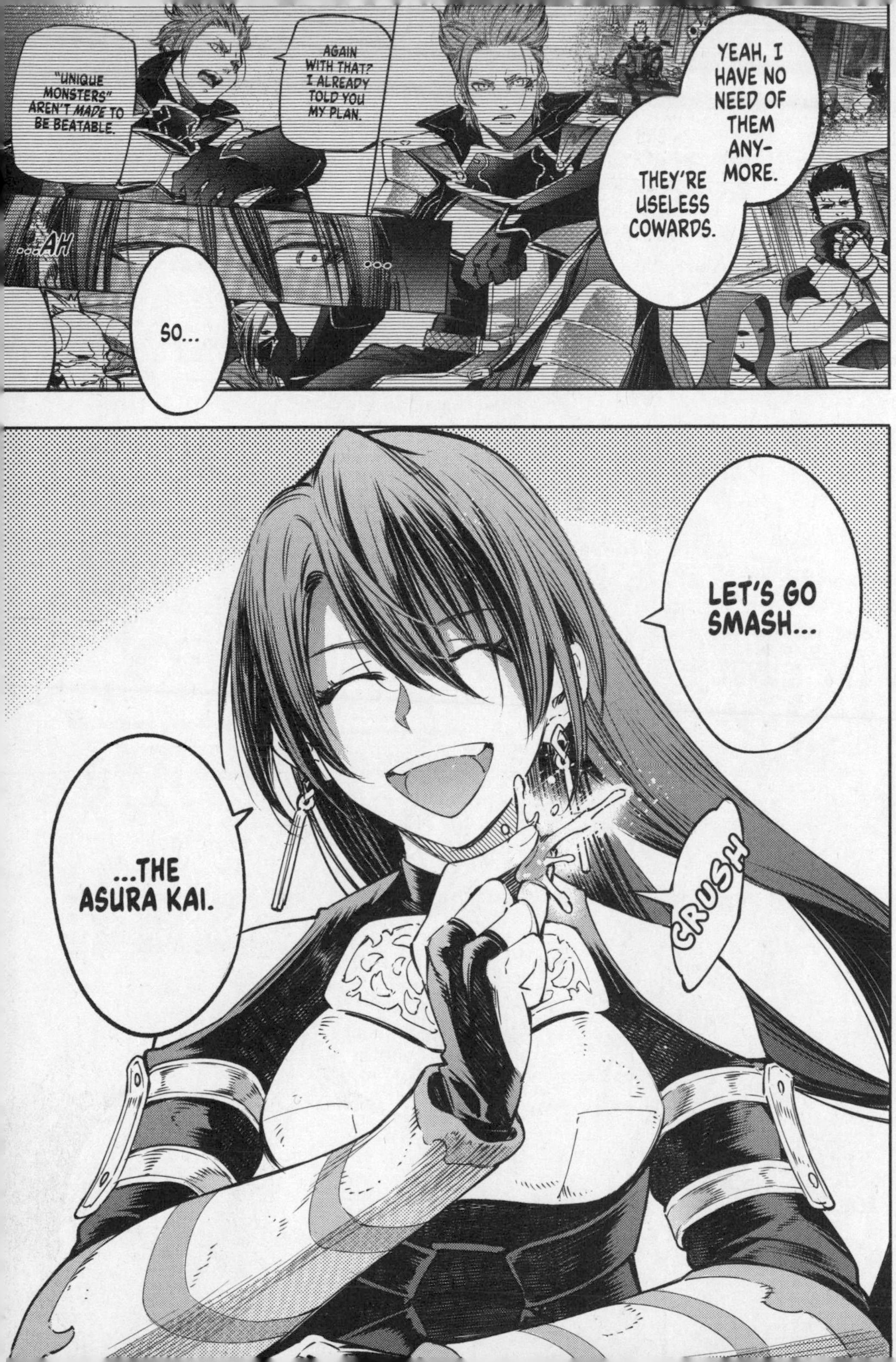
YEAH, I HAVE NO NEED OF THEM ANYMORE.
THEY'RE USELESS COWARDS.
AGAIN WITH THAT? I ALREADY TOLD YOU MY PLAN.
"UNIQUE MONSTERS" AREN'T *MADE* TO BE BEATABLE.
...
...AH
SO...
LET'S GO SMASH...
CRUSH
...THE ASURA KAI.

READ TO LEARN MORE ABOUT THE WORLD OF SLF!

REI-CHAN

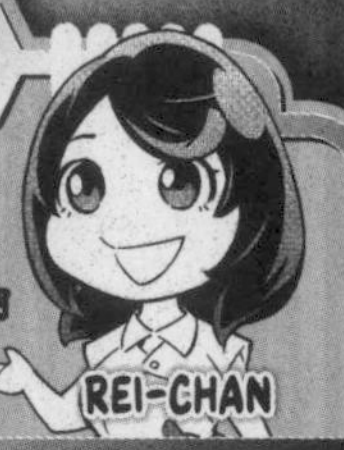

SHANGRI-LA FRONTIER STRATEGY FORUM

VOL. 17

LET SLF MASTER REI-CHAN TAKE YOU THROUGH THE WORLD!

Approaching Battle with the Colossus Wethermon!

Let's check Sunraku's stats after the Skill Gardener visit!

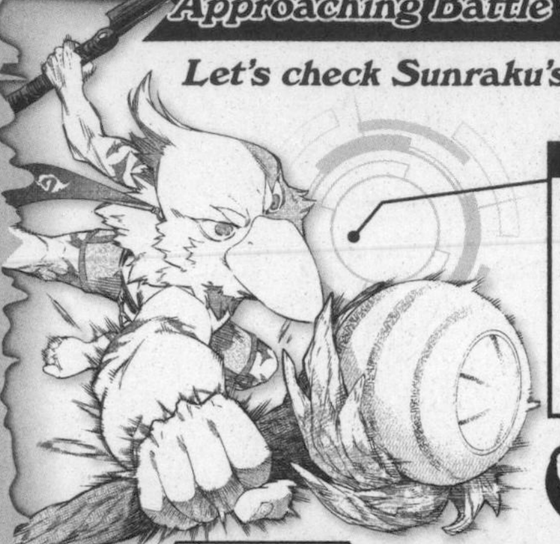

SKILL

*BOUNDLESS SLASH
*PARRYING PROTECT
*CLIMBING GREAT
*5-BOAT LEAP
*OPPRESSION KICK LV. 5
*HUNGER WOLF
*DRILL PIERCER
*HAND OF FORTUNE LV. 1
*CLIMAX BOOST LV. 1
*SHARP TURN
*BEST STEP
*OFF-ROAD LV. 1
*IN-FIGHT LV. 1
*ASSASSIN PIERCE LV. 1
*VORPAL BLADE SKILL, MOON REFLECTION
*SKATE FOOT

SUNRAKU LV. 51

HP: 30	MP: 10
STAMINA: 60	STRENGTH: 40
DEXTERITY: 50	AGILITY: 70
TECH: 55	VITALITY: 7
LUCK: 74	

QUICK LOOK

DRILL PIERCER

EVOLVED FROM SPIRAL EDGE, WITH EXTRA POWER AND MULTILEVEL STRIKES.

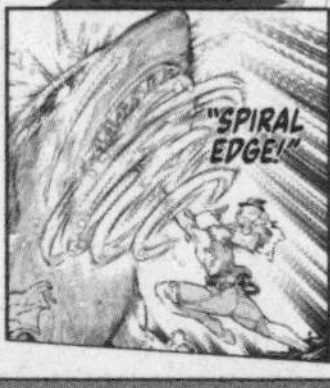

"SPIRAL EDGE!"

PARRYING PROTECT

EVOLVED FROM REPEL COUNTER. DEFLECTS AND DEALS 5% OF THE DAMAGE BACK.

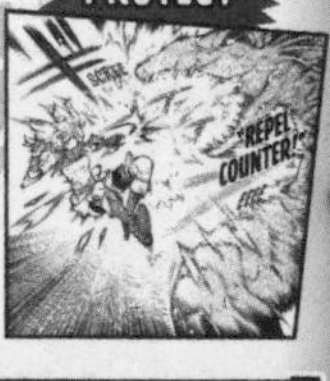

"REPEL COUNTER!"

How will he use these skills? Wethermon is coming!

Peeking into Sunraku's group's hidden NPC café, The Serpent's Apple!

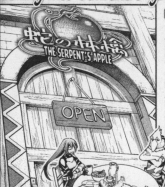

THE SERPENT'S APPLE
OPEN
GREAT FOR SECRET MEETINGS!

Q: WHAT IS IT?

A: THIS BACK-ALLEY CAFÉ EXISTS IN NEARLY ALL CITIES, CATERING TO "UNDERGROUND" TYPES. ONE OF THE FEW PUBLIC FACILITIES PK'ERS ARE ALLOWED TO ENTER, IT'S A NOTORIOUS SPOT, BUT NOT ACTUALLY USED BY PLAYERS MUCH, OFFERING A LOT OF PRIVACY.

SLF'S TASTE SYSTEM!

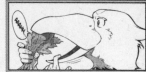

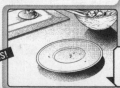

SLF USES THE LATEST TECH TO IMPLEMENT A TASTE SYSTEM. THIS IS DELIBERATELY DIALED BACK DURING REGULAR PLAY; LIMITS ON YOUR SENSE OF TASTE ARE REMOVED AFTER EATING HIGH-QUALITY FOOD.

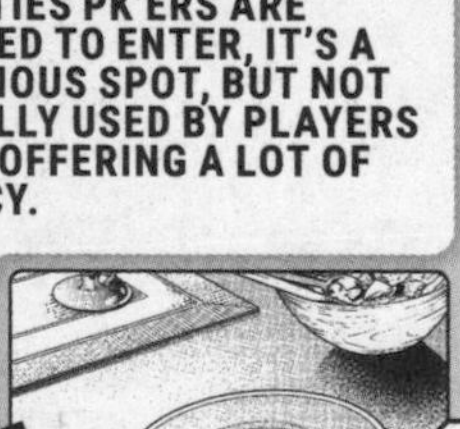

THE SERPENT'S APPLE HAS ALMOST ZERO TASTE LIMITS, LETTING YOU ENJOY CAKE AND TEA ALMOST LIKE IT WAS REAL!

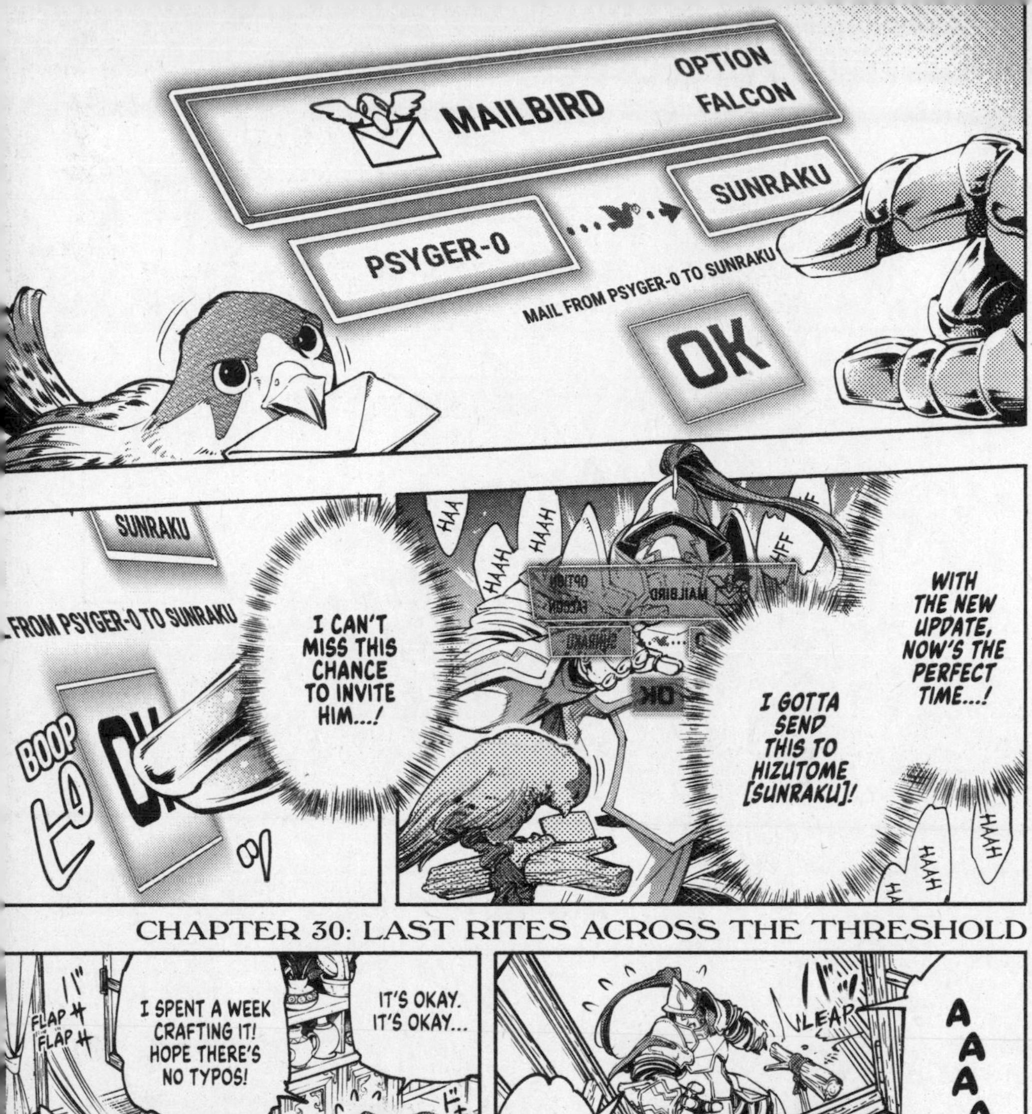
MAILBIRD
OPTION FALCON
PSYGER-0
SUNRAKU
MAIL FROM PSYGER-0 TO SUNRAKU
OK
HAA
HAAH
HAAH
HFF
WITH THE NEW UPDATE, NOW'S THE PERFECT TIME...!
I GOTTA SEND THIS TO HIZUTOME [SUNRAKU]!
HAAH
HAAH
SUNRAKU
FROM PSYGER-0 TO SUNRAKU
I CAN'T MISS THIS CHANCE TO INVITE HIM...!
BOOP

CHAPTER 30: LAST RITES ACROSS THE THRESHOLD

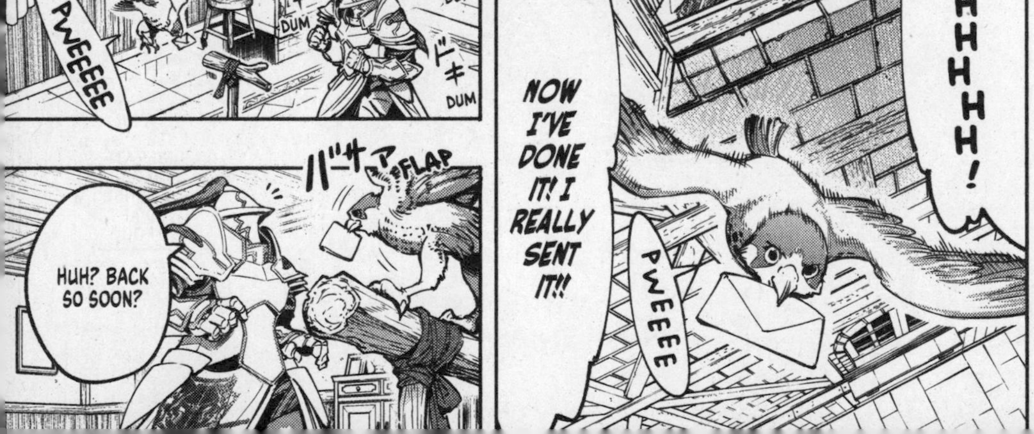
LEAP
AAAAHHHHH!
NOW I'VE DONE IT! I REALLY SENT IT!!
PWEEEE
IT'S OKAY. IT'S OKAY...
I SPENT A WEEK CRAFTING IT! HOPE THERE'S NO TYPOS!
FLAP FLAP
DUM
DUM
DUM
PWEEEEEE
FLAP
HUH? BACK SO SOON?

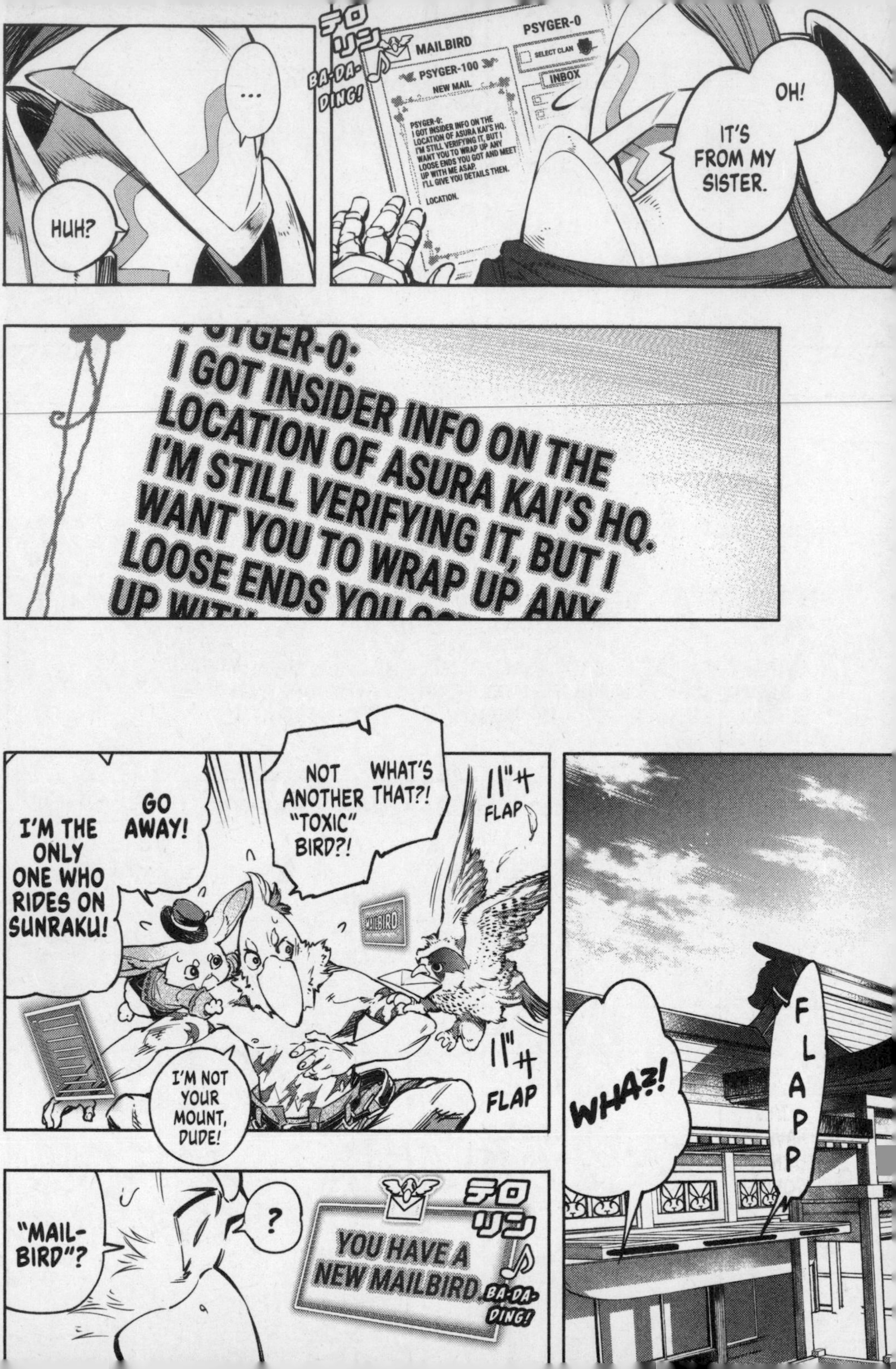
テロリン
BA-DA-DING!
MAILBIRD
PSYGER-0
SELECT CLAN
INBOX
PSYGER-100
NEW MAIL
PSYGER-0:
I GOT INSIDER INFO ON THE
LOCATION OF ASURA KAI'S HQ.
I'M STILL VERIFYING IT, BUT I
WANT YOU TO WRAP UP ANY
LOOSE ENDS YOU GOT AND MEET
UP WITH ME ASAP.
I'LL GIVE YOU DETAILS THEN.
LOCATION.
OH!
IT'S FROM MY SISTER.
...
HUH?
GER-0:
I GOT INSIDER INFO ON THE
LOCATION OF ASURA KAI'S HQ.
I'M STILL VERIFYING IT, BUT I
WANT YOU TO WRAP UP ANY
LOOSE ENDS YOU
FLAPP
WHA?!
WHAT'S THAT?!
NOT ANOTHER "TOXIC" BIRD?!
FLAP
GO AWAY!
I'M THE ONLY ONE WHO RIDES ON SUNRAKU!
MAILBIRD
FLAP
I'M NOT YOUR MOUNT, DUDE!
テロリン
YOU HAVE A NEW MAILBIRD.
BA-DA-DING!
?
"MAIL-BIRD"?

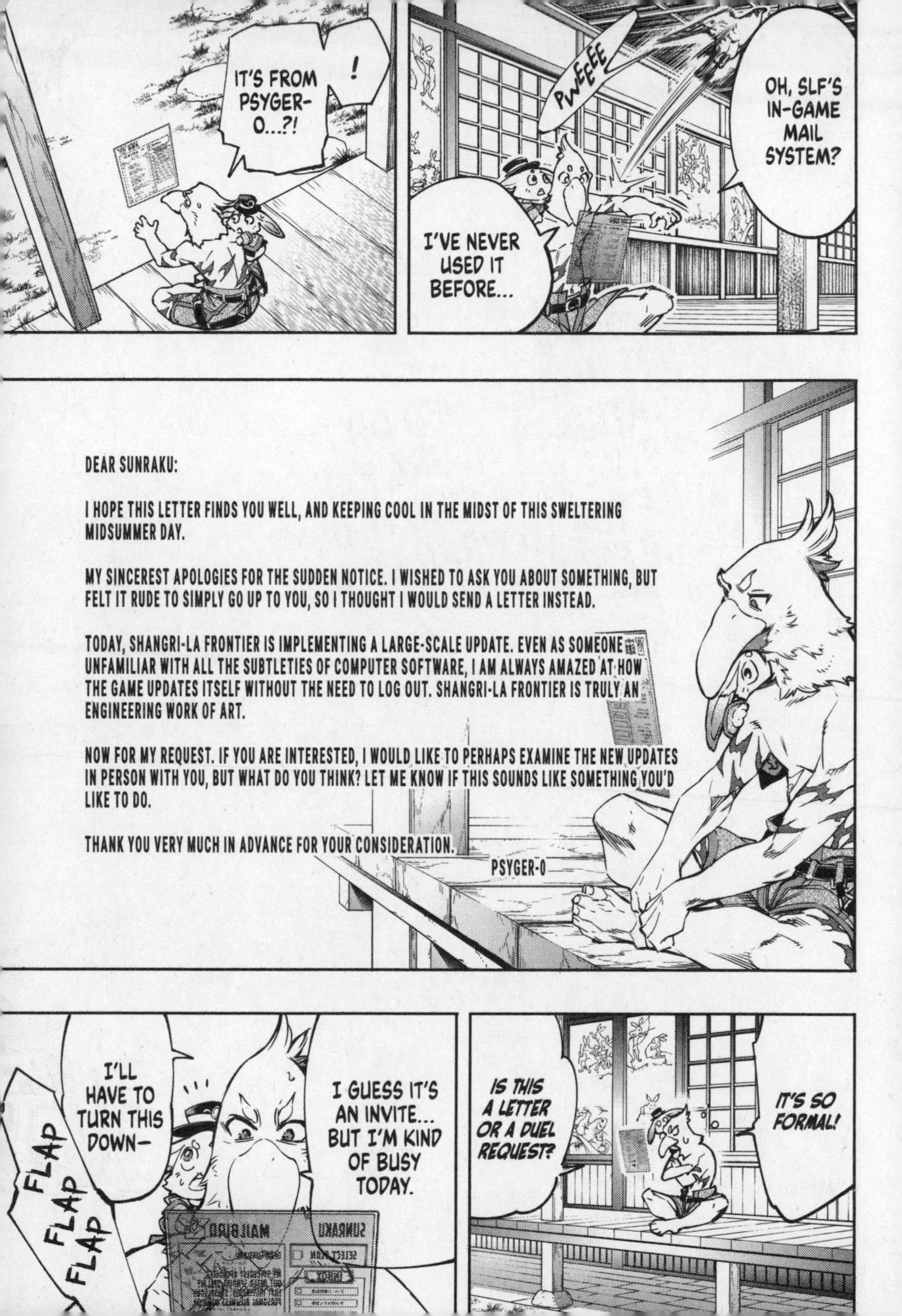
PWEEEE
OH, SLF'S IN-GAME MAIL SYSTEM?
I'VE NEVER USED IT BEFORE...
!
IT'S FROM PSYGER-0...?!
DEAR SUNRAKU:
I HOPE THIS LETTER FINDS YOU WELL, AND KEEPING COOL IN THE MIDST OF THIS SWELTERING MIDSUMMER DAY.
MY SINCEREST APOLOGIES FOR THE SUDDEN NOTICE. I WISHED TO ASK YOU ABOUT SOMETHING, BUT FELT IT RUDE TO SIMPLY GO UP TO YOU, SO I THOUGHT I WOULD SEND A LETTER INSTEAD.
TODAY, SHANGRI-LA FRONTIER IS IMPLEMENTING A LARGE-SCALE UPDATE. EVEN AS SOMEONE UNFAMILIAR WITH ALL THE SUBTLETIES OF COMPUTER SOFTWARE, I AM ALWAYS AMAZED AT HOW THE GAME UPDATES ITSELF WITHOUT THE NEED TO LOG OUT. SHANGRI-LA FRONTIER IS TRULY AN ENGINEERING WORK OF ART.
NOW FOR MY REQUEST. IF YOU ARE INTERESTED, I WOULD LIKE TO PERHAPS EXAMINE THE NEW UPDATES IN PERSON WITH YOU, BUT WHAT DO YOU THINK? LET ME KNOW IF THIS SOUNDS LIKE SOMETHING YOU'D LIKE TO DO.
THANK YOU VERY MUCH IN ADVANCE FOR YOUR CONSIDERATION.
PSYGER-0
IT'S SO FORMAL!
IS THIS A LETTER OR A DUEL REQUEST?
I GUESS IT'S AN INVITE... BUT I'M KIND OF BUSY TODAY.
I'LL HAVE TO TURN THIS DOWN—
FLAP FLAP FLAP

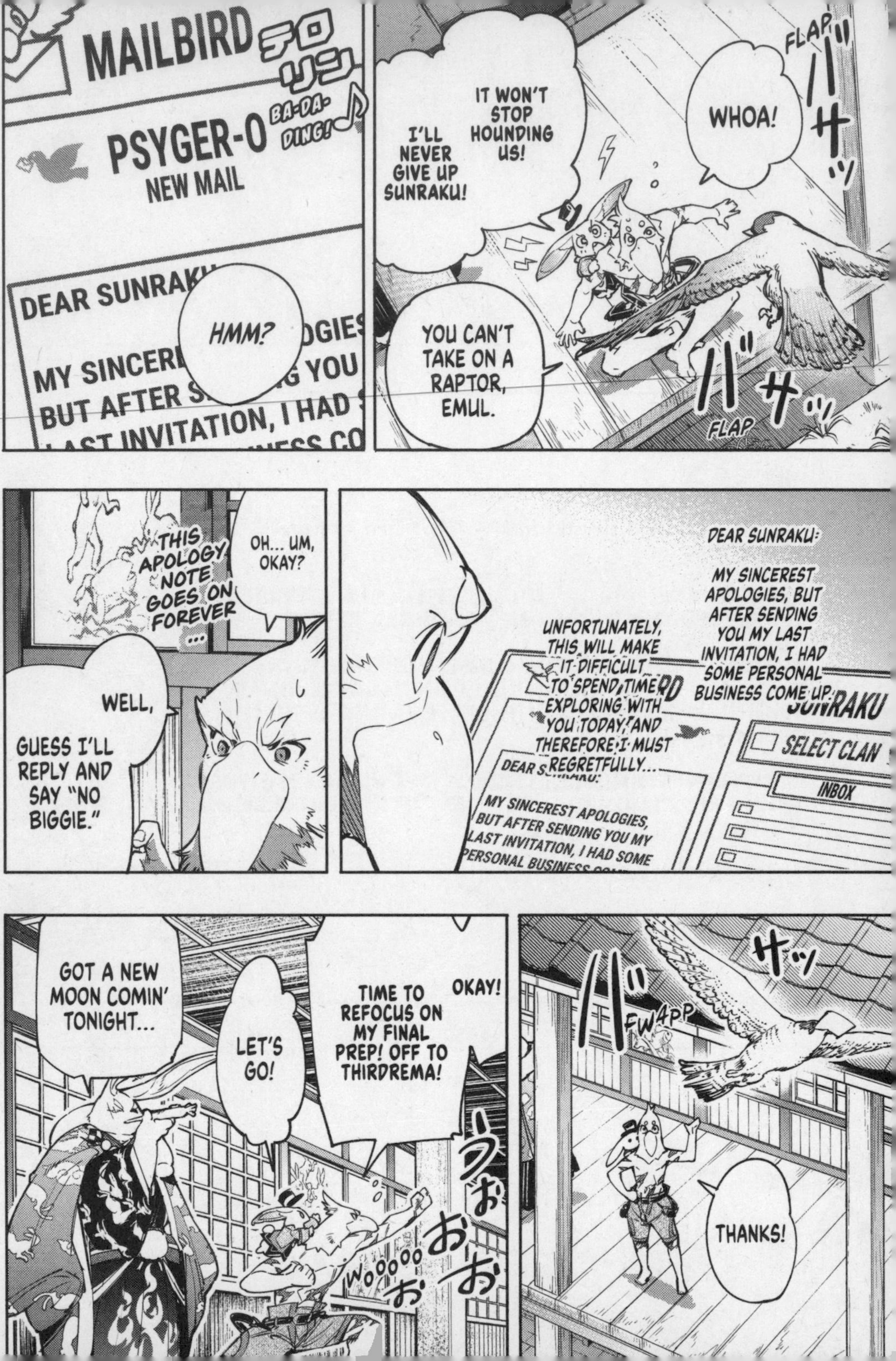
FLAP
WHOA!
IT WON'T STOP HOUNDING US!
I'LL NEVER GIVE UP SUNRAKU!
YOU CAN'T TAKE ON A RAPTOR, EMUL.
FLAP
MAILBIRD
テロリン
BA-DA-DING!
PSYGER-O
NEW MAIL
DEAR SUNRAKU
HMM?
DEAR SUNRAKU:
MY SINCEREST APOLOGIES, BUT AFTER SENDING YOU MY LAST INVITATION, I HAD SOME PERSONAL BUSINESS COME UP.
UNFORTUNATELY, THIS WILL MAKE IT DIFFICULT TO SPEND TIME EXPLORING WITH YOU TODAY, AND THEREFORE I MUST REGRETFULLY...
SUNRAKU
SELECT CLAN
INBOX
MY SINCEREST APOLOGIES, BUT AFTER SENDING YOU MY LAST INVITATION, I HAD SOME PERSONAL BUSINESS
OH... UM, OKAY?
THIS APOLOGY NOTE GOES ON FOREVER...
WELL,
GUESS I'LL REPLY AND SAY "NO BIGGIE."
FWAPP
THANKS!
OKAY!
TIME TO REFOCUS ON MY FINAL PREP! OFF TO THIRDREMA!
LET'S GO!
GOT A NEW MOON COMIN' TONIGHT...
WOOOOO

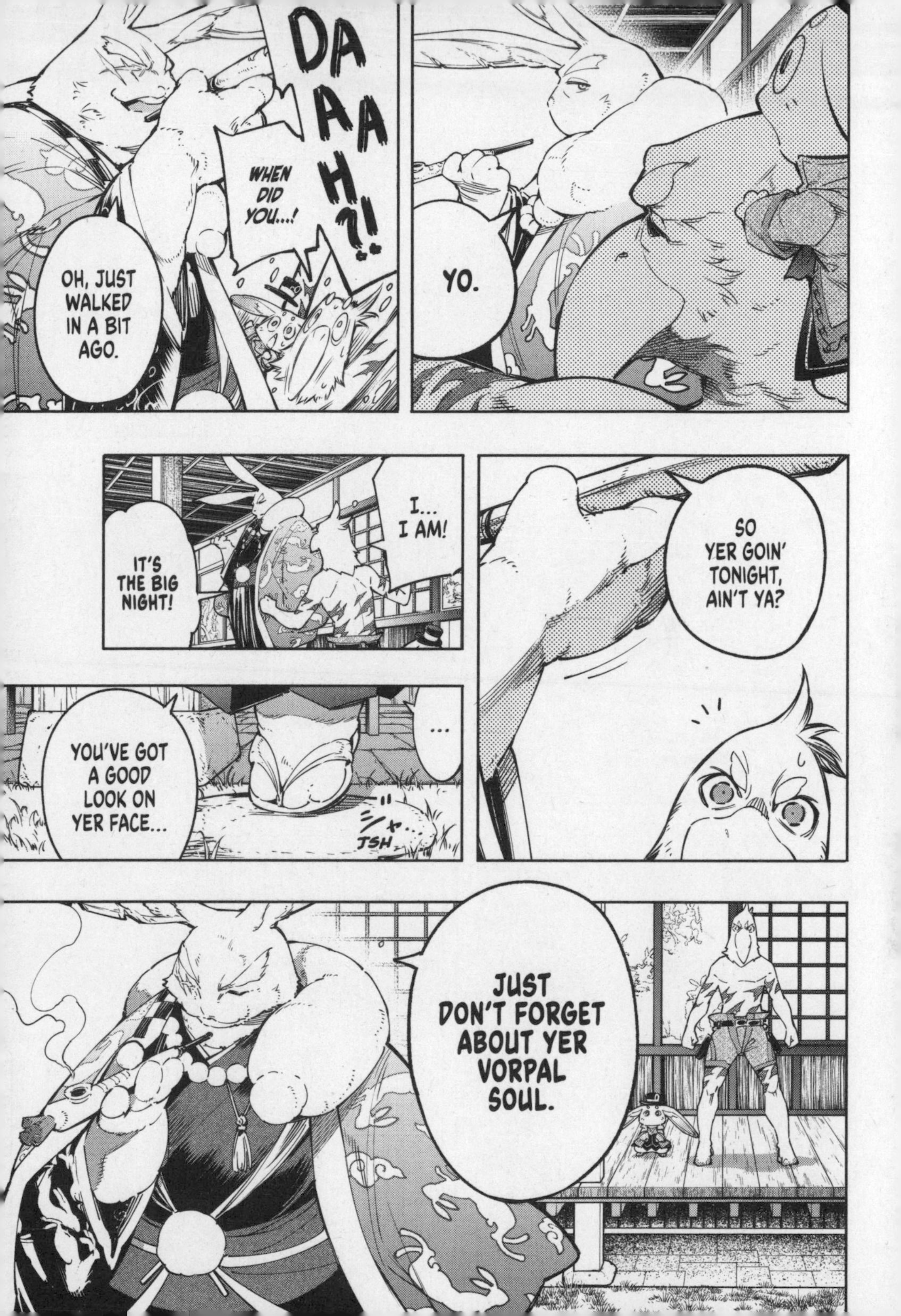
YO.
DAAAH?!
WHEN DID YOU...!
OH, JUST WALKED IN A BIT AGO.
SO YER GOIN' TONIGHT, AIN'T YA?
I... I AM!
IT'S THE BIG NIGHT!
...
YOU'VE GOT A GOOD LOOK ON YER FACE...
TSH
JUST DON'T FORGET ABOUT YER VORPAL SOUL.

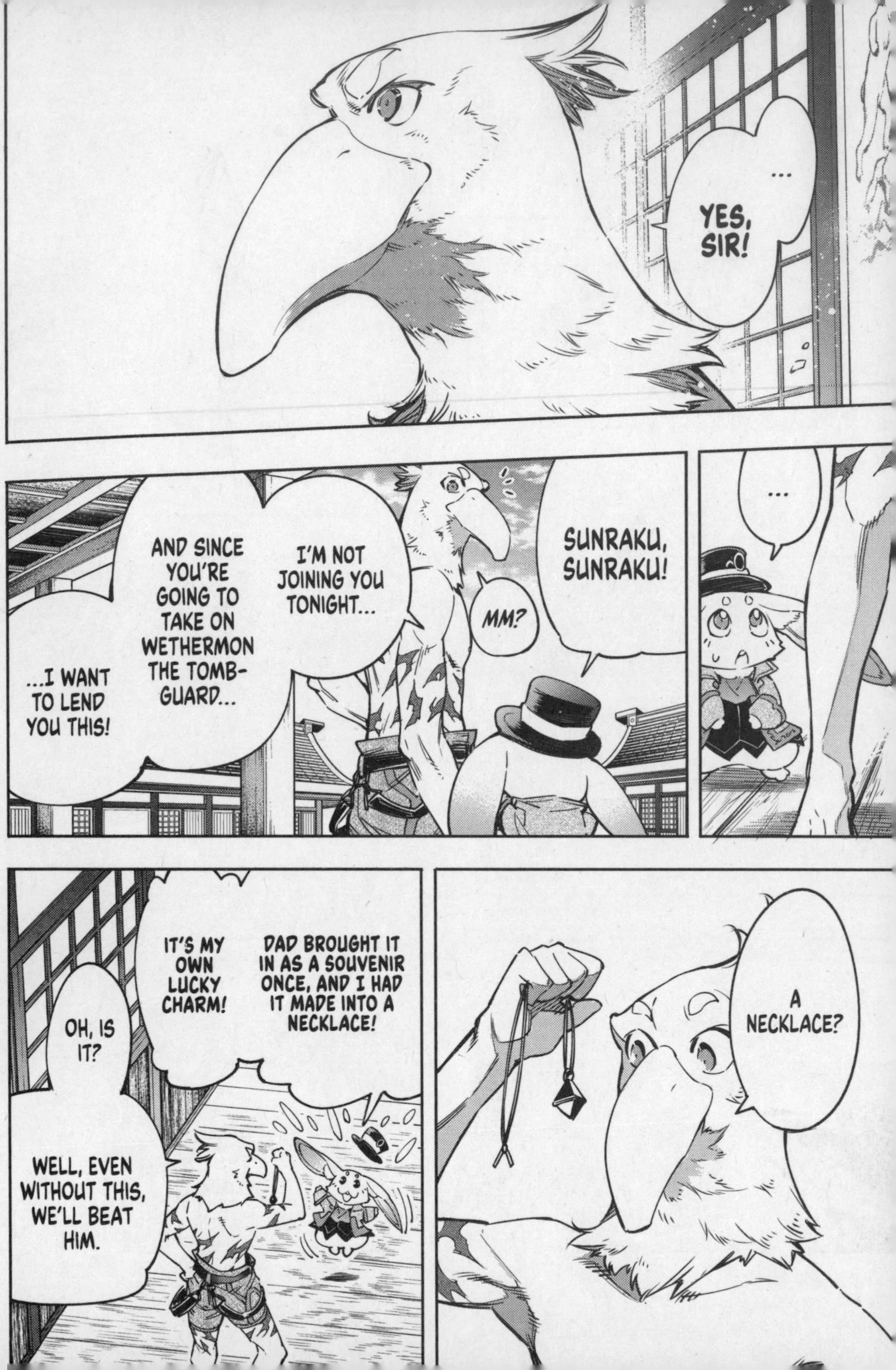
... YES, SIR!
...
SUNRAKU, SUNRAKU!
MM?
I'M NOT JOINING YOU TONIGHT...
AND SINCE YOU'RE GOING TO TAKE ON WETHERMON THE TOMB-GUARD...
...I WANT TO LEND YOU THIS!
A NECKLACE?
IT'S MY OWN LUCKY CHARM!
DAD BROUGHT IT IN AS A SOUVENIR ONCE, AND I HAD IT MADE INTO A NECKLACE!
OH, IS IT?
WELL, EVEN WITHOUT THIS, WE'LL BEAT HIM.

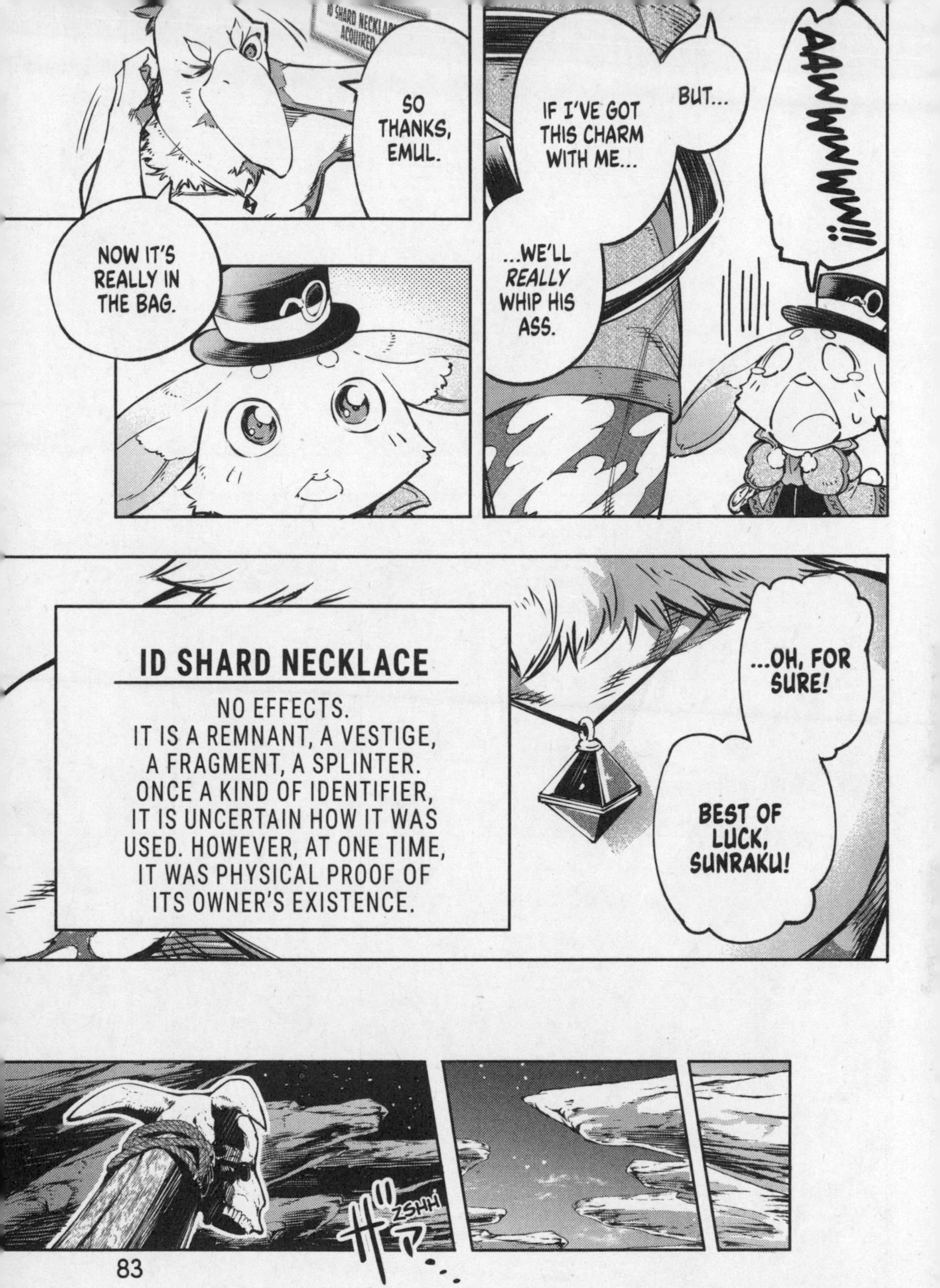
AAWWWWWWW!!
BUT...
IF I'VE GOT THIS CHARM WITH ME...
...WE'LL *REALLY* WHIP HIS ASS.
ID SHARD NECKLACE ACQUIRED
SO THANKS, EMUL.
NOW IT'S REALLY IN THE BAG.
...OH, FOR SURE!
BEST OF LUCK, SUNRAKU!
ID SHARD NECKLACE
NO EFFECTS.
IT IS A REMNANT, A VESTIGE, A FRAGMENT, A SPLINTER. ONCE A KIND OF IDENTIFIER, IT IS UNCERTAIN HOW IT WAS USED. HOWEVER, AT ONE TIME, IT WAS PHYSICAL PROOF OF ITS OWNER'S EXISTENCE.
ZSHH

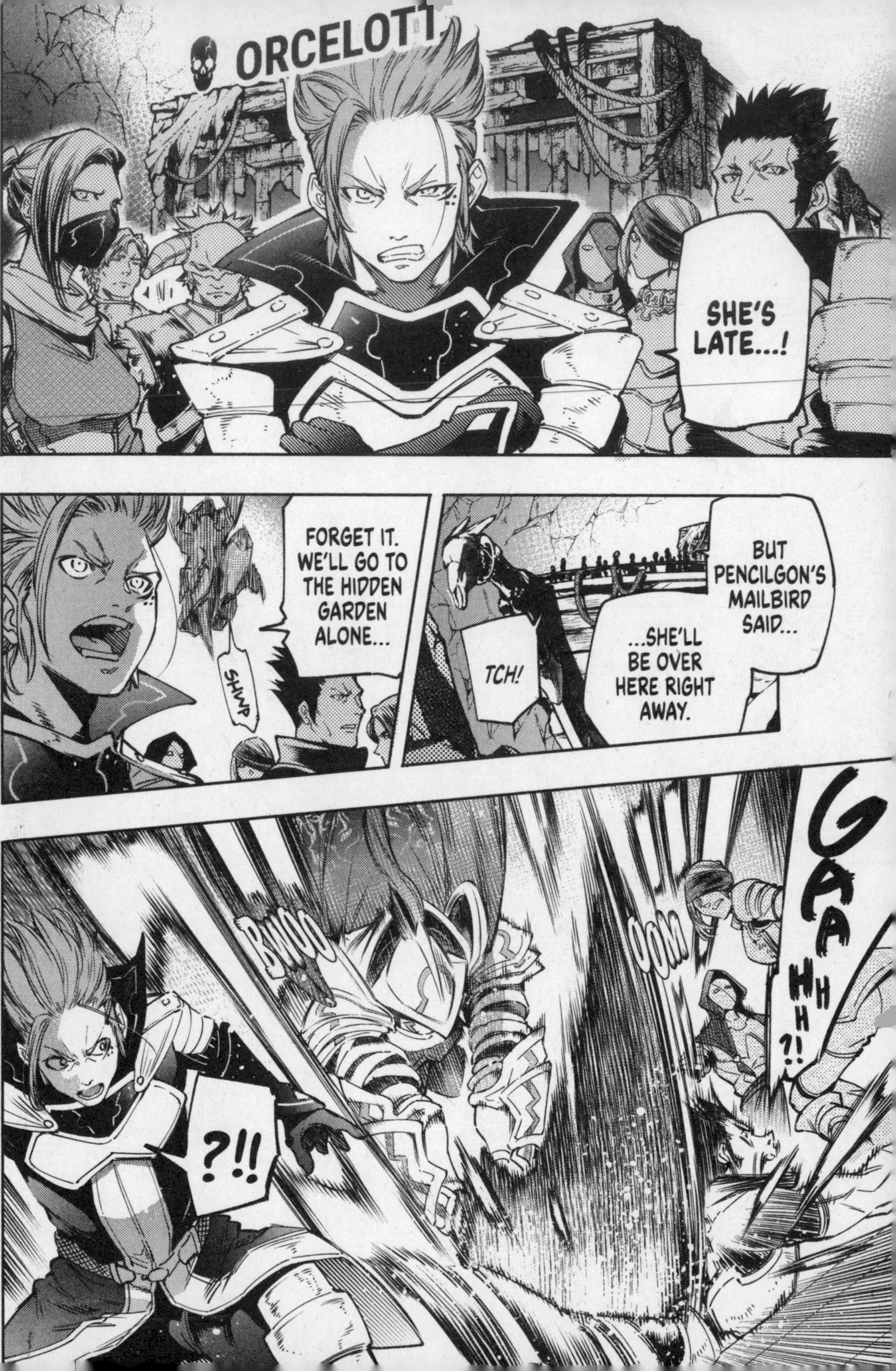
ORCELOT1
SHE'S LATE...!
BUT PENCILGON'S MAILBIRD SAID...
...SHE'LL BE OVER HERE RIGHT AWAY.
TCH!
FORGET IT. WE'LL GO TO THE HIDDEN GARDEN ALONE...
SHWP
GAAHHH?!
BWOOOOM
?!!

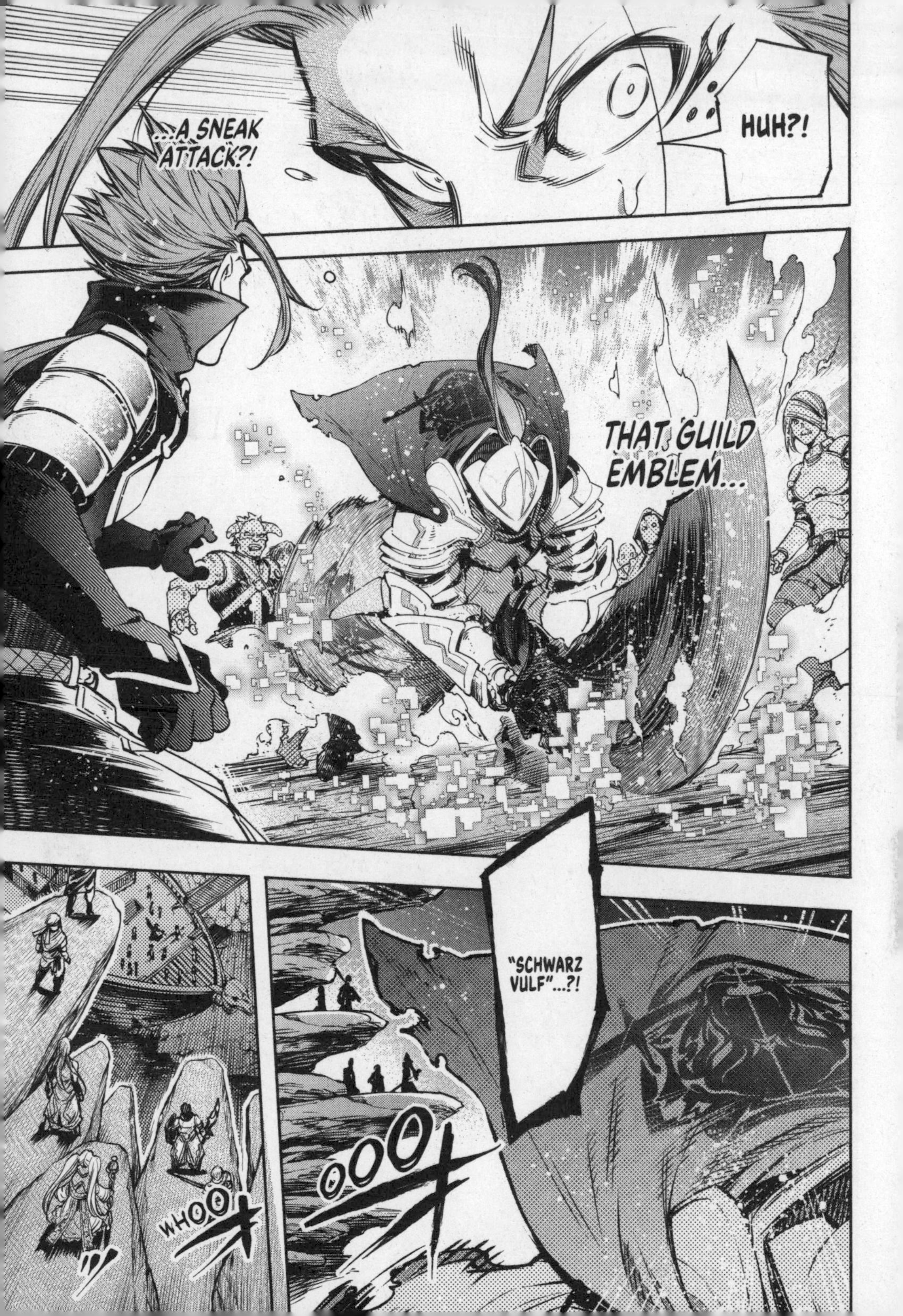
HUH?!
...A SNEAK ATTACK?!
THAT GUILD EMBLEM...
"SCHWARZ VULF"...?!
OOO
WHOO

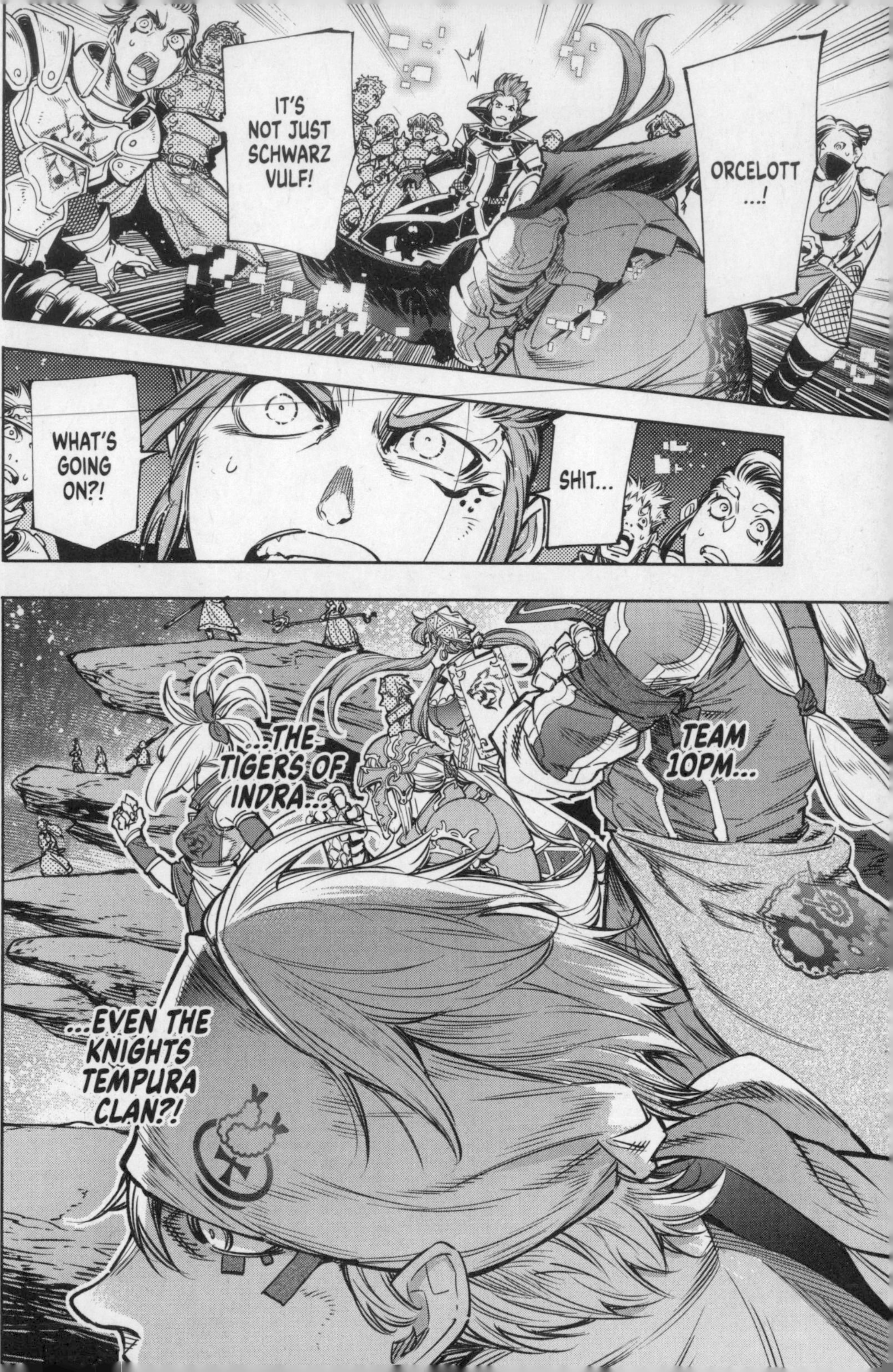
ORCELOTT ...!
IT'S NOT JUST SCHWARZ VULF!
SHIT...
WHAT'S GOING ON?!
TEAM 10PM...
...THE TIGERS OF INDRA...
...EVEN THE KNIGHTS TEMPURA CLAN?!

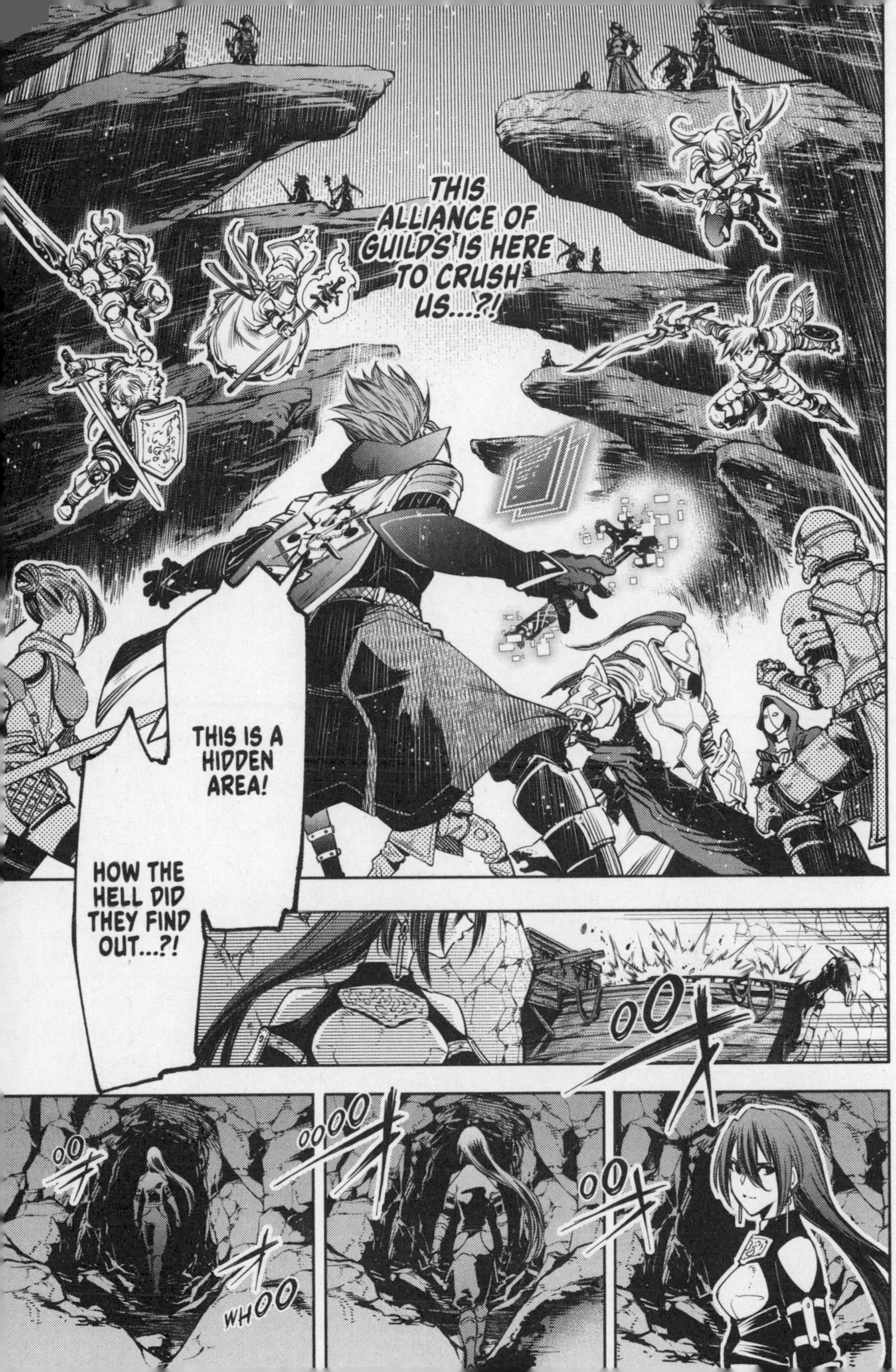
THIS ALLIANCE OF GUILDS IS HERE TO CRUSH US...?!
THIS IS A HIDDEN AREA!
HOW THE HELL DID THEY FIND OUT...?!
WHOO

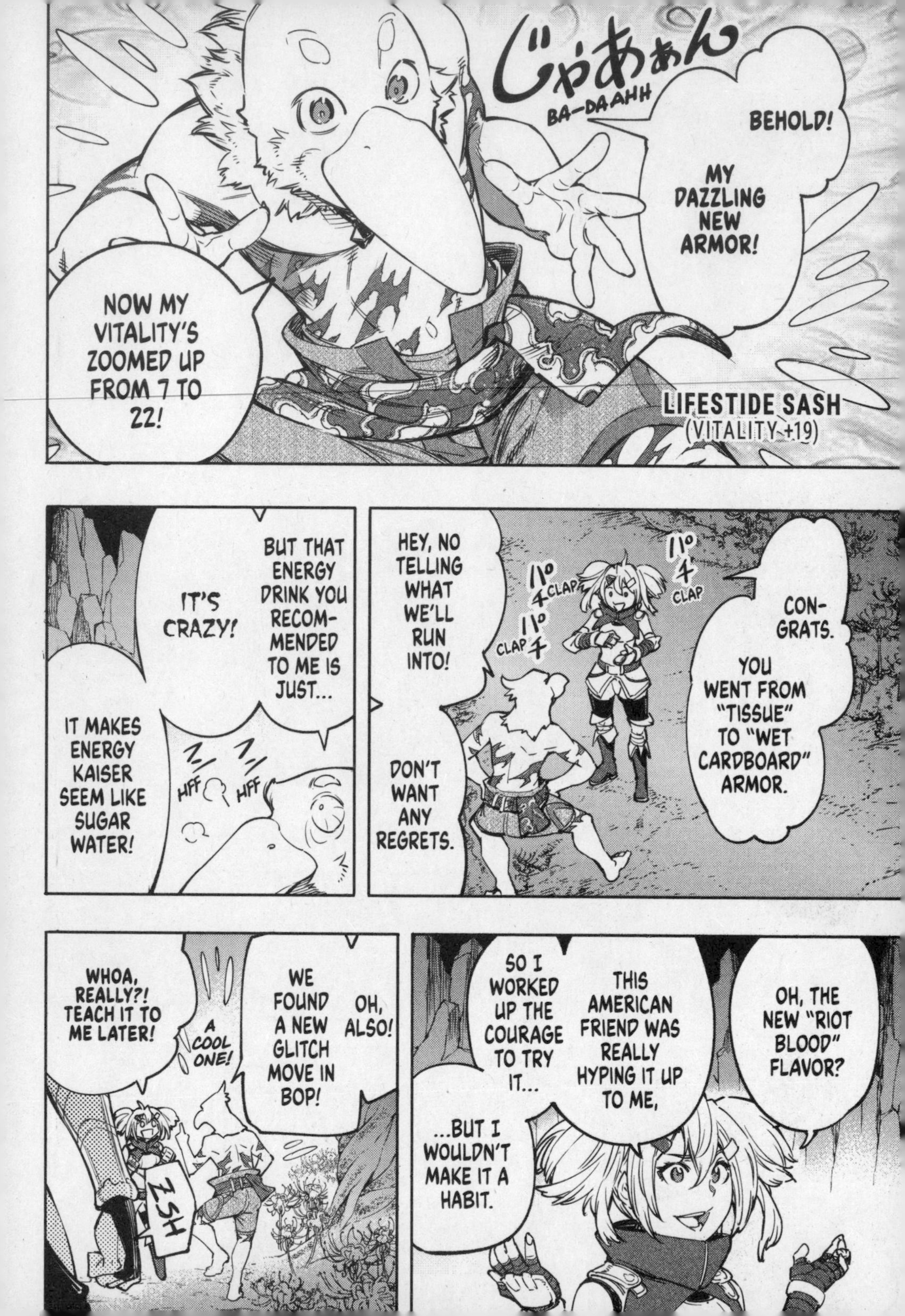
じゃあぁん
BA-DAAHH
BEHOLD!
MY DAZZLING NEW ARMOR!
NOW MY VITALITY'S ZOOMED UP FROM 7 TO 22!
LIFESTIDE SASH (VITALITY +19)
パチ CLAP
パチ CLAP
パチ CLAP
CON-GRATS.
YOU WENT FROM "TISSUE" TO "WET CARDBOARD" ARMOR.
HEY, NO TELLING WHAT WE'LL RUN INTO!
DON'T WANT ANY REGRETS.
BUT THAT ENERGY DRINK YOU RECOMMENDED TO ME IS JUST...
IT'S CRAZY!
HFF HFF
IT MAKES ENERGY KAISER SEEM LIKE SUGAR WATER!
OH, THE NEW "RIOT BLOOD" FLAVOR?
THIS AMERICAN FRIEND WAS REALLY HYPING IT UP TO ME,
SO I WORKED UP THE COURAGE TO TRY IT...
...BUT I WOULDN'T MAKE IT A HABIT.
OH, ALSO!
WE FOUND A NEW GLITCH MOVE IN BOP!
A COOL ONE!
WHOA, REALLY?! TEACH IT TO ME LATER!
ZSH

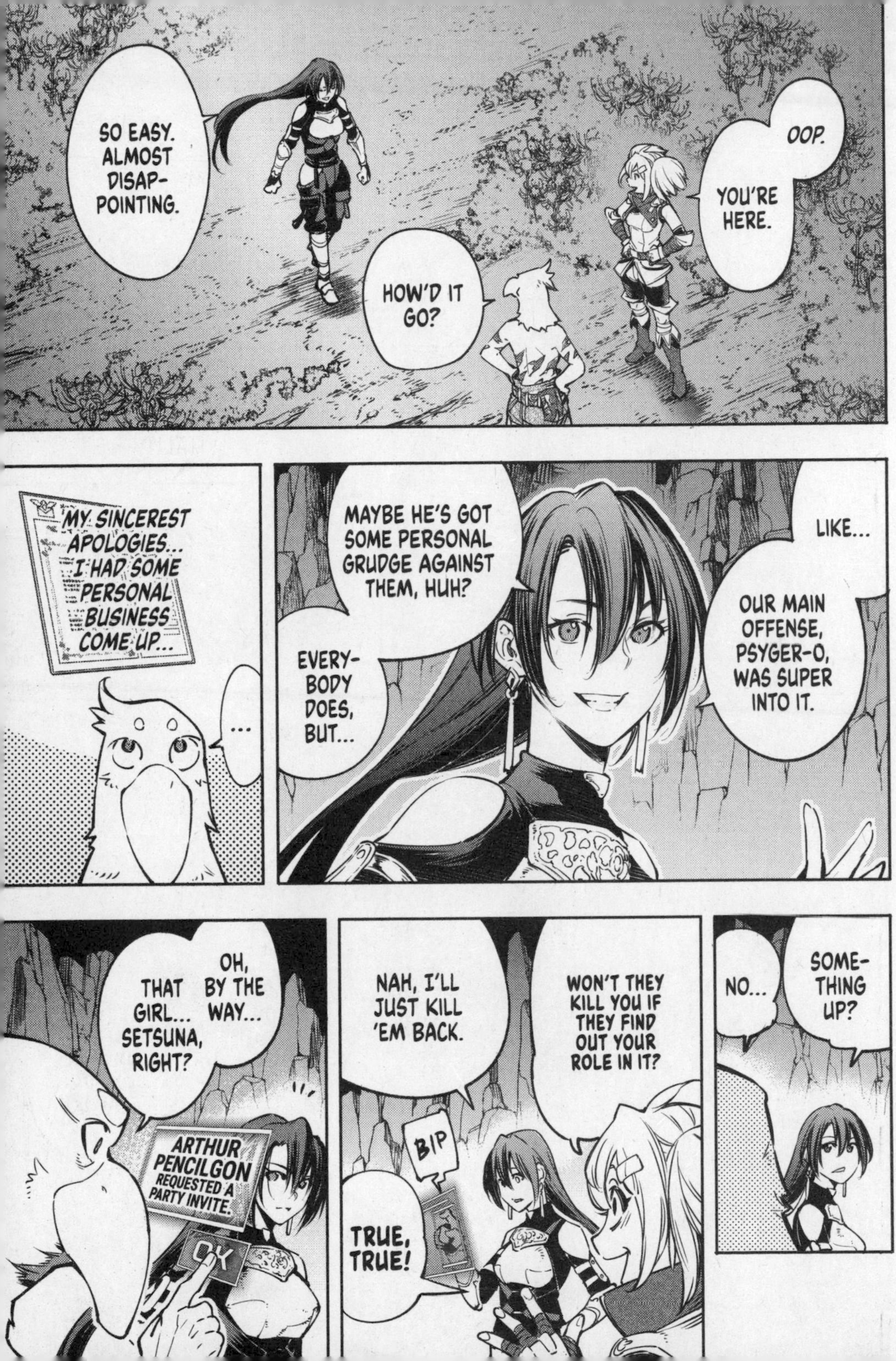
OOP.
YOU'RE HERE.
HOW'D IT GO?
SO EASY. ALMOST DISAP-POINTING.
LIKE...
OUR MAIN OFFENSE, PSYGER-O, WAS SUPER INTO IT.
MAYBE HE'S GOT SOME PERSONAL GRUDGE AGAINST THEM, HUH?
EVERY-BODY DOES, BUT...
MY SINCEREST APOLOGIES... I HAD SOME PERSONAL BUSINESS COME UP...
...
SOME-THING UP?
NO...
WON'T THEY KILL YOU IF THEY FIND OUT YOUR ROLE IN IT?
NAH, I'LL JUST KILL 'EM BACK.
BIP
TRUE, TRUE!
OH, BY THE WAY...
THAT GIRL... SETSUNA, RIGHT?
ARTHUR PENCILGON REQUESTED A PARTY INVITE.
OK

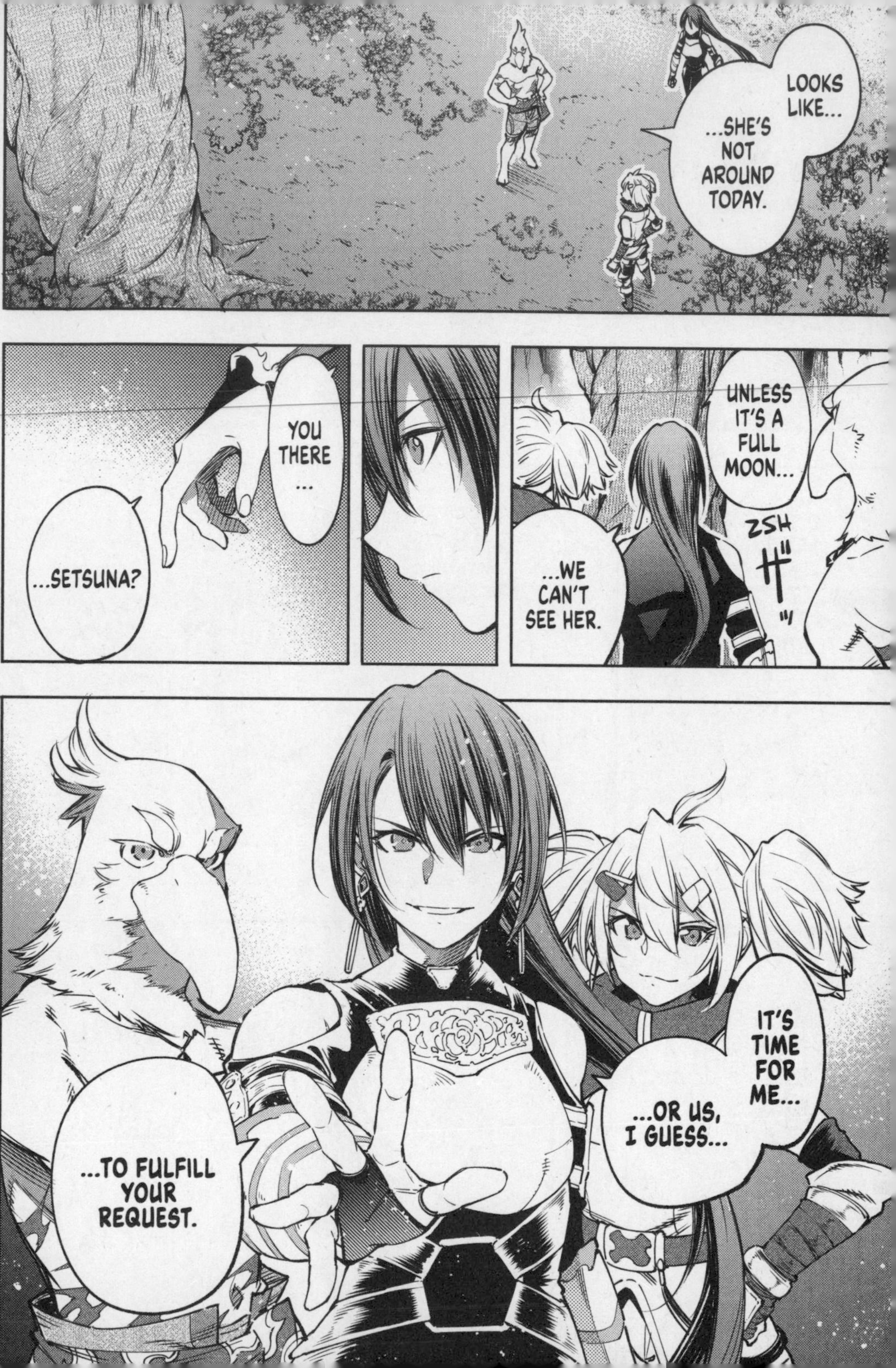
LOOKS LIKE...
...SHE'S NOT AROUND TODAY.
UNLESS IT'S A FULL MOON...
ZSH
ザッ
...WE CAN'T SEE HER.
YOU THERE...
...SETSUNA?
IT'S TIME FOR ME...
...OR US, I GUESS...
...TO FULFILL YOUR REQUEST.

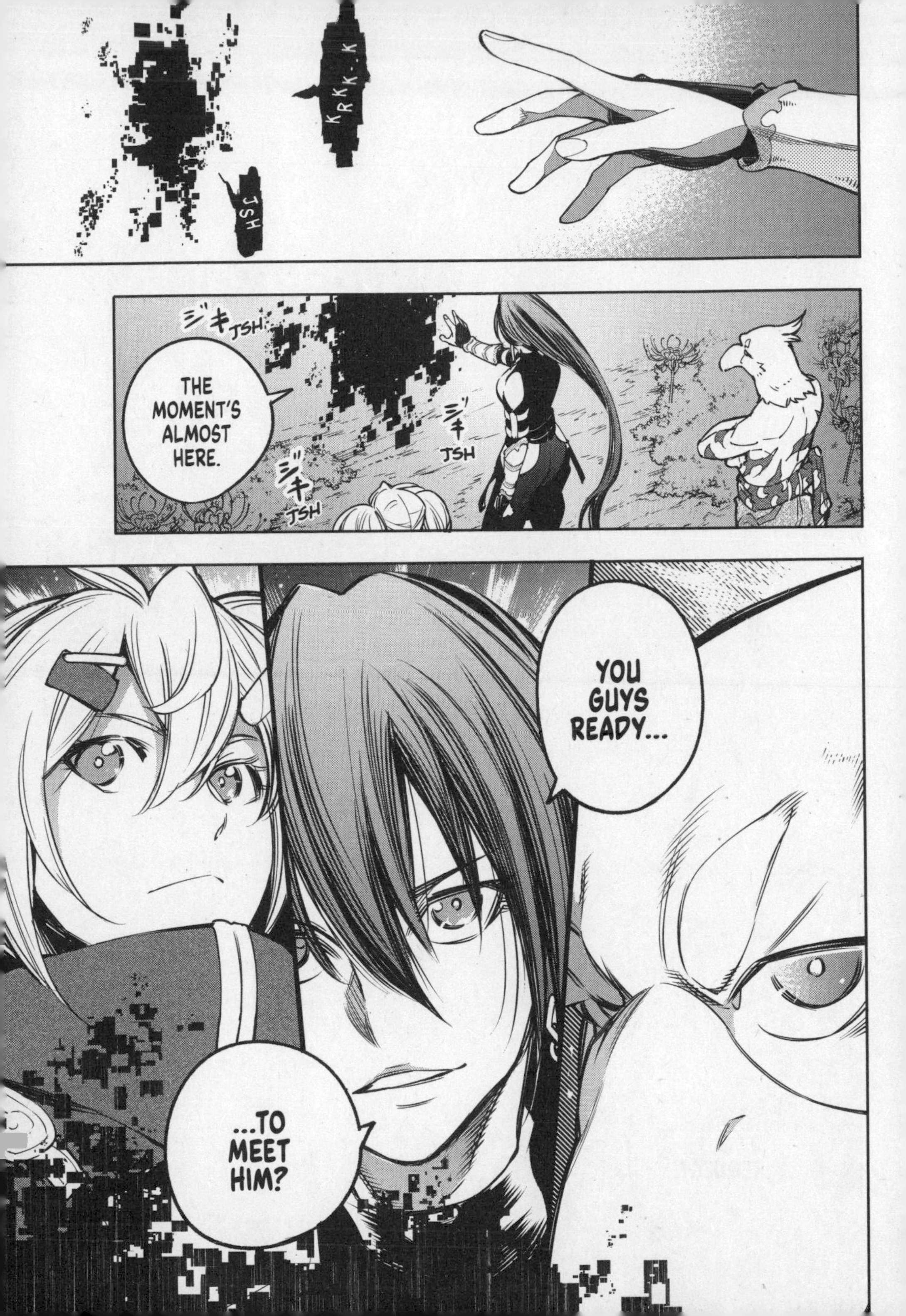
KRKK-K
JSH
ジキ JSH
THE MOMENT'S ALMOST HERE.
ジキ JSH
ジキ JSH
YOU GUYS READY...
...TO MEET HIM?

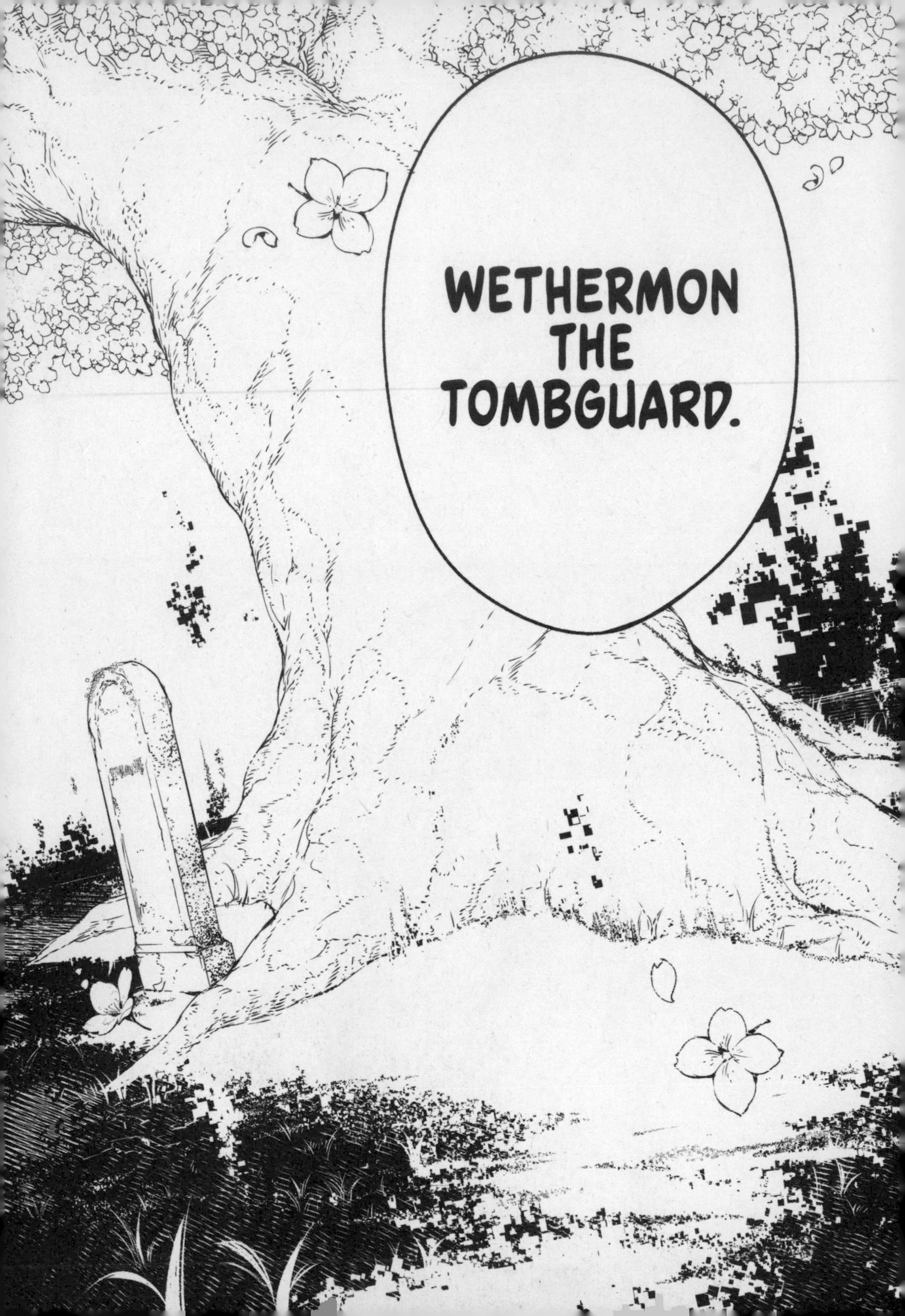
WETHERMON THE TOMBGUARD.

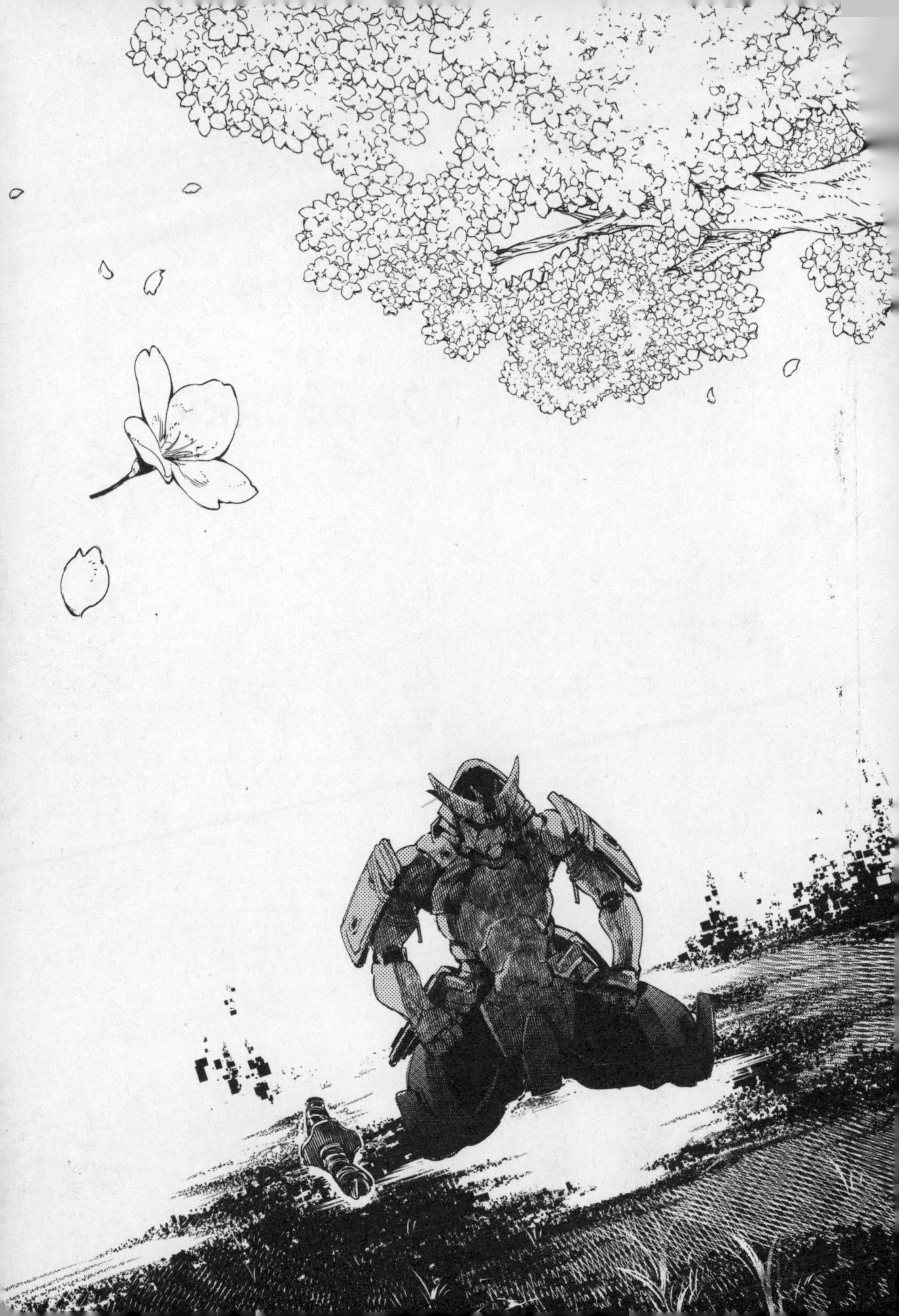

READ TO LEARN MORE ABOUT THE WORLD OF SLF!

SHANGRI-LA FRONTIER STRATEGY FORUM

VOL. 18

LET SLF MASTER REI-CHAN TAKE YOU THROUGH THE WORLD!

REI-CHAN

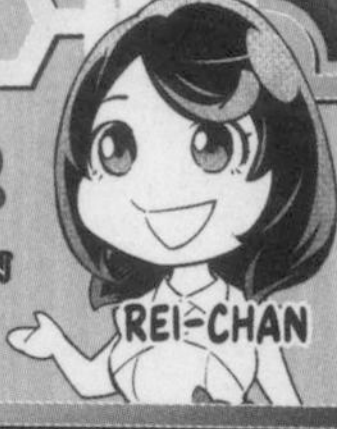

Approaching Battle with the Colossus Wethermon!

Let's check out Arthur Pencilgon and OiKatzo's stats!

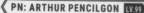

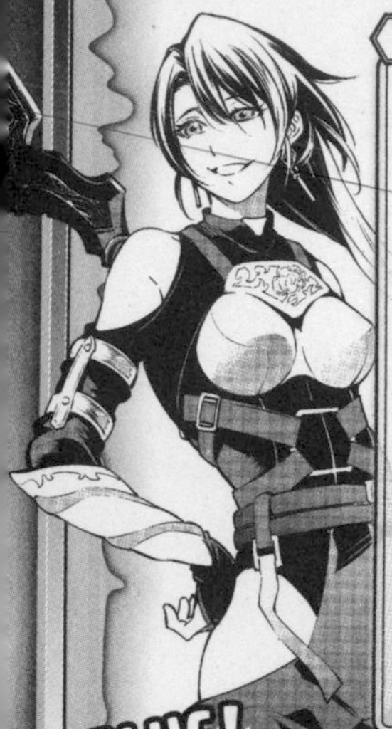

PN: ARTHUR PENCILGON LV.99

JOB

MAIN ??? SUB MAGIC LANCER

MONEY ---------- 5 MAHNI

HP: 400	MP: 150
STAMINA: 210	STRENGTH: 210
DEXTERITY: 310	AGILITY: 210
TECH: 130	VITALITY: 378
LUCK: 100	

EQUIPMENT
- HANDS: ZANBARALIA BLACKSPEAR
- HEAD: NONE
- TORSO: EVIL QUEEN'S BATTLEGEAR
- WAIST: EVIL QUEEN'S BADGEWRAP
- LEGS: EVIL QUEEN'S BOOTS
- ACCESSORY: DEEP SILVER EARRINGS
- ACCESSORY: GHOST REALM BRACELET
- ACCESSORY: ID BRACELET (ASURA KAI)
- ACCESSORY: COWARD CHICKEN
- ACCESSORY: INVENTORY EXTENDER

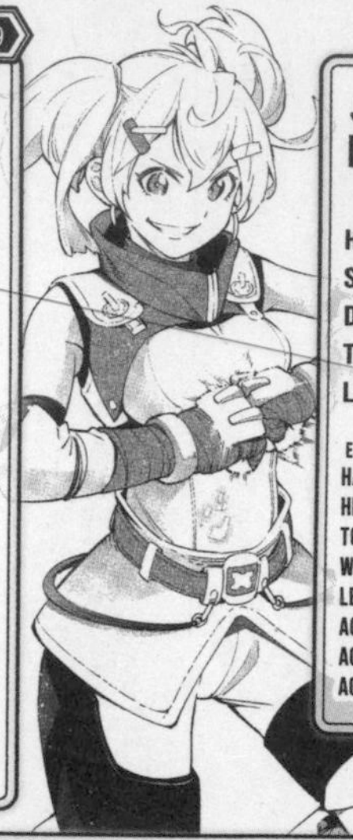

PN: OIKATZO LV.50

JOB

MAIN MONK SUB ????

MONEY ---------- 32050 MAHNI

HP: 90	MP: 35
STAMINA: 30	STRENGTH: 30
DEXTERITY: 41	AGILITY: 30
TECH: 20	VITALITY: 130
LUCK: 40	

EQUIPMENT
- HANDS: NONE
- HEAD: PROUD HAIRSTRING
- TORSO: ASCETIC'S ROBE
- WAIST: ASCETIC'S BELT
- LEGS: ASCETIC'S LEG ARMOR
- ACCESSORY: PIERCING HAIRBAND
- ACCESSORY: INFECTING HAIRBAND
- ACCESSORY: NEAR-PIN HAIRPIN

PLUS!

SUNRAKU'S POWERED UP WITH TRAINING!

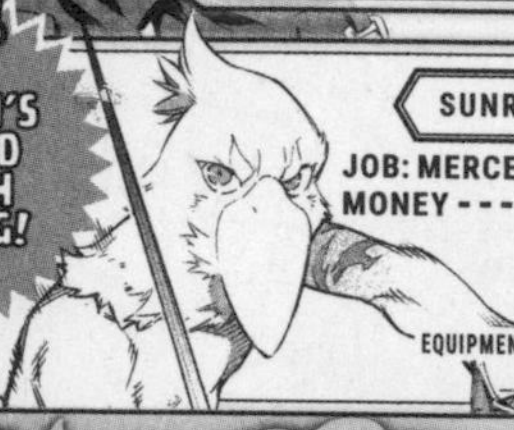

SUNRAKU LV.53

JOB: MERCENARY (TWINBLADE)

MONEY ------150 MAHNI

HP: 30	MP: 10
STAMINA: 60	STRENGTH: 40
DEXTERITY: 50	AGILITY: 70
TECH: 55	VITALITY: 22
LUCK: 74	

EQUIPMENT> HANDS: EMPIRE BEE TWINBLADE, HEAD: STARING BIRD MASK, TORSO: LYCAGON'S MARK, WAIST: LIFESTIDE SASH, LEGS: LYCAGON'S MARK, ACCESSORIES: NONE

BUT!

ALL PLAYERS ARE RESET TO LEVEL 50 AGAINST WETHERMON! THEY MUST WORK TOGETHER TO BEAT HIM!

SLF'S MAILBIRD SYSTEM: MESSAGING IN A FLASH!

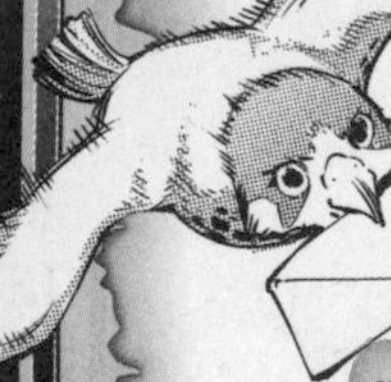

Q: WHAT IS IT?

A: THIS IS SLF'S MESSAGING FEATURE, AVAILABLE TO ESTABLISHED CLANS AND VIA NPC-RUN FACILITIES FOR A FEE. THE MORE MONEY YOU PAY, THE QUICKER YOUR MAIL IS DELIVERED.

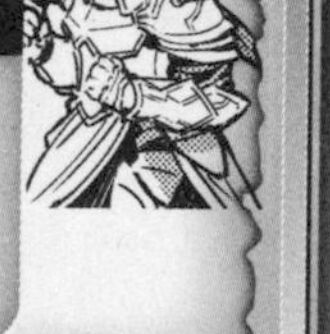

I GOTTA SEND THIS BY FALCON TO HIZUTOME!

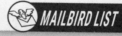

MAILBIRD LIST

SPARROW ---	THE CHEAPEST. ARRIVES IN 5 MINUTES. CONSUMED BY RAPTORS 30% OF THE TIME.
PIGEON -----	STANDARD PRICE. ARRIVES IN 3 MINUTES. FASTER, BUT 5% CHANCE OF RAPTOR ATTACK.
RAVEN -----	PRICEY. ARRIVES IN 4 MINUTES. A BIT SLOWER THAN PIGEONS, BUT IMPERVIOUS TO RAPTORS.
OWL ------	EXPENSIVE. ARRIVES IN 2 SECONDS. AVAILABLE ONLY AFTER DARK.
FALCON ----	FIRST-CLASS. ARRIVES IN 3 SECONDS. SOMETIMES GIVES BONUS ITEMS (LIKE SPARROW FEATHERS).

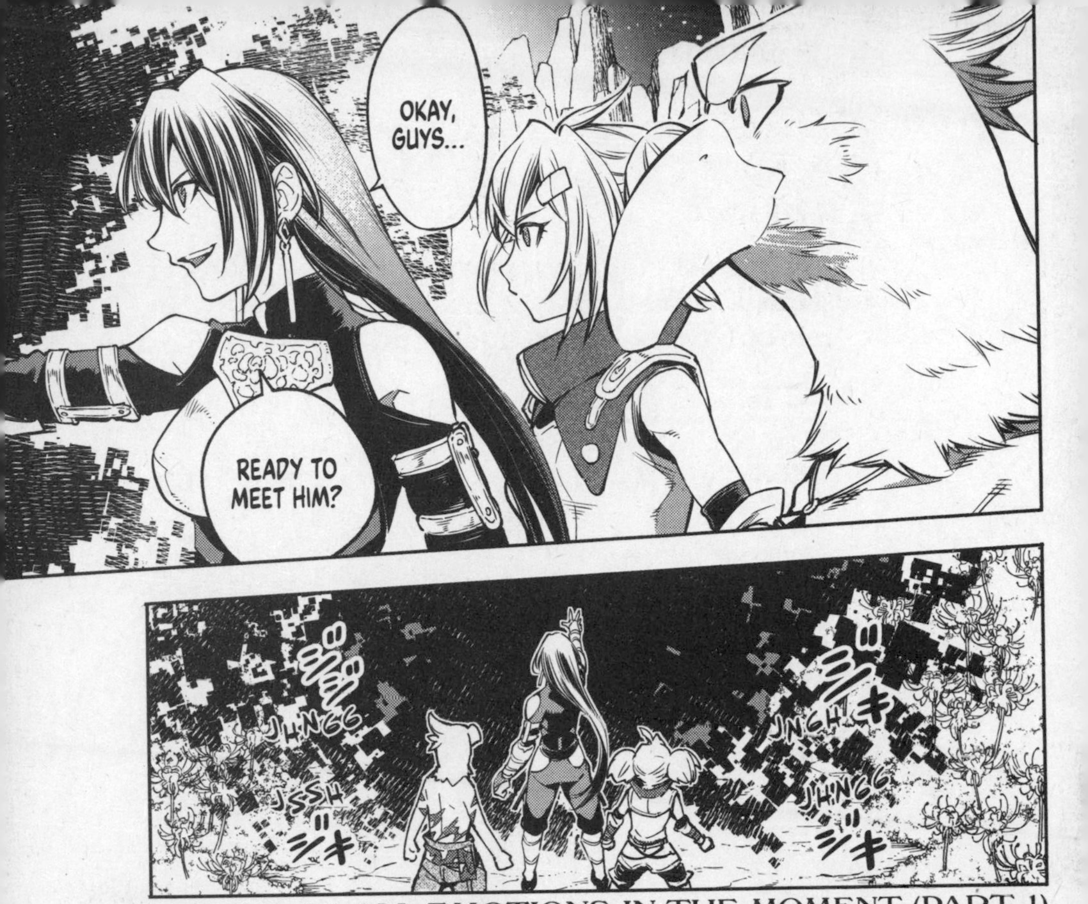
OKAY, GUYS...
READY TO MEET HIM?
JHNGH
JHNGG
JHNGG
JSSH

CHAPTER 31: ALL EMOTIONS IN THE MOMENT (PART 1)

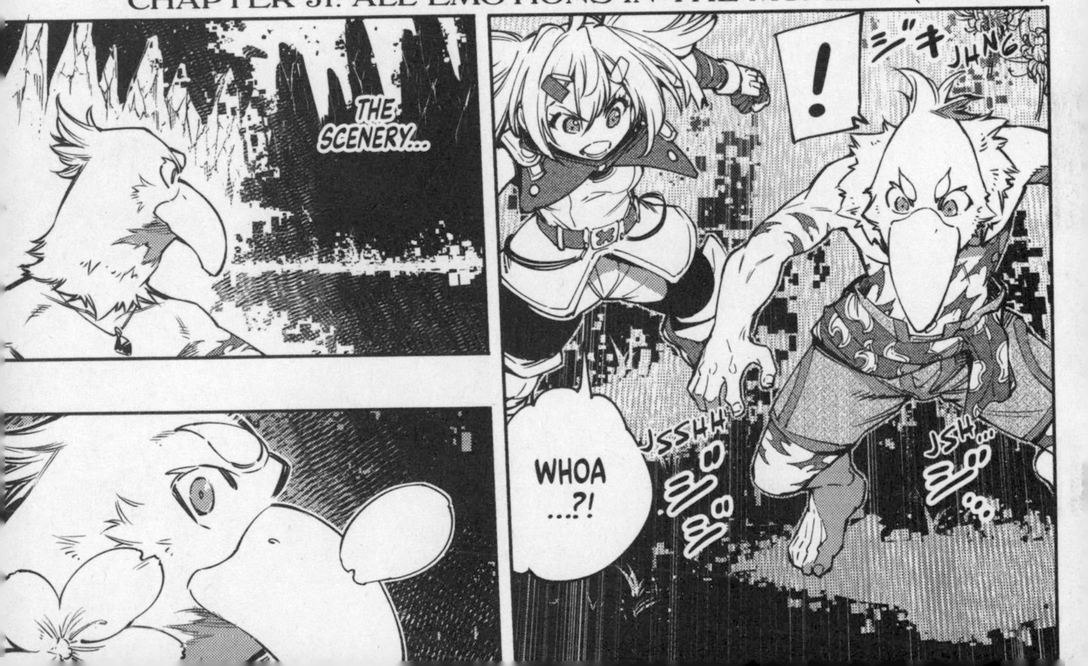
!
JHNG
JSH...
WHOA ...?!
JSSHH
THE SCENERY...

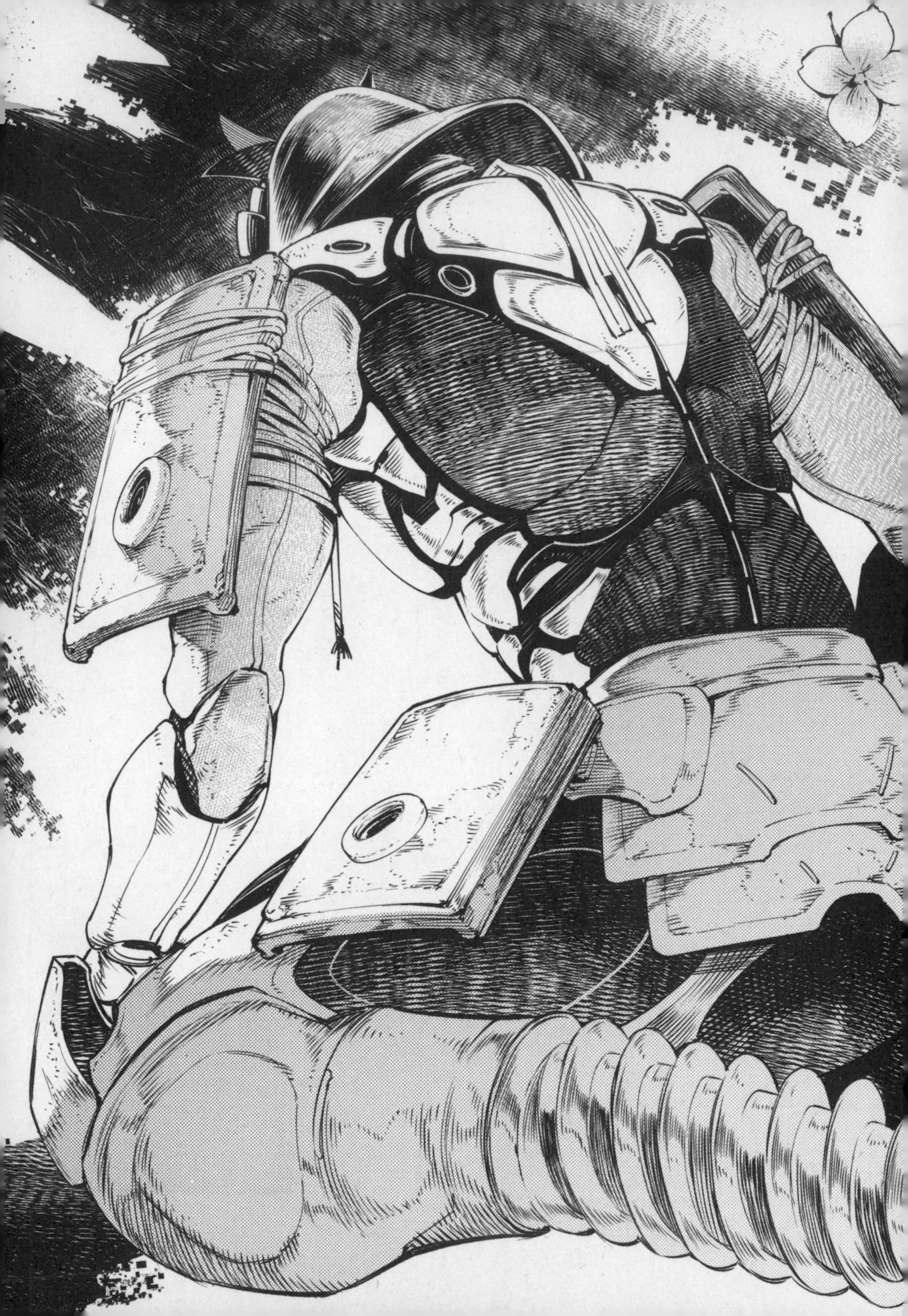

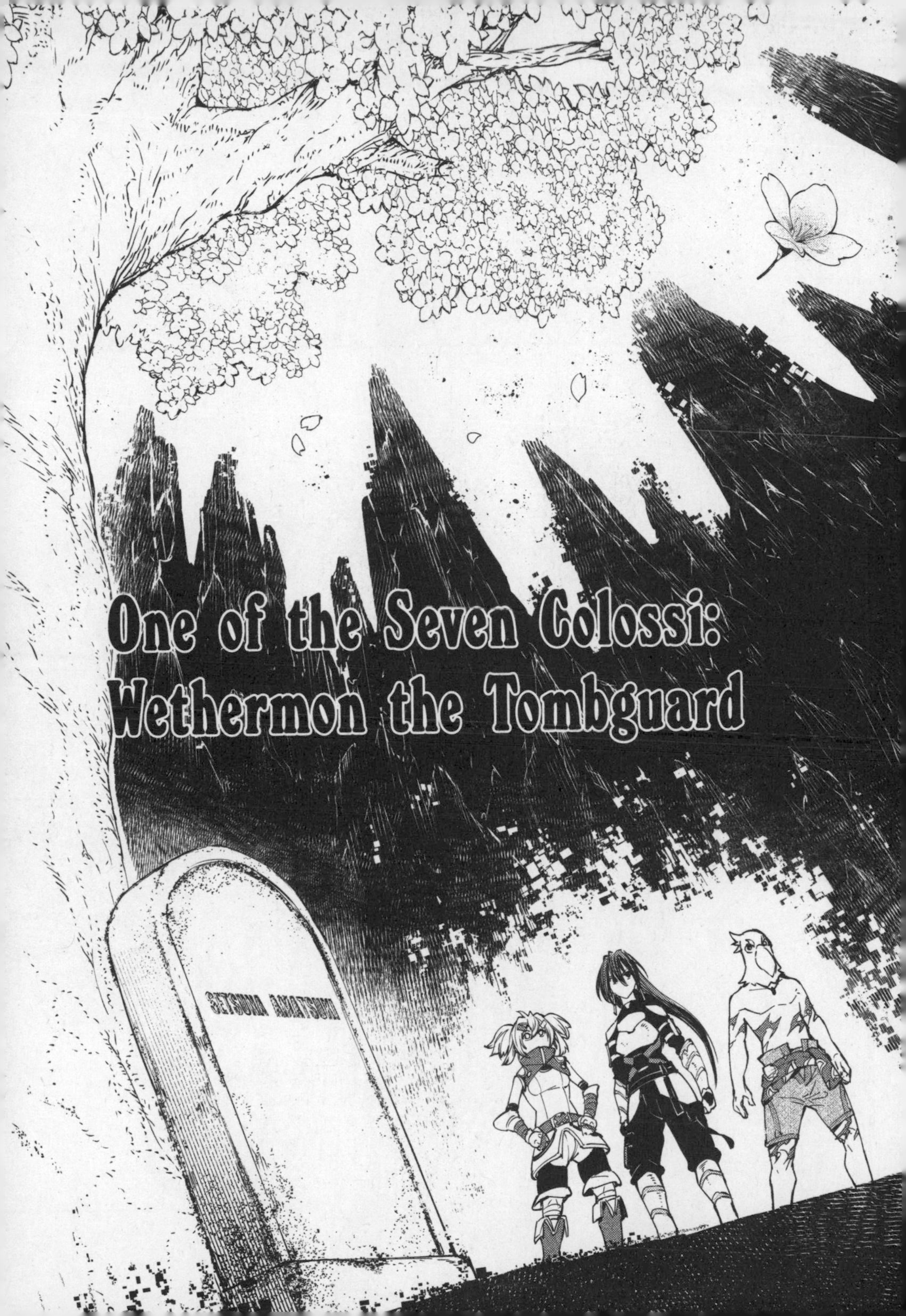
One of the Seven Colossi:
Wethermon the Tombguard
SETSUNA AMATSUKI

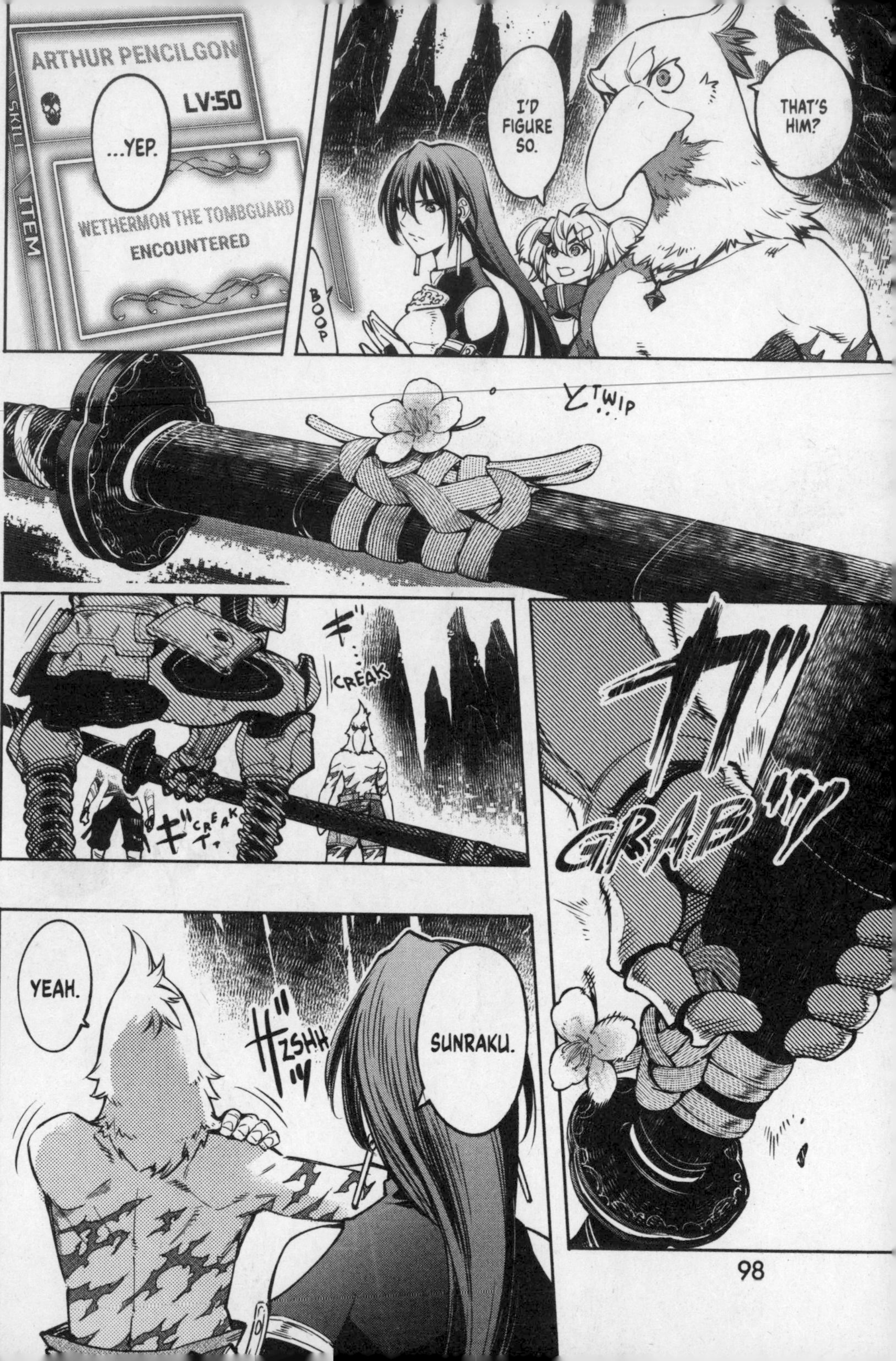
THAT'S HIM?
I'D FIGURE SO.
BOOP
ARTHUR PENCILGON
LV:50
SKILL
ITEM
WETHERMON THE TOMBGUARD ENCOUNTERED
...YEP.
TWIP
GRAB
CREAK
CREAK
SUNRAKU.
ZSHH
YEAH.

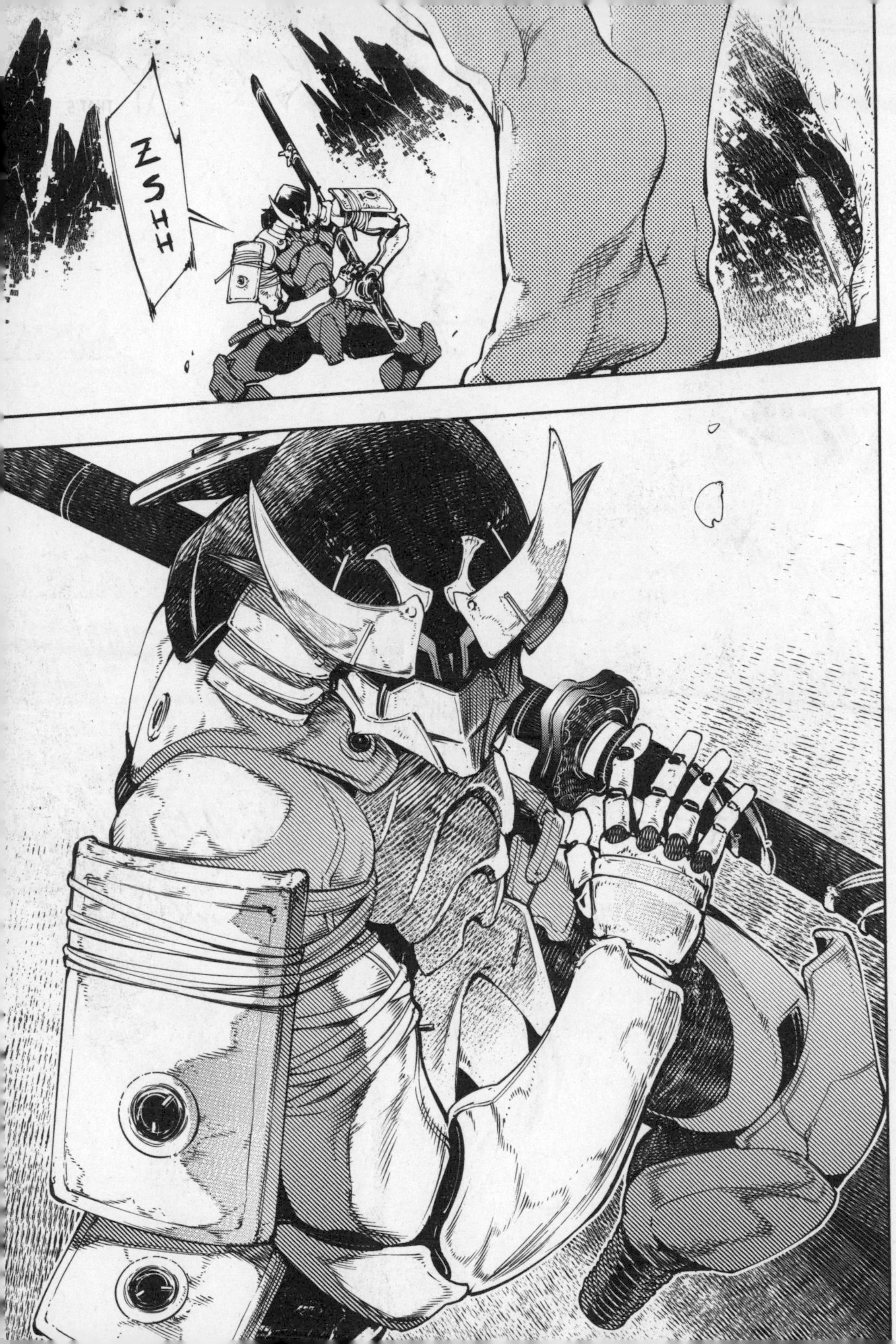
ZSHH

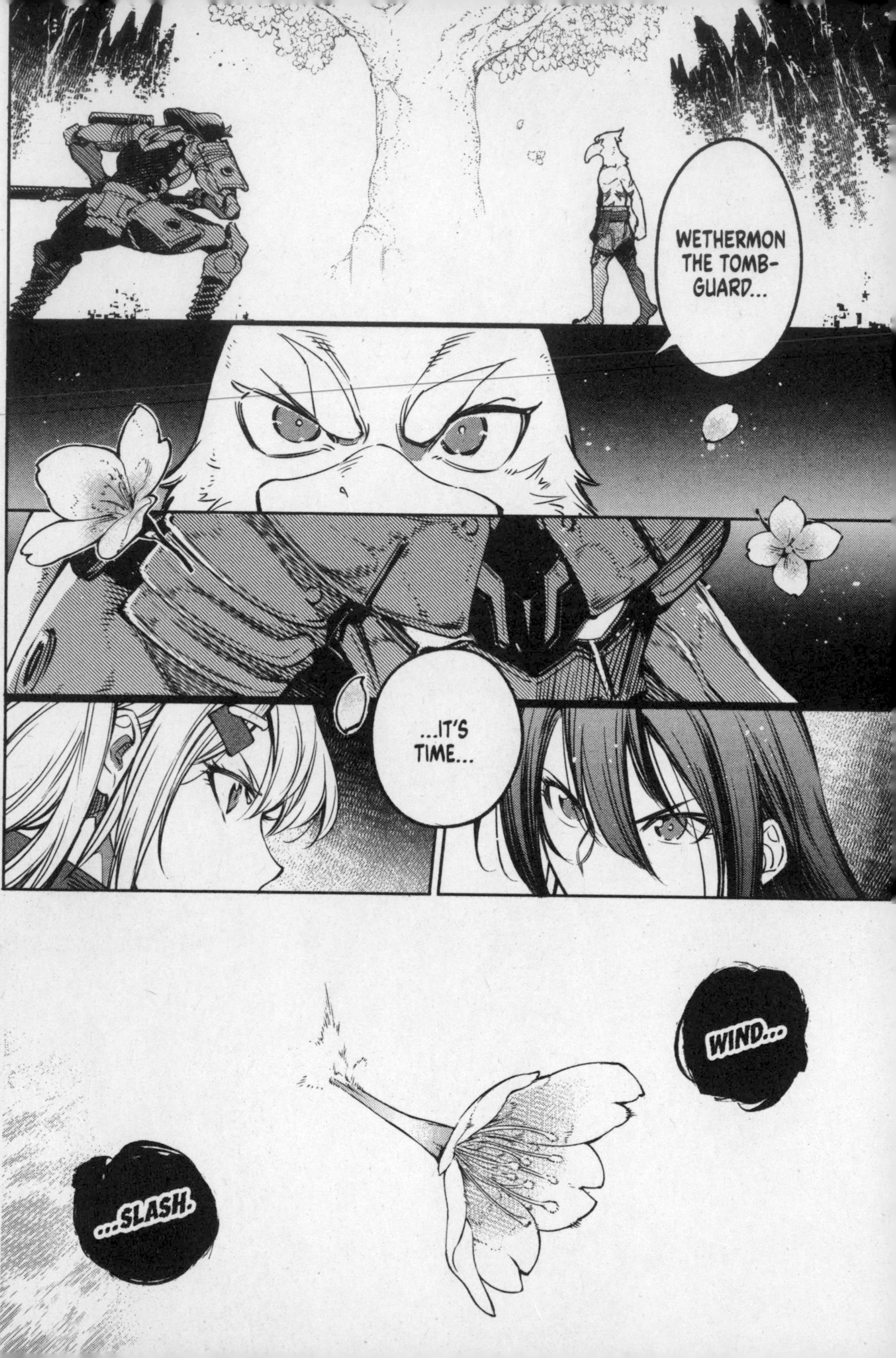
WETHERMON THE TOMB-GUARD...
...IT'S TIME...
WIND...
...SLASH.

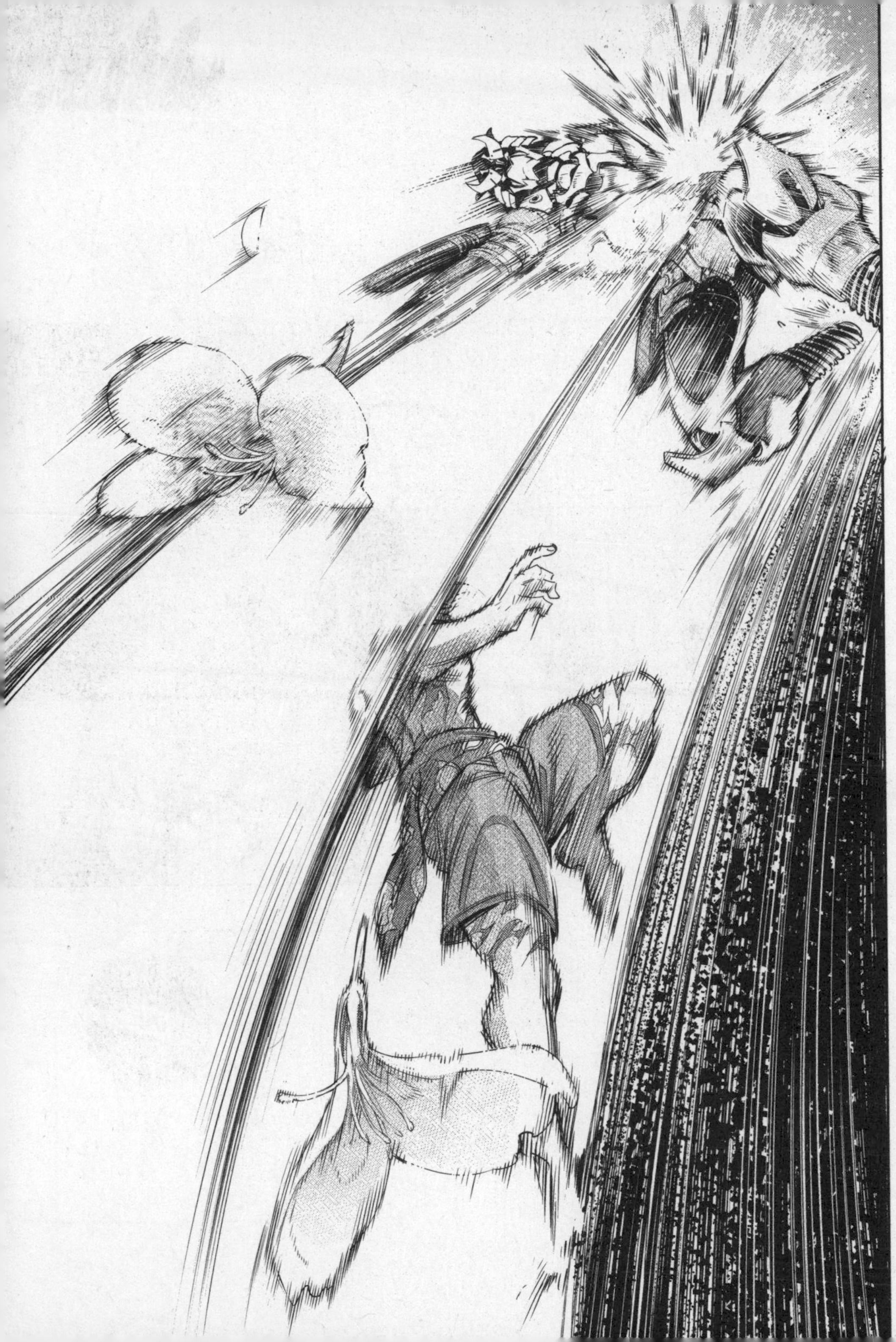

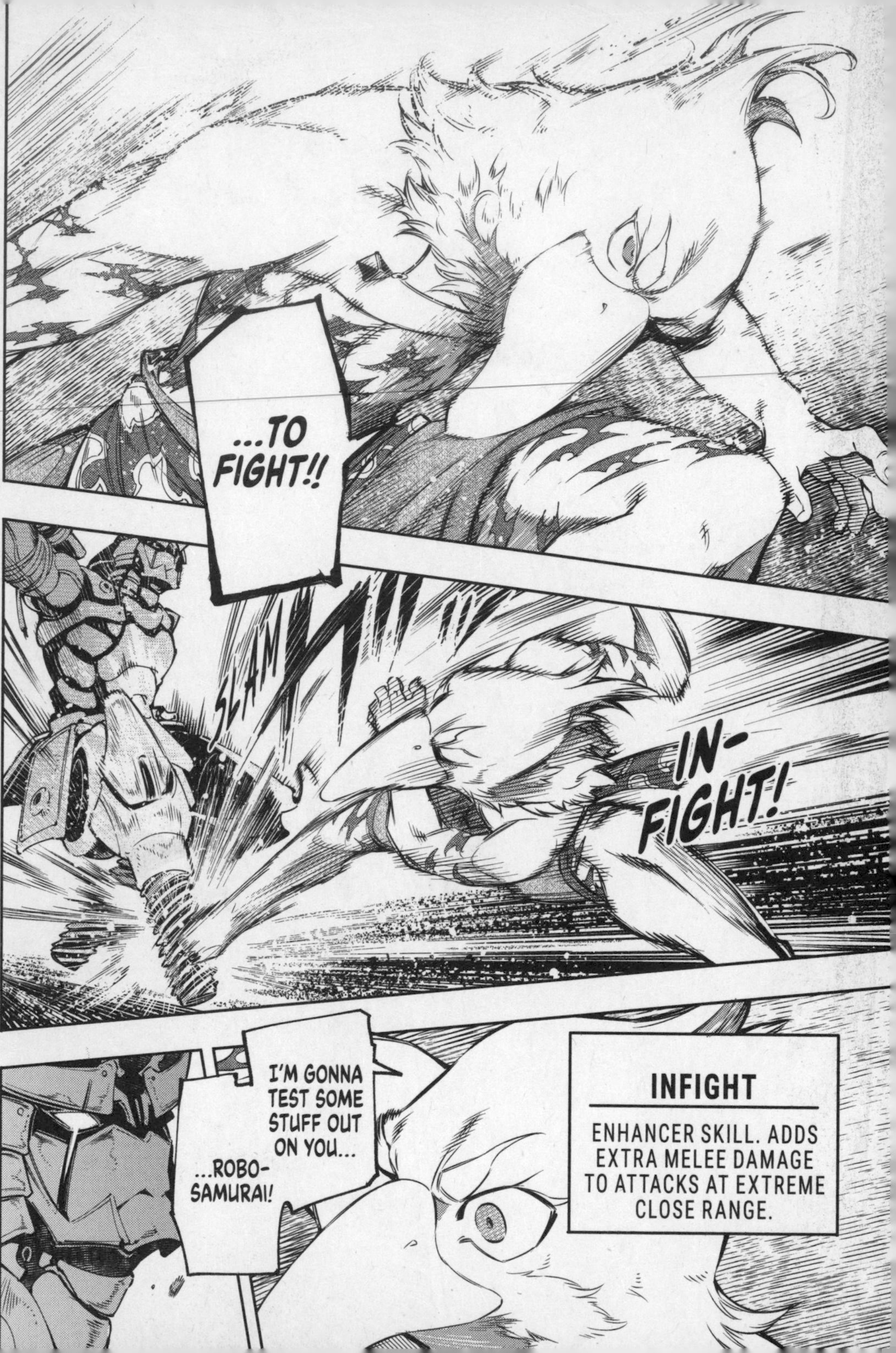
...TO FIGHT!!
SLAM
IN-FIGHT!
INFIGHT
ENHANCER SKILL. ADDS EXTRA MELEE DAMAGE TO ATTACKS AT EXTREME CLOSE RANGE.
I'M GONNA TEST SOME STUFF OUT ON YOU...
...ROBO-SAMURAI!

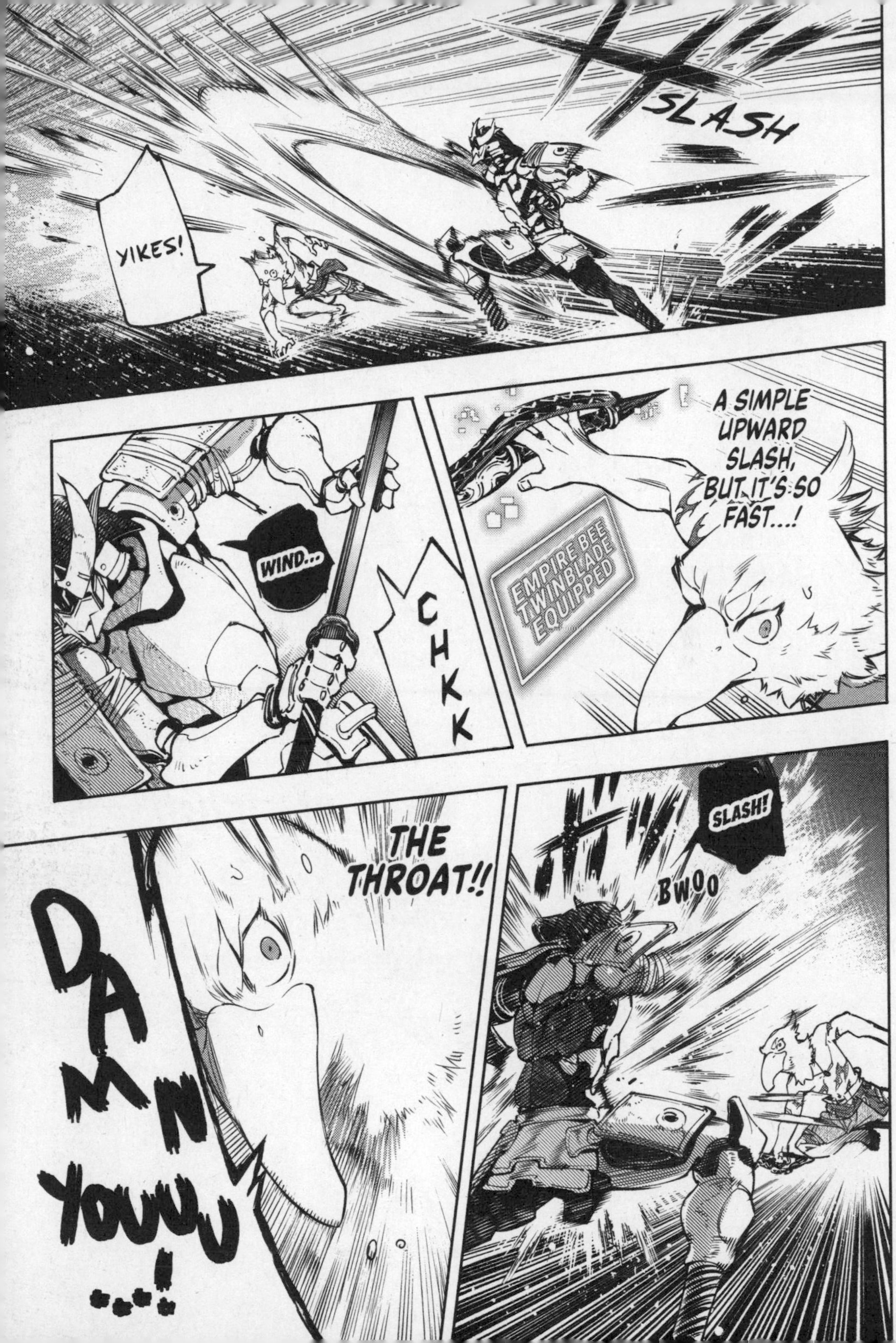
SLASH
YIKES!
A SIMPLE UPWARD SLASH, BUT IT'S SO FAST...!
EMPIRE BEE TWINBLADE EQUIPPED
CHKK
WIND...
SLASH!
BWOO
THE THROAT!!
DAMN YOUUU...!

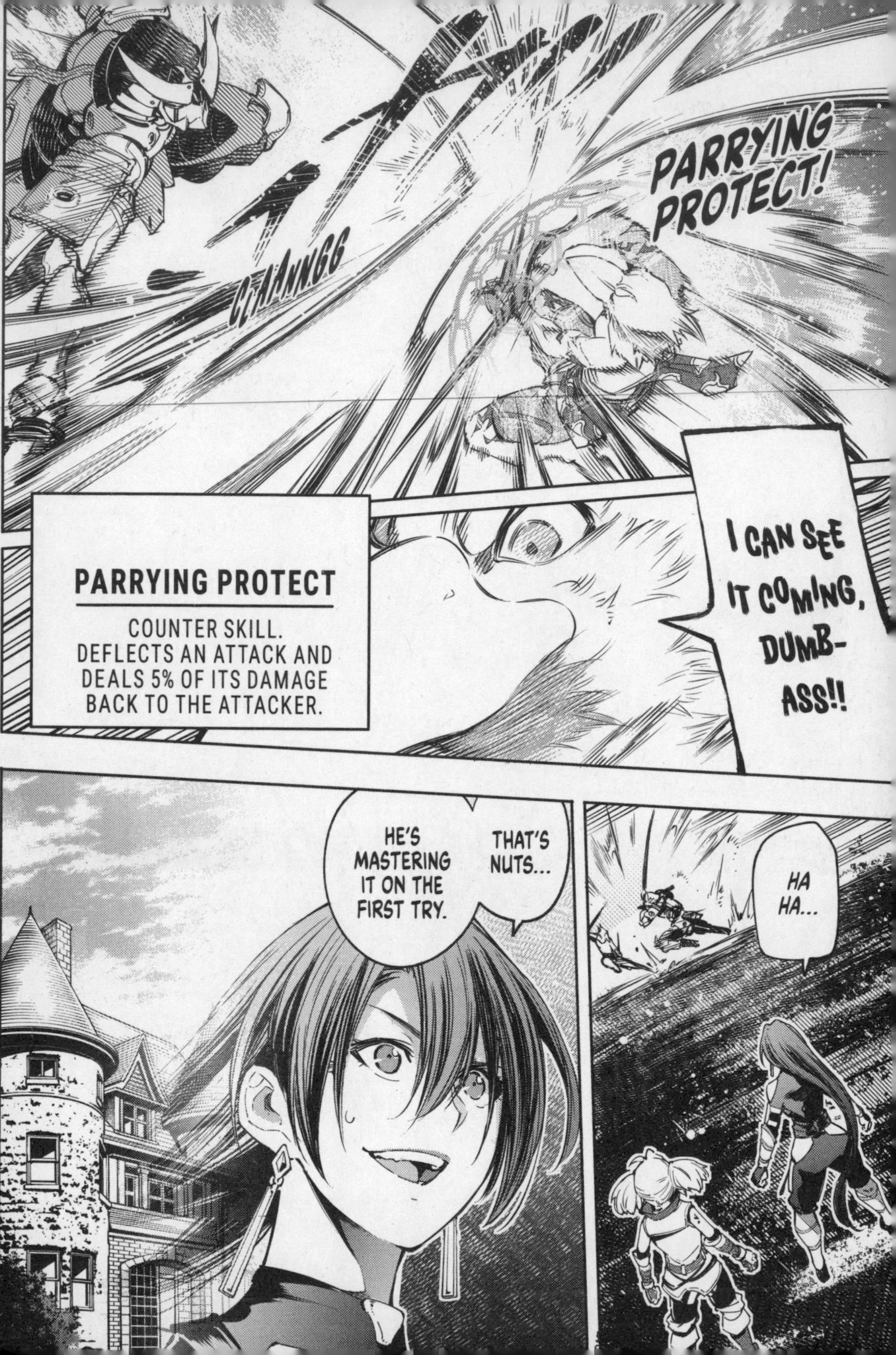
PARRYING PROTECT!
CLAAANNGG
I CAN SEE IT COMING, DUMB-ASS!!
PARRYING PROTECT
COUNTER SKILL. DEFLECTS AN ATTACK AND DEALS 5% OF ITS DAMAGE BACK TO THE ATTACKER.
HA HA...
THAT'S NUTS...
HE'S MASTERING IT ON THE FIRST TRY.

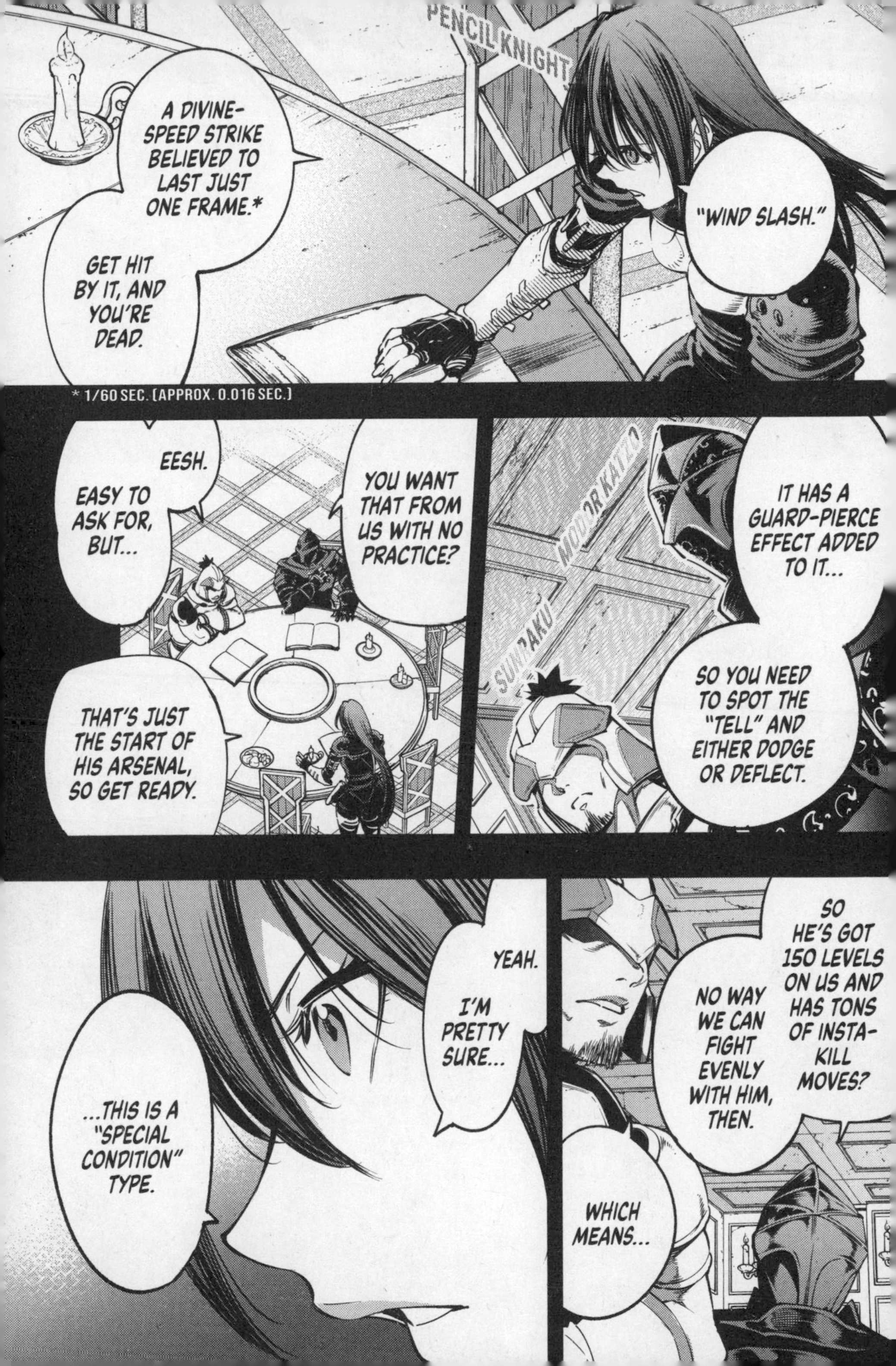
PENCIL KNIGHT
"WIND SLASH."
A DIVINE-SPEED STRIKE BELIEVED TO LAST JUST ONE FRAME.*
GET HIT BY IT, AND YOU'RE DEAD.
* 1/60 SEC. (APPROX. 0.016 SEC.)
SUNRAKU
IT HAS A GUARD-PIERCE EFFECT ADDED TO IT...
SO YOU NEED TO SPOT THE "TELL" AND EITHER DODGE OR DEFLECT.
YOU WANT THAT FROM US WITH NO PRACTICE?
EESH.
EASY TO ASK FOR, BUT...
THAT'S JUST THE START OF HIS ARSENAL, SO GET READY.
SO HE'S GOT 150 LEVELS ON US AND HAS TONS OF INSTA-KILL MOVES?
NO WAY WE CAN FIGHT EVENLY WITH HIM, THEN.
WHICH MEANS...
YEAH.
I'M PRETTY SURE...
...THIS IS A "SPECIAL CONDITION" TYPE.

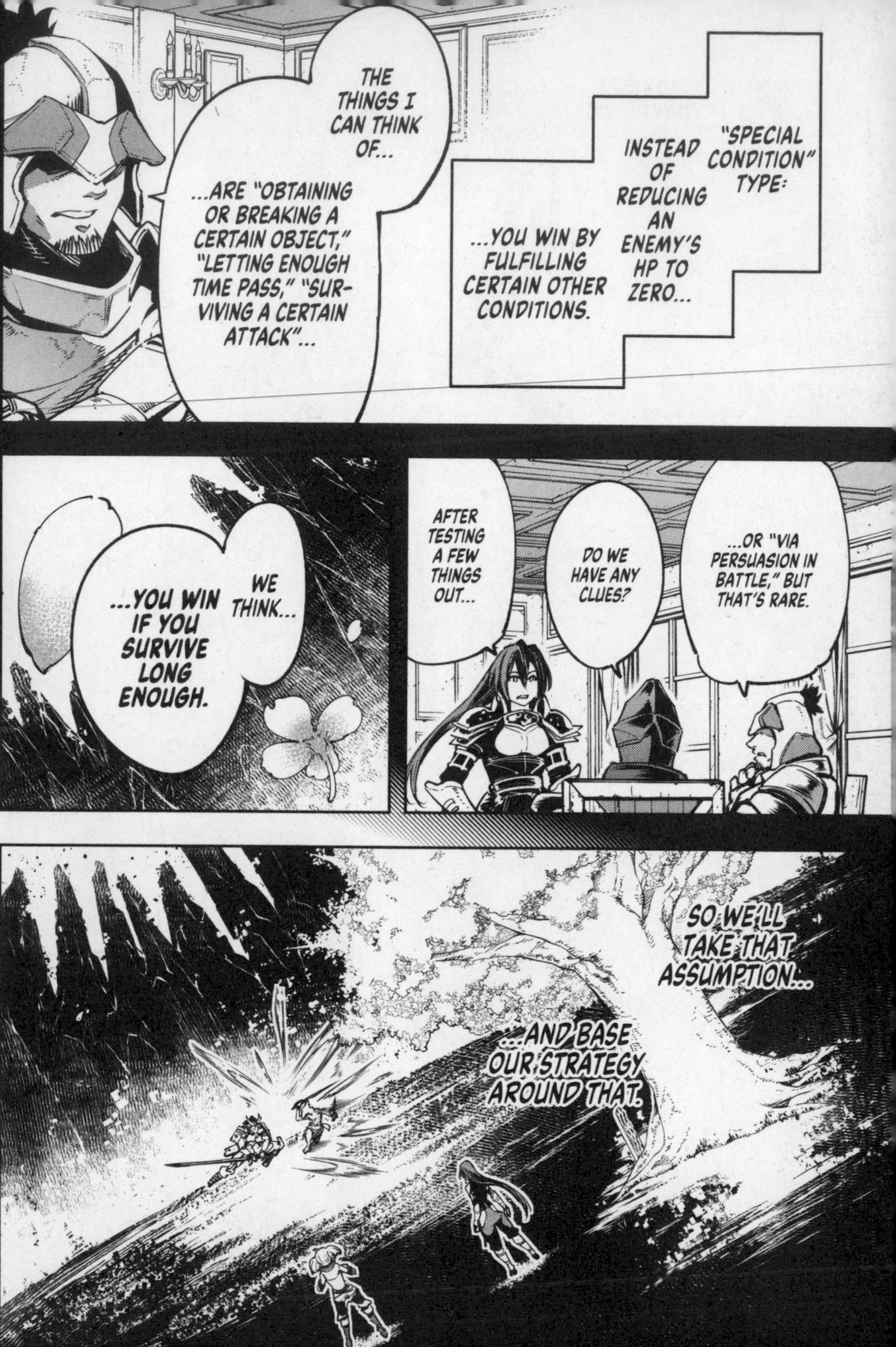
"SPECIAL CONDITION" TYPE:
INSTEAD OF REDUCING AN ENEMY'S HP TO ZERO...
...YOU WIN BY FULFILLING CERTAIN OTHER CONDITIONS.
THE THINGS I CAN THINK OF...
...ARE "OBTAINING OR BREAKING A CERTAIN OBJECT," "LETTING ENOUGH TIME PASS," "SURVIVING A CERTAIN ATTACK"...
...OR "VIA PERSUASION IN BATTLE," BUT THAT'S RARE.
DO WE HAVE ANY CLUES?
AFTER TESTING A FEW THINGS OUT...
WE THINK...
...YOU WIN IF YOU SURVIVE LONG ENOUGH.
SO WE'LL TAKE THAT ASSUMPTION...
...AND BASE OUR STRATEGY AROUND THAT.

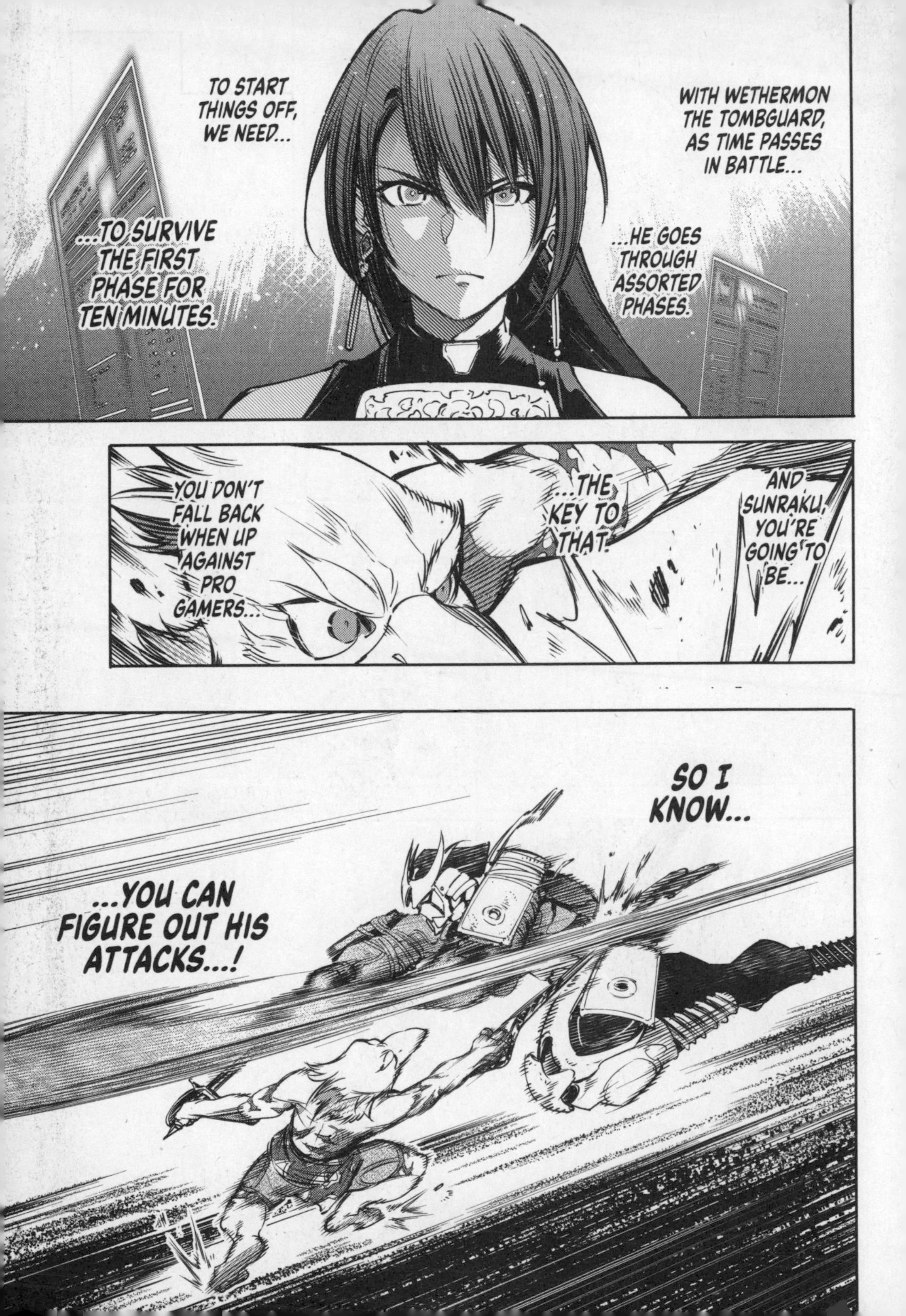
WITH WETHERMON THE TOMBGUARD, AS TIME PASSES IN BATTLE...
...HE GOES THROUGH ASSORTED PHASES.
TO START THINGS OFF, WE NEED...
...TO SURVIVE THE FIRST PHASE FOR TEN MINUTES.
AND SUNRAKU, YOU'RE GOING TO BE...
...THE KEY TO THAT.
YOU DON'T FALL BACK WHEN UP AGAINST PRO GAMERS...
SO I KNOW...
...YOU CAN FIGURE OUT HIS ATTACKS...!

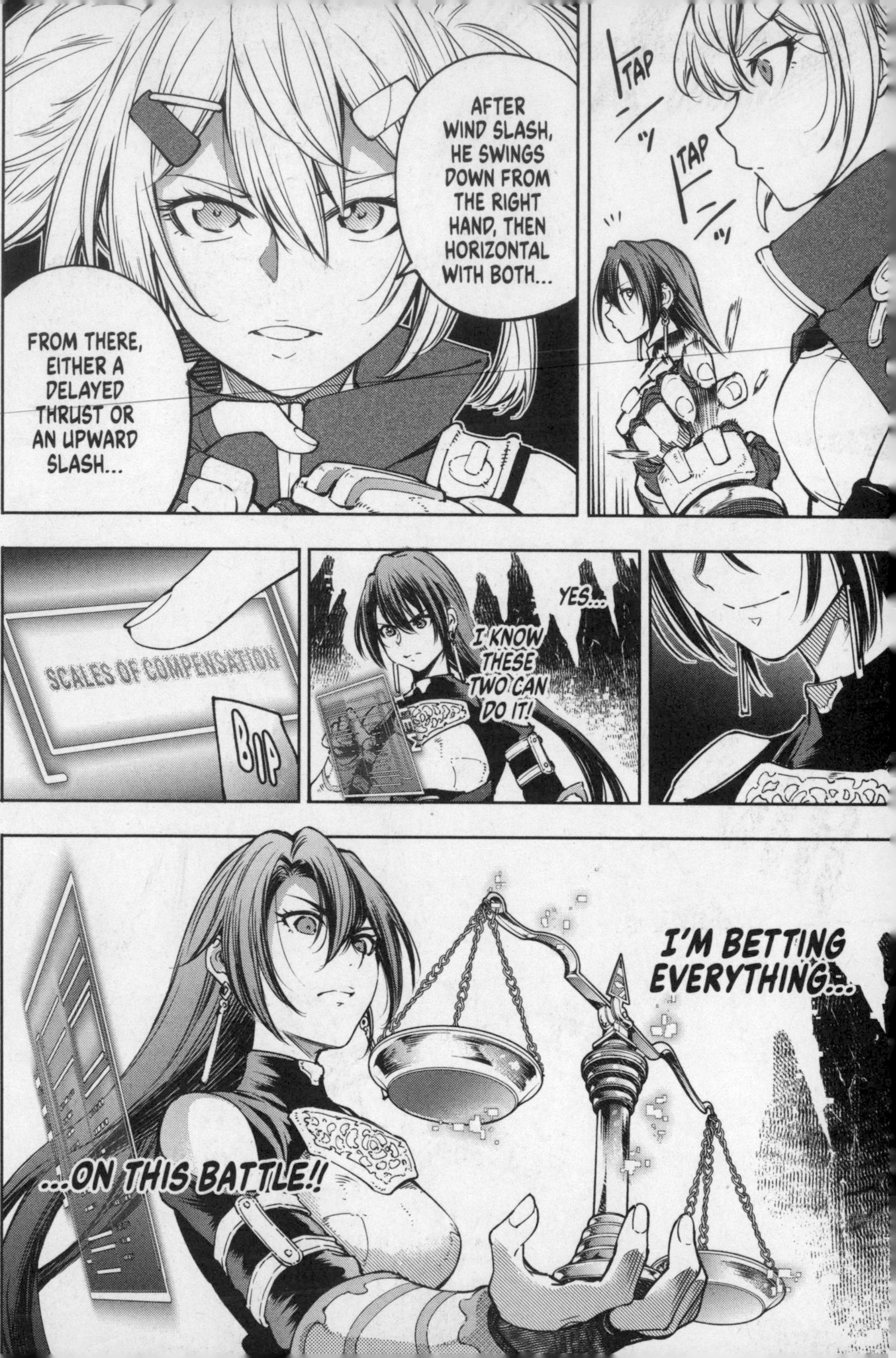
TAP
TAP
AFTER WIND SLASH, HE SWINGS DOWN FROM THE RIGHT HAND, THEN HORIZONTAL WITH BOTH...
FROM THERE, EITHER A DELAYED THRUST OR AN UPWARD SLASH...
YES...
I KNOW THESE TWO CAN DO IT!
SCALES OF COMPENSATION
BIP
I'M BETTING EVERYTHING...
...ON THIS BATTLE!!

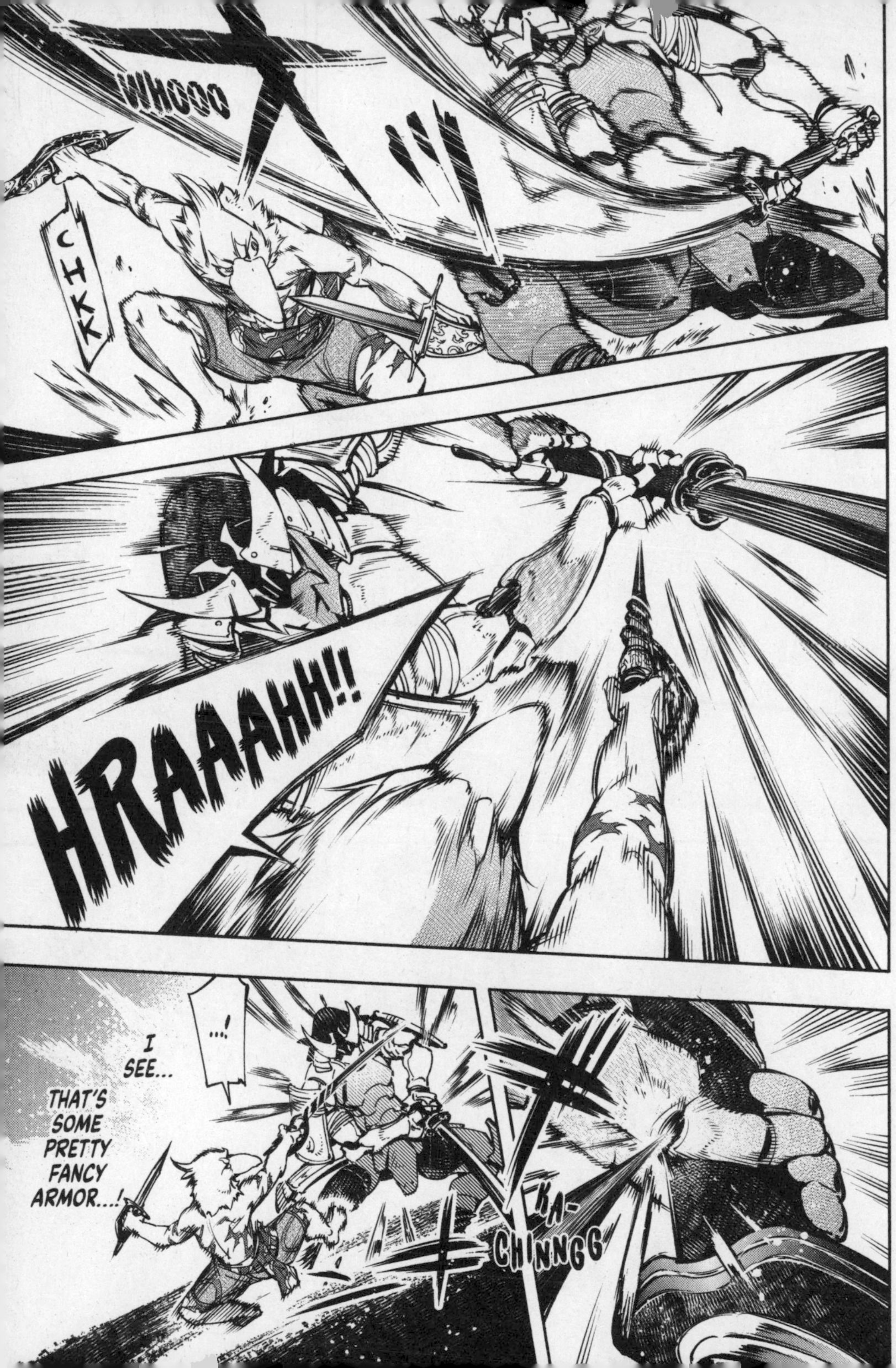
WHOOO
CHKK
HRAAAHH!!
KA-CHINNGG
...!
I SEE... THAT'S SOME PRETTY FANCY ARMOR...!

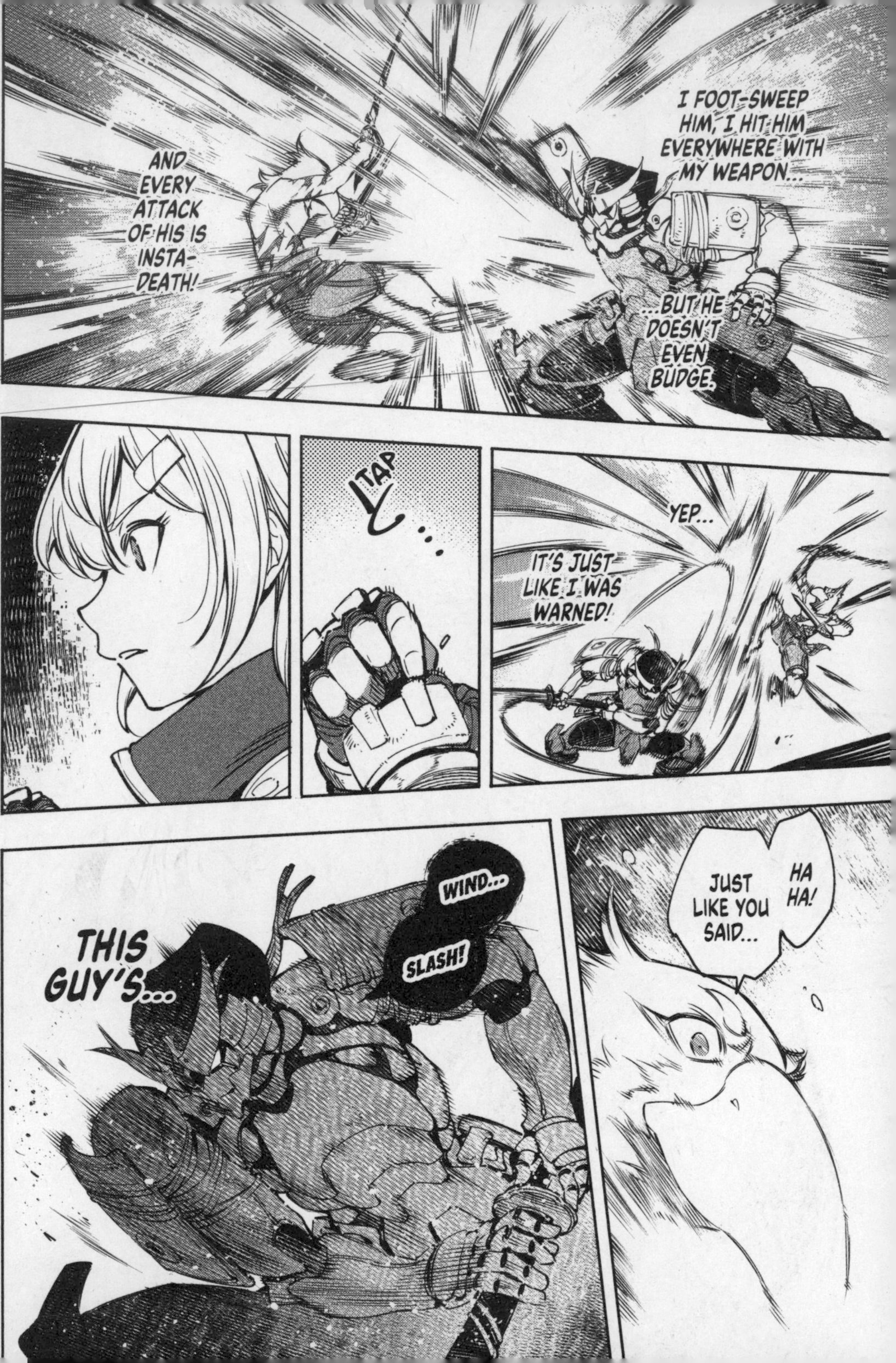
I FOOT-SWEEP HIM, I HIT HIM EVERYWHERE WITH MY WEAPON...
...BUT HE DOESN'T EVEN BUDGE.
AND EVERY ATTACK OF HIS IS INSTA-DEATH!
YEP...
IT'S JUST LIKE I WAS WARNED!
TAP
HA HA!
JUST LIKE YOU SAID...
WIND...
SLASH!
THIS GUY'S...

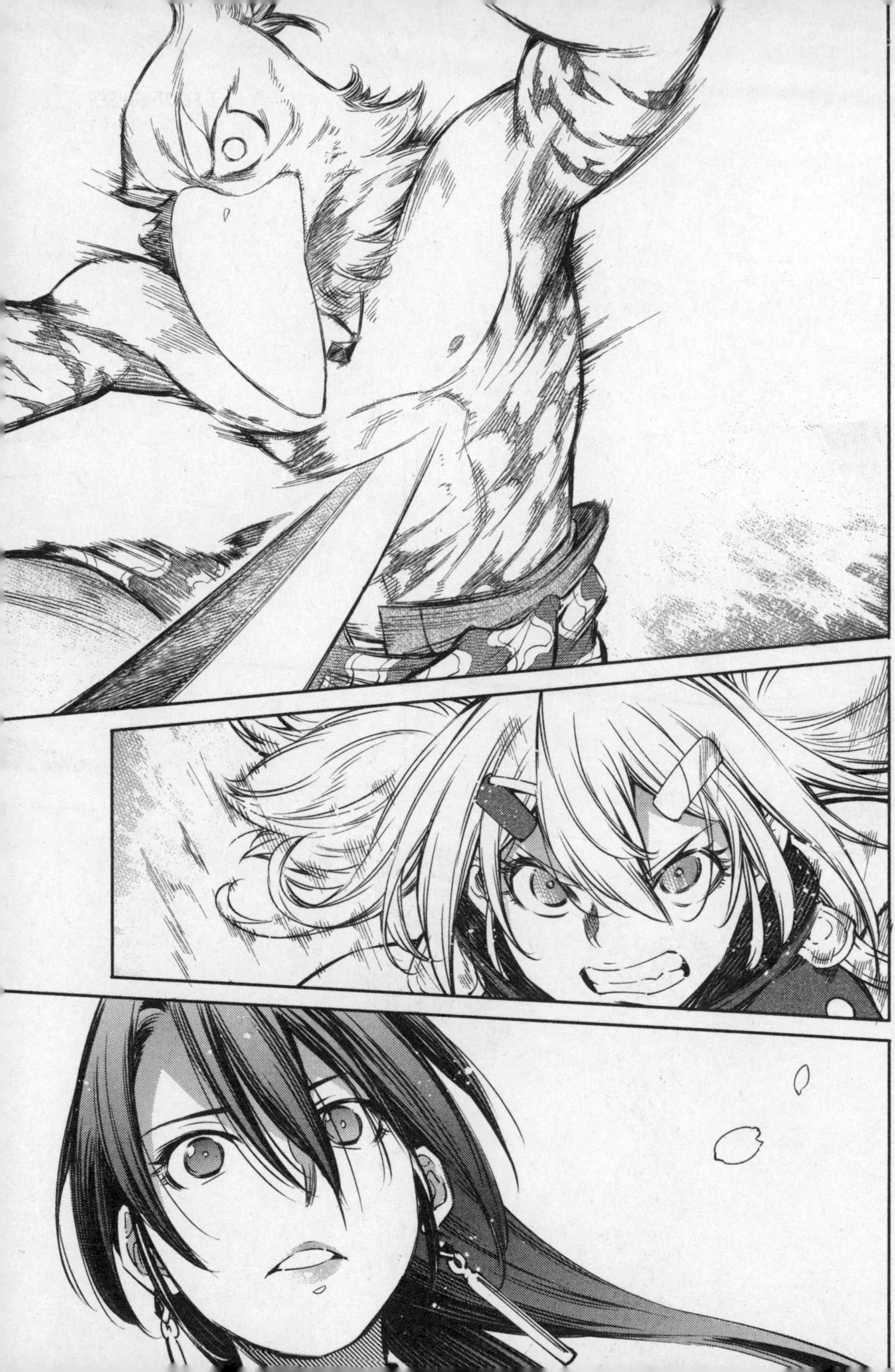

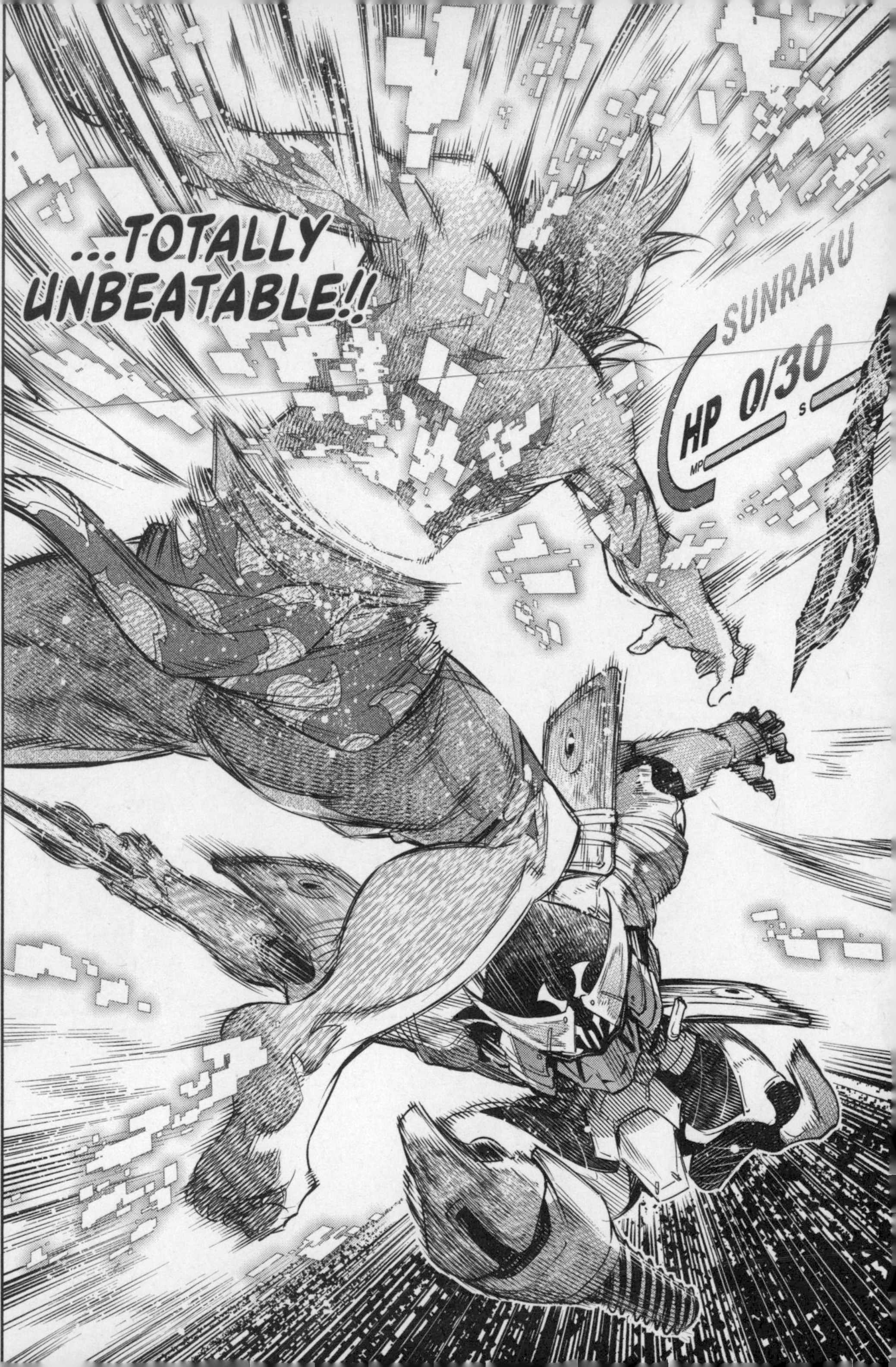
...TOTALLY UNBEATABLE!!
SUNRAKU
HP 0/30
MP
S

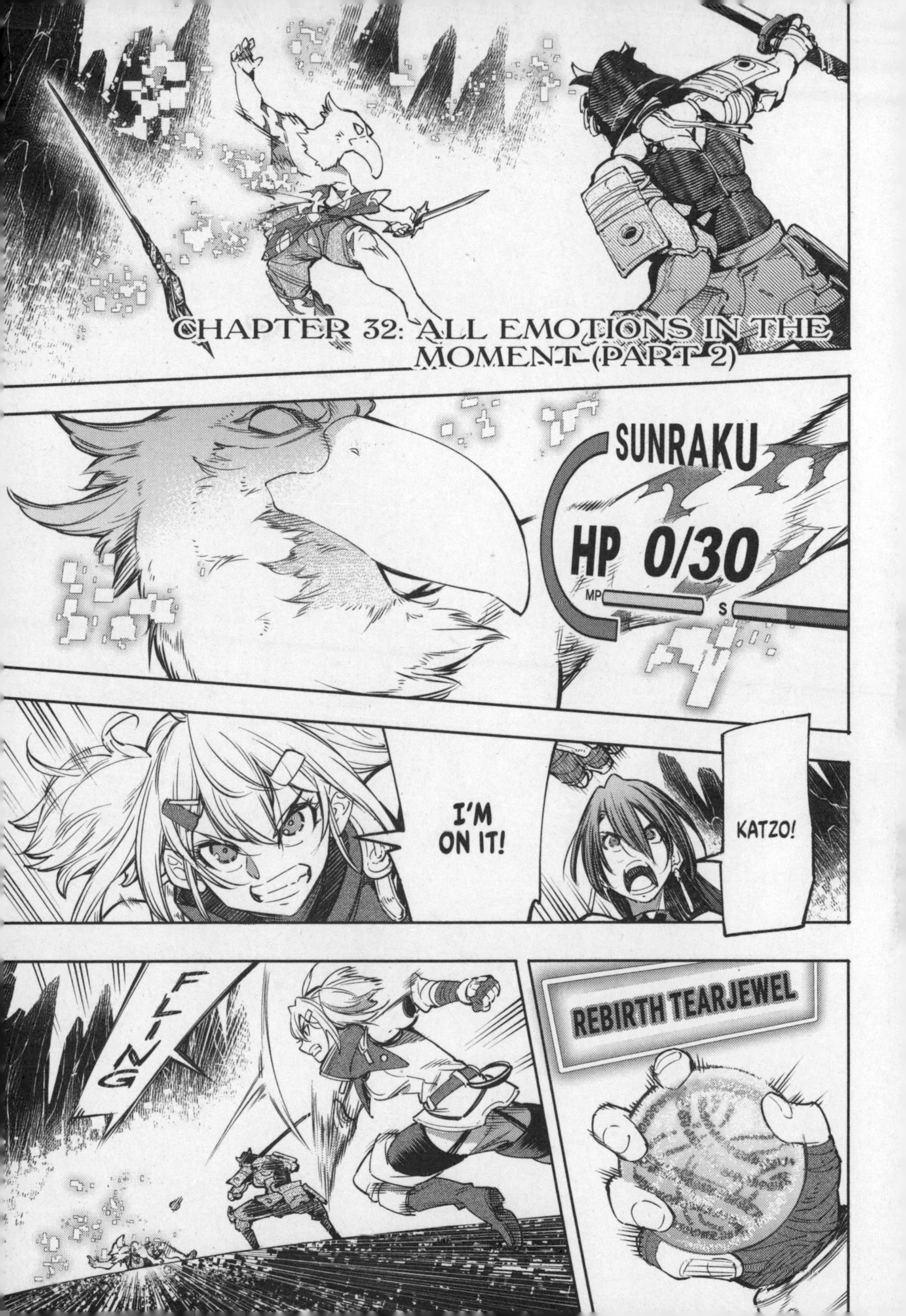
CHAPTER 32: ALL EMOTIONS IN THE MOMENT (PART 2)
SUNRAKU
HP 0/30
MP
S
KATZO!
I'M ON IT!
REBIRTH TEARJEWEL
FLING

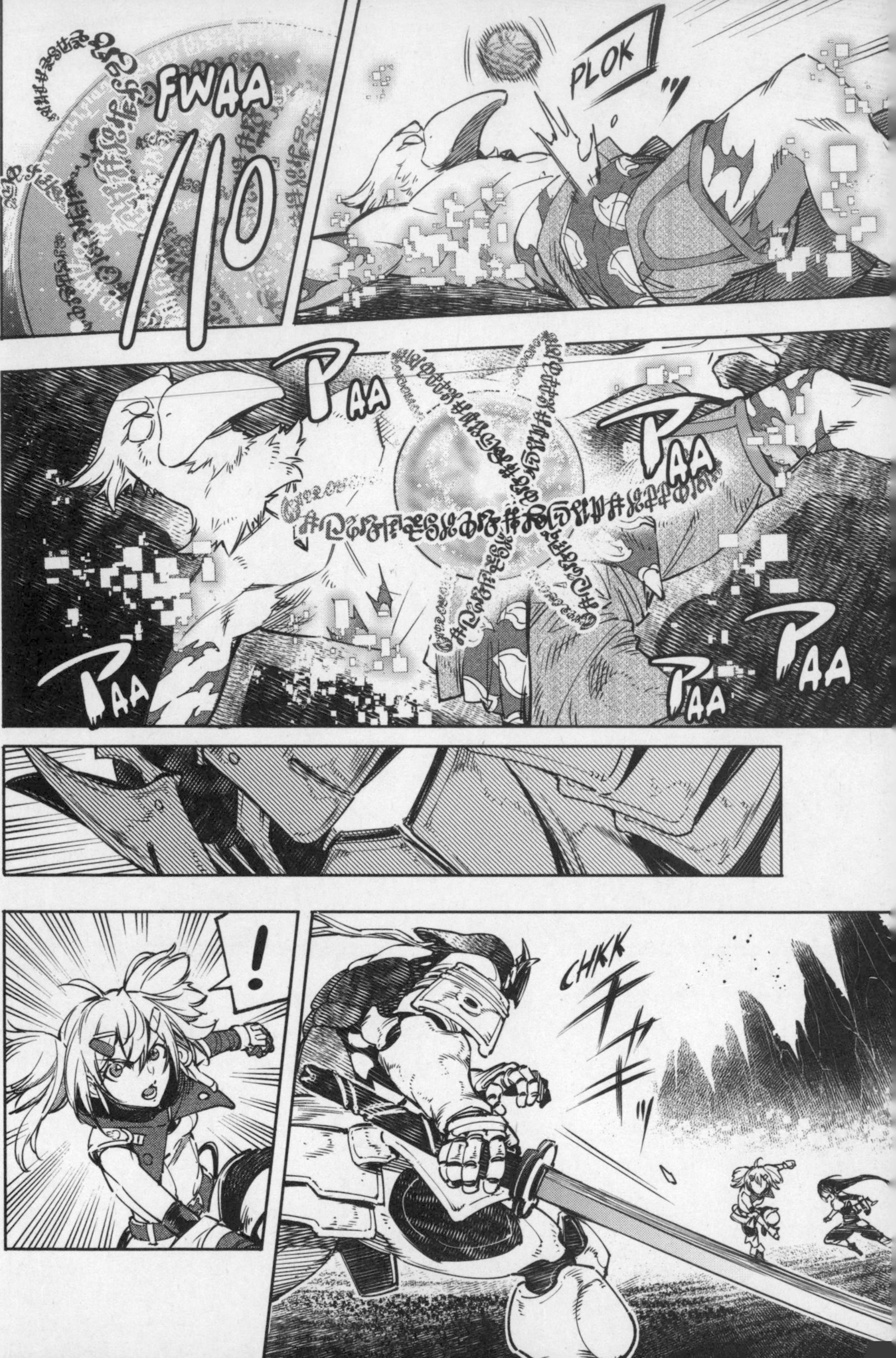
PLOK
FWAA
PAA
PAA
PAA
PAA
PAA
CHKK
!

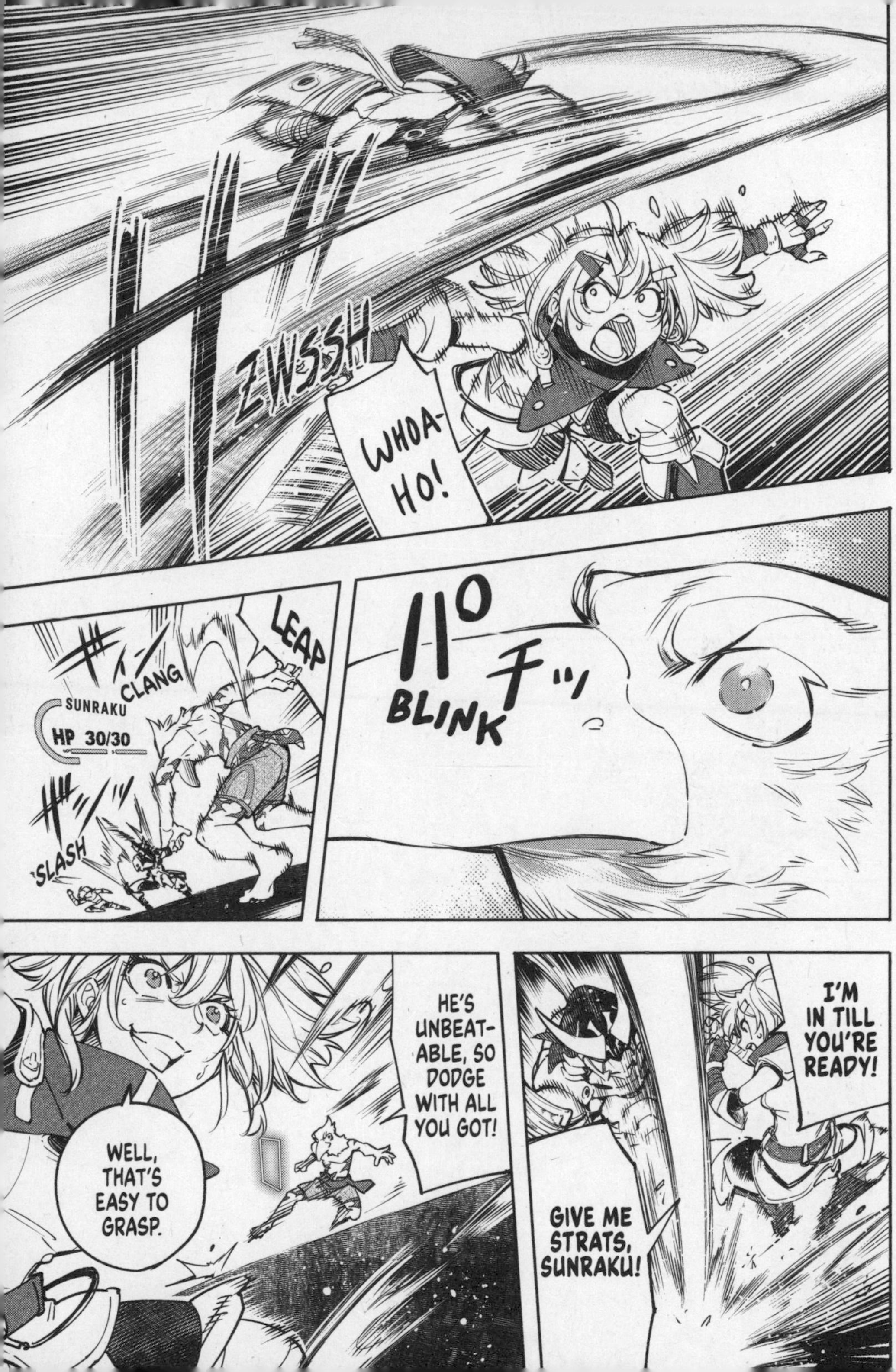
ZWSSH
WHOA-HO!
パチッ
BLINK
LEAP
CLANG
SUNRAKU
HP 30/30
SLASH
I'M IN TILL YOU'RE READY!
GIVE ME STRATS, SUNRAKU!
HE'S UNBEAT-ABLE, SO DODGE WITH ALL YOU GOT!
WELL, THAT'S EASY TO GRASP.

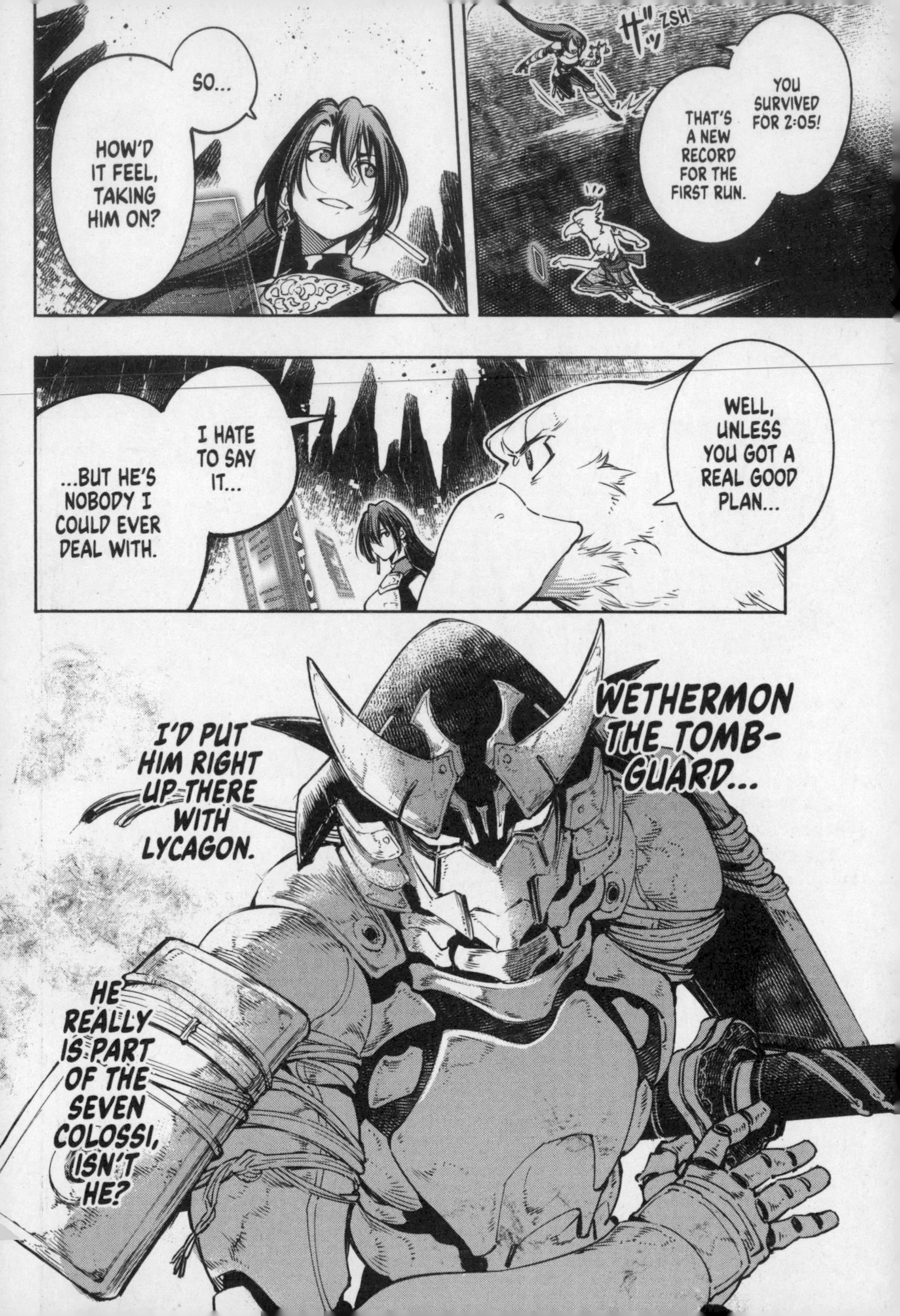
ザッ ZSH
YOU SURVIVED FOR 2:05!
THAT'S A NEW RECORD FOR THE FIRST RUN.
SO...
HOW'D IT FEEL, TAKING HIM ON?
WELL, UNLESS YOU GOT A REAL GOOD PLAN...
I HATE TO SAY IT...
...BUT HE'S NOBODY I COULD EVER DEAL WITH.
WETHERMON THE TOMB-GUARD...
I'D PUT HIM RIGHT UP THERE WITH LYCAGON.
HE REALLY IS PART OF THE SEVEN COLOSSI, ISN'T HE?

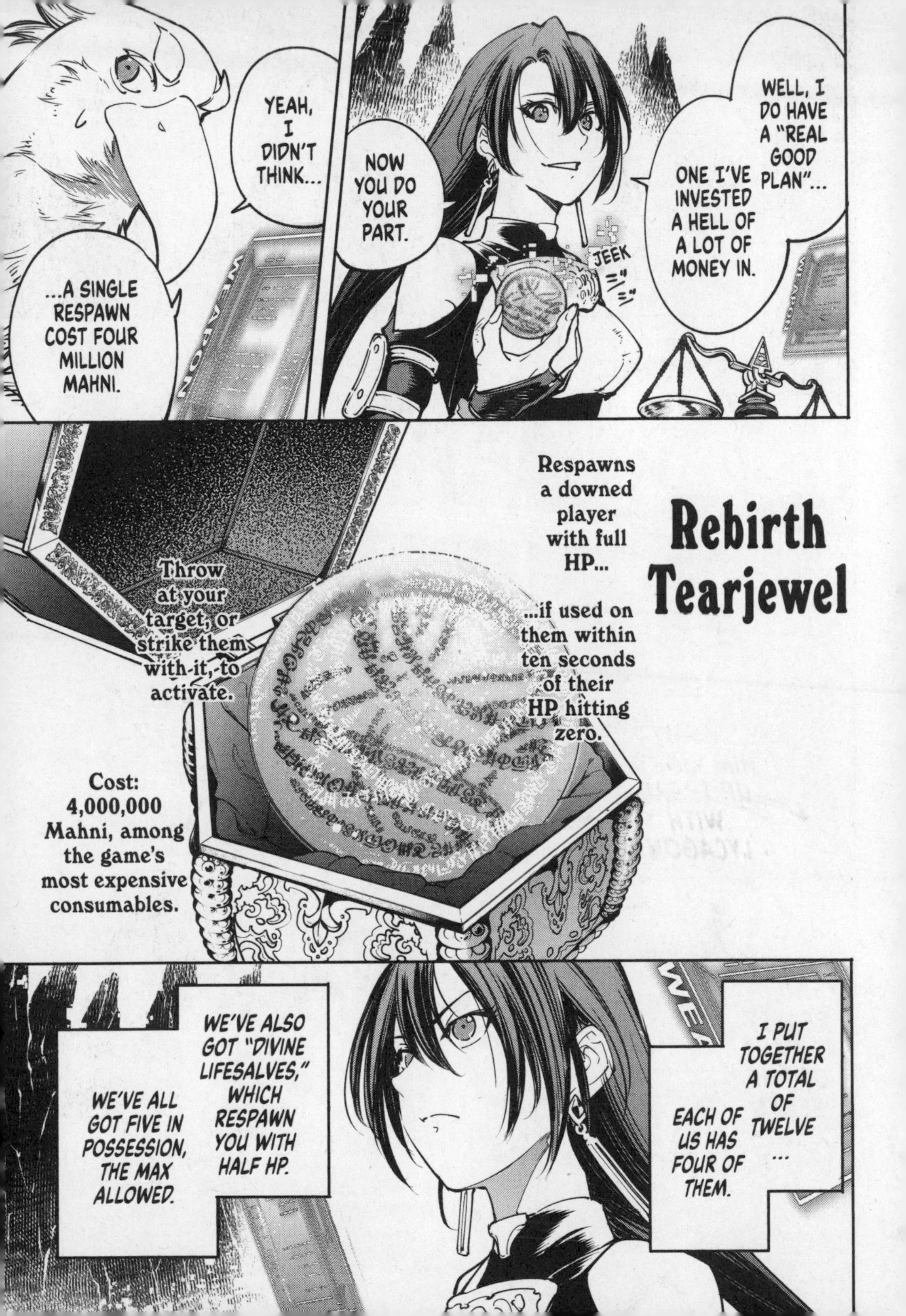
WELL, I DO HAVE A "REAL GOOD PLAN"...
ONE I'VE INVESTED A HELL OF A LOT OF MONEY IN.
JEEK
NOW YOU DO YOUR PART.
YEAH, I DIDN'T THINK...
...A SINGLE RESPAWN COST FOUR MILLION MAHNI.
Rebirth Tearjewel
Respawns a downed player with full HP...
...if used on them within ten seconds of their HP hitting zero.
Throw at your target, or strike them with it, to activate.
Cost: 4,000,000 Mahni, among the game's most expensive consumables.
I PUT TOGETHER A TOTAL OF TWELVE ...
EACH OF US HAS FOUR OF THEM.
WE'VE ALSO GOT "DIVINE LIFESALVES," WHICH RESPAWN YOU WITH HALF HP.
WE'VE ALL GOT FIVE IN POSSESSION, THE MAX ALLOWED.

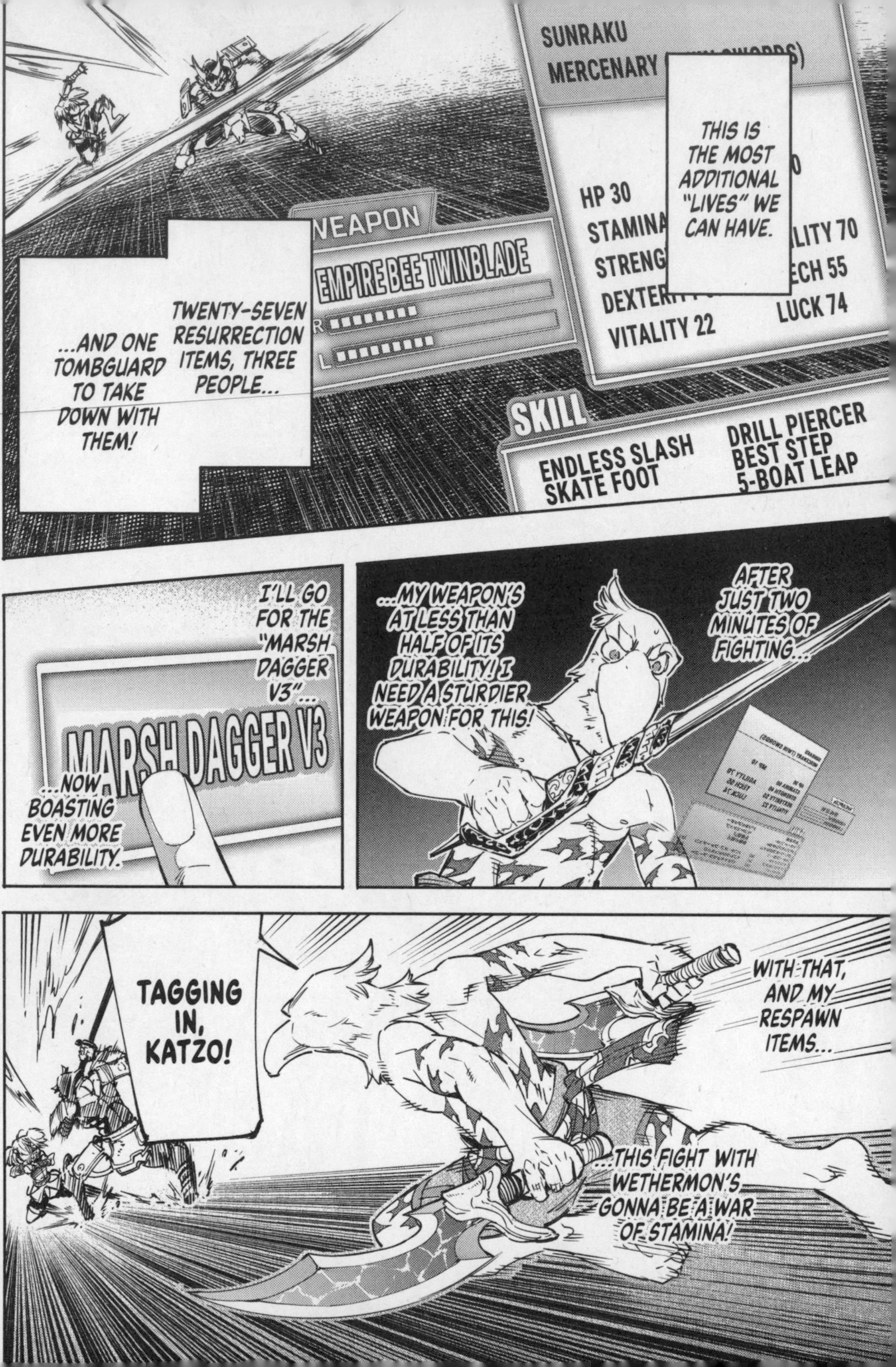
SUNRAKU
MERCENARY
THIS IS THE MOST ADDITIONAL "LIVES" WE CAN HAVE.
HP 30
STAMINA
VITALITY 22
LUCK 74
WEAPON
EMPIRE BEE TWINBLADE
TWENTY-SEVEN RESURRECTION ITEMS, THREE PEOPLE...
...AND ONE TOMBGUARD TO TAKE DOWN WITH THEM!
SKILL
ENDLESS SLASH
SKATE FOOT
DRILL PIERCER
BEST STEP
5-BOAT LEAP
AFTER JUST TWO MINUTES OF FIGHTING...
...MY WEAPON'S AT LESS THAN HALF OF ITS DURABILITY! I NEED A STURDIER WEAPON FOR THIS!
I'LL GO FOR THE "MARSH DAGGER V3"...
MARSH DAGGER V3
...NOW BOASTING EVEN MORE DURABILITY.
WITH THAT, AND MY RESPAWN ITEMS...
...THIS FIGHT WITH WETHERMON'S GONNA BE A WAR OF STAMINA!
TAGGING IN, KATZO!

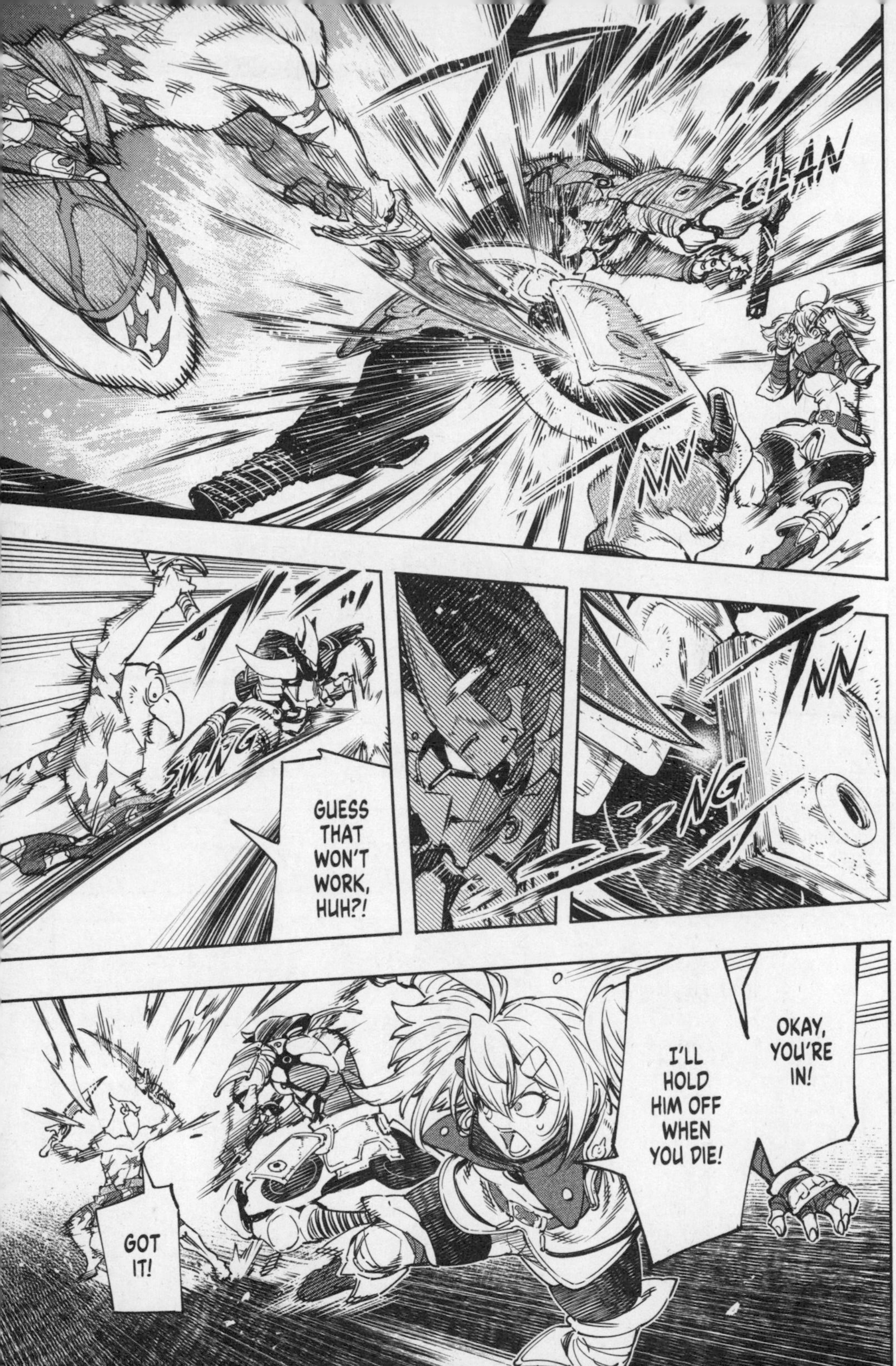
CLAN
NN
NN
SWING
GUESS THAT WON'T WORK, HUH?!
OKAY, YOU'RE IN!
I'LL HOLD HIM OFF WHEN YOU DIE!
GOT IT!

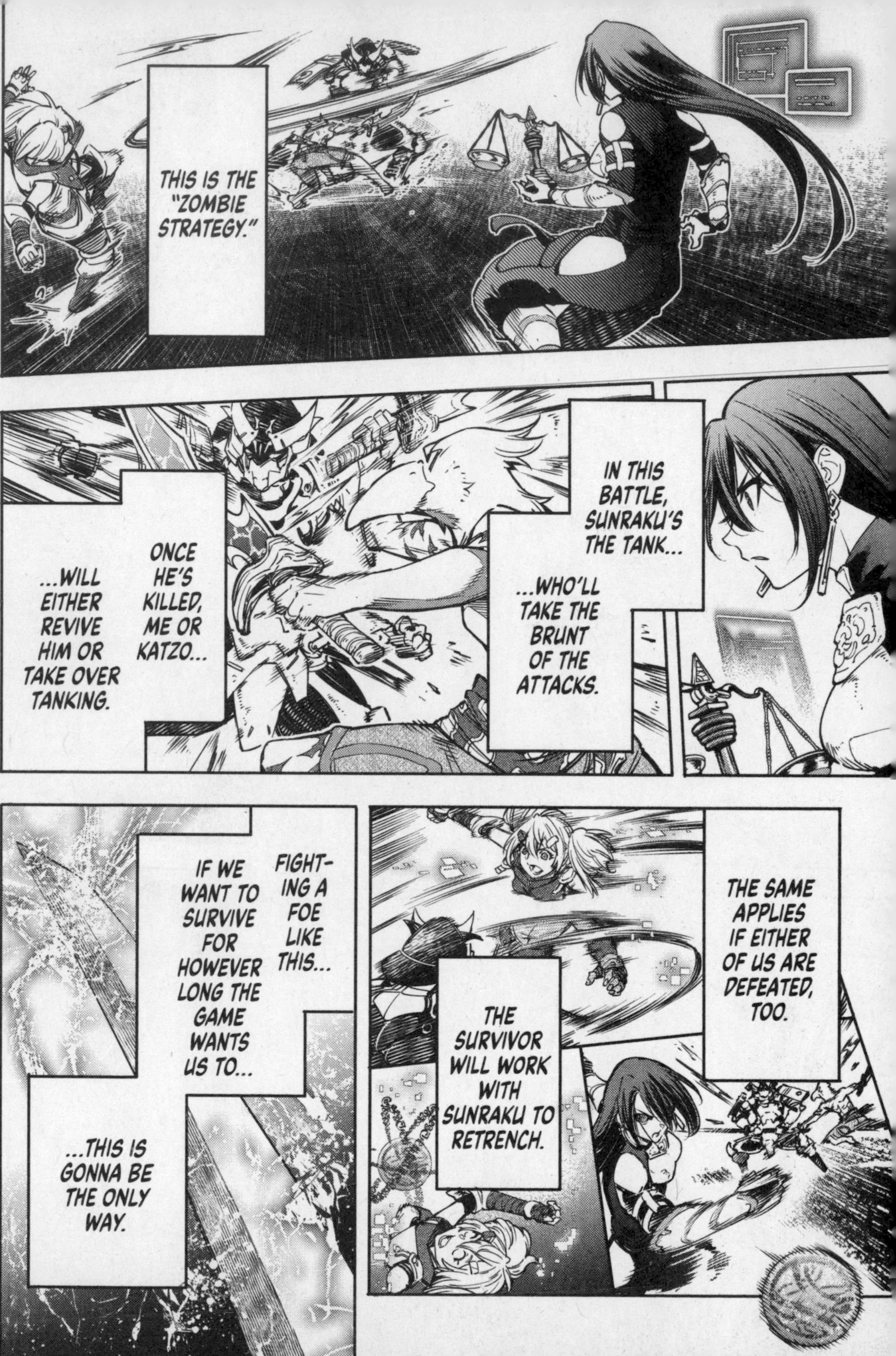
THIS IS THE "ZOMBIE STRATEGY."
IN THIS BATTLE, SUNRAKU'S THE TANK...
...WHO'LL TAKE THE BRUNT OF THE ATTACKS.
ONCE HE'S KILLED, ME OR KATZO...
...WILL EITHER REVIVE HIM OR TAKE OVER TANKING.
THE SAME APPLIES IF EITHER OF US ARE DEFEATED, TOO.
THE SURVIVOR WILL WORK WITH SUNRAKU TO RETRENCH.
FIGHTING A FOE LIKE THIS...
IF WE WANT TO SURVIVE FOR HOWEVER LONG THE GAME WANTS US TO...
...THIS IS GONNA BE THE ONLY WAY.

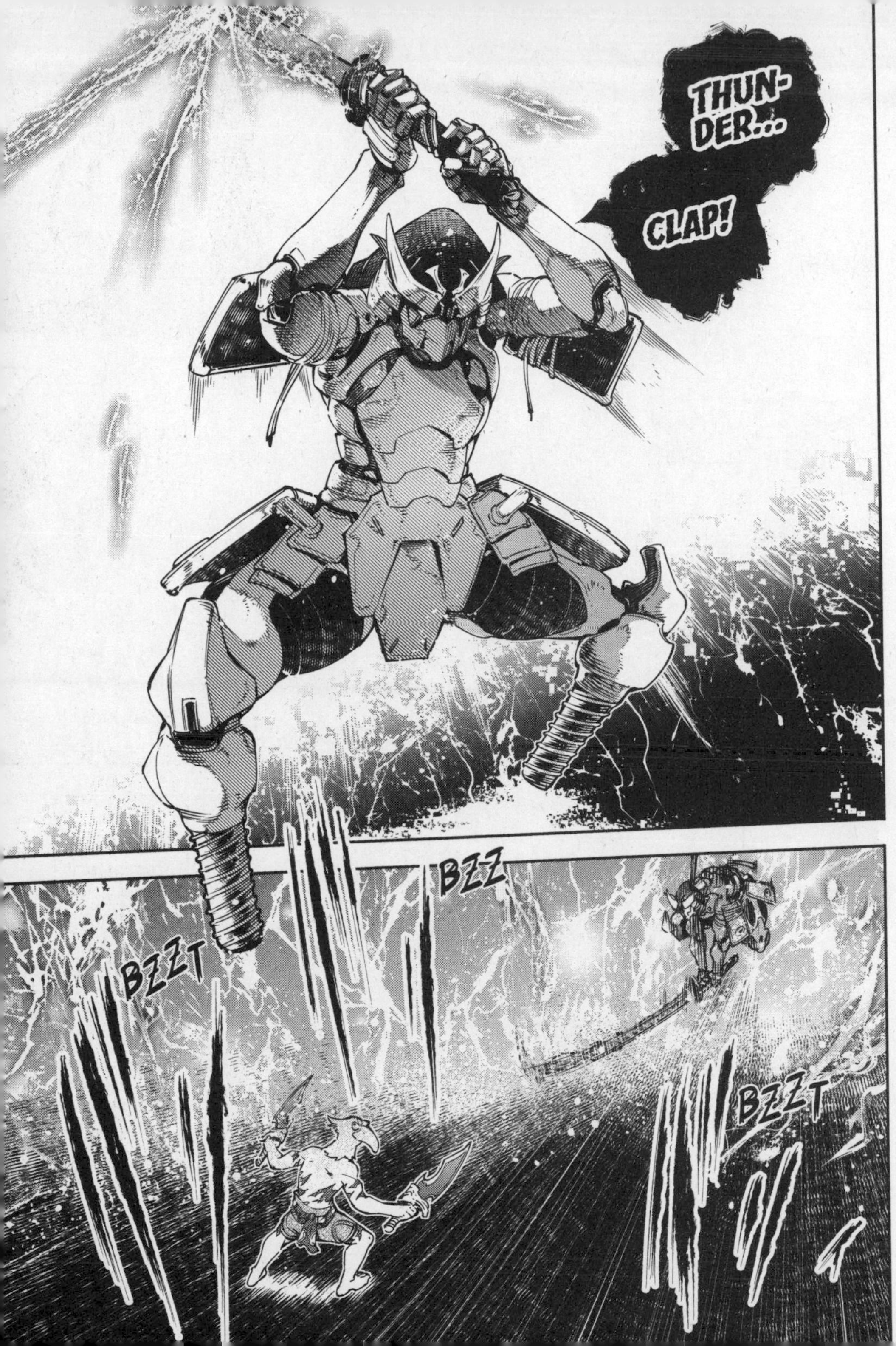
THUN-
DER...
CLAP!
BZZ
BZZT
BZZT

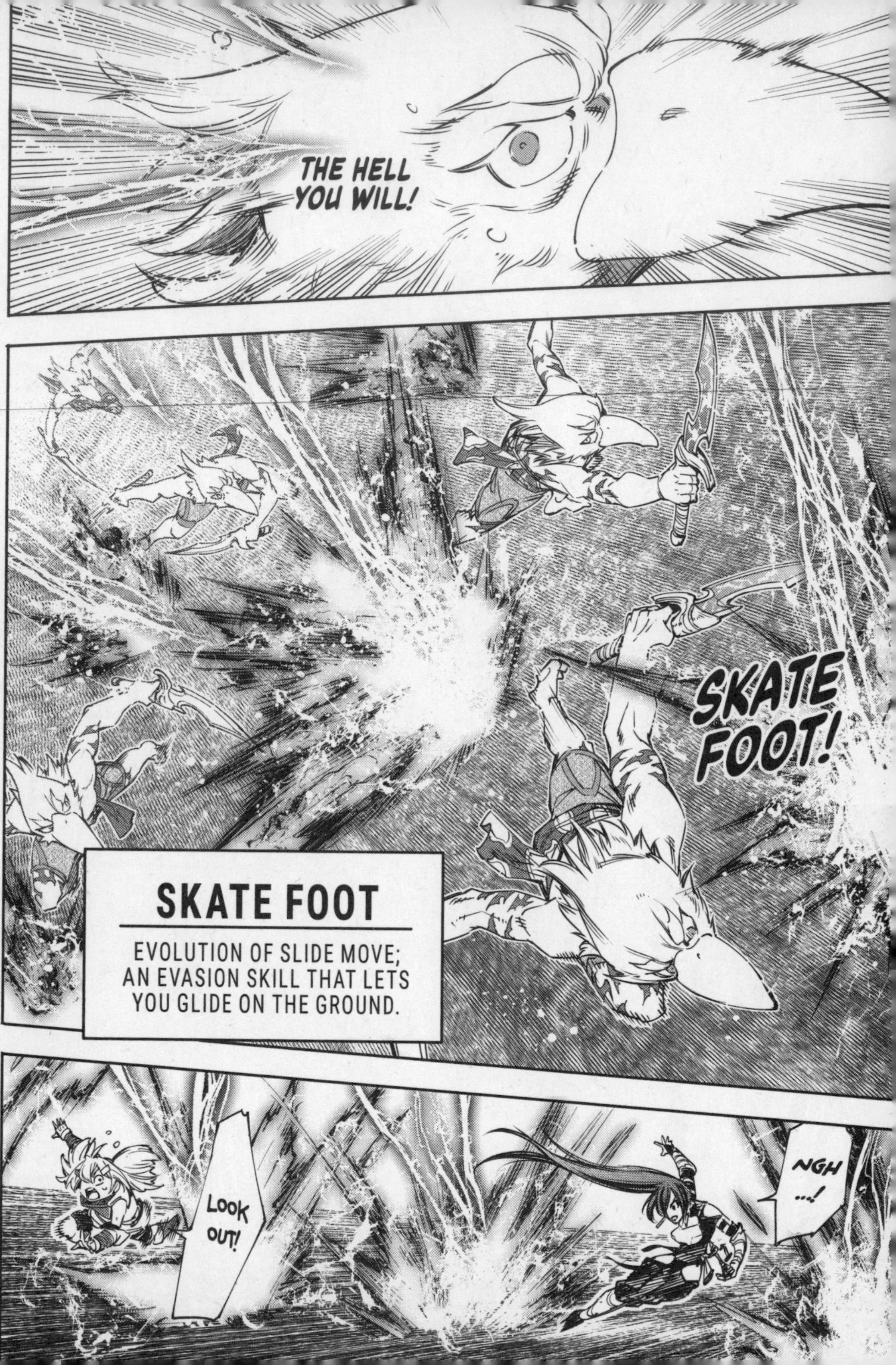
THE HELL YOU WILL!
SKATE FOOT!
SKATE FOOT
EVOLUTION OF SLIDE MOVE; AN EVASION SKILL THAT LETS YOU GLIDE ON THE GROUND.
NGH ...!
LOOK OUT!

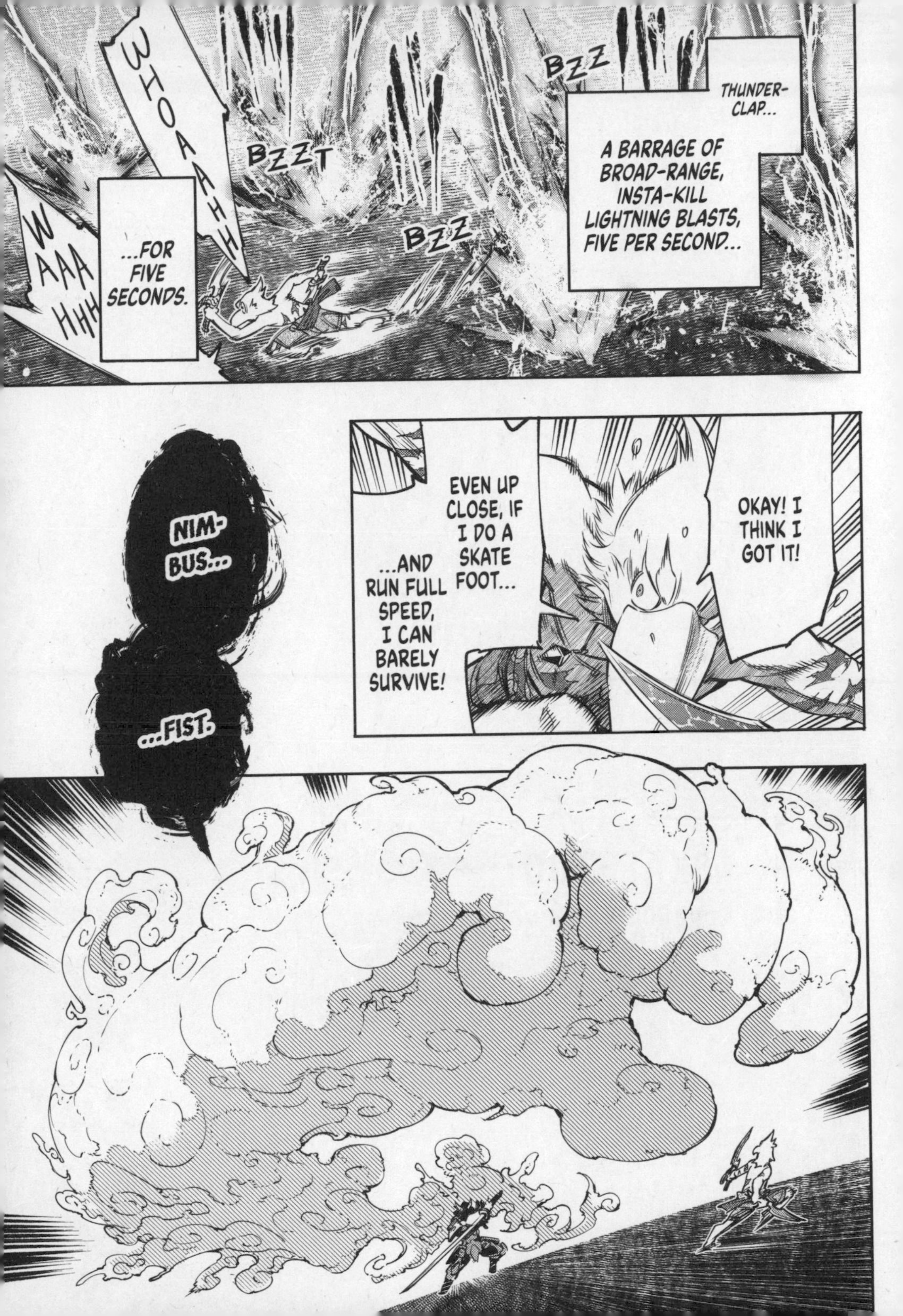
THUNDER-CLAP...
A BARRAGE OF BROAD-RANGE, INSTA-KILL LIGHTNING BLASTS, FIVE PER SECOND...
BZZ
BZZ
BZZT
WHOAAAHH
...FOR FIVE SECONDS.
WAAAHHH
OKAY! I THINK I GOT IT!
EVEN UP CLOSE, IF I DO A SKATE FOOT...
...AND RUN FULL SPEED, I CAN BARELY SURVIVE!
NIM-BUS...
...FIST.

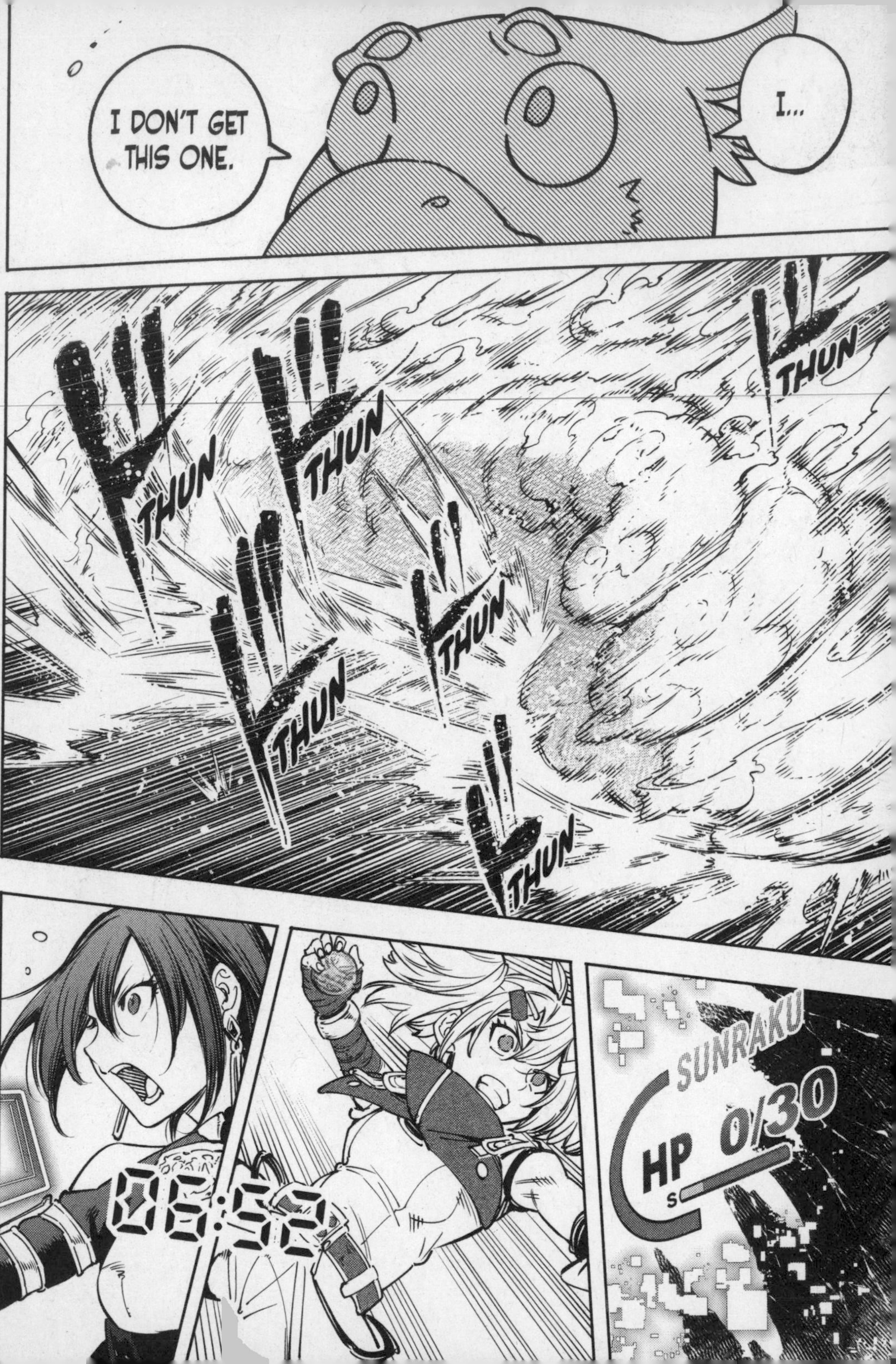
I...
I DON'T GET THIS ONE.
THUN
THUN
THUN
THUN
THUN
THUN
THUN
SUNRAKU
HP 0/30
06:52

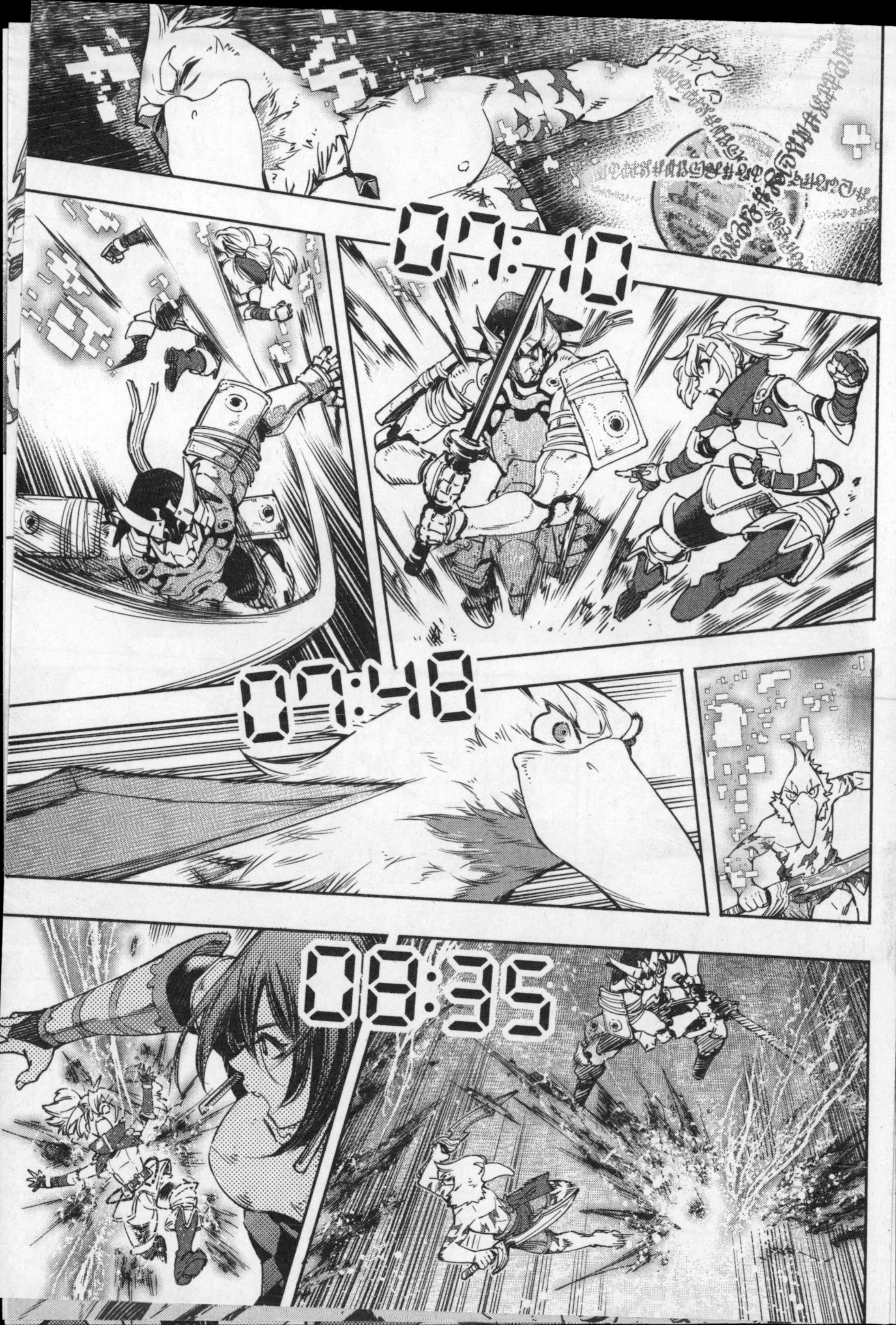
07:10
07:48
08:35

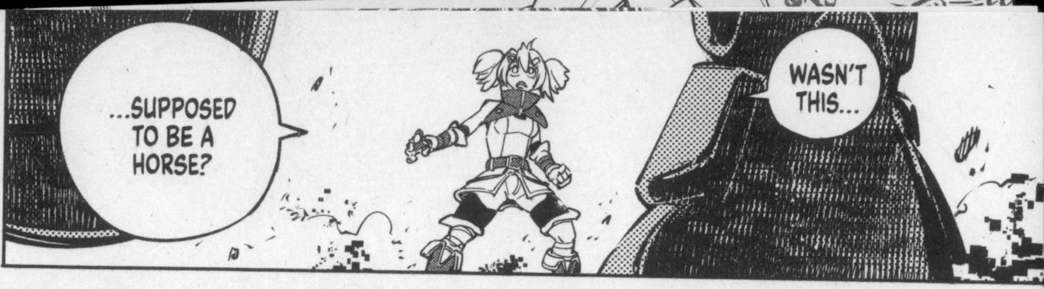
WASN'T THIS...
...SUPPOSED TO BE A HORSE?

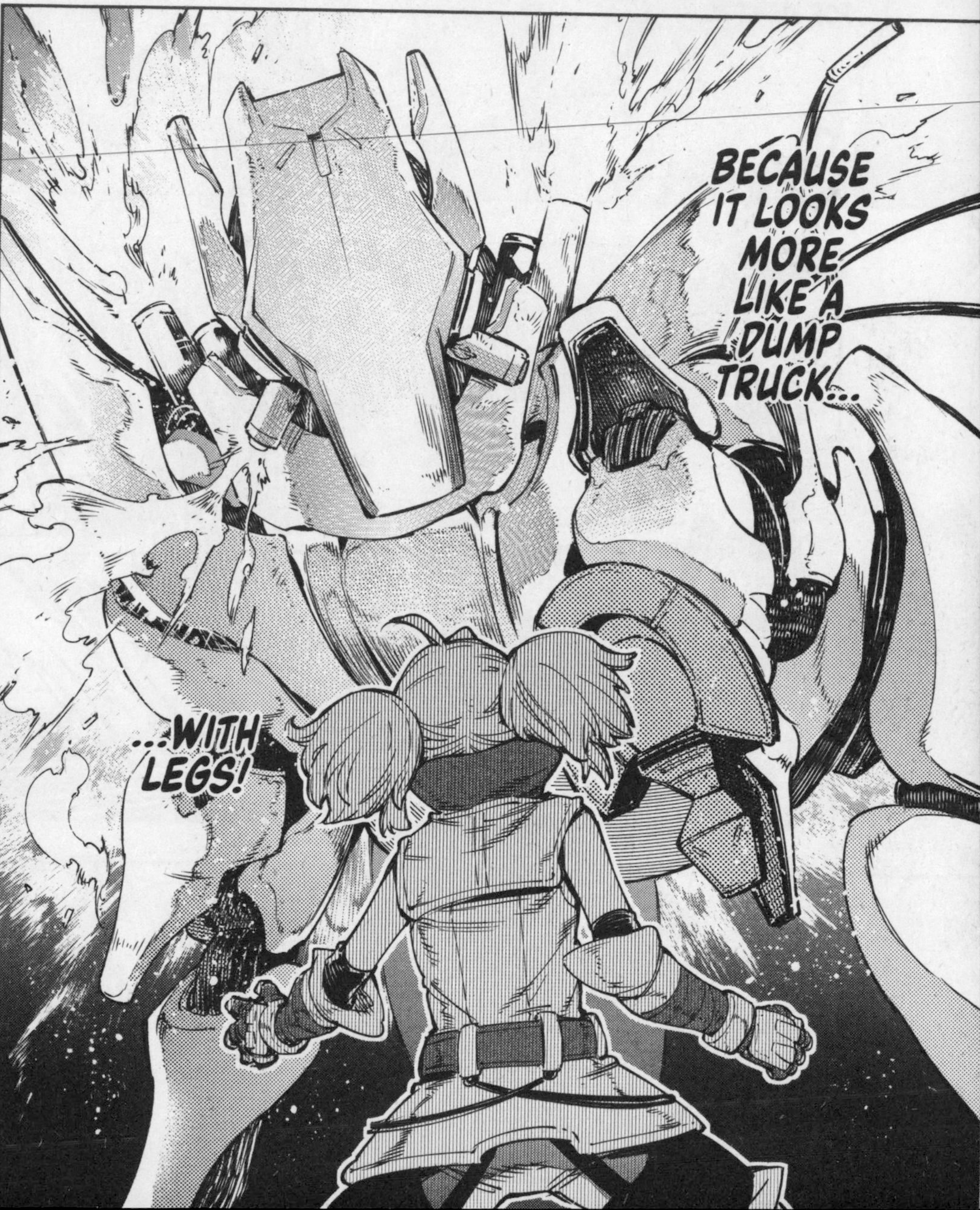
BECAUSE IT LOOKS MORE LIKE A DUMP TRUCK...
...WITH LEGS!

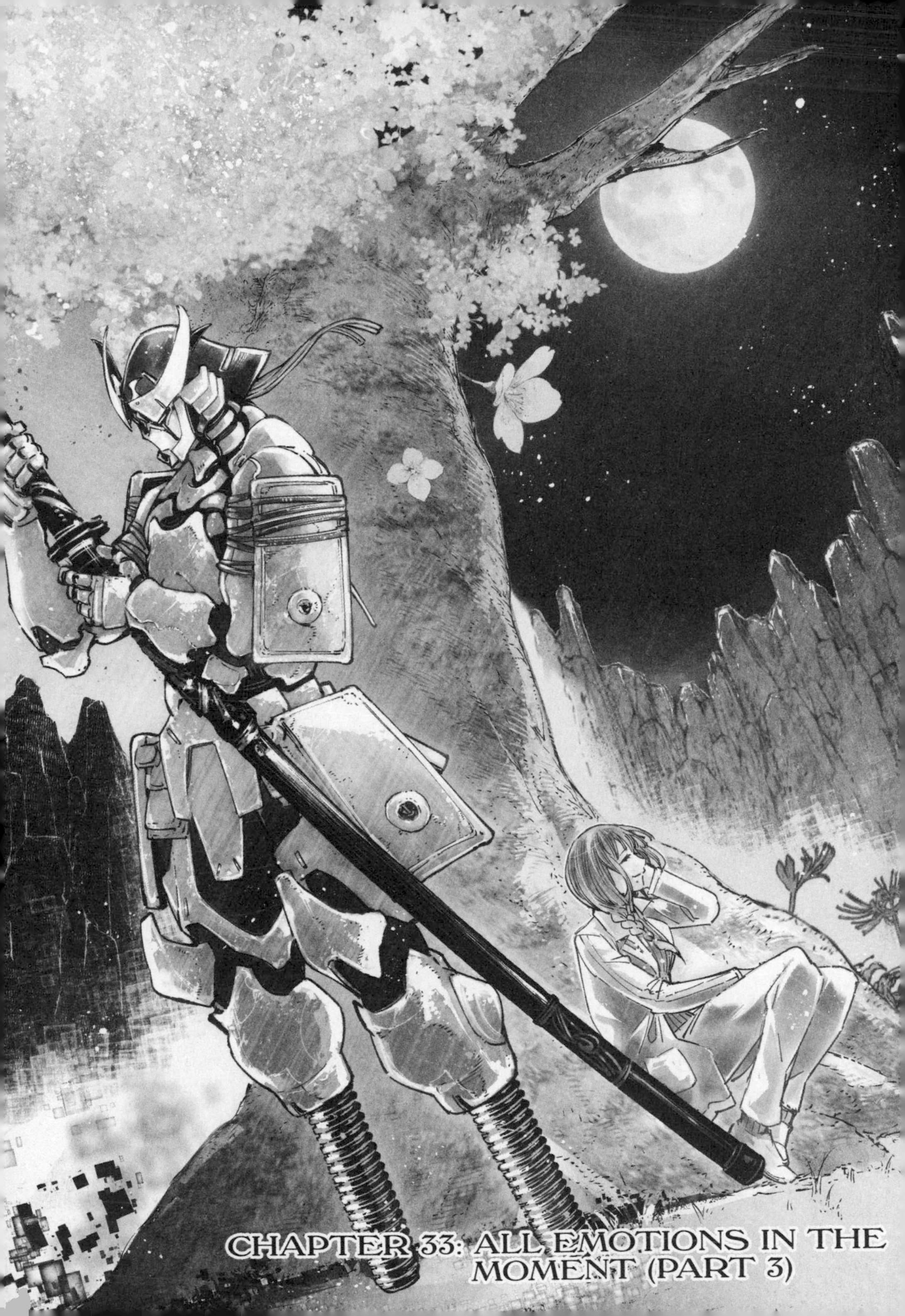

CHAPTER 33: ALL EMOTIONS IN THE MOMENT (PART 3)

SHANGRI-LA
FRONTIER

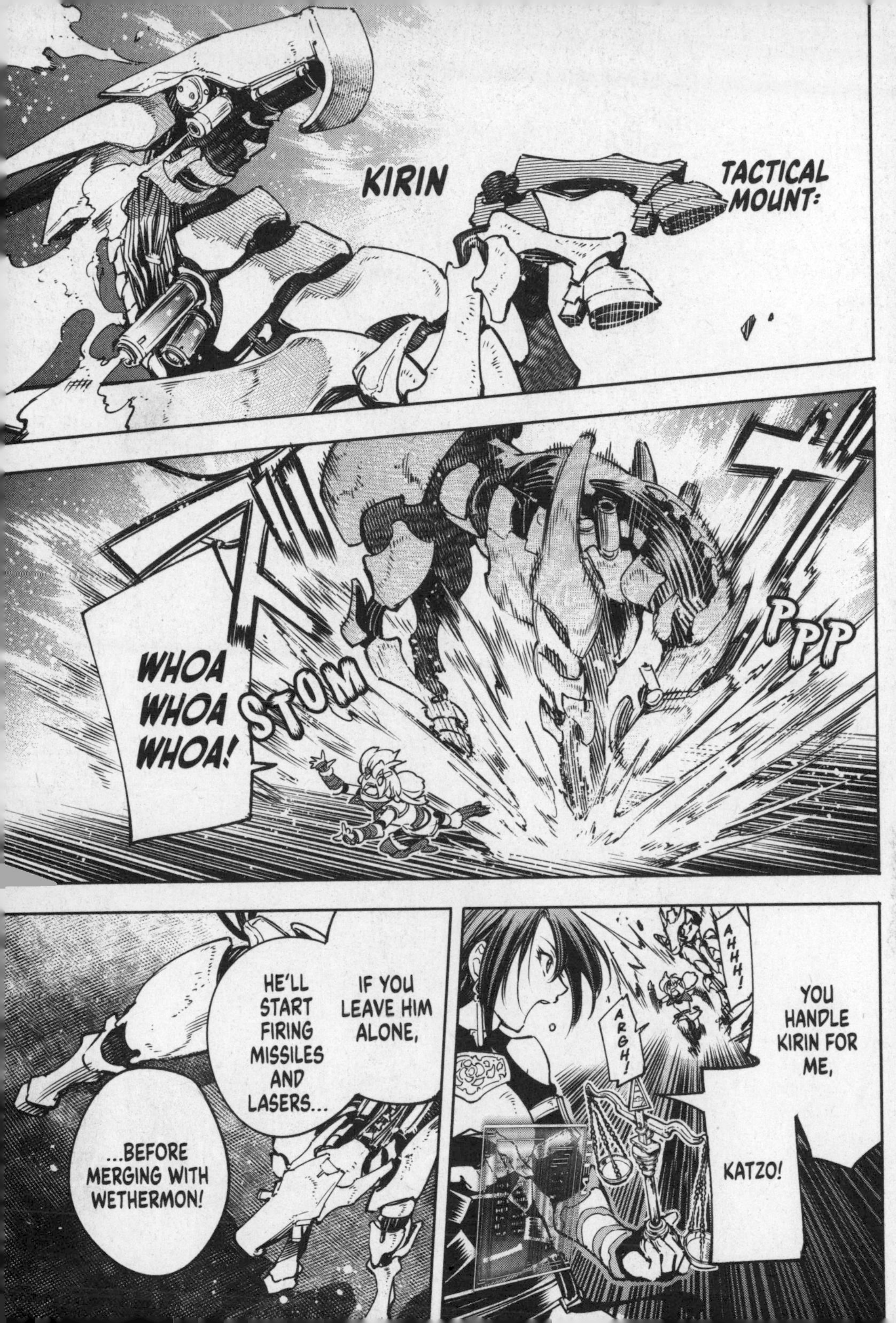
TACTICAL MOUNT:
KIRIN
PPP
STOM
WHOA WHOA WHOA!
YOU HANDLE KIRIN FOR ME,
AHHH!
ARGH!
KATZO!
IF YOU LEAVE HIM ALONE,
HE'LL START FIRING MISSILES AND LASERS...
...BEFORE MERGING WITH WETHERMON!

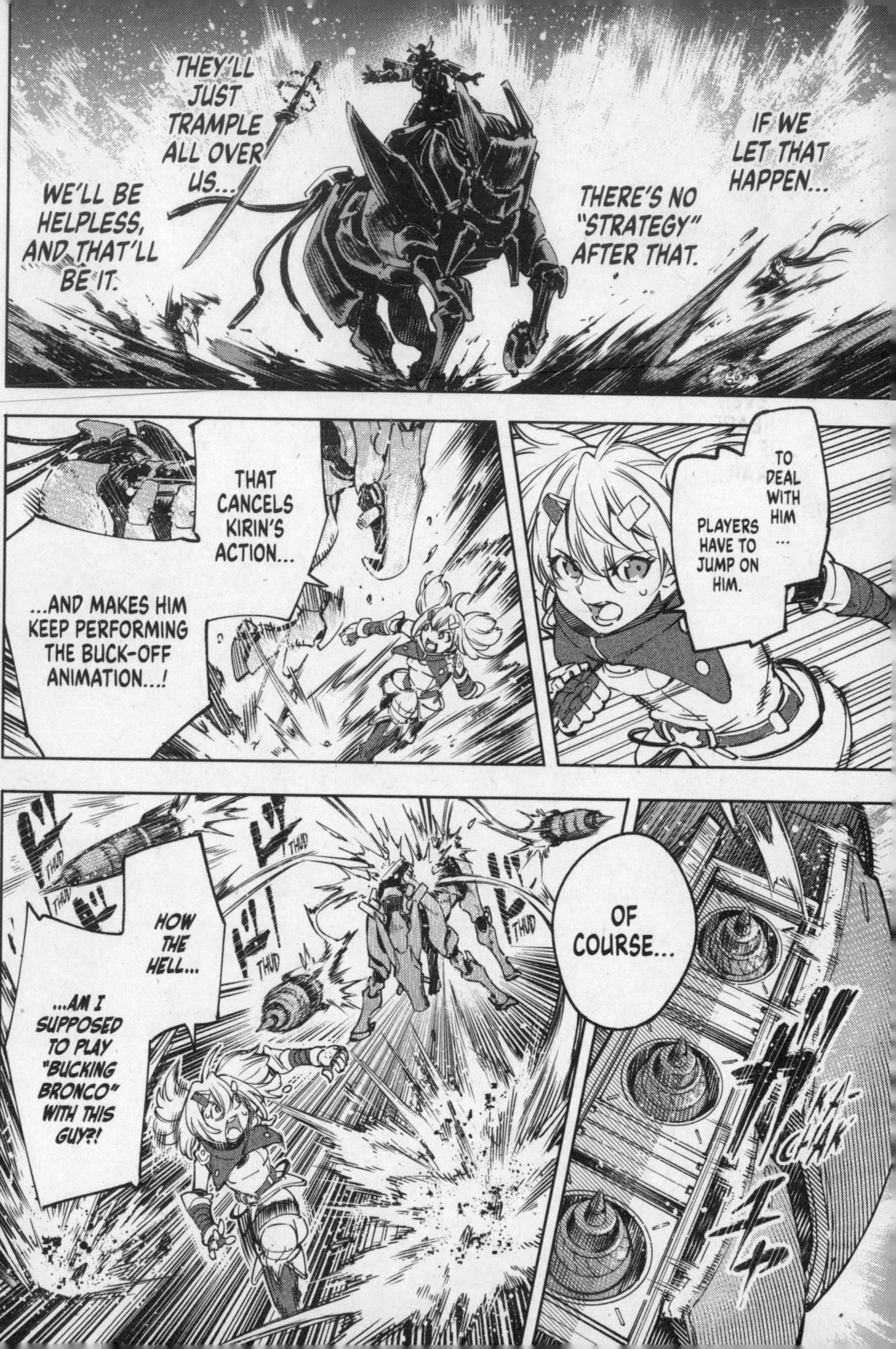
IF WE LET THAT HAPPEN...
THERE'S NO "STRATEGY" AFTER THAT.
THEY'LL JUST TRAMPLE ALL OVER US...
WE'LL BE HELPLESS, AND THAT'LL BE IT.
TO DEAL WITH HIM...
PLAYERS HAVE TO JUMP ON HIM.
THAT CANCELS KIRIN'S ACTION...
...AND MAKES HIM KEEP PERFORMING THE BUCK-OFF ANIMATION...!
OF COURSE...
KA-CHAK
THUD
THUD
THUD
THUD
THUD
HOW THE HELL...
...AM I SUPPOSED TO PLAY "BUCKING BRONCO" WITH THIS GUY?!

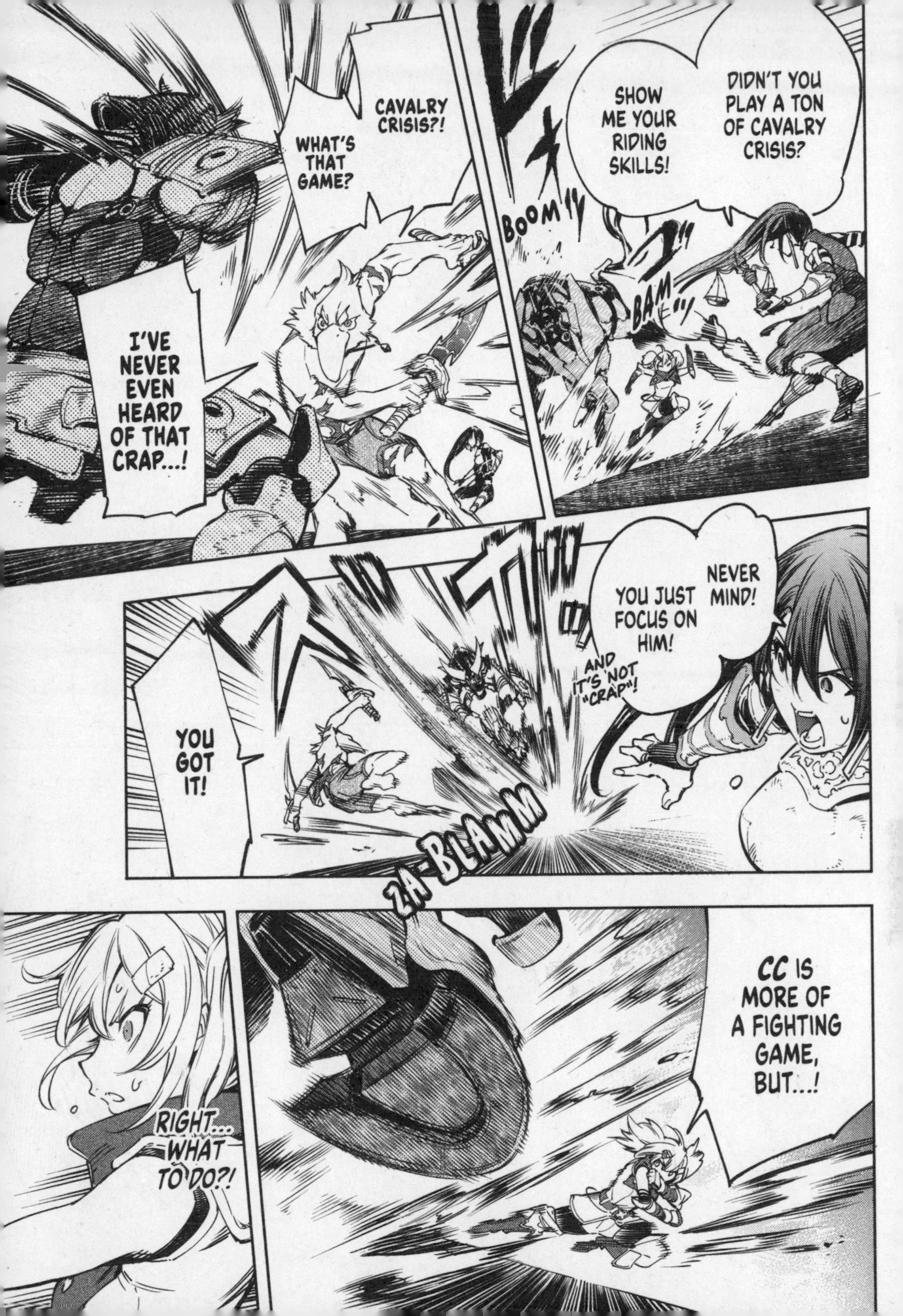
DIDN'T YOU PLAY A TON OF CAVALRY CRISIS?
SHOW ME YOUR RIDING SKILLS!
BOOM
BAM
CAVALRY CRISIS?!
WHAT'S THAT GAME?
I'VE NEVER EVEN HEARD OF THAT CRAP...!
NEVER MIND!
YOU JUST FOCUS ON HIM!
AND IT'S NOT "CRAP"!
YOU GOT IT!
ZA-BLAMM
CC IS MORE OF A FIGHTING GAME, BUT...!
RIGHT... WHAT TO DO?!

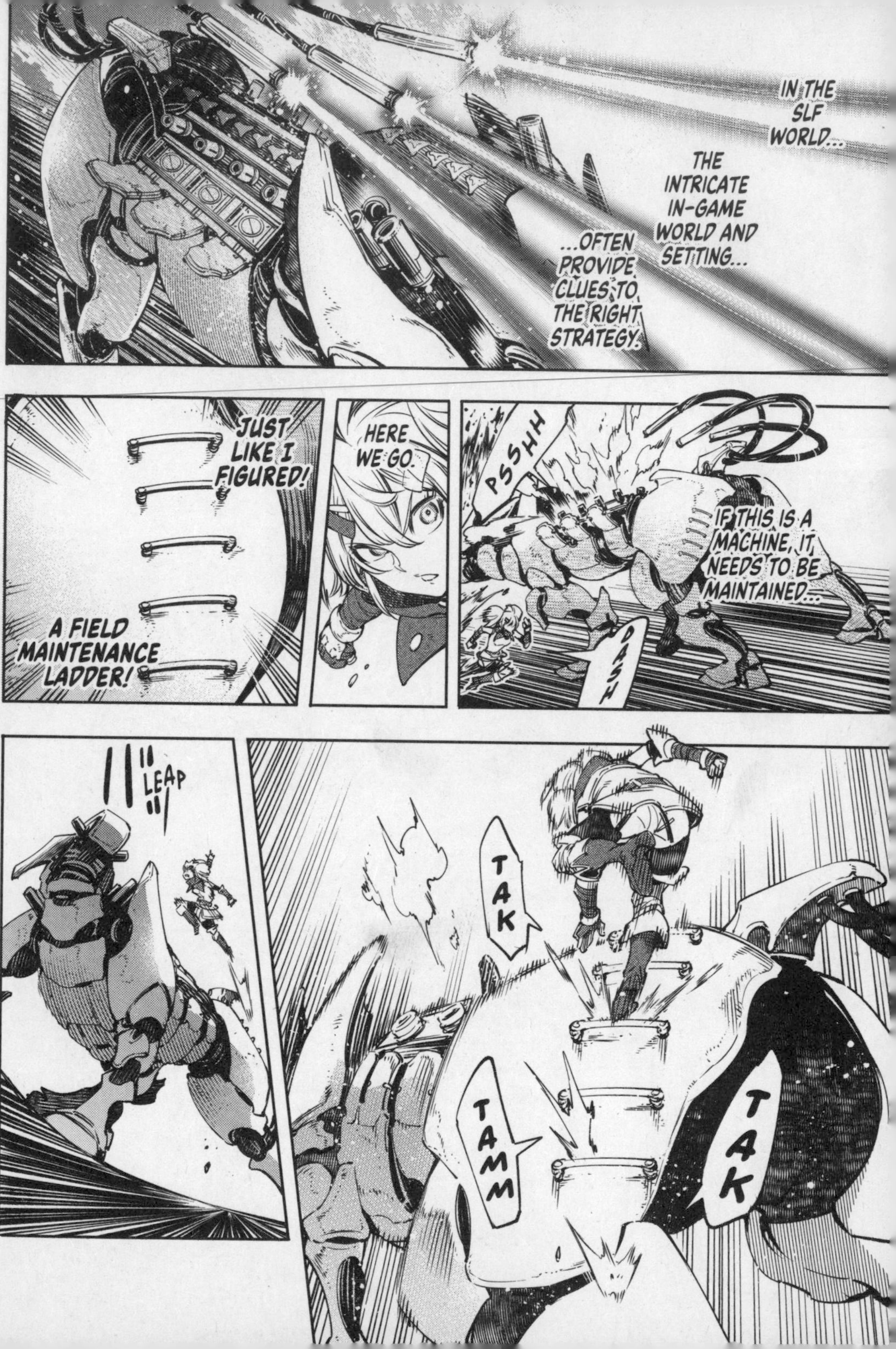
IN THE SLF WORLD...
THE INTRICATE IN-GAME WORLD AND SETTING...
...OFTEN PROVIDE CLUES TO THE RIGHT STRATEGY.
PSSHH
IF THIS IS A MACHINE, IT NEEDS TO BE MAINTAINED...
DASH
HERE WE GO.
JUST LIKE I FIGURED!
A FIELD MAINTENANCE LADDER!
TAK
TAK
TAMM
LEAP

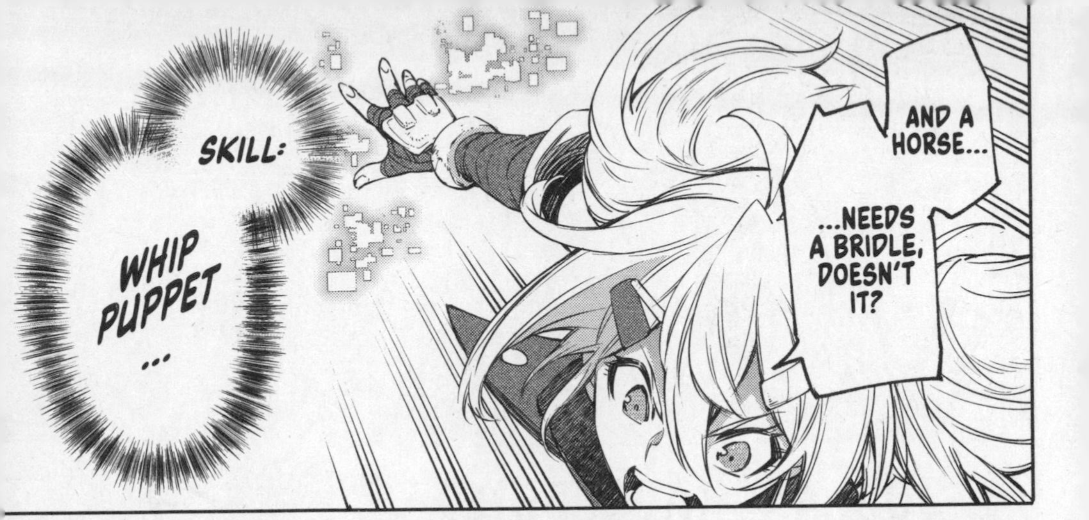
AND A HORSE...
...NEEDS A BRIDLE, DOESN'T IT?
SKILL:
WHIP PUPPET ...

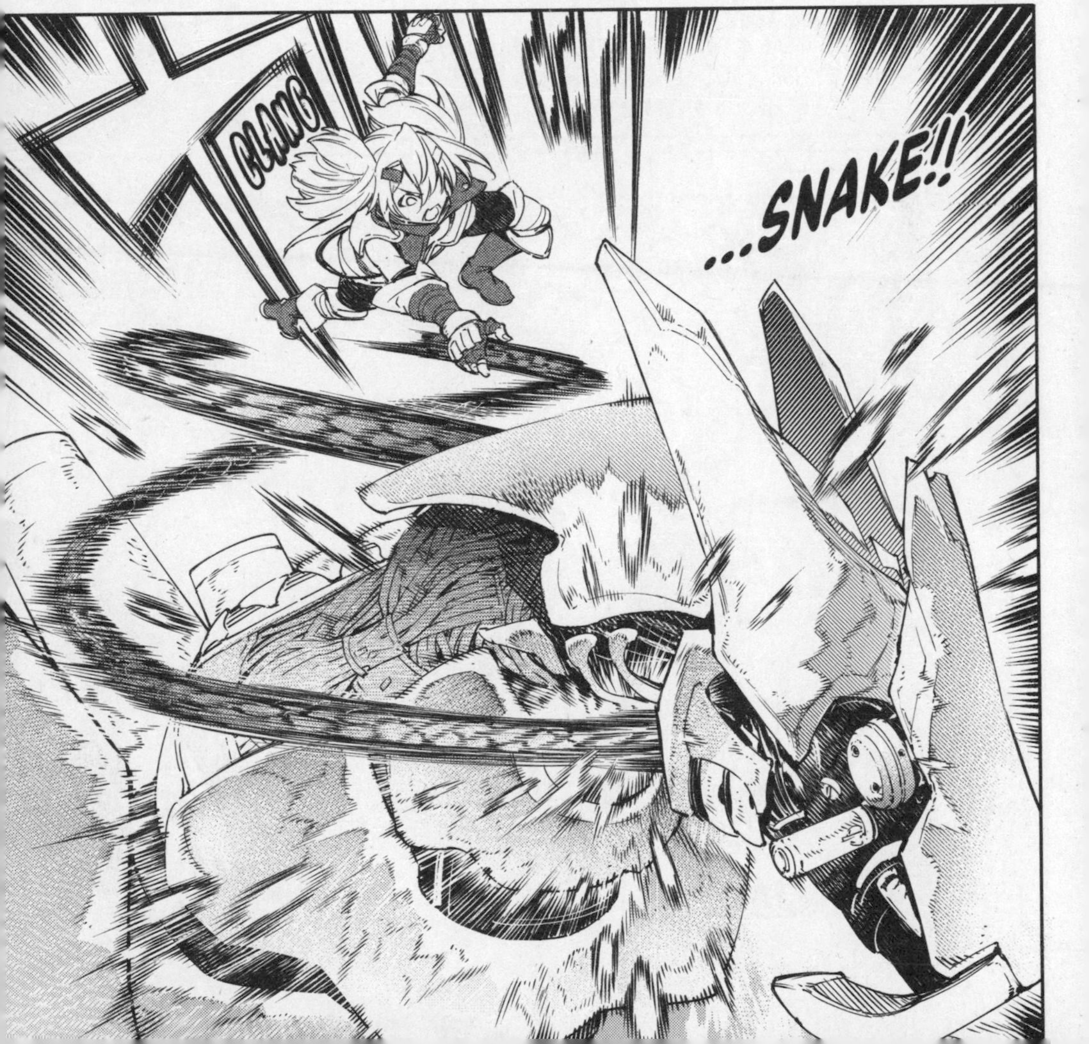
...SNAKE!!
CLANG

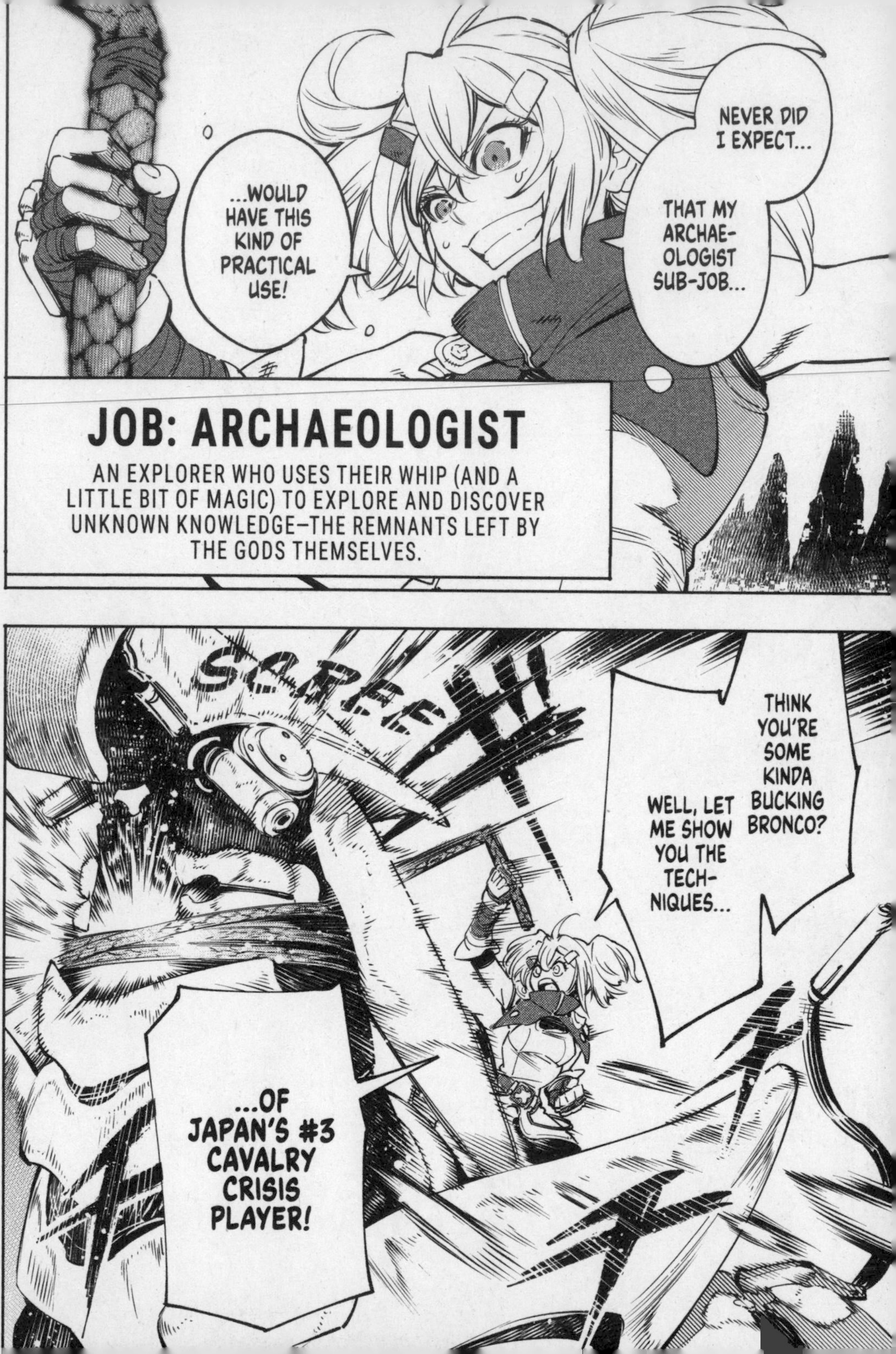

NEVER DID I EXPECT...
THAT MY ARCHAEOLOGIST SUB-JOB...
...WOULD HAVE THIS KIND OF PRACTICAL USE!
JOB: ARCHAEOLOGIST
AN EXPLORER WHO USES THEIR WHIP (AND A LITTLE BIT OF MAGIC) TO EXPLORE AND DISCOVER UNKNOWN KNOWLEDGE—THE REMNANTS LEFT BY THE GODS THEMSELVES.
THINK YOU'RE SOME KINDA BUCKING BRONCO?
WELL, LET ME SHOW YOU THE TECHNIQUES...
SCREE
...OF JAPAN'S #3 CAVALRY CRISIS PLAYER!

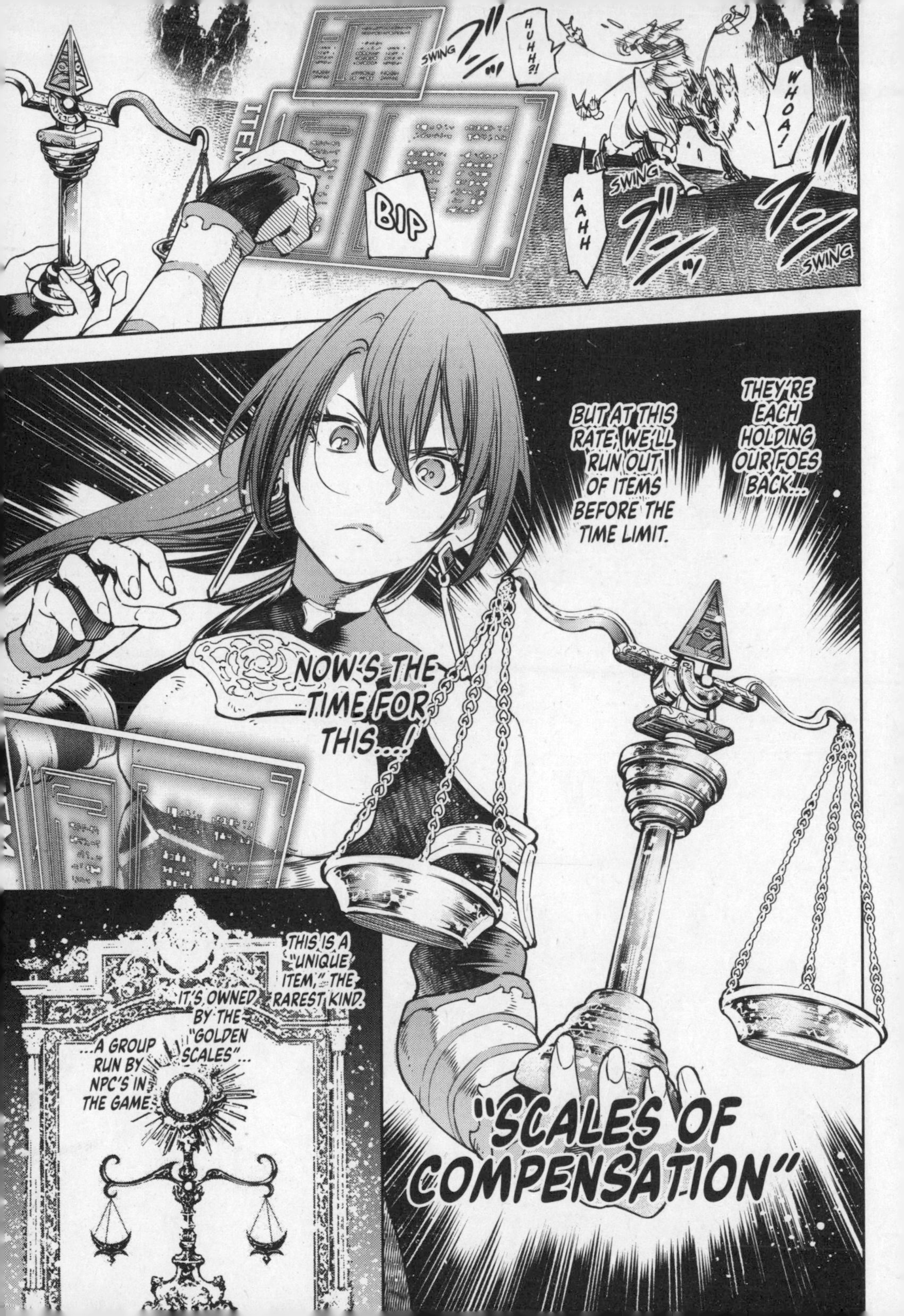
WHOA!
SWING
AAHH
SWING
HUHH?!
SWING
BIP
THEY'RE EACH HOLDING OUR FOES BACK...
BUT AT THIS RATE, WE'LL RUN OUT OF ITEMS BEFORE THE TIME LIMIT.
NOW'S THE TIME FOR THIS...!
"SCALES OF COMPENSATION"
THIS IS A "UNIQUE ITEM," THE RAREST KIND.
IT'S OWNED BY THE "GOLDEN SCALES"...
...A GROUP RUN BY NPC'S IN THE GAME.

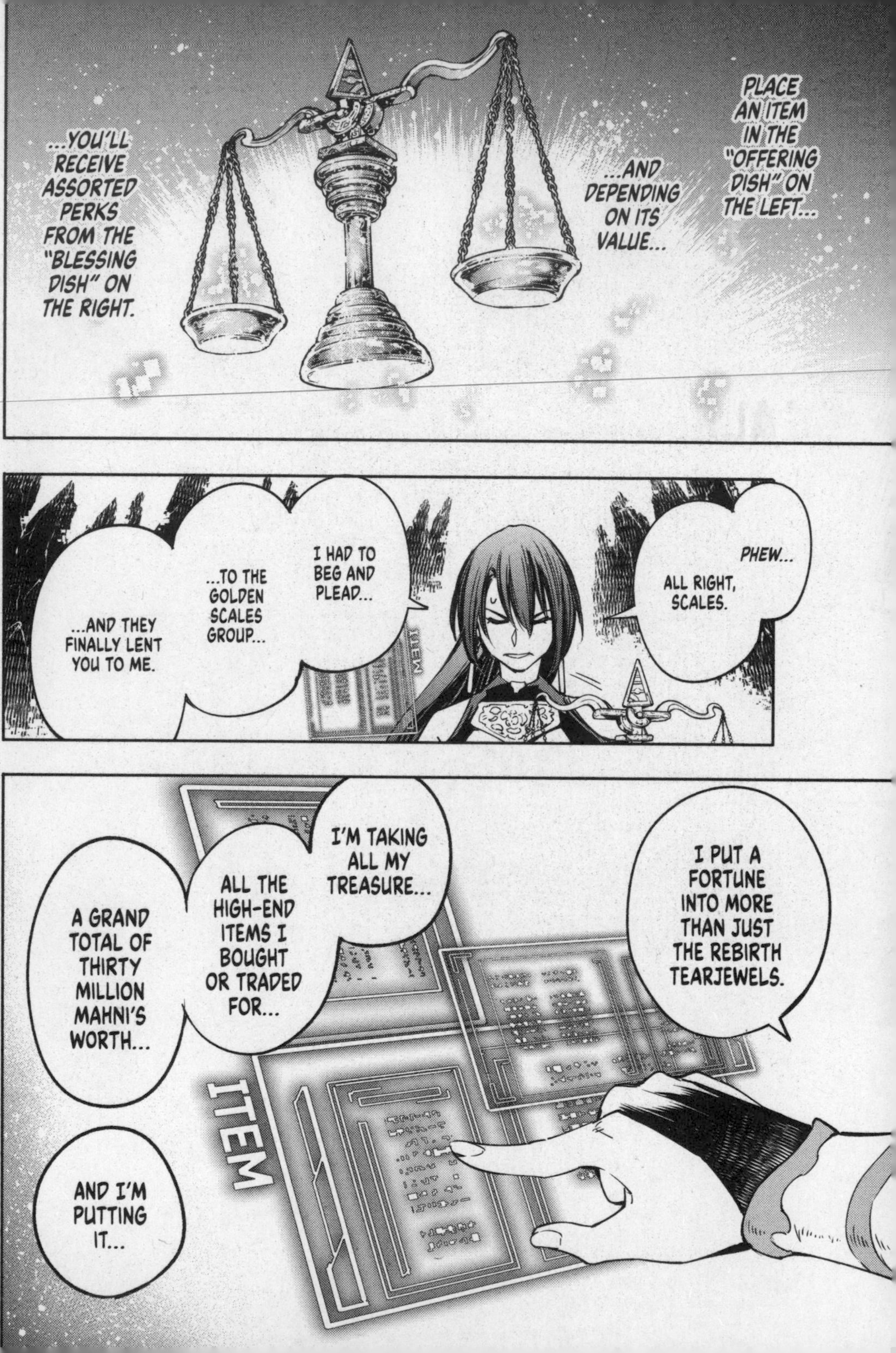
PLACE AN ITEM IN THE "OFFERING DISH" ON THE LEFT...
...AND DEPENDING ON ITS VALUE...
...YOU'LL RECEIVE ASSORTED PERKS FROM THE "BLESSING DISH" ON THE RIGHT.
PHEW...
ALL RIGHT, SCALES.
I HAD TO BEG AND PLEAD...
...TO THE GOLDEN SCALES GROUP...
...AND THEY FINALLY LENT YOU TO ME.
ITEM
I PUT A FORTUNE INTO MORE THAN JUST THE REBIRTH TEARJEWELS.
I'M TAKING ALL MY TREASURE...
ALL THE HIGH-END ITEMS I BOUGHT OR TRADED FOR...
A GRAND TOTAL OF THIRTY MILLION MAHNI'S WORTH...
ITEM
AND I'M PUTTING IT...

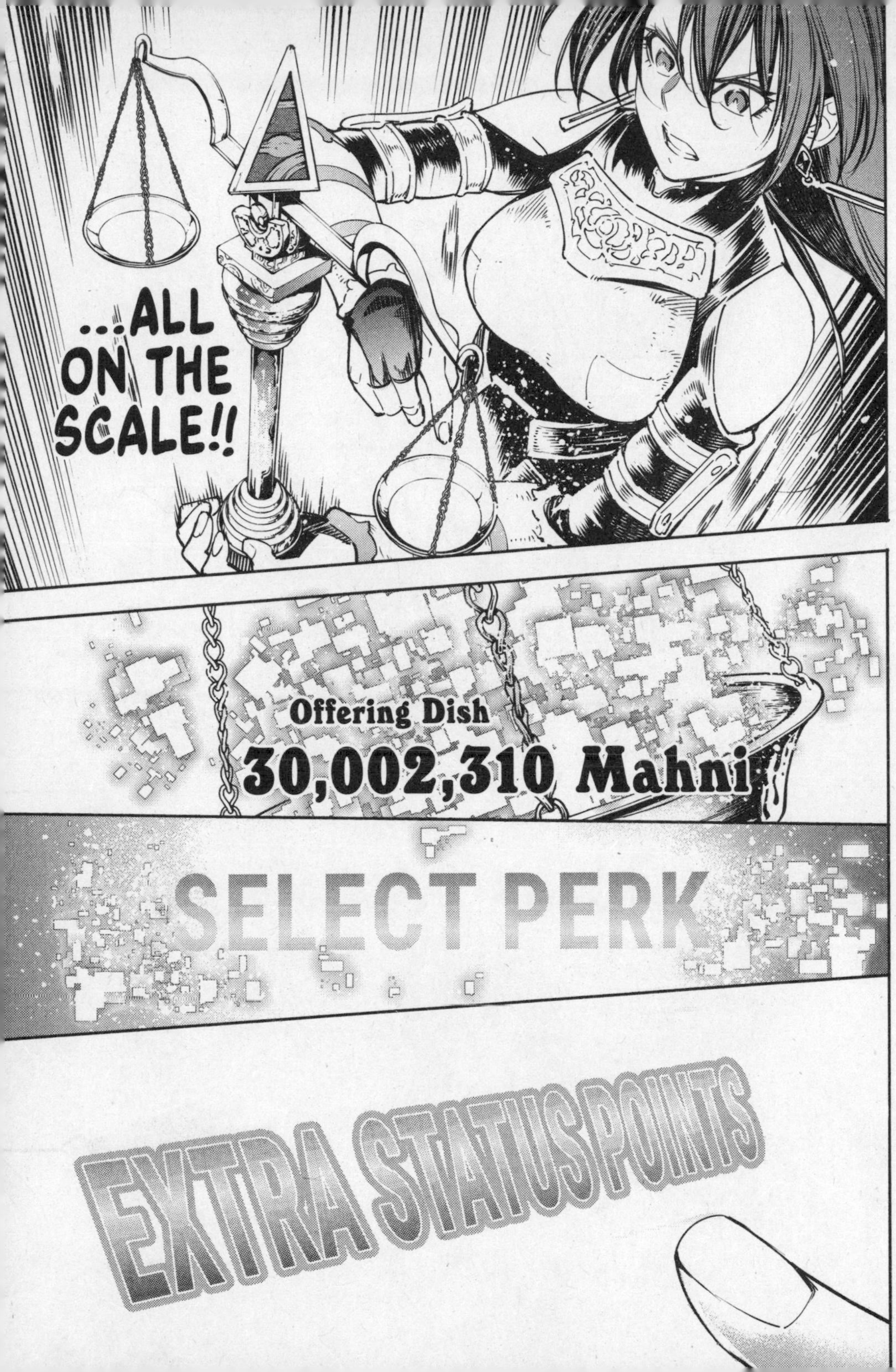
...ALL ON THE SCALE!!
Offering Dish
30,002,310 Mahni
SELECT PERK
EXTRA STATUS POINTS

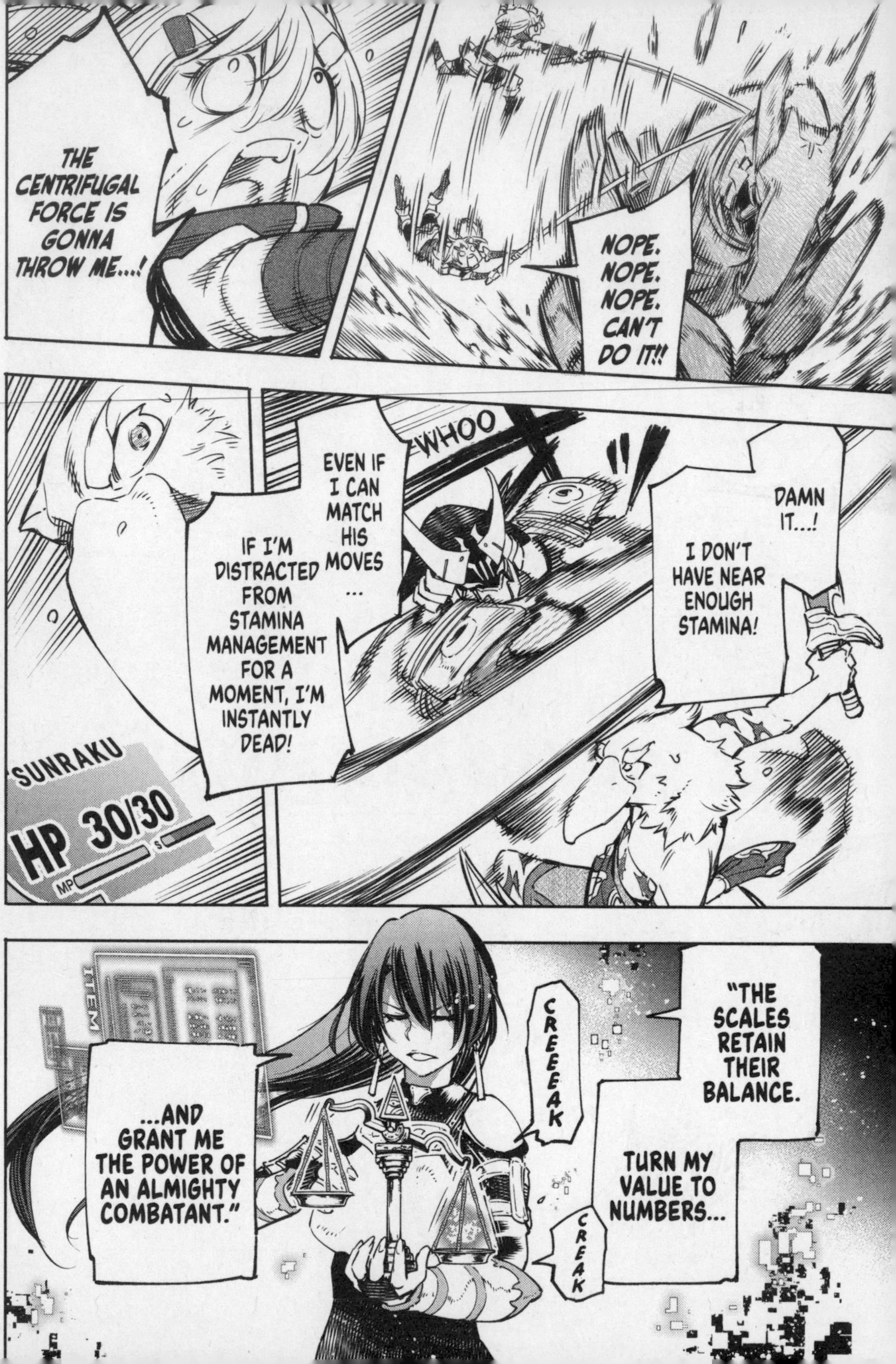
NOPE. NOPE. NOPE. CAN'T DO IT!!
THE CENTRIFUGAL FORCE IS GONNA THROW ME...!
DAMN IT...!
I DON'T HAVE NEAR ENOUGH STAMINA!
WHOO
EVEN IF I CAN MATCH HIS MOVES...
IF I'M DISTRACTED FROM STAMINA MANAGEMENT FOR A MOMENT, I'M INSTANTLY DEAD!
SUNRAKU
HP 30/30
MP
S
"THE SCALES RETAIN THEIR BALANCE.
TURN MY VALUE TO NUMBERS...
CREEEAK
CREAK
...AND GRANT ME THE POWER OF AN ALMIGHTY COMBATANT."
ITEM

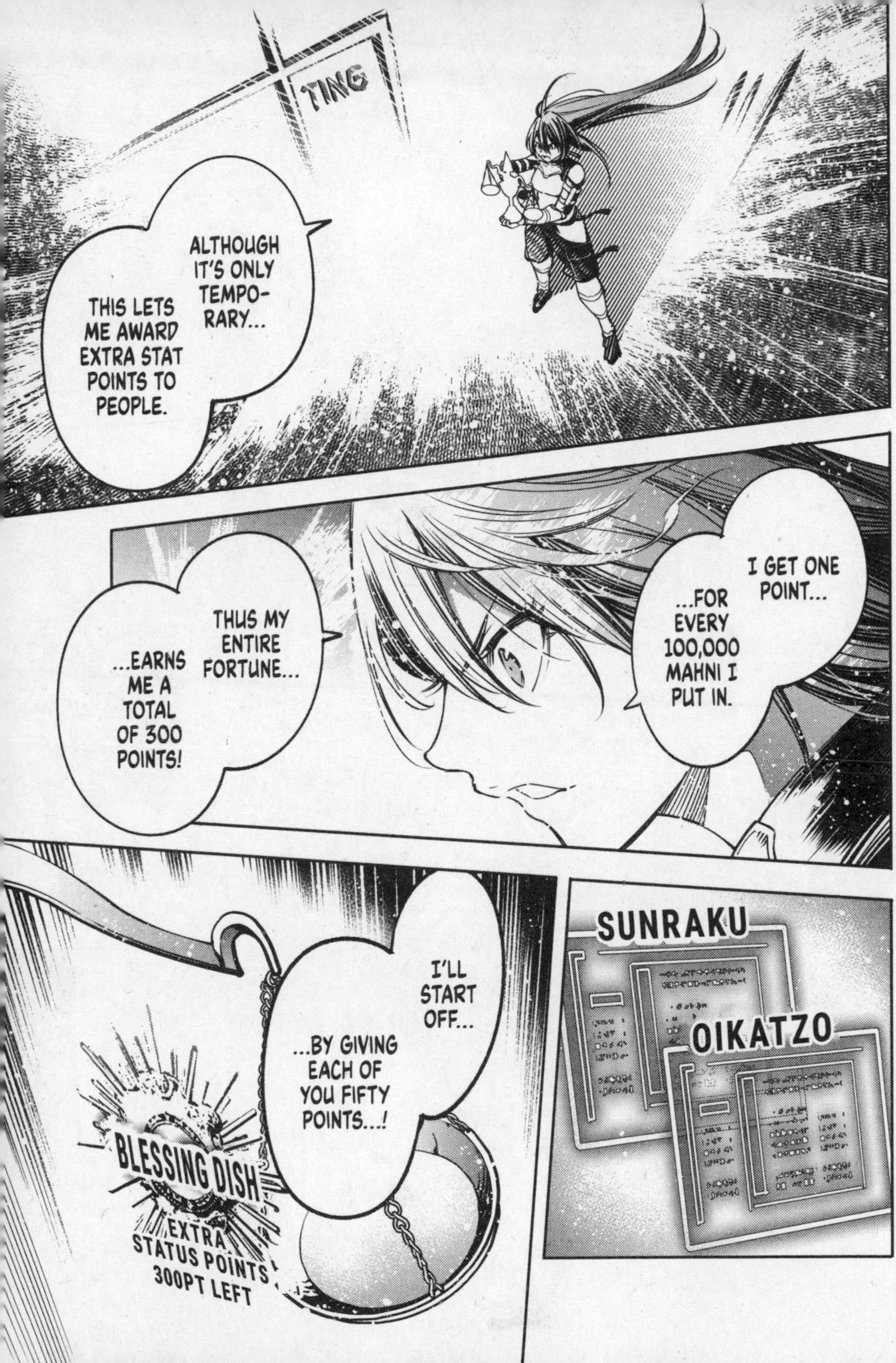
TING
ALTHOUGH IT'S ONLY TEMPORARY... THIS LETS ME AWARD EXTRA STAT POINTS TO PEOPLE.
I GET ONE POINT... ...FOR EVERY 100,000 MAHNI I PUT IN.
THUS MY ENTIRE FORTUNE... ...EARNS ME A TOTAL OF 300 POINTS!
SUNRAKU
OIKATZO
I'LL START OFF... ...BY GIVING EACH OF YOU FIFTY POINTS...!
BLESSING DISH
EXTRA STATUS POINTS 300PT LEFT

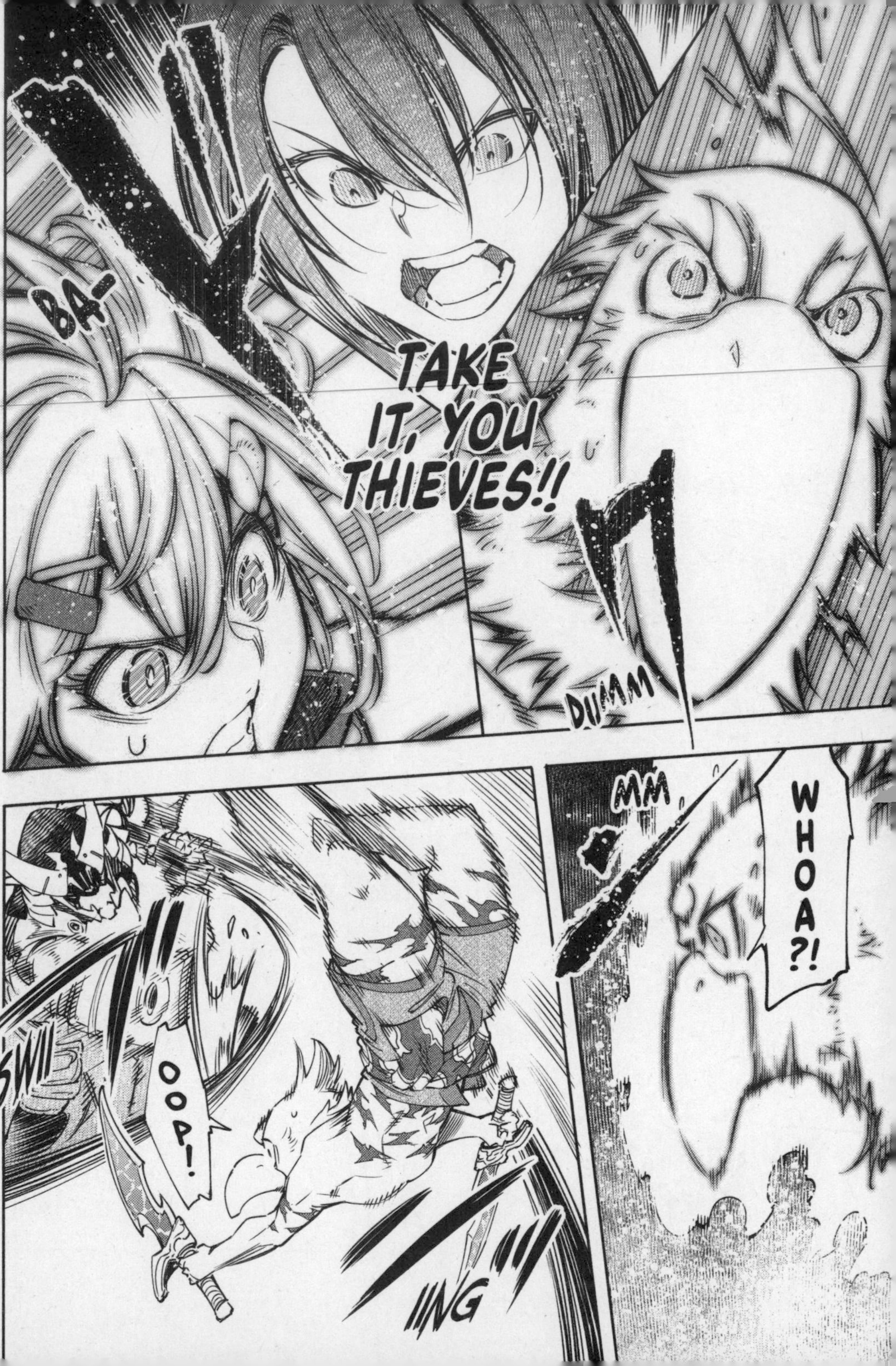
TAKE IT, YOU THIEVES!!
BA-
DUMM
MM
WHOA?!
OOP!
SWII
IING

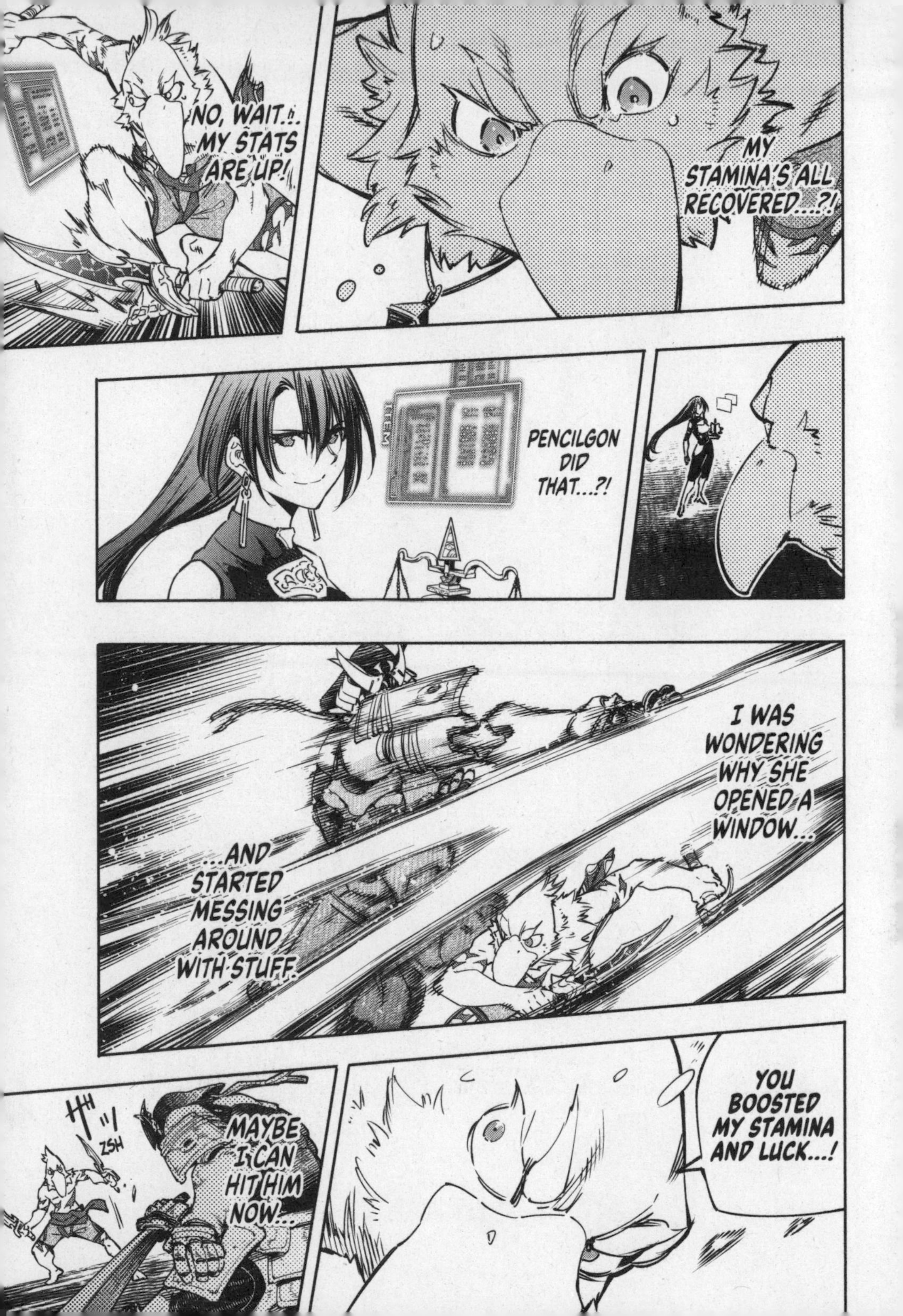
MY STAMINA'S ALL RECOVERED...?!
NO, WAIT...! MY STATS ARE UP!
PENCILGON DID THAT...?!
I WAS WONDERING WHY SHE OPENED A WINDOW...
...AND STARTED MESSING AROUND WITH STUFF.
YOU BOOSTED MY STAMINA AND LUCK...!
ZSH
MAYBE I CAN HIT HIM NOW...

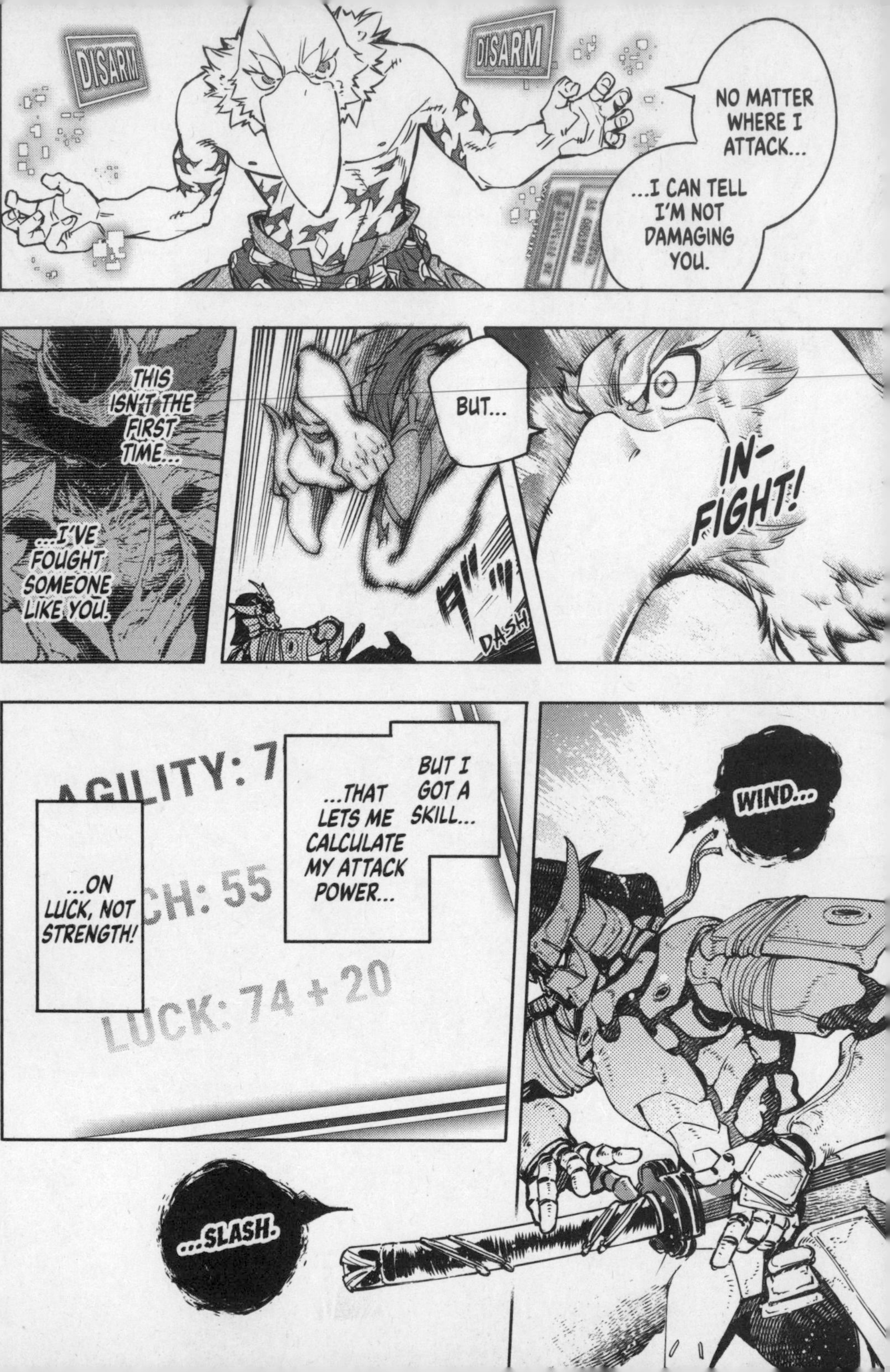
DISARM
DISARM
NO MATTER WHERE I ATTACK...
...I CAN TELL I'M NOT DAMAGING YOU.
BUT...
IN-FIGHT!
DASH
THIS ISN'T THE FIRST TIME...
...I'VE FOUGHT SOMEONE LIKE YOU.
WIND...
BUT I GOT A SKILL...
...THAT LETS ME CALCULATE MY ATTACK POWER...
AGILITY: 7
CH: 55
LUCK: 74 + 20
...ON LUCK, NOT STRENGTH!
...SLASH.

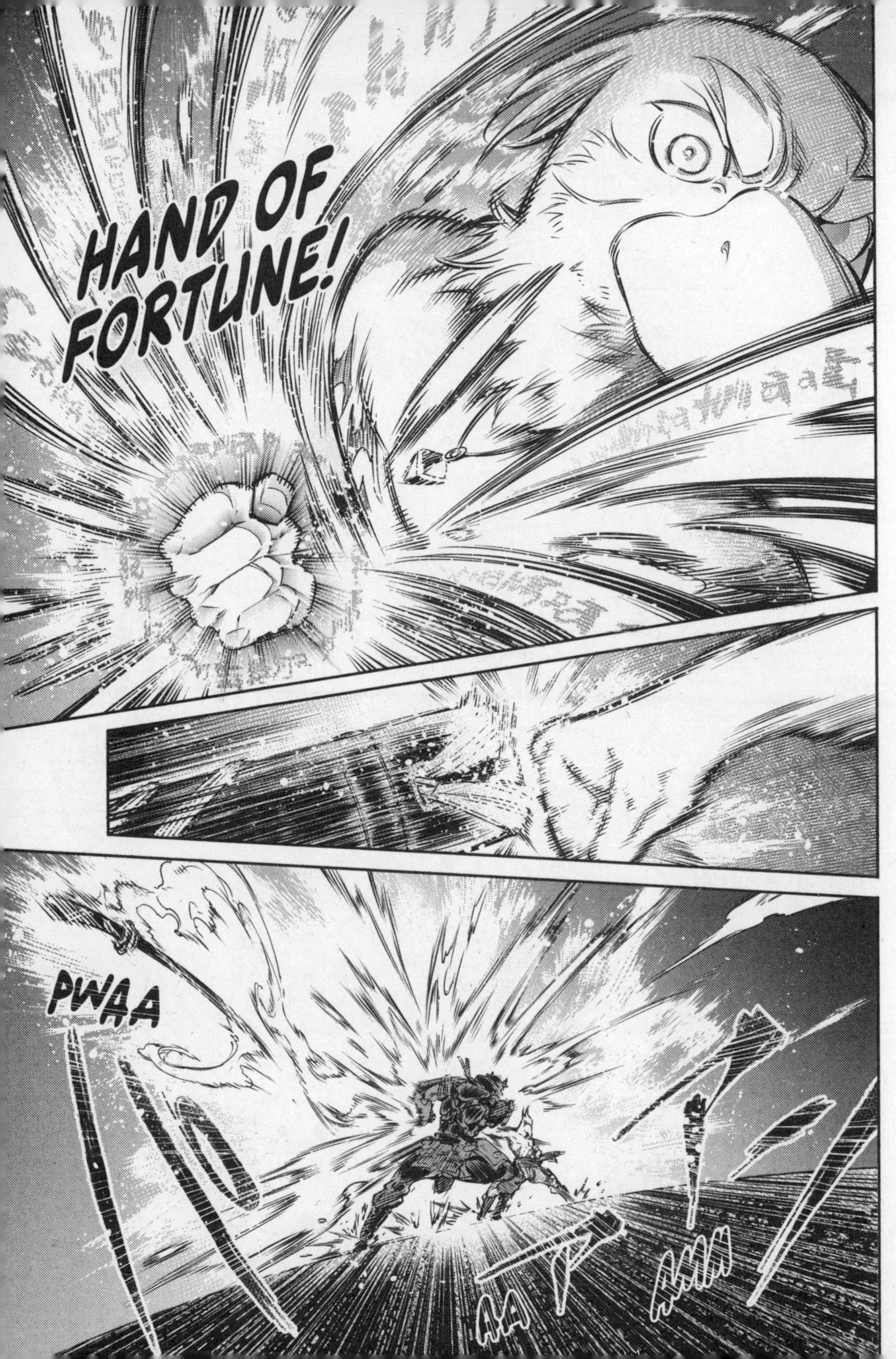
HAND OF FORTUNE!
PWAA

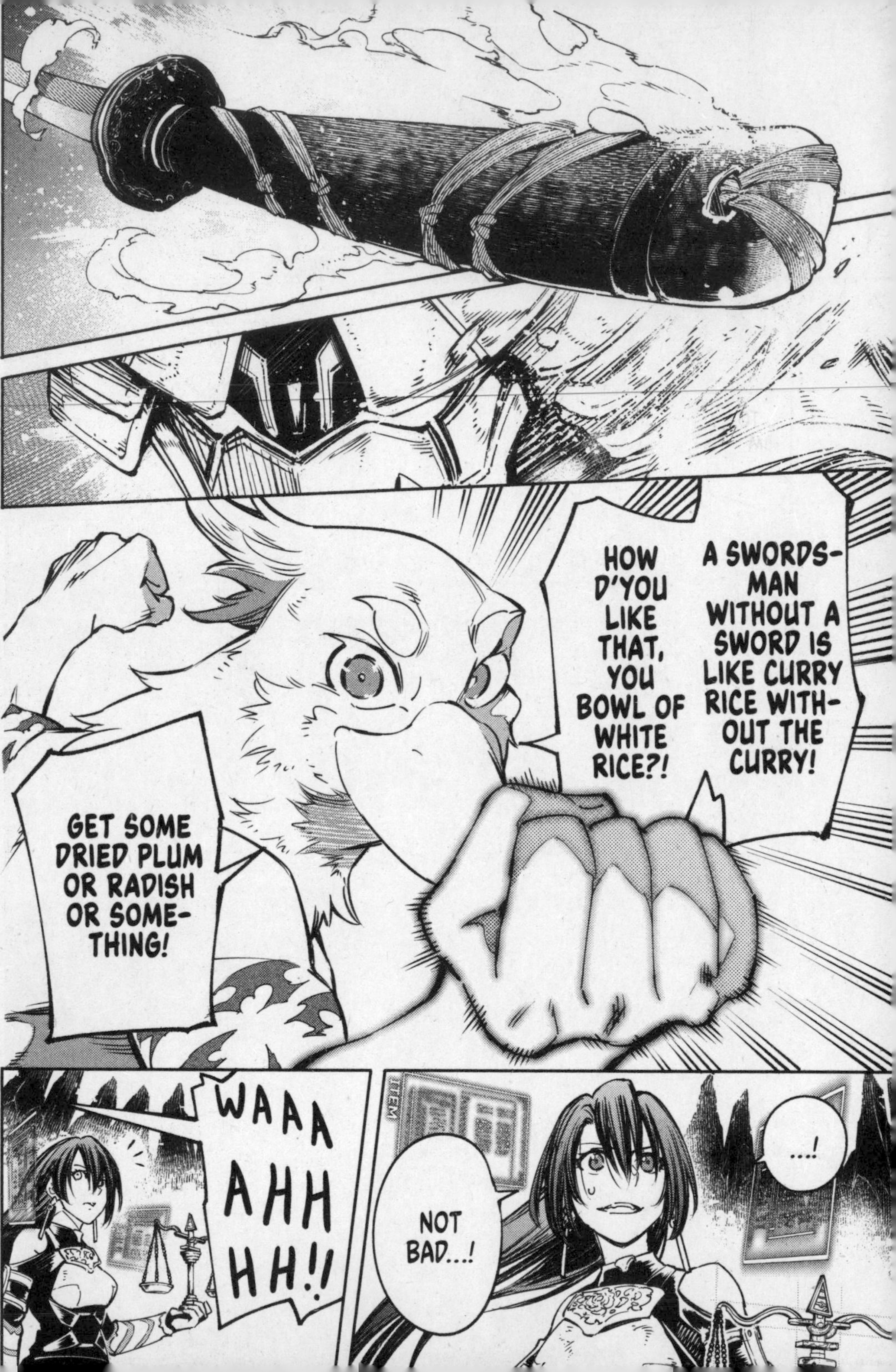
A SWORDS-MAN WITHOUT A SWORD IS LIKE CURRY RICE WITH-OUT THE CURRY!
HOW D'YOU LIKE THAT, YOU BOWL OF WHITE RICE?!
GET SOME DRIED PLUM OR RADISH OR SOME-THING!
...!
ITEM
NOT BAD...!
WAAAAHHHH!!

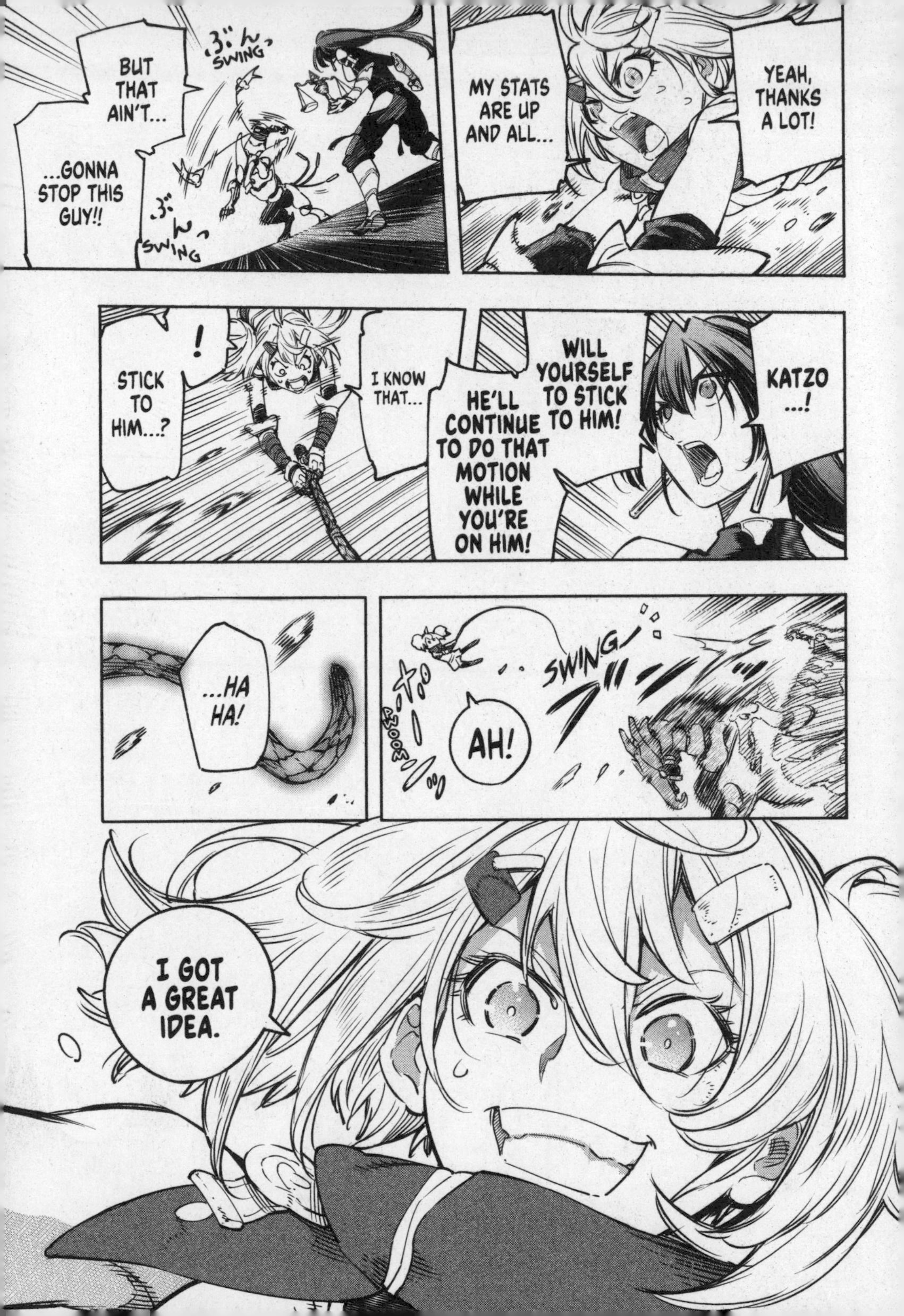
YEAH, THANKS A LOT!
MY STATS ARE UP AND ALL...
SWING
BUT THAT AIN'T...
...GONNA STOP THIS GUY!!
SWING
KATZO...!
WILL YOURSELF TO STICK TO HIM!
HE'LL CONTINUE TO DO THAT MOTION WHILE YOU'RE ON HIM!
I KNOW THAT...
!
STICK TO HIM...?
SWING!
AH!
...HA HA!
I GOT A GREAT IDEA.

READ TO LEARN MORE ABOUT THE WORLD OF SLF!

SHANGRI-LA FRONTIER STRATEGY FORUM

VOL. 19

LET SLF MASTER REI-CHAN TAKE YOU THROUGH THE WORLD!

REI-CHAN

IN DEPTH!! Wethermon the Tombguard's Moves (Part 1)

WETHERMON THE TOMBGUARD, ONE OF THE SEVEN COLOSSI, CAN KILL WITH EACH OF HIS ATTACKS—BUT HIS SPECIAL MOVES ARE EVEN TRICKIER! LET'S TAKE A LOOK!

Wind Slash

A LETHAL GUARD-BREAKING STRIKE, SAID TO LAST 1 FRAME (1/60 SEC). PLAYERS MUST READ ITS "TELL" IN ADVANCE, BUT IT'S TOO SHORT TO SPOT ON THE FIRST TRY.

Thunderclap

雷鐘

RAINS FIVE LETHAL LIGHTNING BOLTS PER SECOND FOR FIVE SECONDS. THESE HOME IN ON PLAYERS TO SOME EXTENT AND CAN BUNCH TOGETHER, WIPING OUT A WHOLE PARTY AT ONCE.

Nimbus Fist

AFTER CHARGING, UNLEASHES A "CLOUD" HAND THAT RAZES THE AREA AND KILLS ON CONTACT. IT IS SAFEST ABOVE IT OR CLOSE TO WETHERMON. WITH ENOUGH AGILITY, YOU CAN OUTRUN IT...?

Shangri-LA's Clans – Part 2

HERE ARE THE 3 CLANS WHO TOOK ON ASURA KAI!

THIS ALLIANCE OF GUILDS IS HERE TO CRUSH US...?!

TIGERS OF INDRA

A CLAN MADE OF ANTI-ASURA PLAYERS. THEY'VE ATTACKED ASURA BEFORE, BUT PENCILGON'S TRAP ONCE NEARLY WIPED THEM OUT.

MAIN MEMBER: TIGERSHARK X

TEAM 10PM

YOU MUST HAVE A FULL-TIME JOB TO ENTER THIS CLAN, WHOSE WORKING-ADULT MEMBERS ONLY BEGIN PLAYING AFTER 10 P.M.

MAIN MEMBER: UQ LOAD LETTER

KNIGHTS TEMPURA

THE LARGEST SLF CLAN, POSITIONED BETWEEN MID-TIER AND HARDCORE. THE MEMBER PERKS ATTRACT A LOT OF PLAYERS.

MAIN MEMBER: TEN-DON

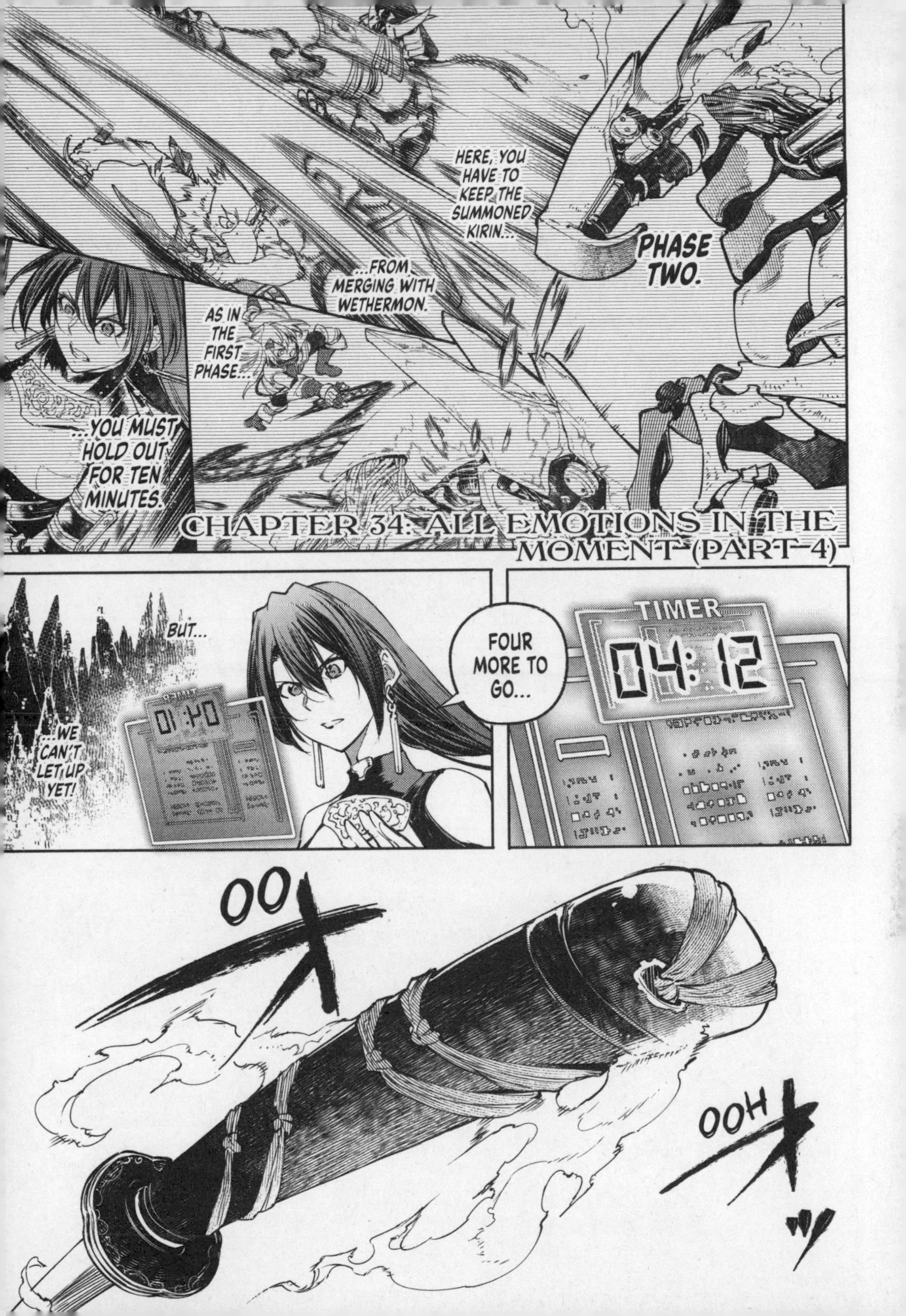
PHASE TWO.
HERE, YOU HAVE TO KEEP THE SUMMONED KIRIN...
...FROM MERGING WITH WETHERMON.
AS IN THE FIRST PHASE...
...YOU MUST HOLD OUT FOR TEN MINUTES.
CHAPTER 34: ALL EMOTIONS IN THE MOMENT (PART 4)
TIMER
04:12
FOUR MORE TO GO...
01:40
BUT...
...WE CAN'T LET UP YET!
OO
OOH

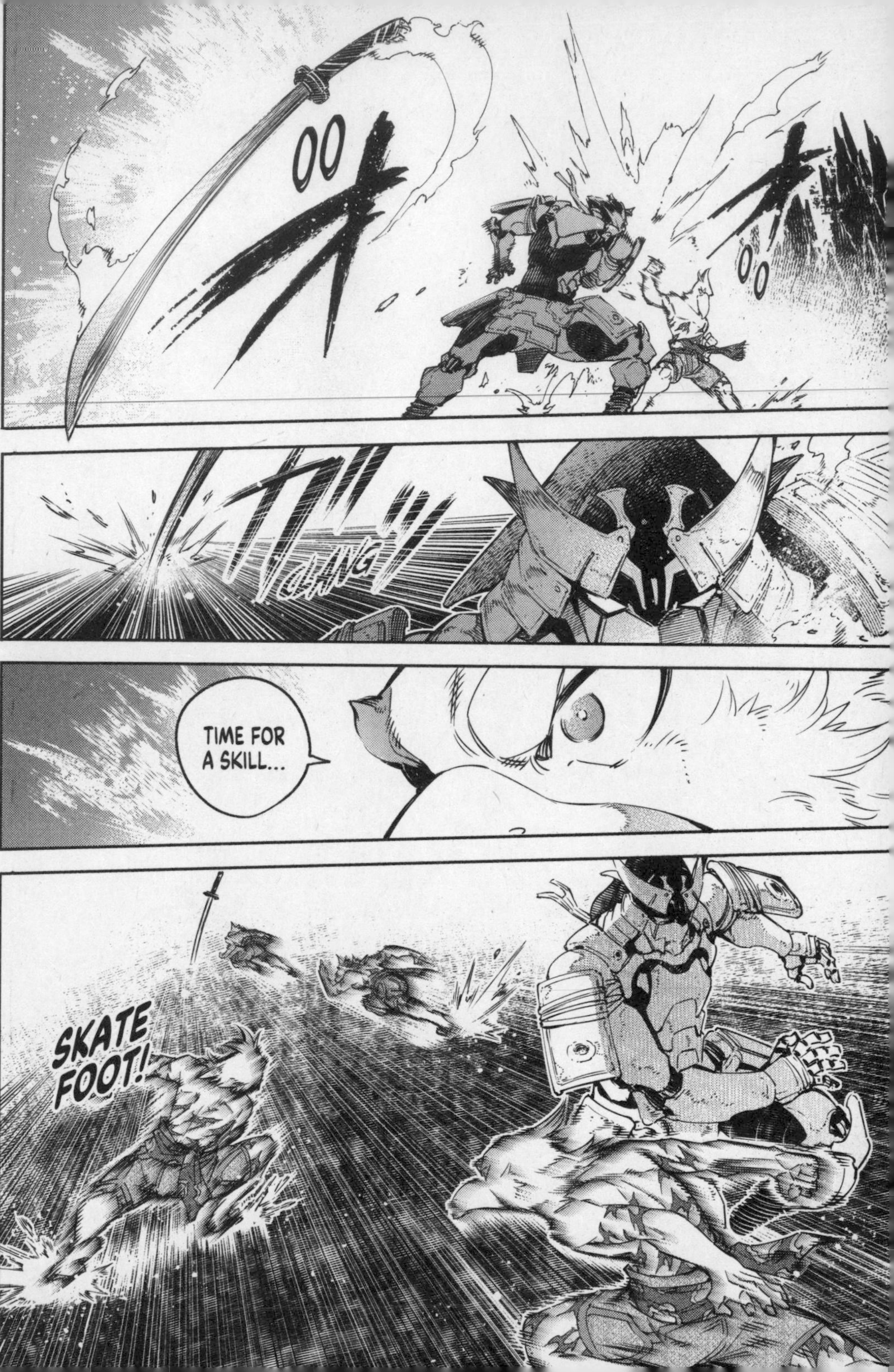
CHANG
TIME FOR A SKILL...
SKATE FOOT!

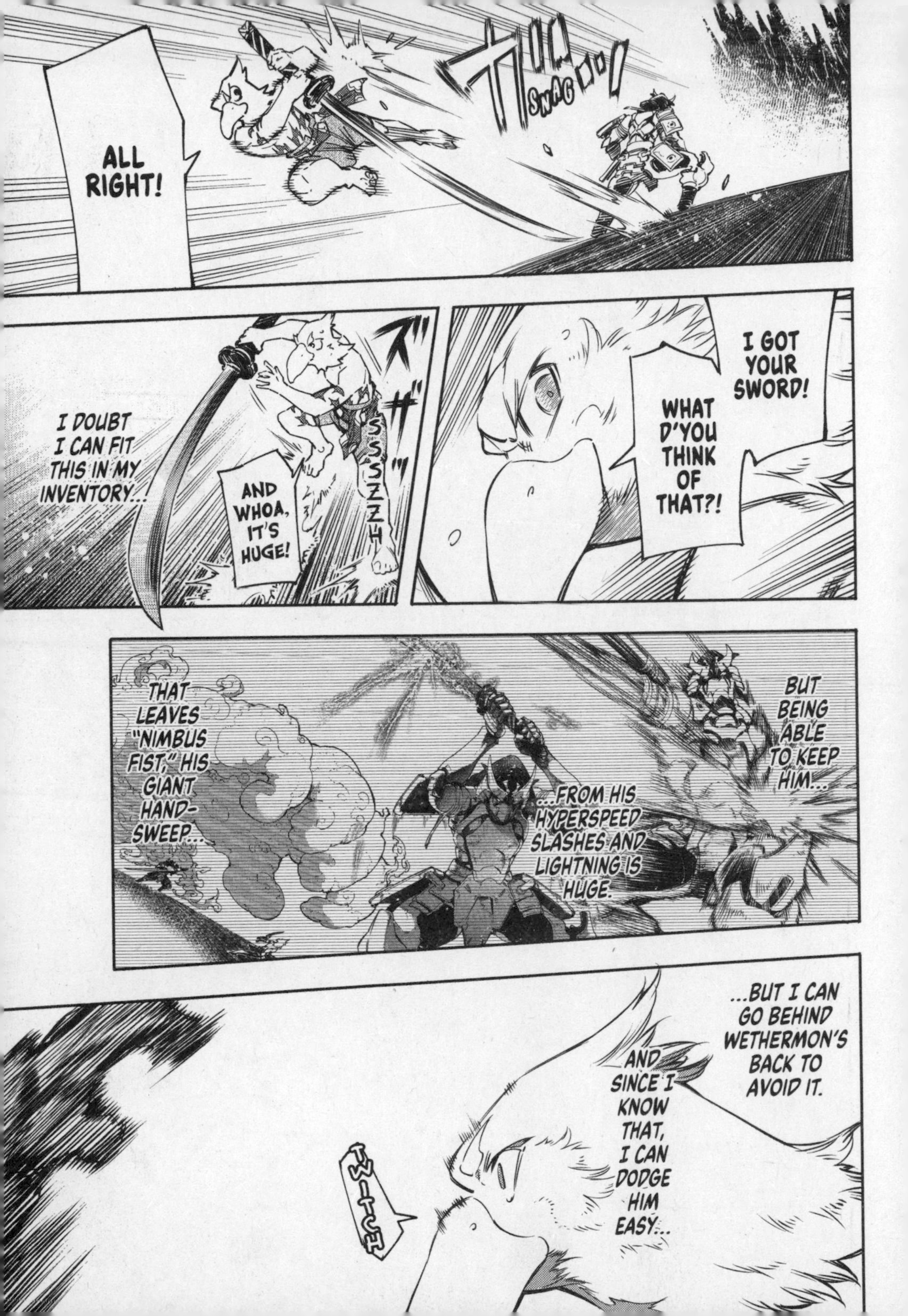
SNAG
ALL RIGHT!
I GOT YOUR SWORD!
WHAT D'YOU THINK OF THAT?!
SSSZZZH
AND WHOA, IT'S HUGE!
I DOUBT I CAN FIT THIS IN MY INVENTORY...
BUT BEING ABLE TO KEEP HIM...
...FROM HIS HYPERSPEED SLASHES AND LIGHTNING IS HUGE.
THAT LEAVES "NIMBUS FIST," HIS GIANT HAND-SWEEP...
...BUT I CAN GO BEHIND WETHERMON'S BACK TO AVOID IT.
AND SINCE I KNOW THAT, I CAN DODGE HIM EASY...
TWITCH

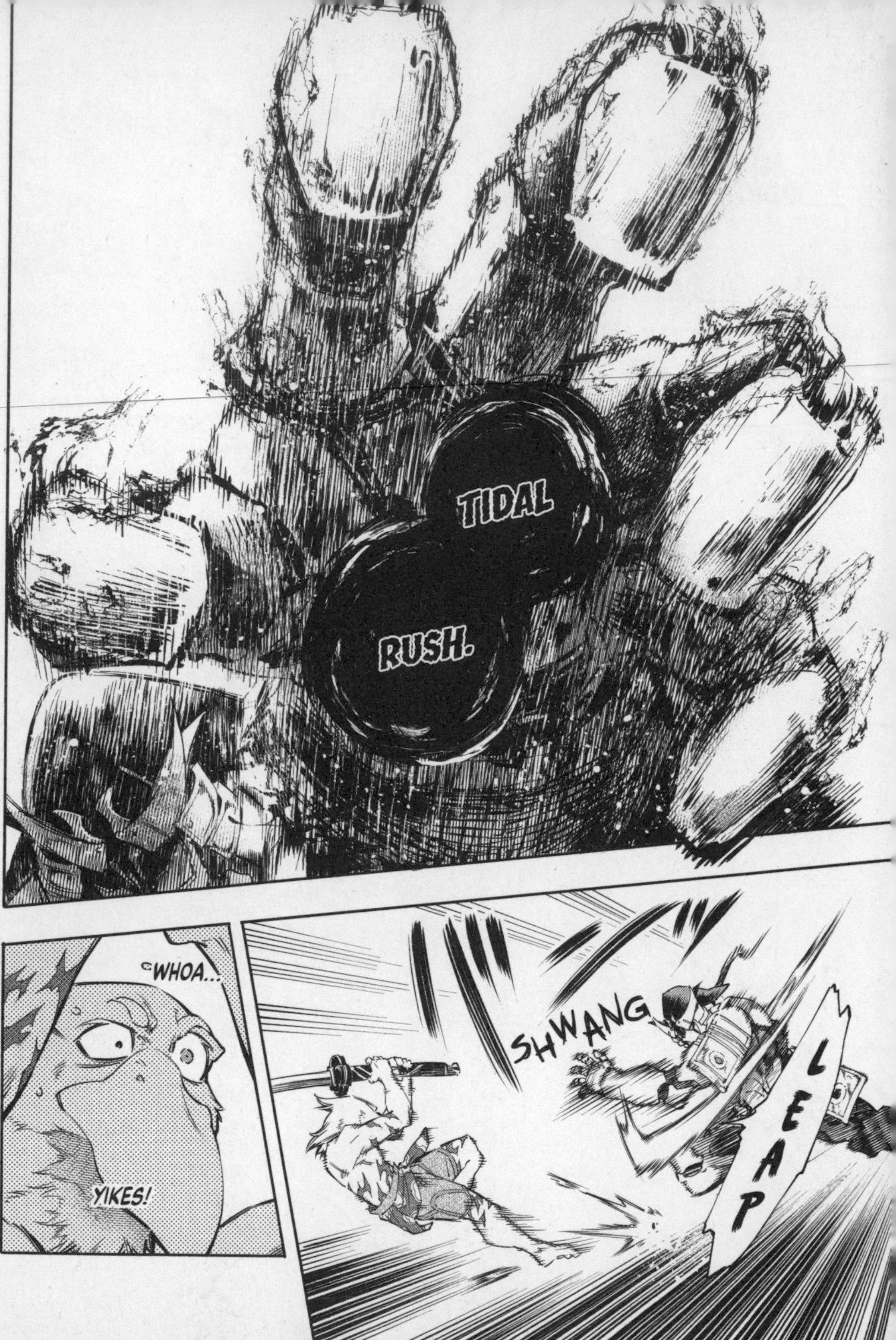
TIDAL
RUSH.
SHWANG
LEAP
WHOA...
YIKES!

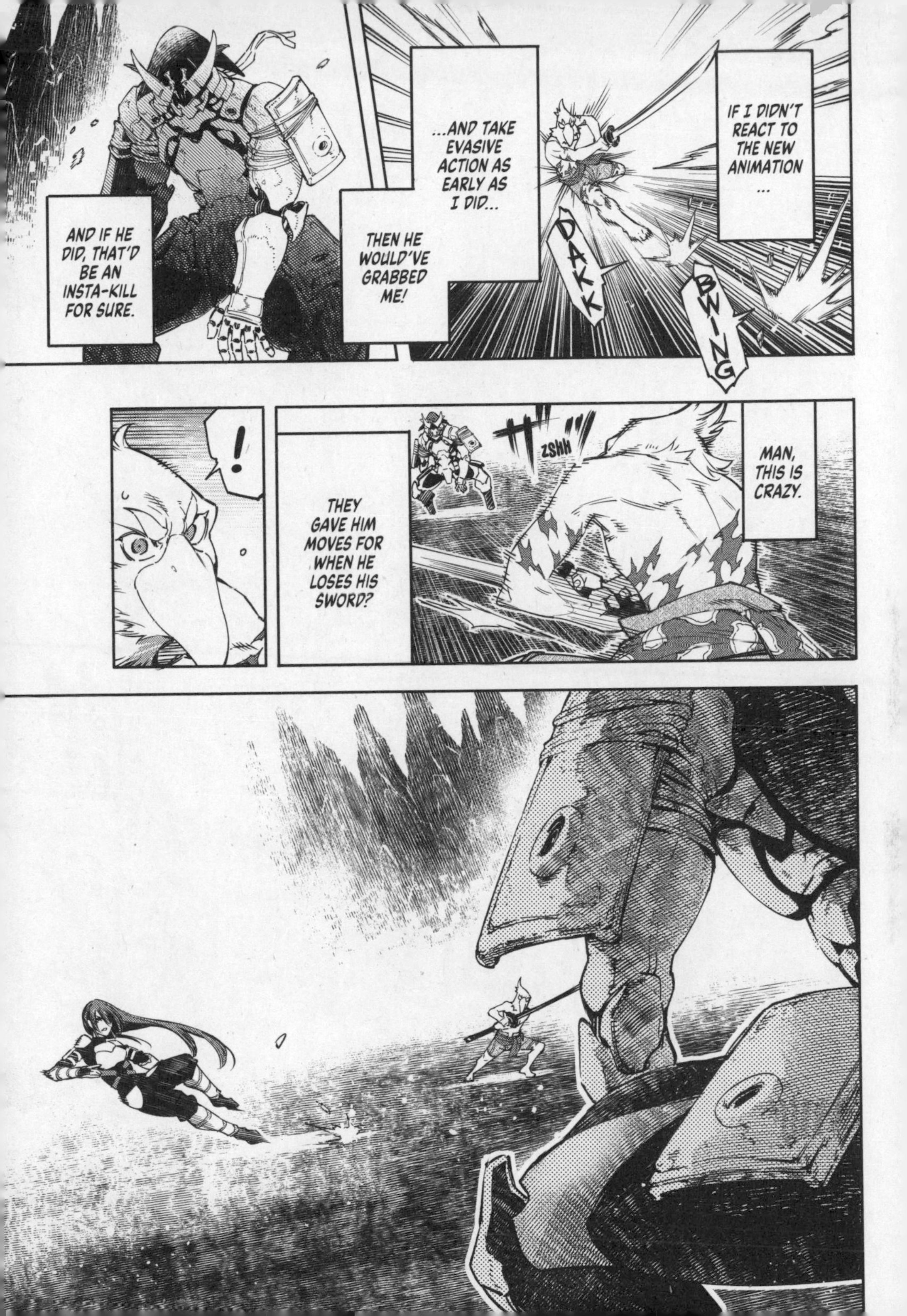
IF I DIDN'T REACT TO THE NEW ANIMATION ...
...AND TAKE EVASIVE ACTION AS EARLY AS I DID...
BWING
DAKK
THEN HE WOULD'VE GRABBED ME!
AND IF HE DID, THAT'D BE AN INSTA-KILL FOR SURE.
MAN, THIS IS CRAZY.
ZSHH
THEY GAVE HIM MOVES FOR WHEN HE LOSES HIS SWORD?
!

PENCILGON!!

WE'RE BADLY OUT OF POSITION...!

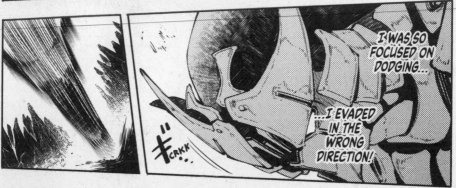

I WAS SO FOCUSED ON DODGING...

...I EVADED IN THE WRONG DIRECTION!

CRKK

AND NOW HIS SIGHTS...

TCH....!

DASH!!

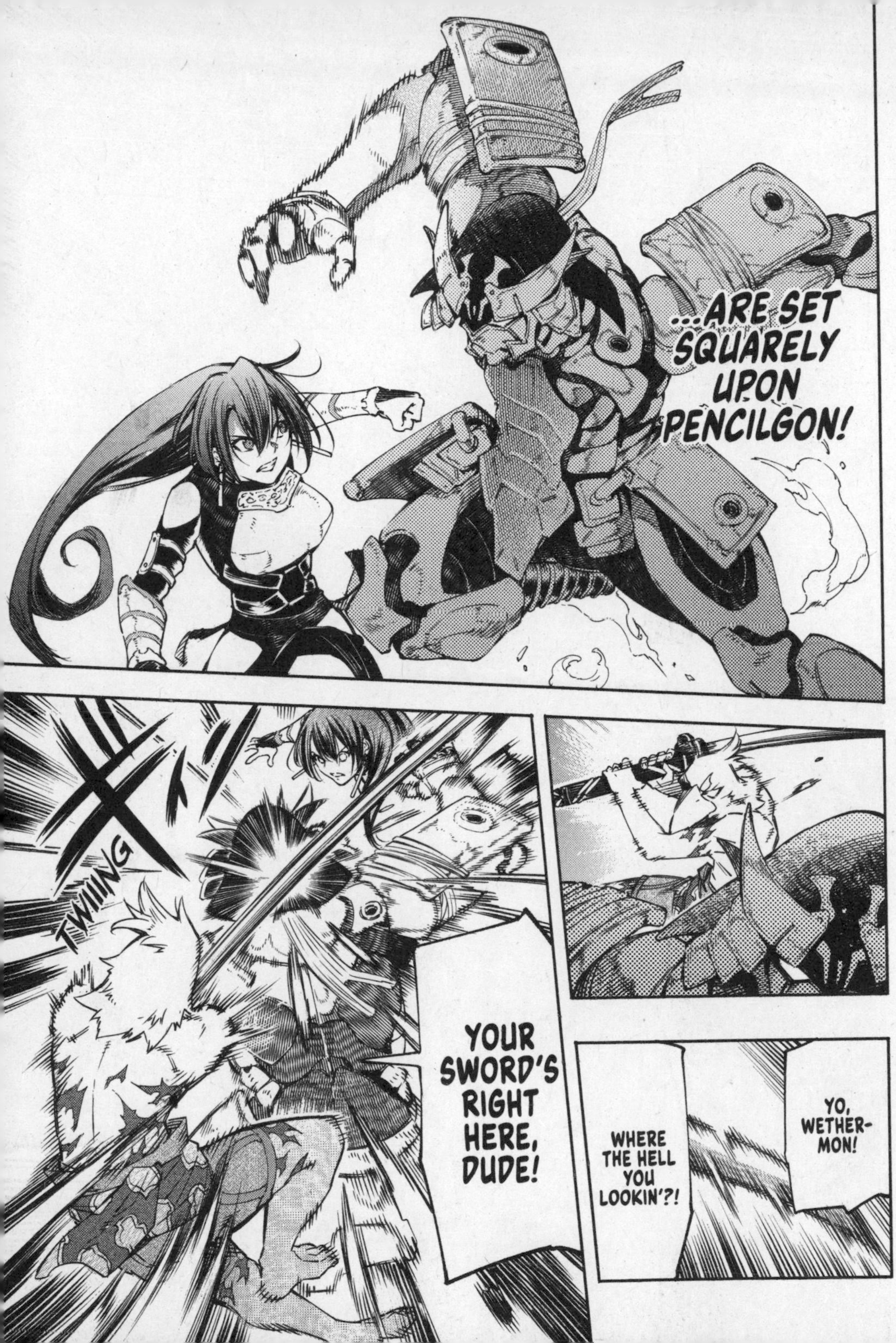
...ARE SET SQUARELY UPON PENCILGON!
YO, WETHER-MON!
WHERE THE HELL YOU LOOKIN'?!
TWIIING
YOUR SWORD'S RIGHT HERE, DUDE!

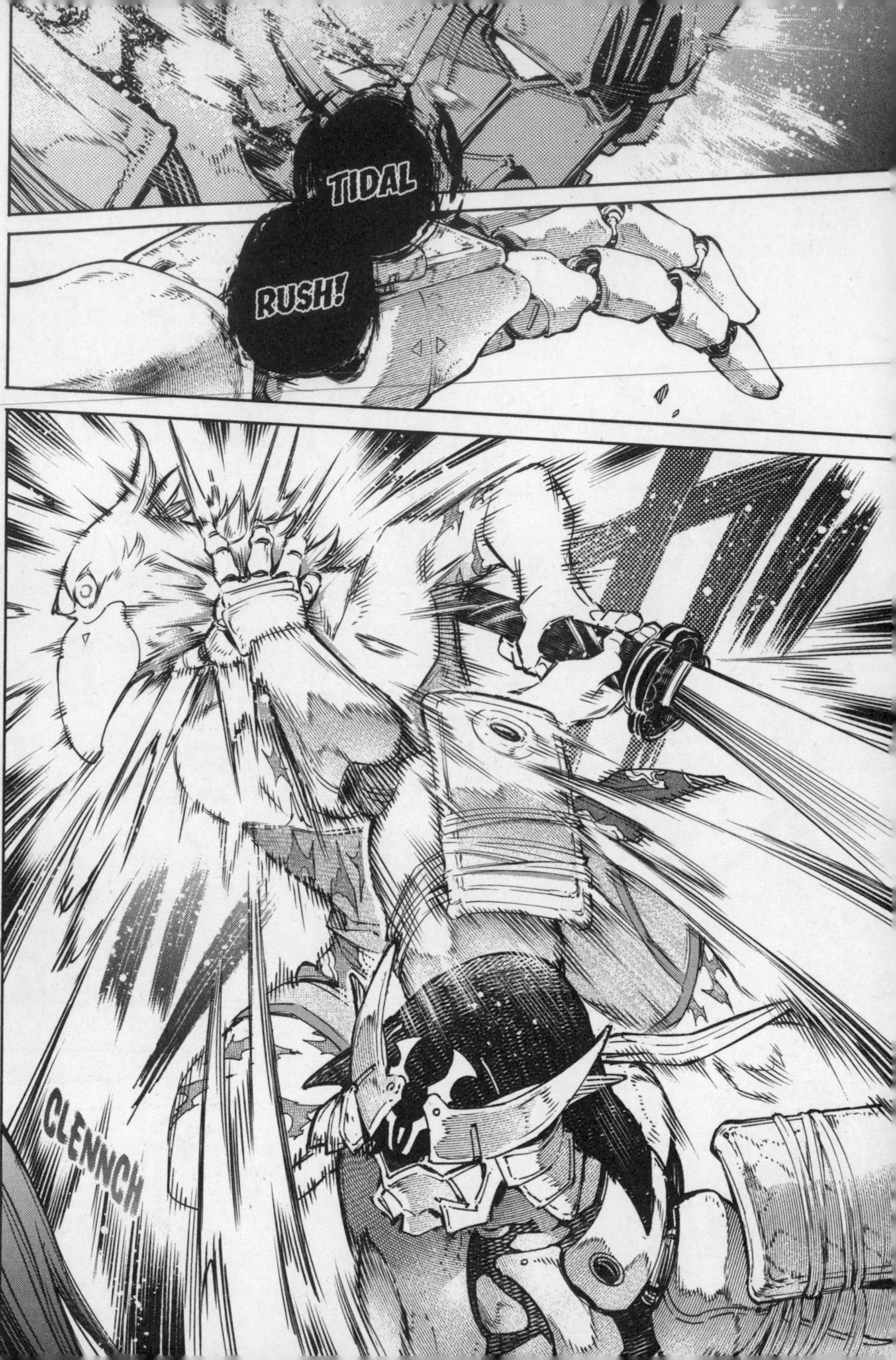
TIDAL
RUSH!
CLENNCH

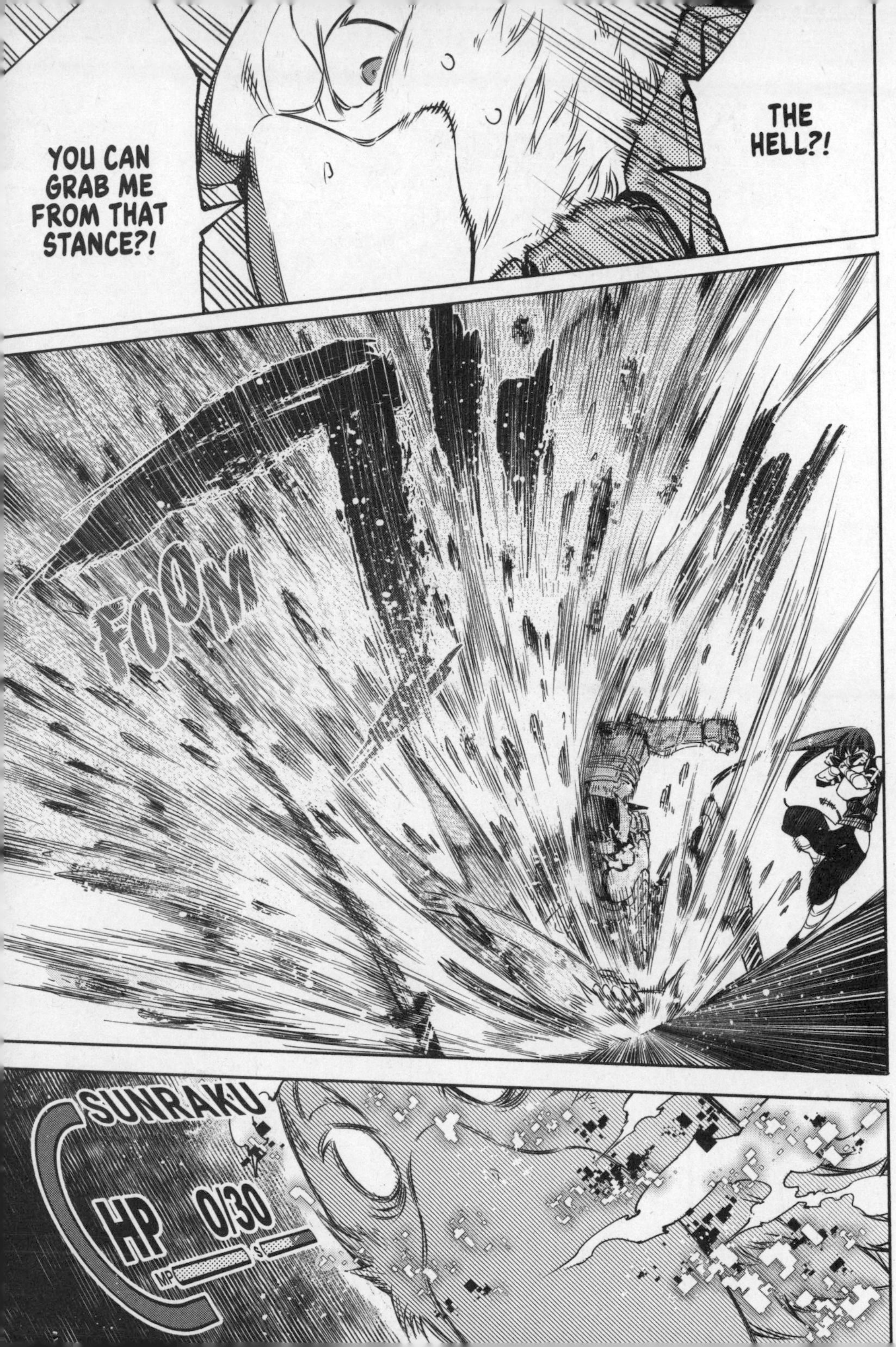
THE HELL?!
YOU CAN GRAB ME FROM THAT STANCE?!
FOOM
SUNRAKU
HP 0/30
MP

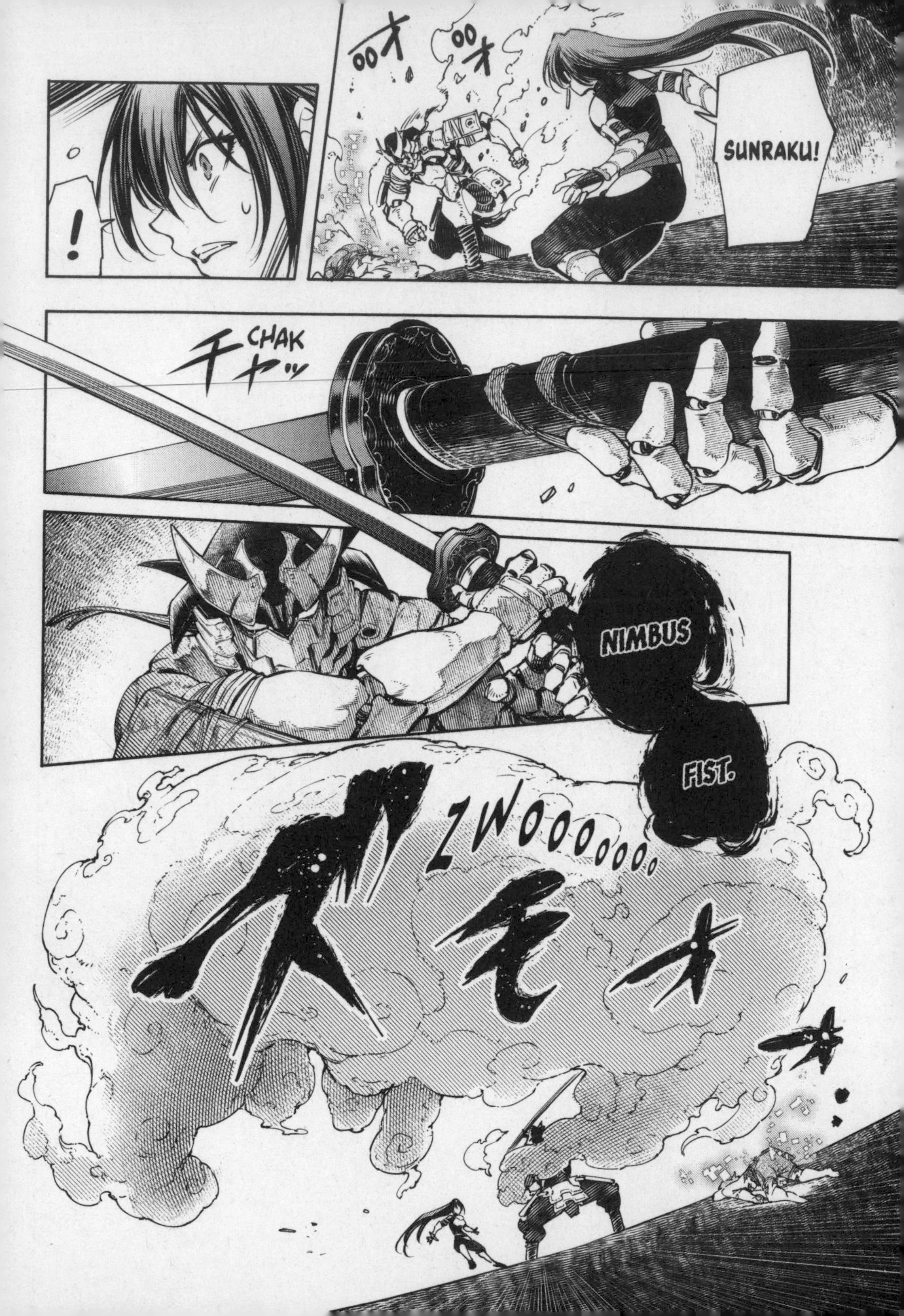
SUNRAKU!
!
CHAK
NIMBUS
FIST.
ZWOOOOOOO

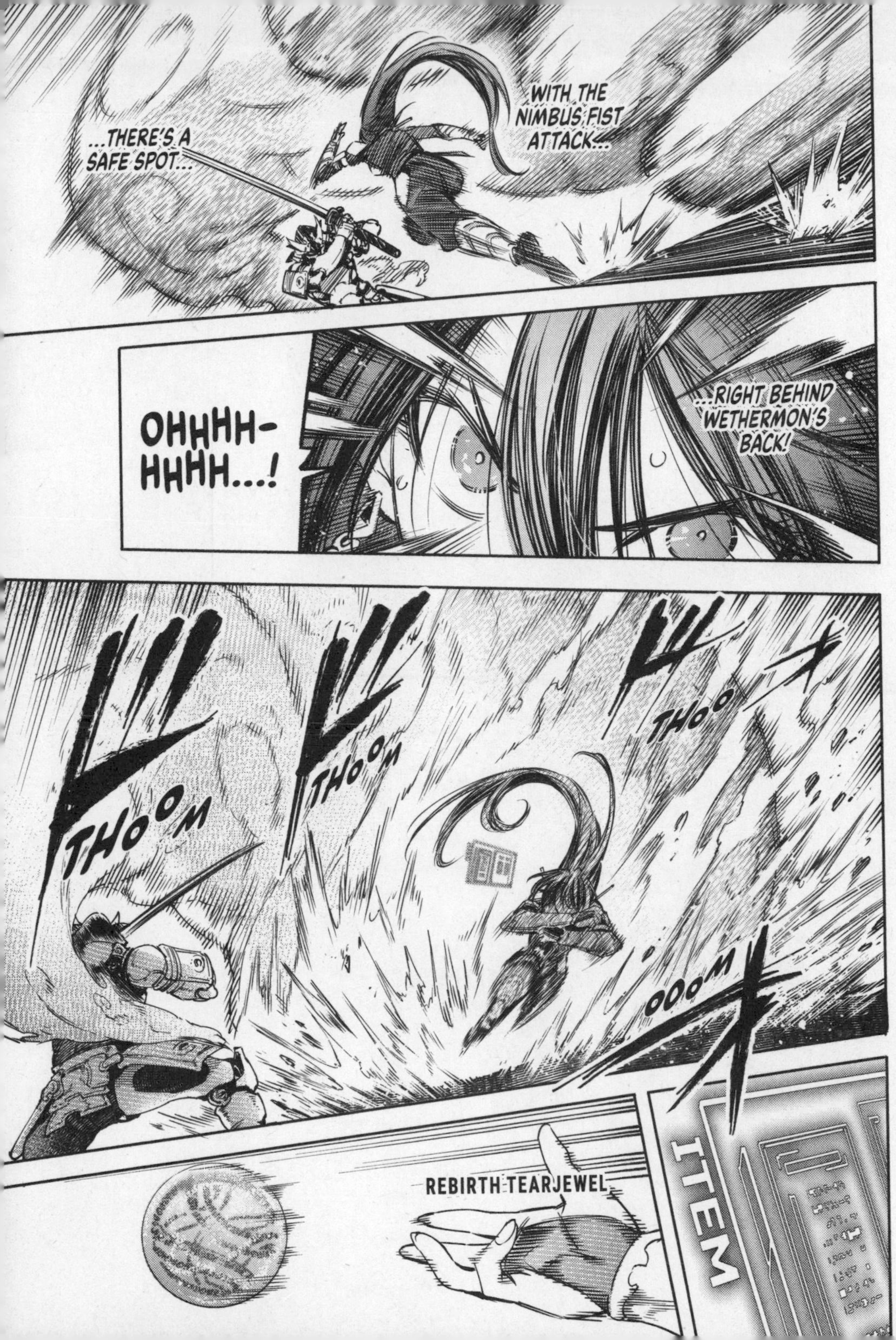
WITH THE NIMBUS FIST ATTACK...
...THERE'S A SAFE SPOT...
...RIGHT BEHIND WETHERMON'S BACK!
OHHHH-HHHH...!
THOOOM
THOOOM
THOOOM
ITEM
REBIRTH TEARJEWEL

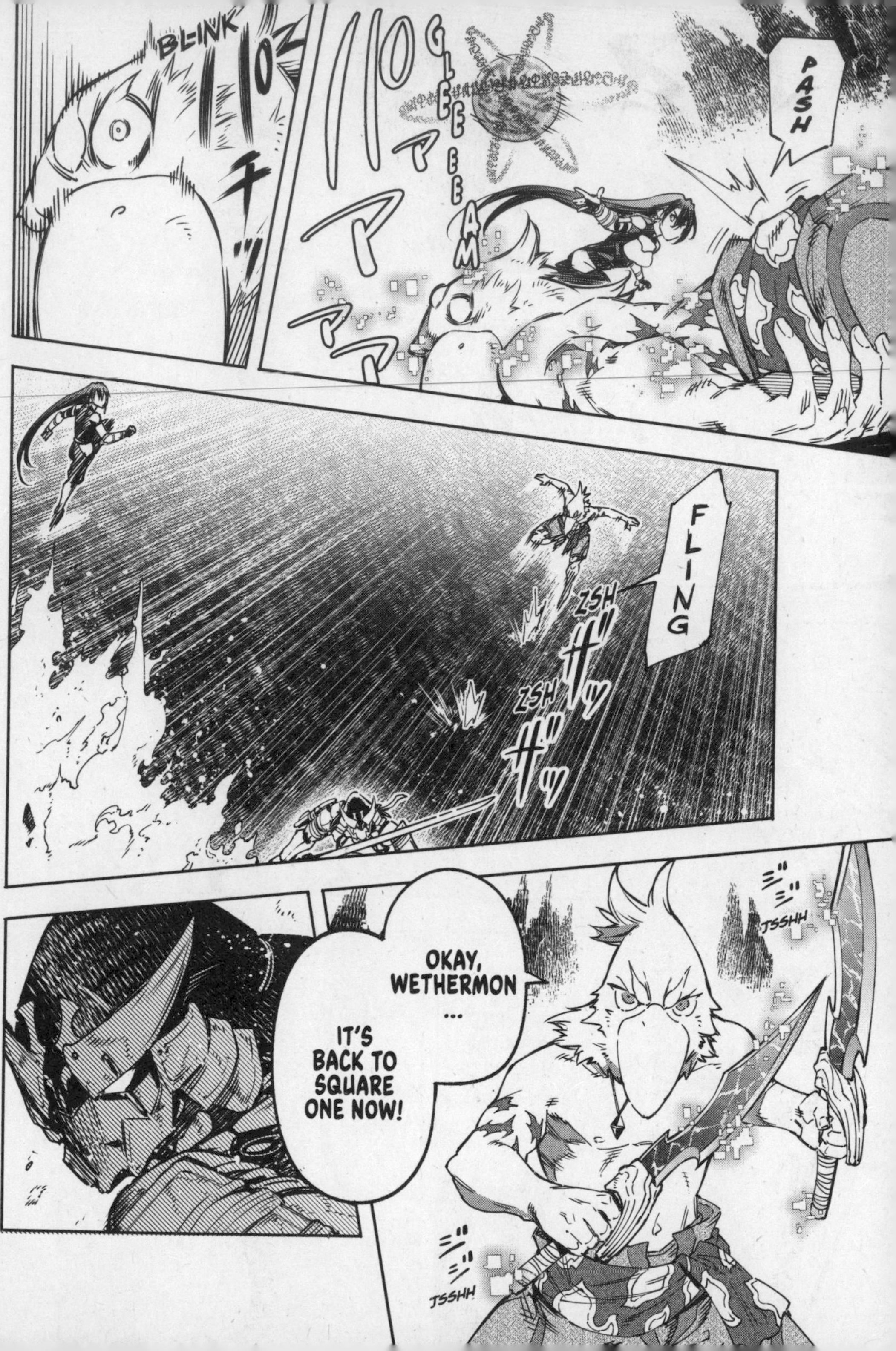
PASH
GLEEEEAM
BLINK
FLING
ZSH
ZSH
JSSHH
OKAY, WETHERMON ...
IT'S BACK TO SQUARE ONE NOW!
JSSHH

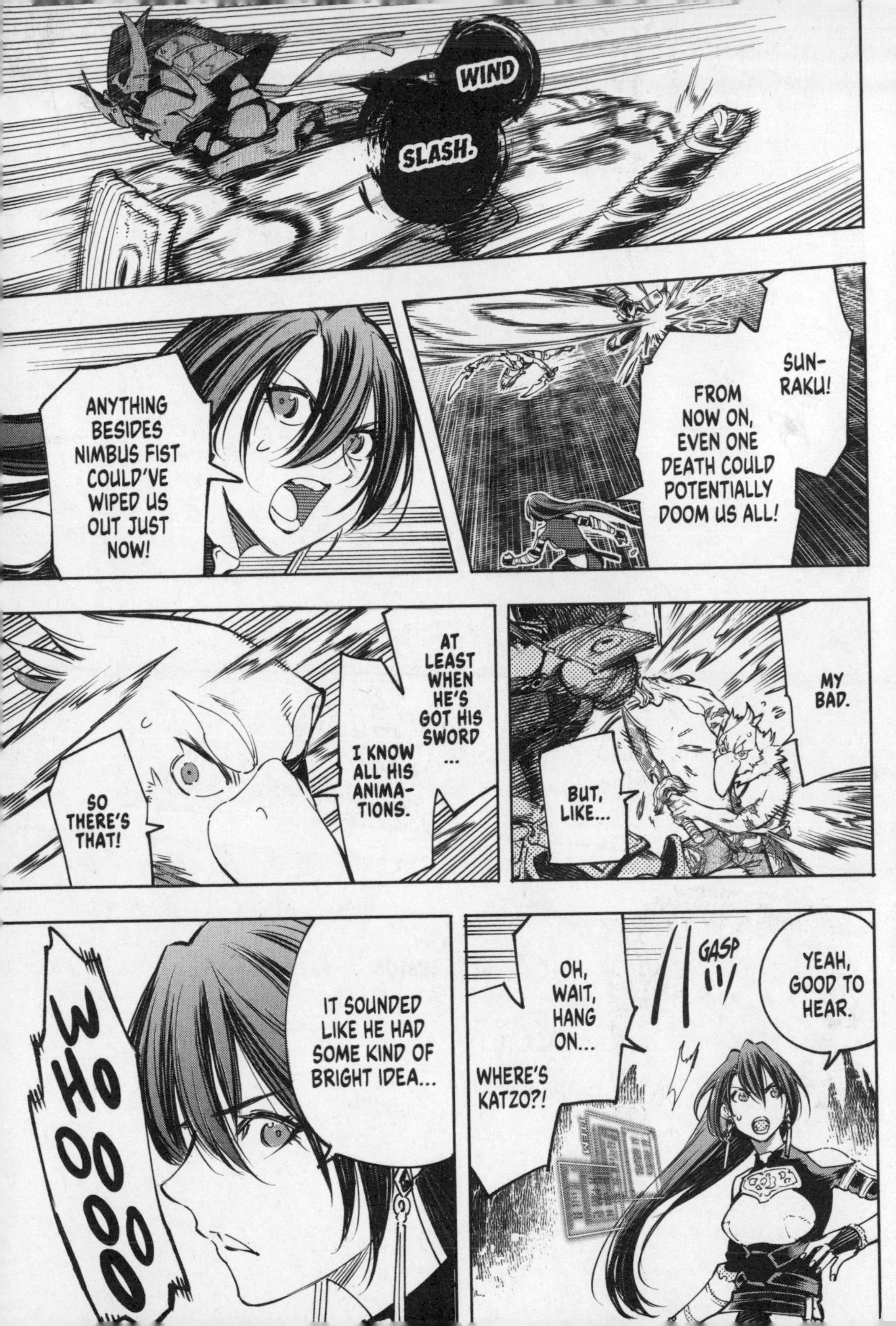
WIND
SLASH.
SUN-RAKU!
FROM NOW ON, EVEN ONE DEATH COULD POTENTIALLY DOOM US ALL!
ANYTHING BESIDES NIMBUS FIST COULD'VE WIPED US OUT JUST NOW!
MY BAD.
BUT, LIKE...
AT LEAST WHEN HE'S GOT HIS SWORD...
I KNOW ALL HIS ANIMATIONS.
SO THERE'S THAT!
YEAH, GOOD TO HEAR.
GASP!!
OH, WAIT, HANG ON...
WHERE'S KATZO?!
IT SOUNDED LIKE HE HAD SOME KIND OF BRIGHT IDEA...
WHOOOOOO

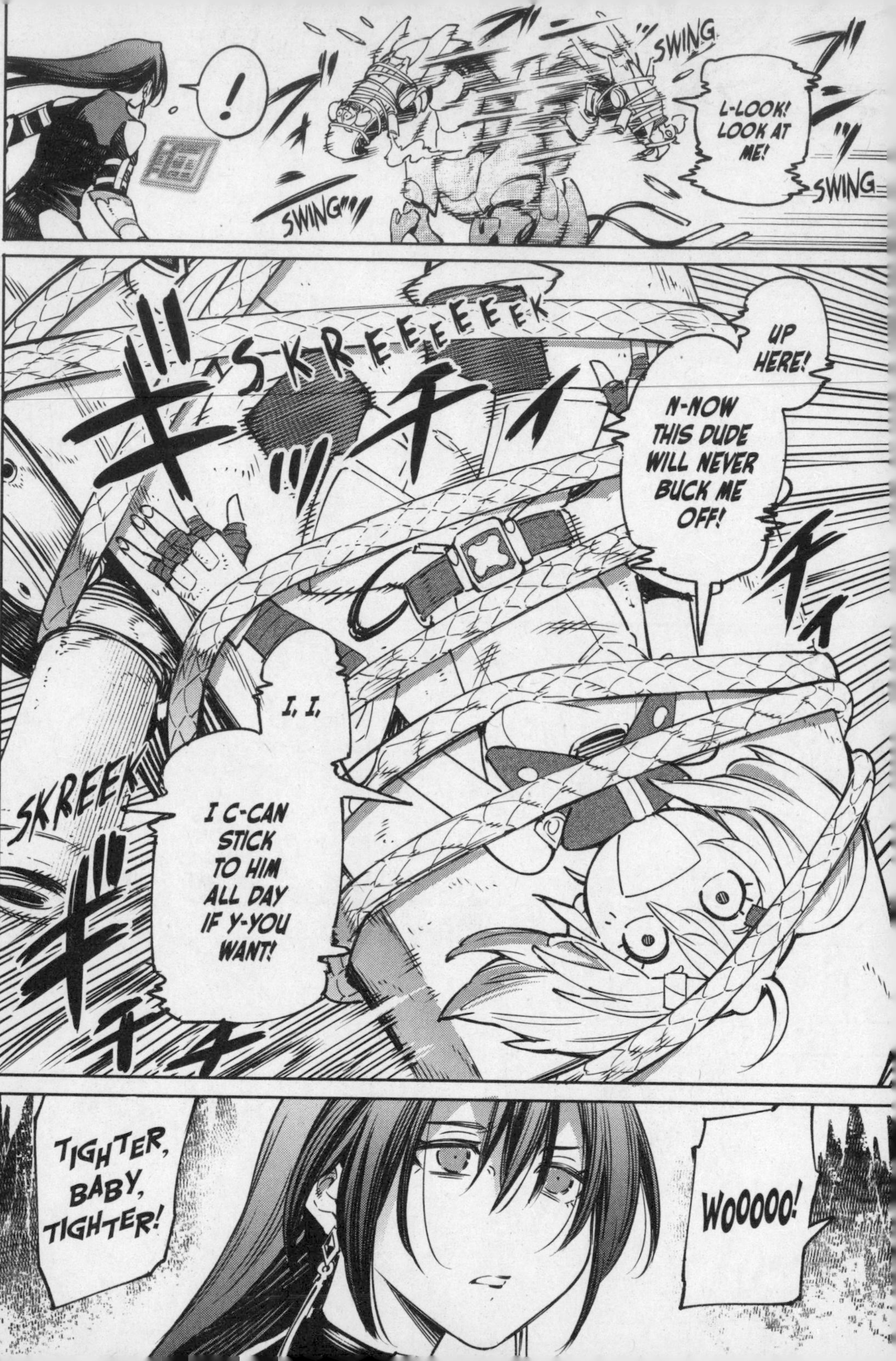
SWING
L-LOOK! LOOK AT ME!
SWING
!
SWING
SKREEEEEEEK
UP HERE!
N-NOW THIS DUDE WILL NEVER BUCK ME OFF!
I, I,
I C-CAN STICK TO HIM ALL DAY IF Y-YOU WANT!
SKREEK
WOOOOO!
TIGHTER, BABY, TIGHTER!

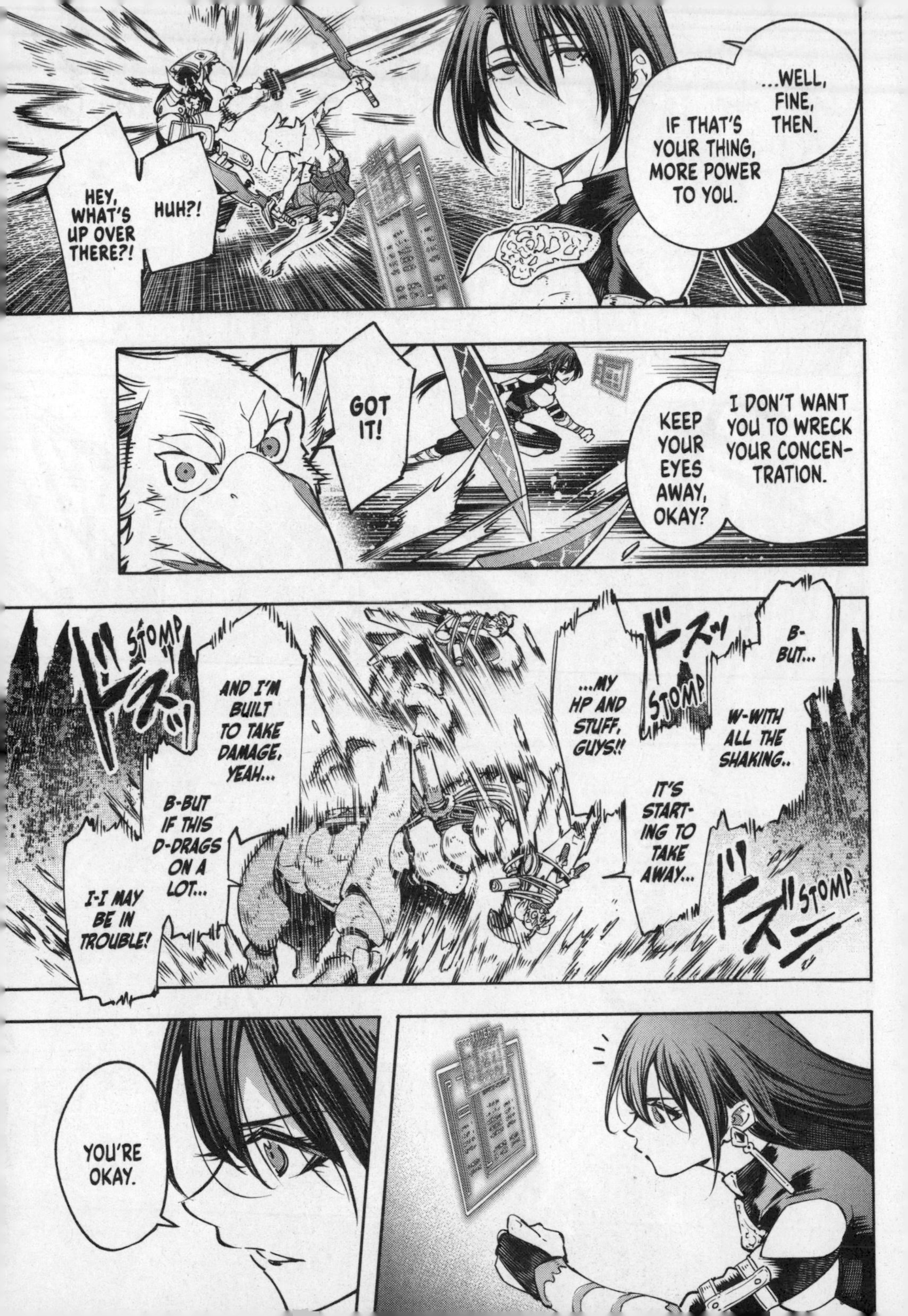

...WELL, FINE, THEN.
IF THAT'S YOUR THING, MORE POWER TO YOU.
HUH?!
HEY, WHAT'S UP OVER THERE?!
I DON'T WANT YOU TO WRECK YOUR CONCENTRATION.
KEEP YOUR EYES AWAY, OKAY?
GOT IT!
B-BUT...
STOMP
W-WITH ALL THE SHAKING..
IT'S STARTING TO TAKE AWAY...
STOMP
...MY HP AND STUFF, GUYS!!
AND I'M BUILT TO TAKE DAMAGE, YEAH...
B-BUT IF THIS D-DRAGS ON A LOT...
I-I MAY BE IN TROUBLE!
STOMP
YOU'RE OKAY.

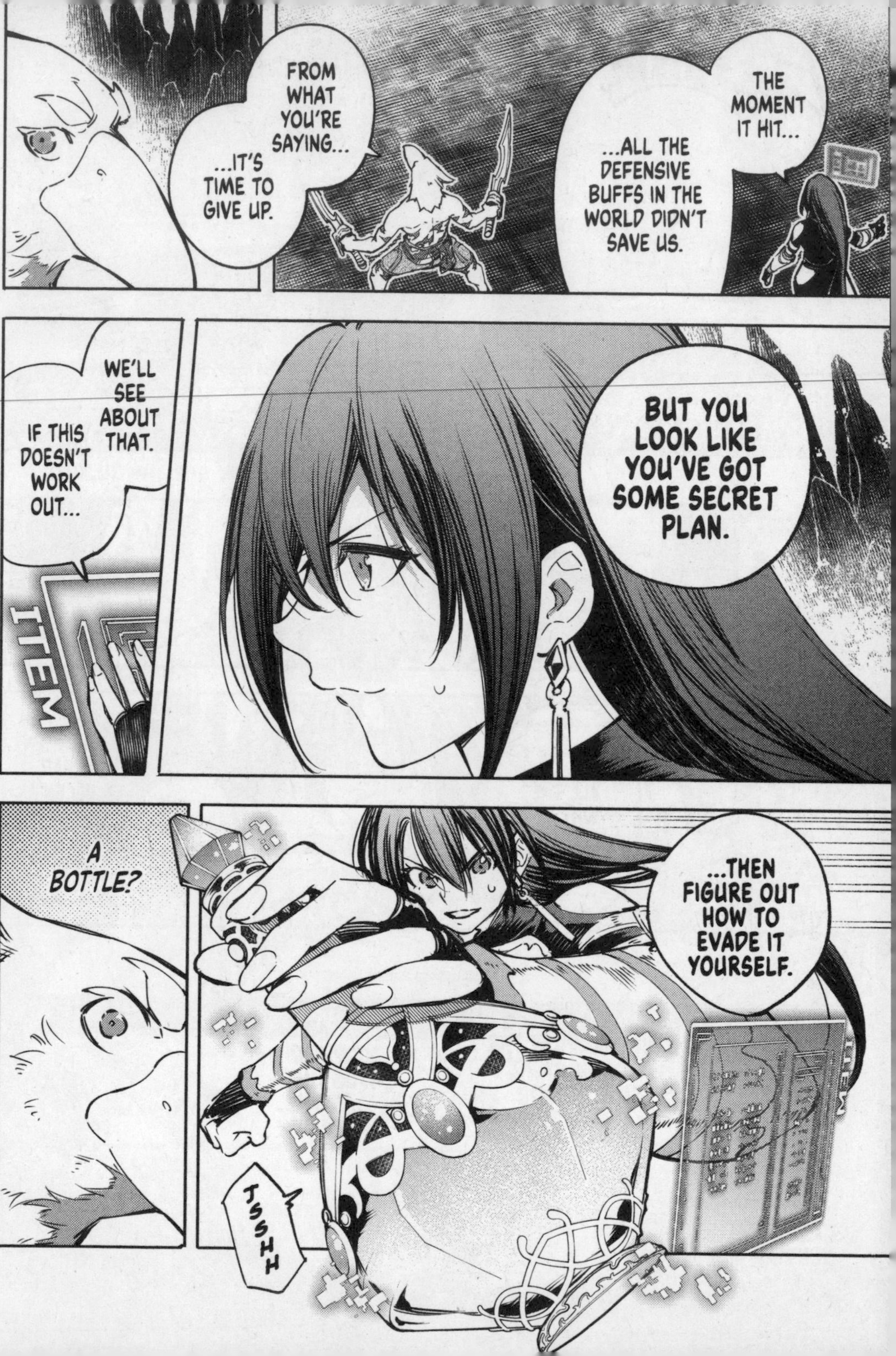
THE MOMENT IT HIT...
...ALL THE DEFENSIVE BUFFS IN THE WORLD DIDN'T SAVE US.
FROM WHAT YOU'RE SAYING...
...IT'S TIME TO GIVE UP.
BUT YOU LOOK LIKE YOU'VE GOT SOME SECRET PLAN.
WE'LL SEE ABOUT THAT.
IF THIS DOESN'T WORK OUT...
ITEM
...THEN FIGURE OUT HOW TO EVADE IT YOURSELF.
ITEM
TSSHH
A BOTTLE?

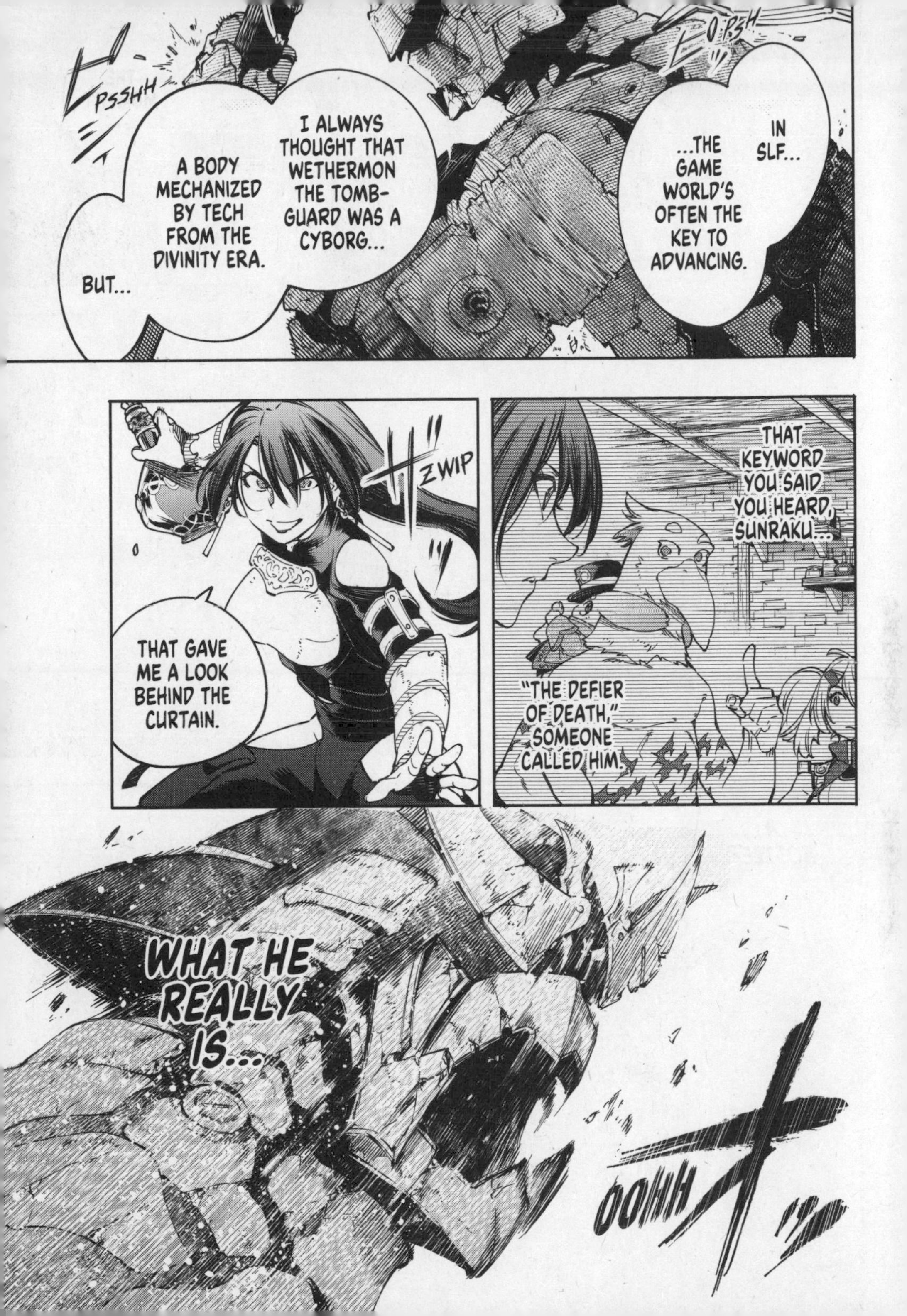
IN SLF...
...THE GAME WORLD'S OFTEN THE KEY TO ADVANCING.
I ALWAYS THOUGHT THAT WETHERMON THE TOMB-GUARD WAS A CYBORG...
A BODY MECHANIZED BY TECH FROM THE DIVINITY ERA.
BUT...
PSSHH
THAT KEYWORD YOU SAID YOU HEARD, SUNRAKU...
"THE DEFIER OF DEATH," SOMEONE CALLED HIM.
ZWIP
THAT GAVE ME A LOOK BEHIND THE CURTAIN.
WHAT HE REALLY IS...
OOHH

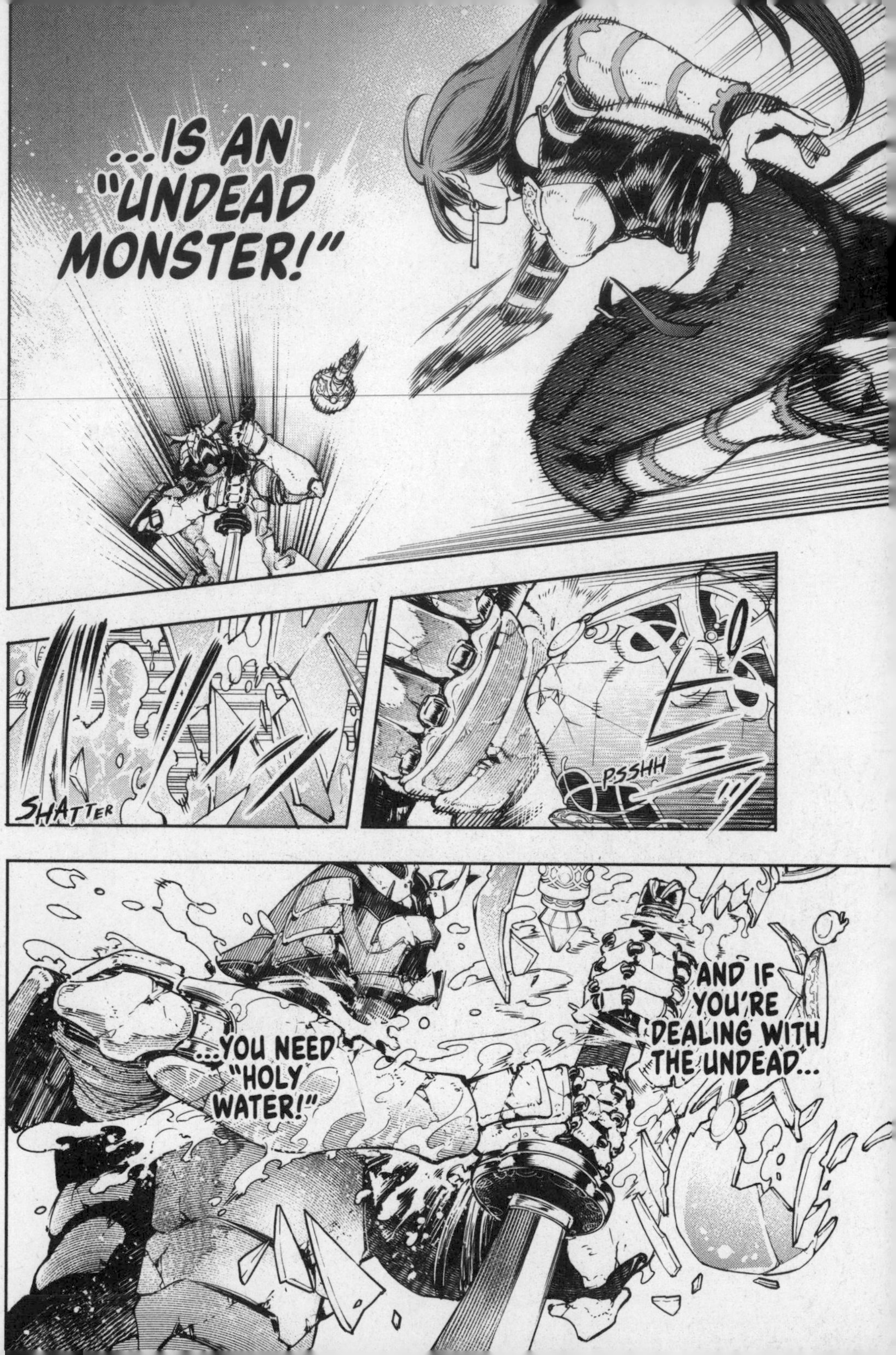
...IS AN "UNDEAD MONSTER!"
PSSHH
!!
SHATTER
AND IF YOU'RE DEALING WITH THE UNDEAD...
...YOU NEED "HOLY WATER!"

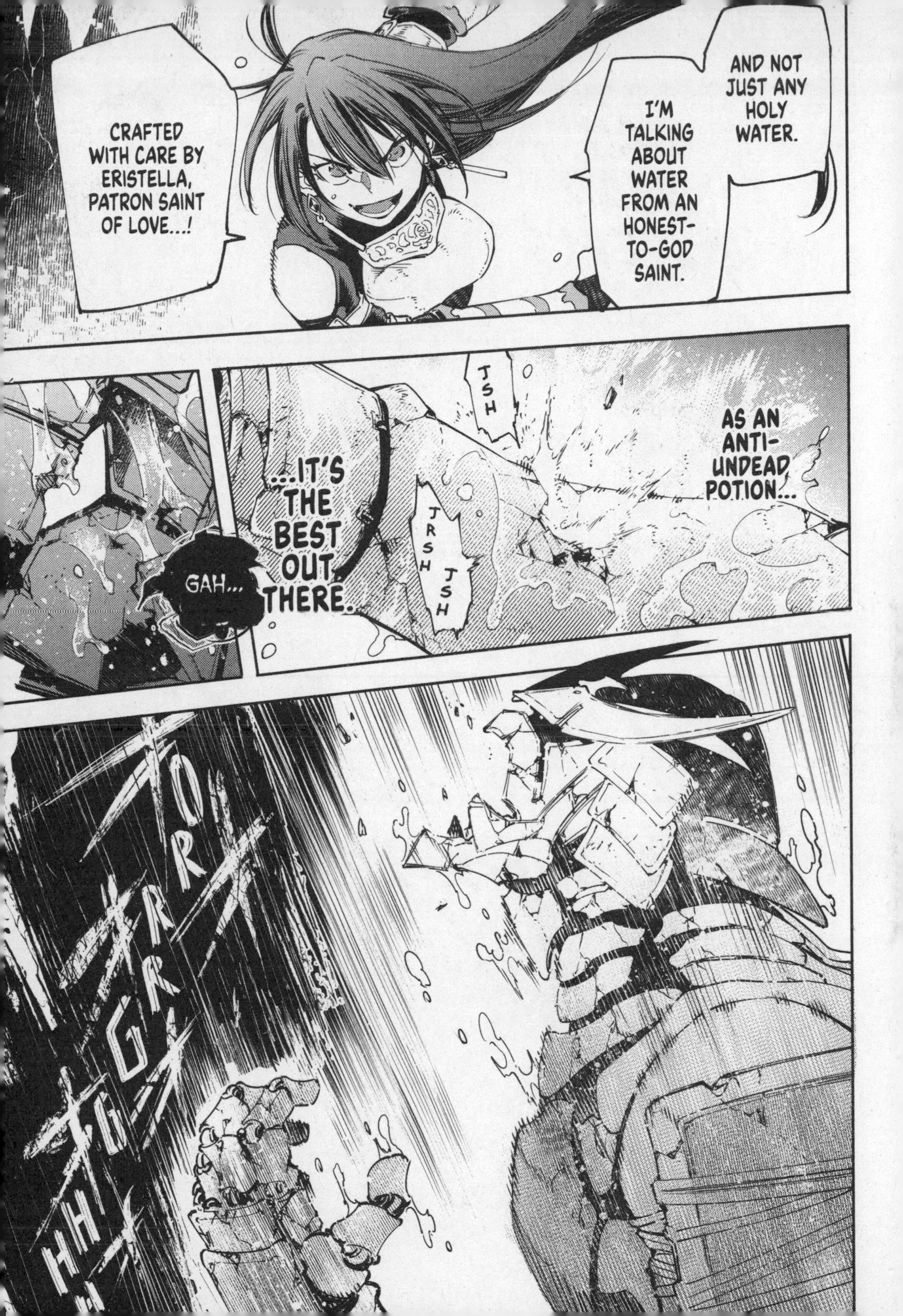
AND NOT JUST ANY HOLY WATER.
I'M TALKING ABOUT WATER FROM AN HONEST-TO-GOD SAINT.
CRAFTED WITH CARE BY ERISTELLA, PATRON SAINT OF LOVE...!
JSH
AS AN ANTI-UNDEAD POTION...
JRSH JSH
...IT'S THE BEST OUT THERE.
GAH...

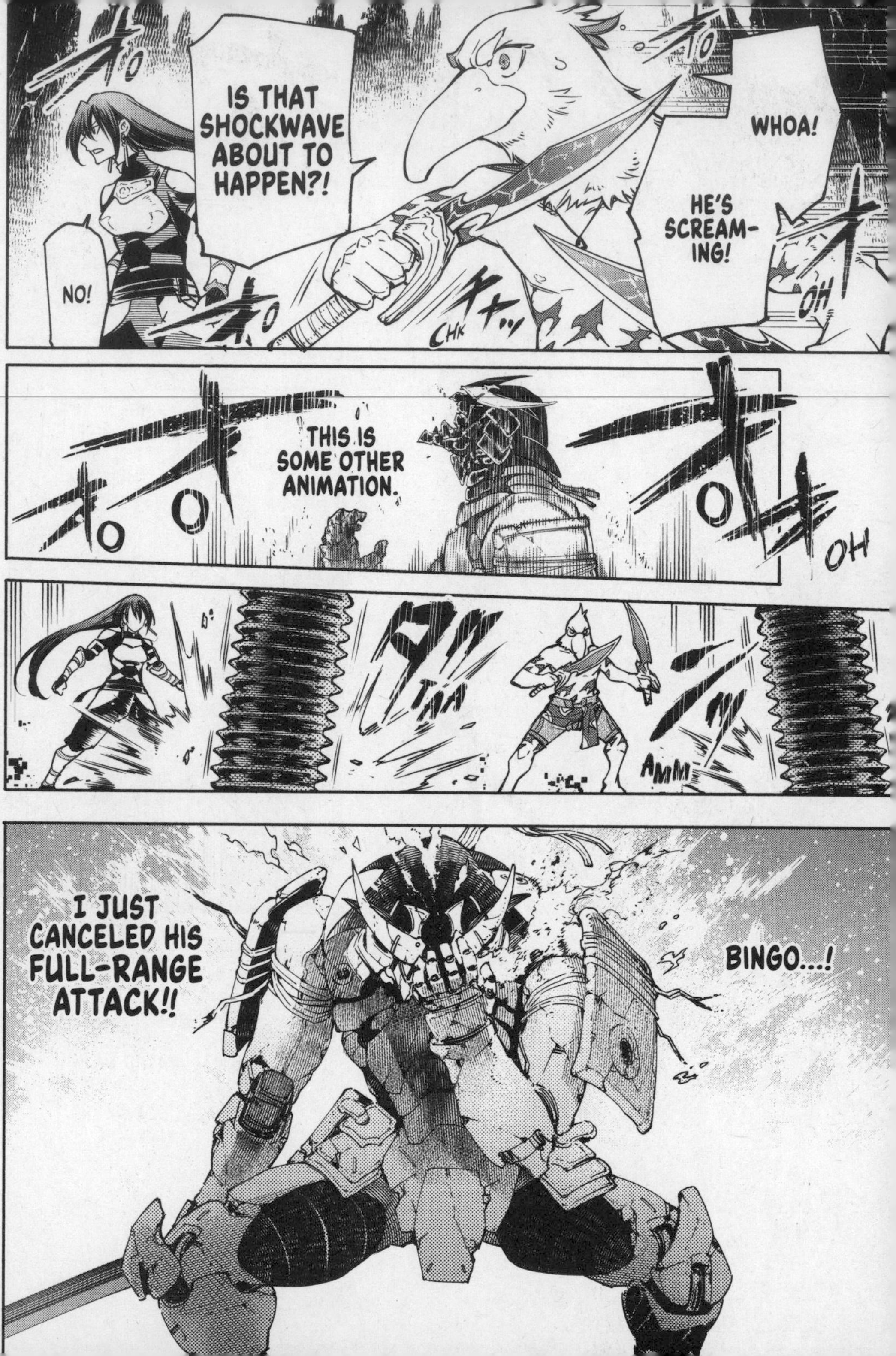
WHOA!
HE'S SCREAMING!
OH
IS THAT SHOCKWAVE ABOUT TO HAPPEN?!
CHK
NO!
OH
THIS IS SOME OTHER ANIMATION.
AMM
TAA
BINGO...!
I JUST CANCELED HIS FULL-RANGE ATTACK!!

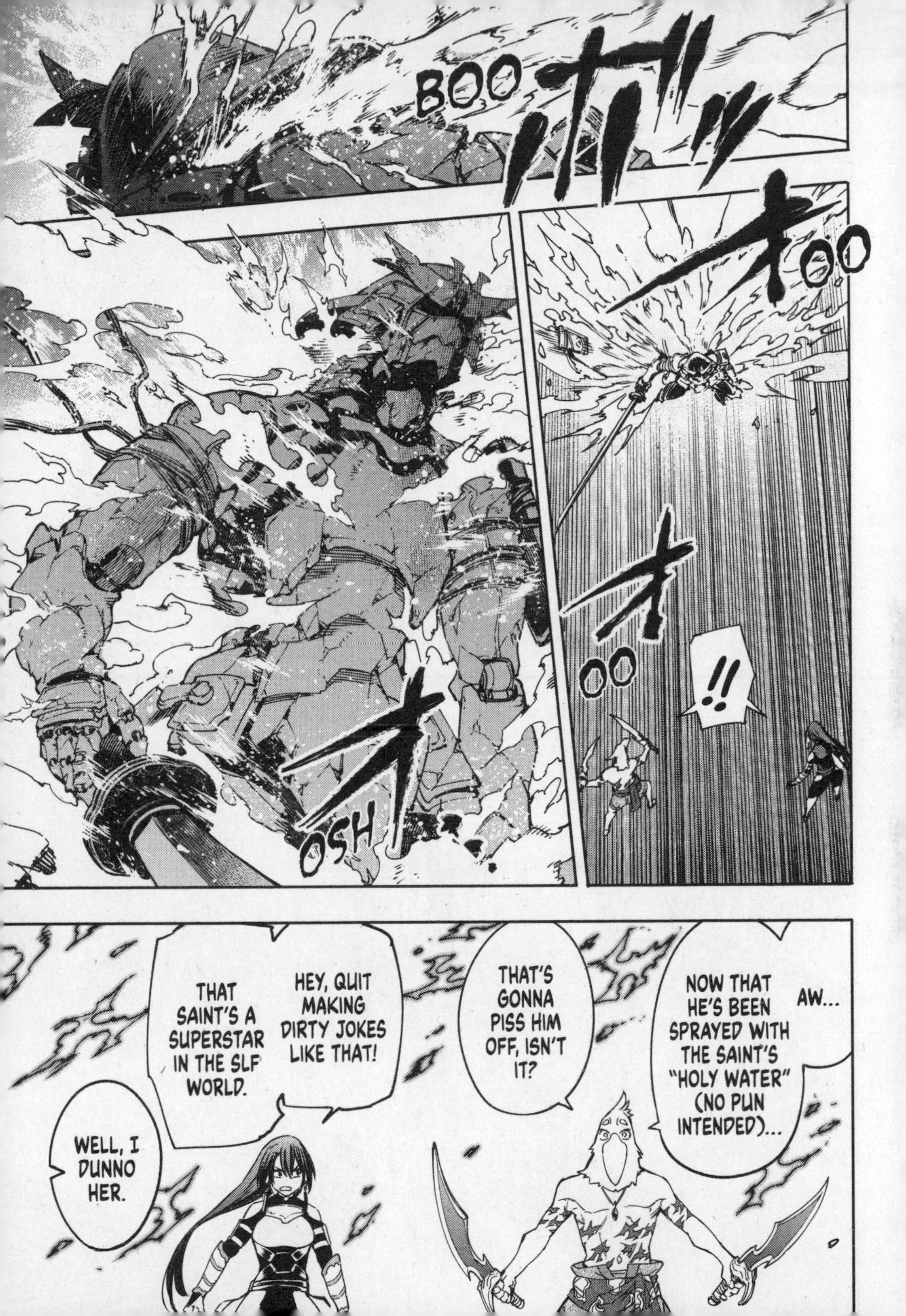
BOO
OO
OO
!!
OSH
AW...
NOW THAT HE'S BEEN SPRAYED WITH THE SAINT'S "HOLY WATER" (NO PUN INTENDED)...
THAT'S GONNA PISS HIM OFF, ISN'T IT?
HEY, QUIT MAKING DIRTY JOKES LIKE THAT!
THAT SAINT'S A SUPERSTAR IN THE SLF WORLD.
WELL, I DUNNO HER.

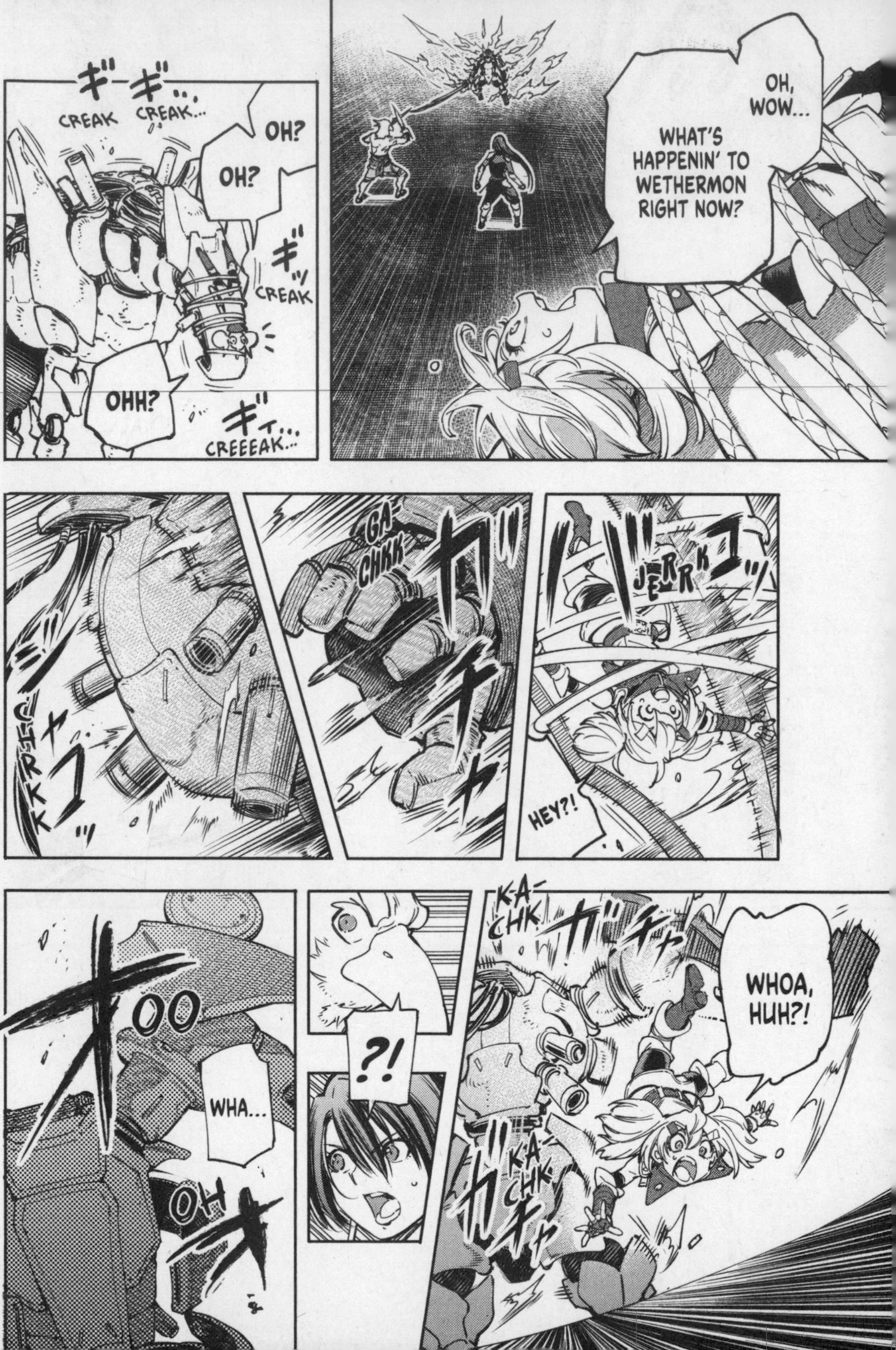
OH, WOW...
WHAT'S HAPPENIN' TO WETHERMON RIGHT NOW?
CREAK CREAK...
OH?
OH?
CREAK
OHH?
CREEEAK...
JERRK
HEY?!
GA CHKK
CHRKK
KA-CHK
WHOA, HUH?!
KA-CHK
?!
OO
WHA...
OH

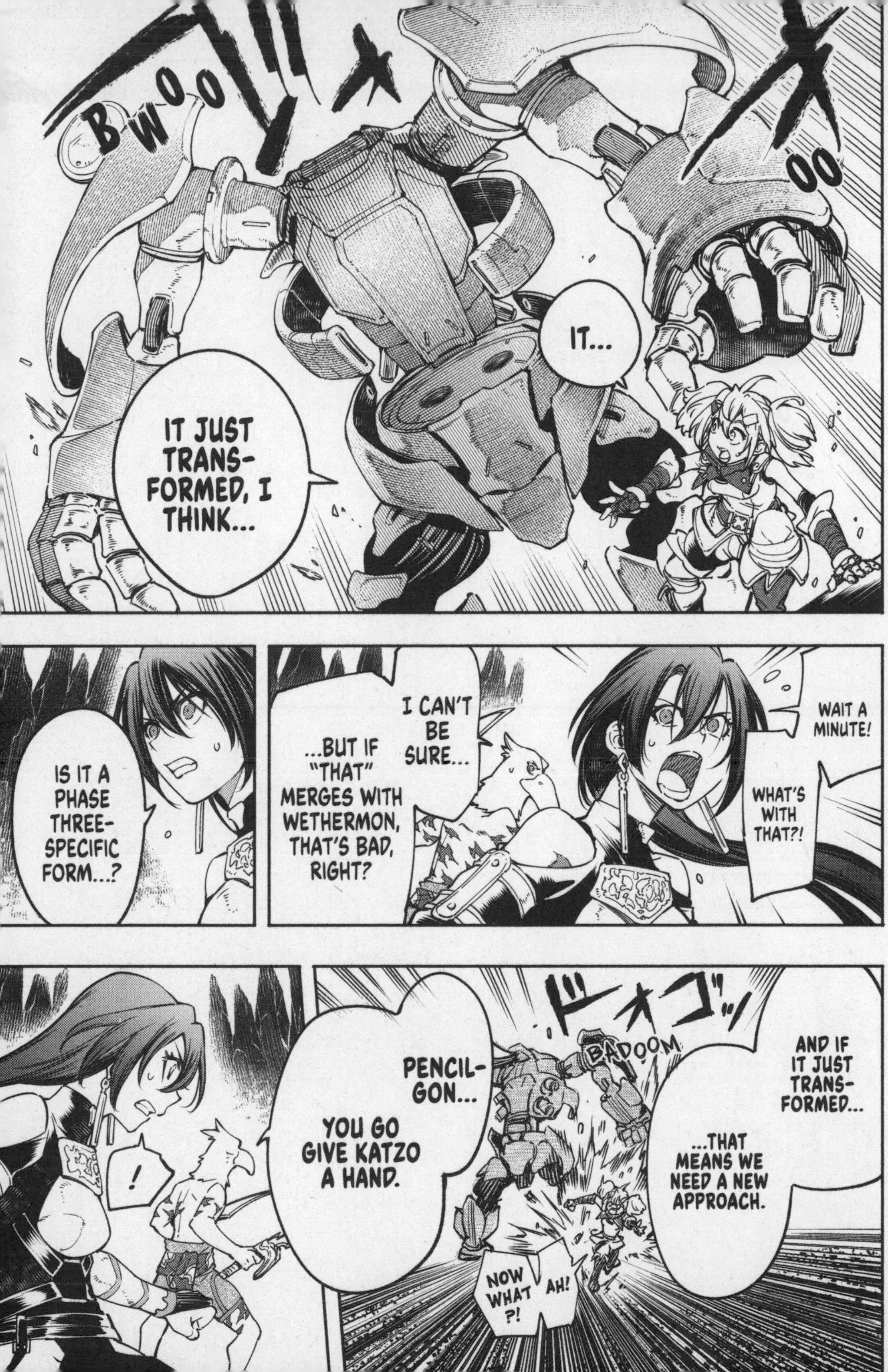
BWOOOO
IT...
IT JUST TRANS-FORMED, I THINK...
WAIT A MINUTE!
WHAT'S WITH THAT?!
I CAN'T BE SURE...
...BUT IF "THAT" MERGES WITH WETHERMON, THAT'S BAD, RIGHT?
IS IT A PHASE THREE-SPECIFIC FORM...?
ドオゴッ
BADOOM
AND IF IT JUST TRANS-FORMED...
...THAT MEANS WE NEED A NEW APPROACH.
AH!
NOW WHAT?!
PENCIL-GON...
YOU GO GIVE KATZO A HAND.
!

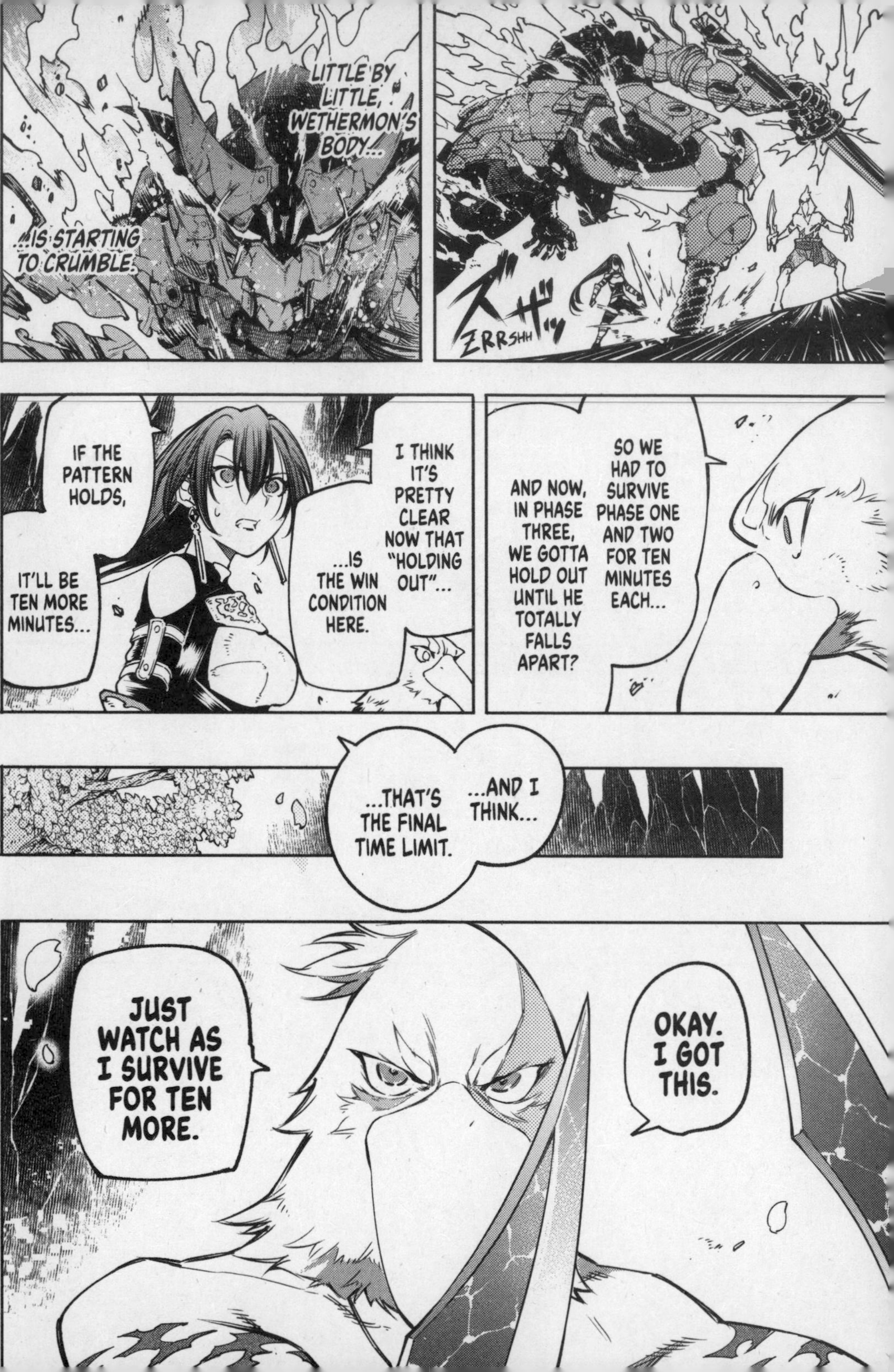
ZRRSHH
LITTLE BY LITTLE, WETHERMON'S BODY...
...IS STARTING TO CRUMBLE.
SO WE HAD TO SURVIVE PHASE ONE AND TWO FOR TEN MINUTES EACH...
AND NOW, IN PHASE THREE, WE GOTTA HOLD OUT UNTIL HE TOTALLY FALLS APART?
I THINK IT'S PRETTY CLEAR NOW THAT "HOLDING OUT"...
...IS THE WIN CONDITION HERE.
IF THE PATTERN HOLDS,
IT'LL BE TEN MORE MINUTES...
...AND I THINK...
...THAT'S THE FINAL TIME LIMIT.
OKAY. I GOT THIS.
JUST WATCH AS I SURVIVE FOR TEN MORE.

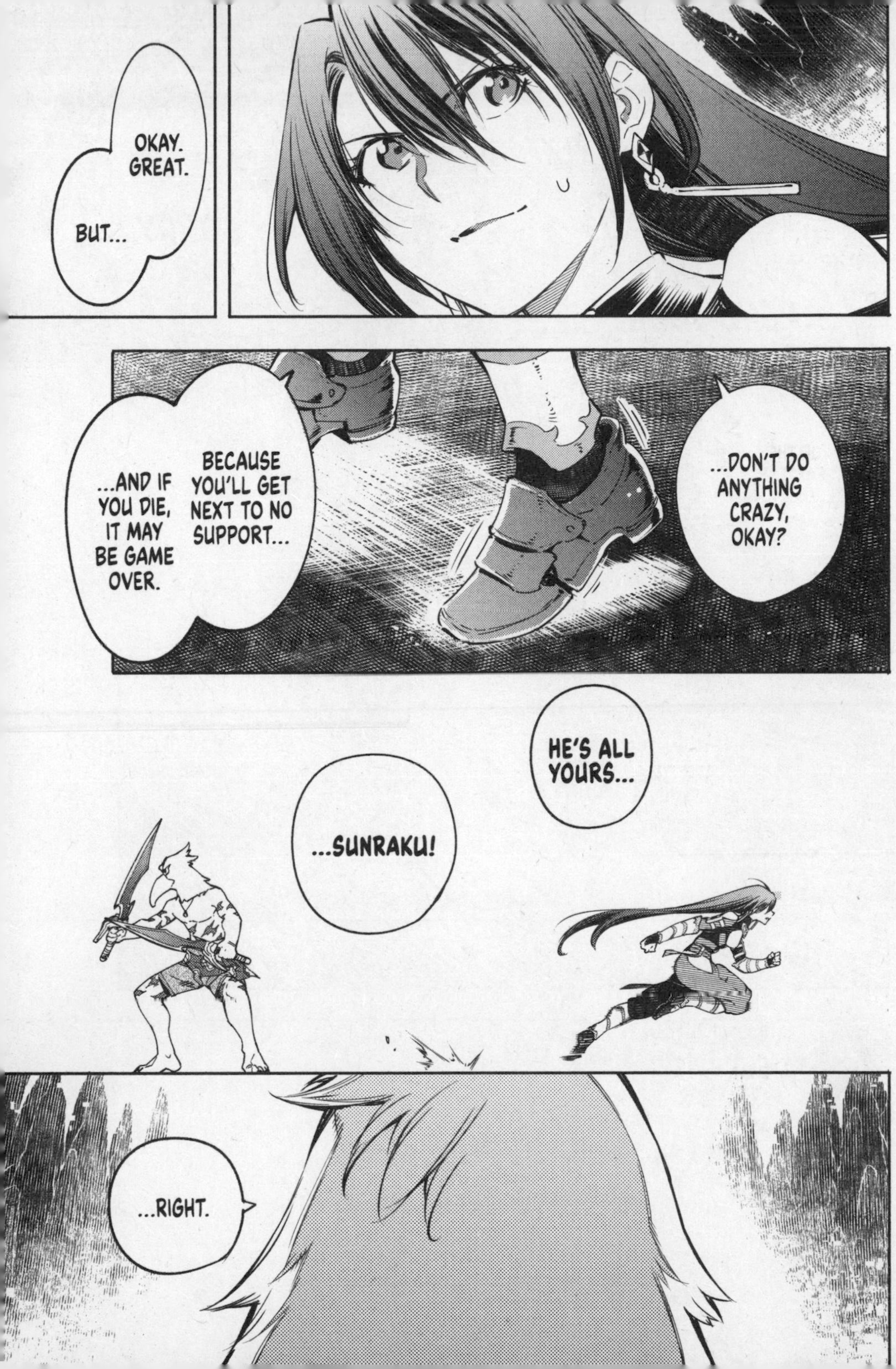
OKAY. GREAT.
BUT...
...DON'T DO ANYTHING CRAZY, OKAY?
BECAUSE YOU'LL GET NEXT TO NO SUPPORT...
...AND IF YOU DIE, IT MAY BE GAME OVER.
HE'S ALL YOURS...
...SUNRAKU!
...RIGHT.

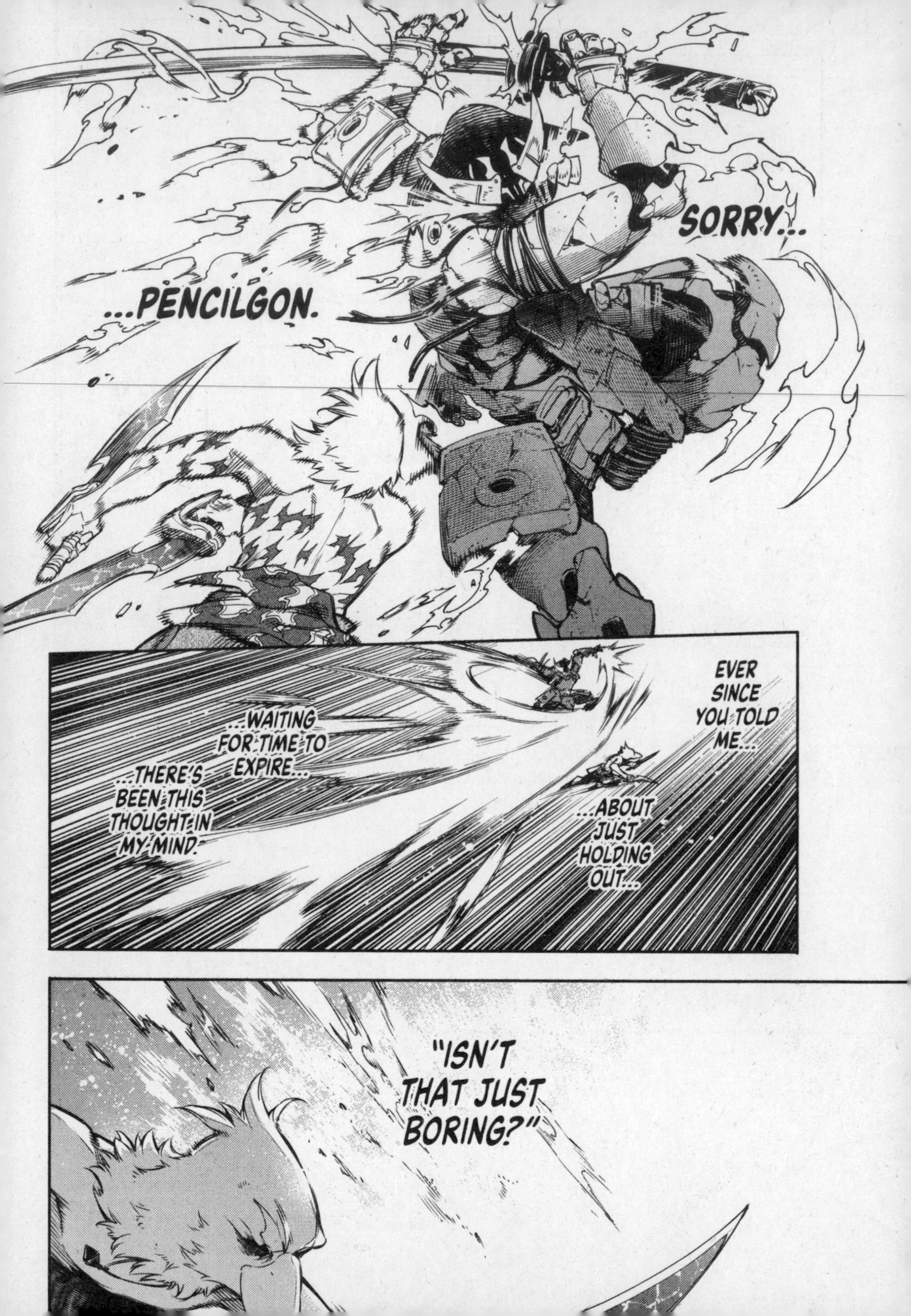
SORRY...
...PENCILGON.
EVER SINCE YOU TOLD ME...
...ABOUT JUST HOLDING OUT...
...WAITING FOR TIME TO EXPIRE...
...THERE'S BEEN THIS THOUGHT IN MY MIND.
"ISN'T THAT JUST BORING?"

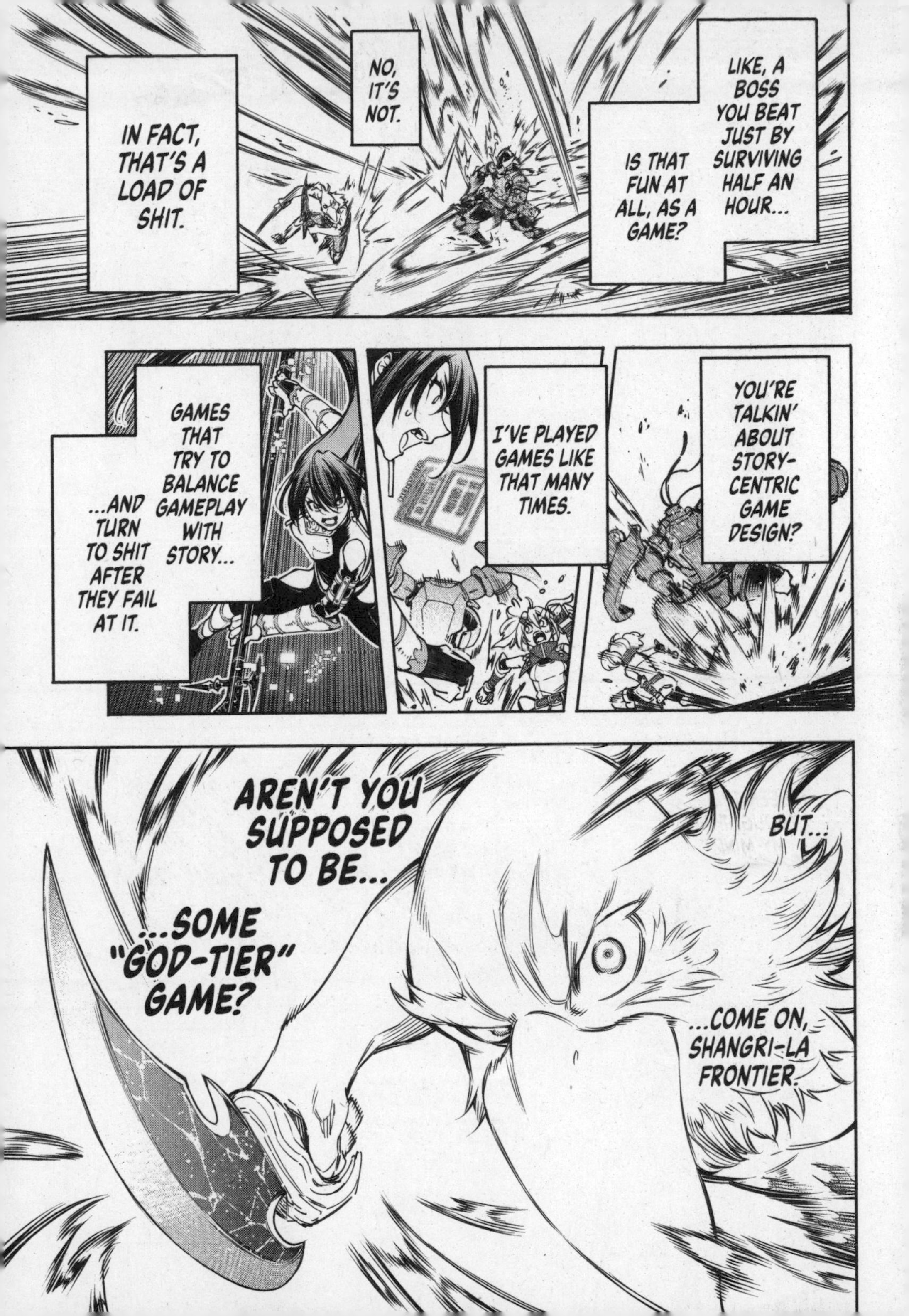
LIKE, A BOSS YOU BEAT JUST BY SURVIVING HALF AN HOUR...
IS THAT FUN AT ALL, AS A GAME?
NO, IT'S NOT.
IN FACT, THAT'S A LOAD OF SHIT.
YOU'RE TALKIN' ABOUT STORY-CENTRIC GAME DESIGN?
I'VE PLAYED GAMES LIKE THAT MANY TIMES.
GAMES THAT TRY TO BALANCE GAMEPLAY WITH STORY...
...AND TURN TO SHIT AFTER THEY FAIL AT IT.
BUT...
...COME ON, SHANGRI-LA FRONTIER.
AREN'T YOU SUPPOSED TO BE...
...SOME "GOD-TIER" GAME?

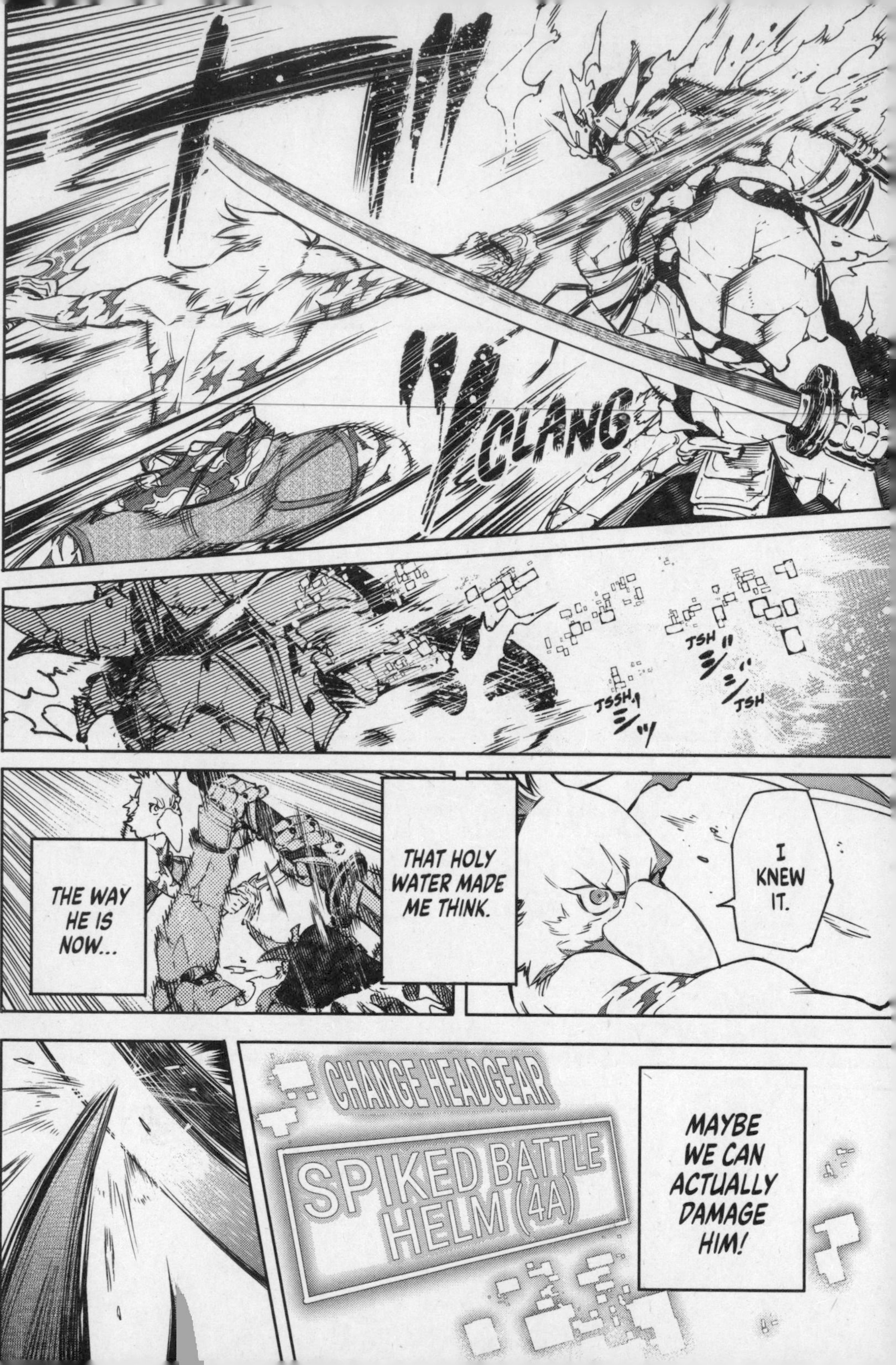
CLANG
JSH
JSH
JSSH
I KNEW IT.
THAT HOLY WATER MADE ME THINK.
THE WAY HE IS NOW...
CHANGE HEADGEAR
SPIKED BATTLE HELM (4A)
MAYBE WE CAN ACTUALLY DAMAGE HIM!

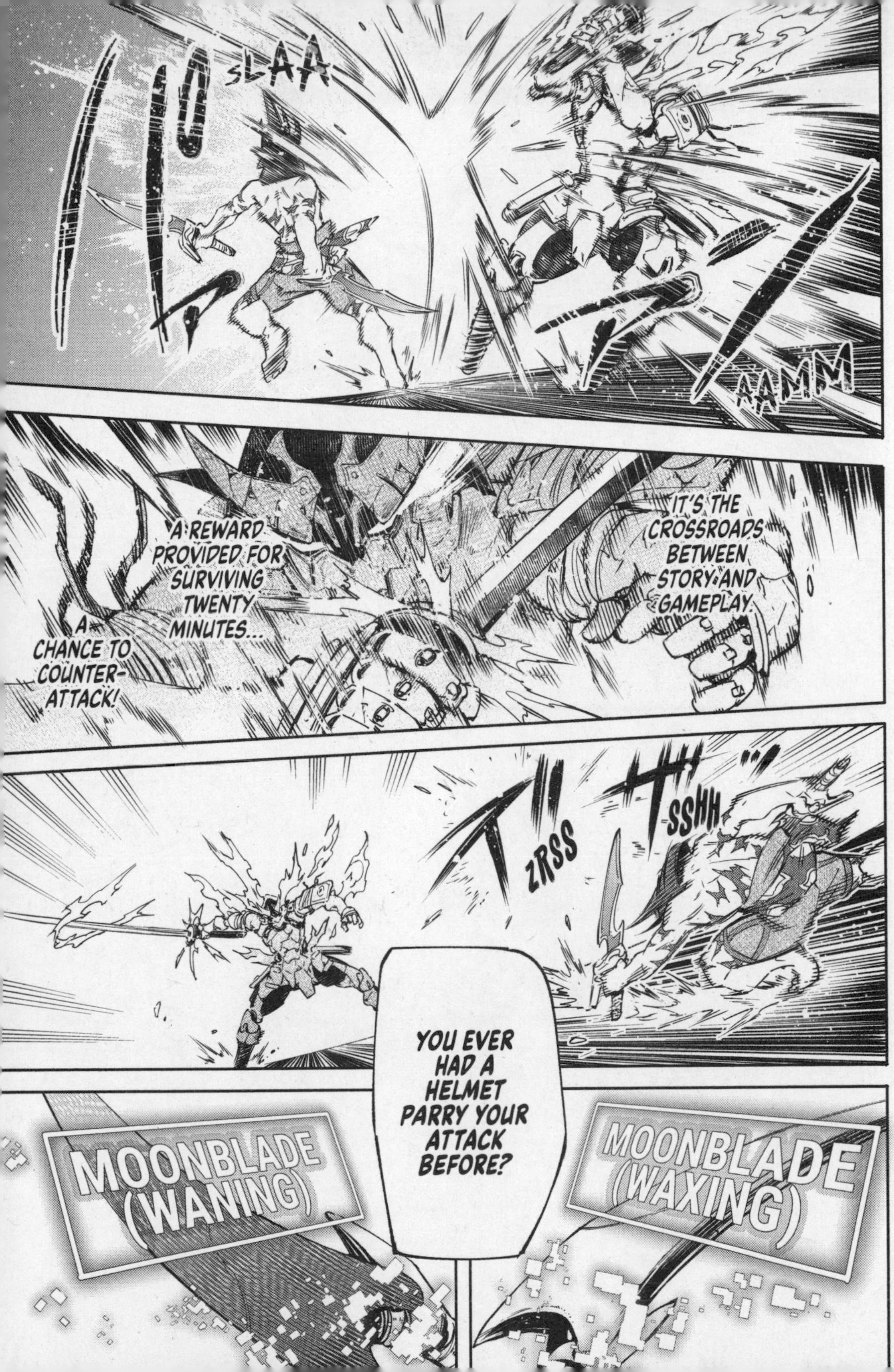
SLAA
AAMM
IT'S THE CROSSROADS BETWEEN STORY AND GAMEPLAY.
A REWARD PROVIDED FOR SURVIVING TWENTY MINUTES...
A CHANCE TO COUNTER-ATTACK!
SSHH
ZRSS
MOONBLADE (WAXING)
YOU EVER HAD A HELMET PARRY YOUR ATTACK BEFORE?
MOONBLADE (WANING)

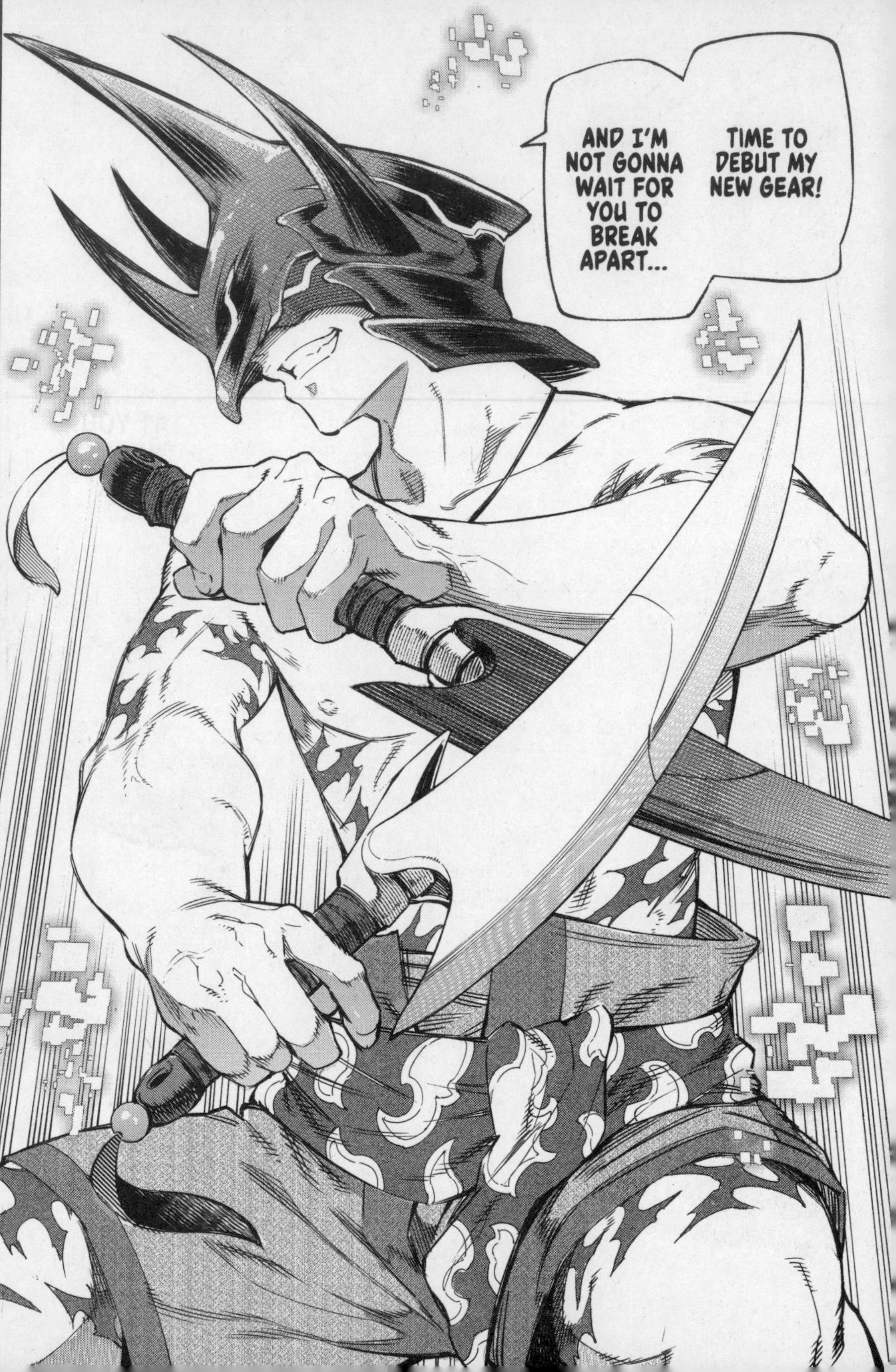
AND I'M NOT GONNA WAIT FOR YOU TO BREAK APART...
TIME TO DEBUT MY NEW GEAR!

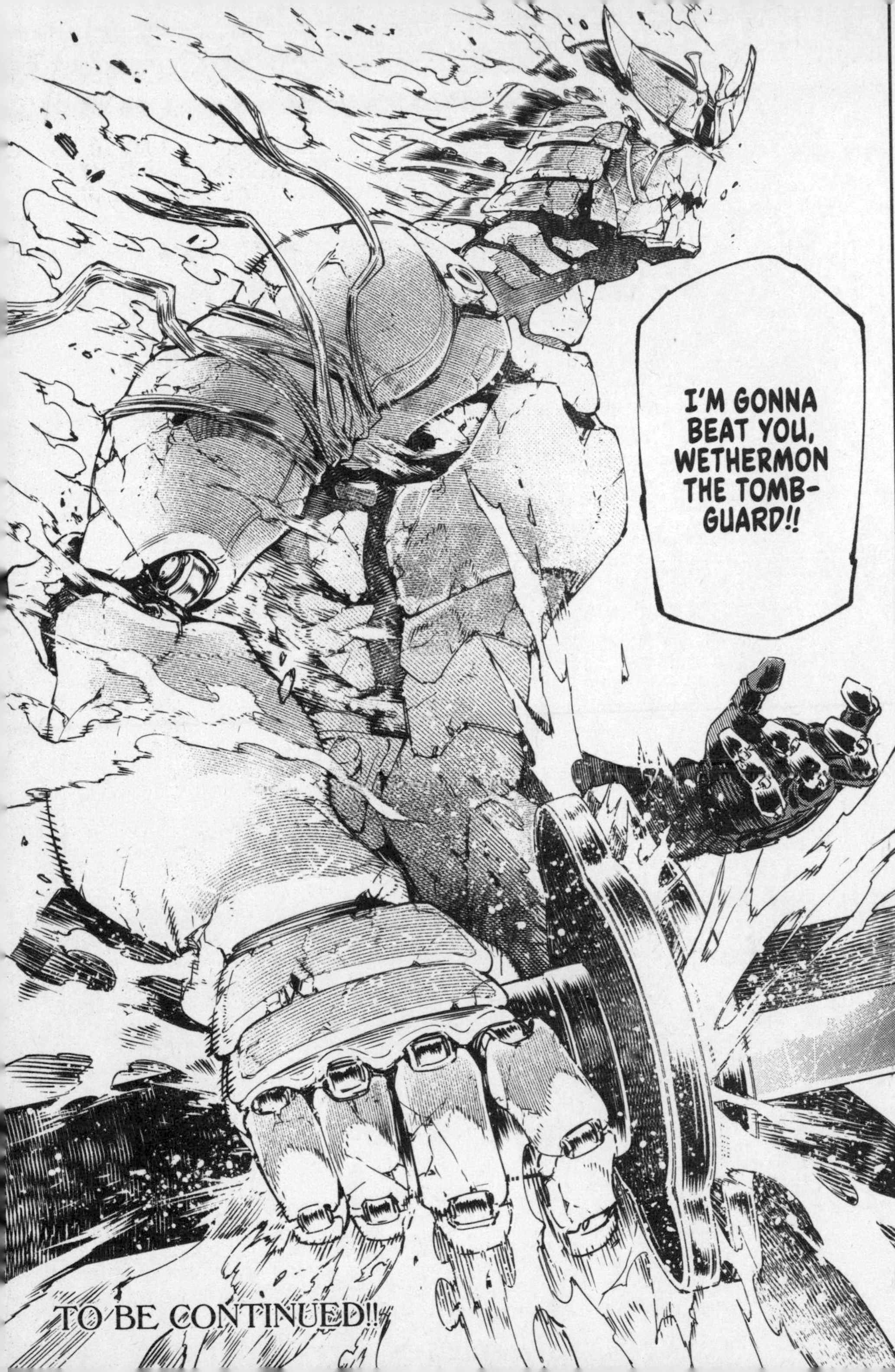
I'M GONNA BEAT YOU, WETHERMON THE TOMB-GUARD!!
TO BE CONTINUED!!

READ TO LEARN MORE ABOUT THE WORLD OF SLF!

SHANGRI-LA FRONTIER STRATEGY FORUM

VOL. 21

LET SLF MASTER REI-CHAN TAKE YOU THROUGH THE WORLD!

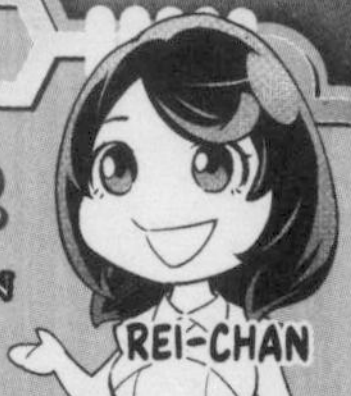
REI-CHAN

A MUST FOR YOUR ADVENTURES!

Shangri-La Item Intro Part 1

IN THE VAST WORLD OF SHANGRI-LA FRONTIER, YOU'LL FIND FOOD, MONSTER PARTS, ORE, AND MANY OTHER ITEMS. SOME HELP YOU IN YOUR ADVENTURE; OTHERS PROVIDE HINTS TO THE RIDDLES LURKING IN THE SLF WORLD. HERE ARE A FEW OF THEM!

1: USEFUL TO HAVE! HELPFUL ITEMS!

SAVE TENT

EFFECT

LETS YOU SAVE IN AREAS WITH MONSTERS. UP TO 10 USES.

DESCRIPTION

A QUICK SAVE-POINT ITEM THAT NOT EVEN SHANGRI-LA DIEHARDS CAN CORNER THE MARKET ON. MONSTERS STILL MAY ATTACK THEM SOMETIMES.

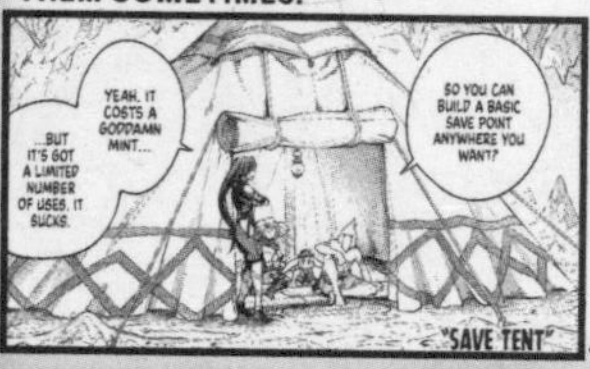
SO YOU CAN BUILD A BASIC SAVE POINT ANYWHERE YOU WANT?
YEAH, IT COSTS A GODDAMN MINT...
...BUT IT'S GOT A LIMITED NUMBER OF USES. IT SUCKS.
"SAVE TENT"

REBIRTH TEARJEWEL

EFFECT

IF A PLAYER REACHES 0 HP, USE WITHIN 10 SECONDS TO REVIVE AND FULLY HEAL THEM.

DESCRIPTION

ONE OF THE MOST EXPENSIVE CONSUMABLES, SOLD ON THE MARKET FOR 4 MILLION MAHNI.

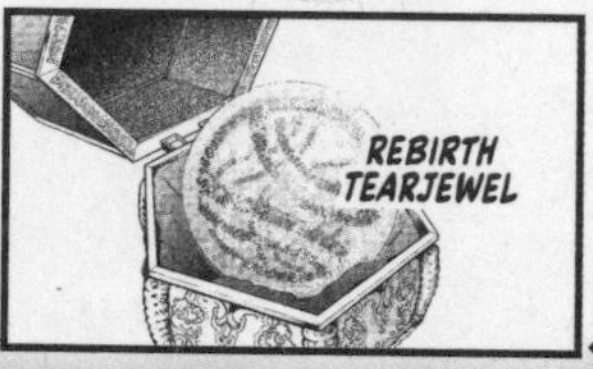
REBIRTH TEARJEWEL

SAINT'S HOLY WATER

EFFECT

STOPS MOST UNDEAD MONSTERS IN THEIR TRACKS, FORCING THEM INTO THE AFTERLIFE. PLAYERS DO NOT EARN EXPERIENCE POINTS.

DESCRIPTION

THE GREATEST OF UNDEAD POTIONS. CRAFTED BY ERISTELLA, THE "SAINT OF LOVE."

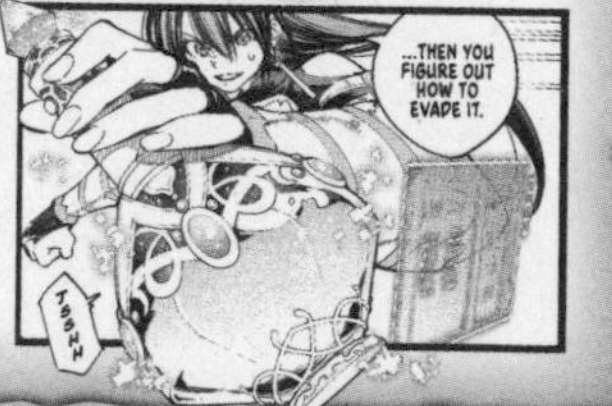
...THEN YOU FIGURE OUT HOW TO EVADE IT.
TSSHH

2: SUPER STRONG! UNIQUE ITEMS!

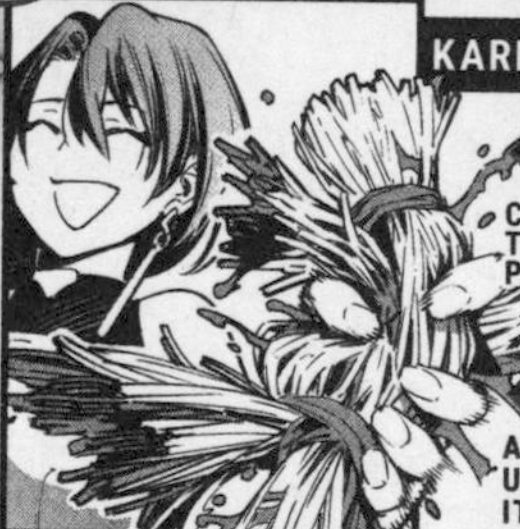

KARMIC STRAW DOLL

EFFECT

CRUSH IN YOUR HAND TO DEFLECT CURSES PLACED ON YOU.

DESCRIPTION

A CONSUMABLE UNIQUE ITEM. GIVEN ITS POWER, THE DOLL CAN DEFLECT A MAXIMUM OF FIVE DEBUFFS. TRYING TO REVEAL THE "ESSENCE" INSIDE OF IT KILLS YOU.

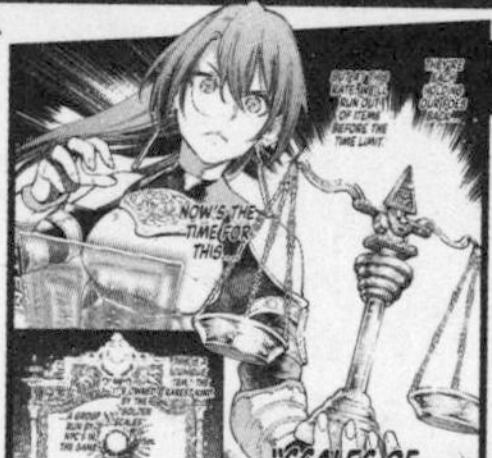
NOW'S THE TIME FOR THIS!!
"SCALES OF COMPENSATION"

SCALES OF COMPENSATION

EFFECT

PUT AN ITEM ON THE "OFFERING DISH ON THE LEFT" AND "BLESSING DISH ON THE RIGHT" AND YOU'LL RECEIVE A COMMENSURATE REWARD ON THE "BLESSING DISH." CAN GIVE YOU ONE STATUS POINT FOR EVERY 100,000 MAHNI YOU OFFER. "BLESSINGS" CAN BE ASSIGNED TO OTHER PLAYERS.

DESCRIPTION

A UNIQUE ITEM OWNED BY THE GOLDEN SCALES NPC GROUP. AS A TOP-CLASS UNIQUE, ITS EFFECTS TAKE PRECEDENT OVER THE ANTI-BUFF EFFECTS OF LYCAON'S MARK.

The Shit-Game Hunter's Early Morning   BY KATARINA

The shit-game hunter wakes up early.

In my case, I was up at four in the morning, before the sun rose, and nimbly changing into the T-shirt and shorts I had prepared in advance.

"Right... Let's go."

I was headed west—toward the site of something I had been constantly seeking. It was...

"Just you wait, *Sushi Chef of the Dead: Premium Sushi Debut Edition*! I'm comin' for you!!!"

...A shit game.

◆

There's a certain phenomenon known in the business as "sell and dash."

Generally, in the game industry, it's common to see a release go on sale, followed by a steady stream of updates, bugfixes, or additional content. It's not a matter of selling an incomplete game; in most cases, it's just the developer cutting the project length before the sale date to reduce the burden on everyone involved, or attracting new users (or bringing back lapsed ones) with extra content. Of course, sometimes games get released with so many bugs and glitches that you wonder if they even bothered debugging them before release, but...well, accidents happen.

The classic "sell and dash" in gaming involves releasing a title, then going completely hands-off with it—no updates, no bugfixes, no extra content. Most full-dive VR games have online features, but you still see that dynamic. No real fixes, no updates, previously-announced DLC turning into vaporware... Sadly, there are still a few game makers who take a "not my problem anymore" approach.

Either way, the "sell and dash" mentality is a common tactic among game publishers. The practice is akin to giving birth to a baby and then not bothering to take care of it at all.

Sushi Chef of the Dead, my current target, is one of those abandoned babies. It was developed and released, but the labor conditions must've been pretty shit, because the staff went on strike and the upper management fled the company and went into hiding. (Reportedly this was due to excessive unpaid overtime, as well as people not being paid at all—a one-two punch of awfulness.)

So thanks to the company breaking apart, only the game exists. It's a sad story, but one that's irrelevant to my purpose. What I'm looking for right now is the *Premium Sushi Debut Edition*. There are tons of out-of-print shit games, but the special edition of *Sushi Chef of the Dead* not only features the original game that self-destructed out of the gate in such a dramatic fashion; it includes a limited edition cutting board with the logo of the company etched into it, as if it were a shield of victory. Owning it would let you lord it over all the other trash game aficionados out there. In a way, it's an even more cruel way to deride the game, besides just ripping on the gameplay itself.

"I can't believe they have an unopened special edition... I should've known better than to doubt that shit game shop."

The unopened copies of *Sushi Chef of the Dead: Premium Sushi Debut Edition* were reportedly discovered at a certain game store, a veritable dodo munching on bread in the middle of a flock of sparrows.

"The first train of the day's in another twenty minutes. Gotta find a way to kill time..."

This living fossil was found at Masquerade, a game store in Tottori Prefecture, in the rural southwestern side of Japan. People in the crap game scene call it a "holy land," or a "place of restful sanctuary." The kinds of games that usually take up discount bins elsewhere are carefully lined on the shelves here—and if you can't find what you want there, ask the manager and he'll supposedly take out anything you want from storage, no matter how obscure.

"Mint special editions...and if that post was true, they have ten in stock... There's already a bloodstorm forming among western Japan's kusoge gamers..."

Good games often go for a premium on the collector's market because they're, well, worth it. Shitty games, on the other hand, go for big bucks chiefly because they're absolutely impossible to find. When word leaks out about this discovery, will the trash game collectors of the nation manage to retain their sanity? Not a chance.

"Well, it's almost time. Let's get going."

◆

In Tottori Prefecture, about fifteen minutes by foot from the station, after a one-hour journey by train, quietly stood the game store.

"So this is Masquerade..."

The restful sanctuary for shit. A place on the lips of any crap game fan. This didn't exactly sound like high praise, admittedly. But…how to put it? It was smaller than I imagined. It was easy to imagine a place like this being run entirely by one person.

"Half an hour until opening? Guess I'll line up—"

"Hold it, kid."

"Huh?"

Out of nowhere, this man on the street started talking to me like I was an RPG protagonist.

"You here looking for the unopened *Sushi Chef of the Dead Special Edition*?"

"Y-Yeah…um…"

"Well, me too. But by the looks of things, you don't know how things work at Masquerade."

The man, who must've been here for the same reason I was, pointed toward the shuttered store. At the entrance I could see a robot, looking a bit like those inflatable punching bags, standing in the way.

"Masquerade bans people from lining up at the door until five minutes before opening. That droid's on the lookout for that."

What kind of rule was that? And why was a game store requiring this RPG-style subquest to get in? And why did people accept this?? No answers seemed to be forthcoming, but this guy (I still had no idea who he was) kept on talking.

"So… Well, take a look around you."

Hmm…?

Looking where the man pointed, I found…a woman standing in the shade of a light pole, a sweet roll in her mouth. No way.

I recalled the words of the elderly lady seated next to me on the train here.

"Hee hee hee! Well, I hope you manage to find what you're looking for!"

"Yeah, well, it's first come, first served, so it'll kind of be a competition."

"Ah! In that case, you'll need to expend every effort you can! What you need the most…"

"What I need the most?"

"…is power."

Ma'am, I think it's gonna be a tougher battle than I thought.

Six minutes to open.

Already, there were more people mulling around the Masquerade game store than available hiding places. None of them approached the entrance, eyes trained on the store from a prudent distance. Seeing this, I began to wonder just what I had gotten myself into.

"Umm... If I could ask, there isn't gonna be bloodshed over this, is there?"

"Of course not. If people started shedding blood, they'd have to go to the hospital before they could buy the game."

Right. Yeah. That was obvious.

Again, what the hell was I doing here? The tension in me began to rise. I was only here to purchase a special edition, so what was with this giant game of Red Light, Green Light? Did the mad scramble have to be quite this mad?

The more I thought about it, the more common sense began to dull my mind. My sensible side sounded an alarm bell, asking if it was really right to dive into this. Whether you can buy it or not, wasn't it saner to just have people line up? ...Oh, it was five minutes, five seconds to open.

"Whoa! What the hell?! My digital timer bugged out! It skipped thirty seconds!"

"?!"

"Gotcha!"

Everyone on hand looked down at their devices, scowling. The moment they did, I unleashed all of my charged power and made a dash for the door. The unknown stranger gave me a stupefied look. I decided to give him a choice quote from Pencil Knight:

"No matter what your strategy, victory always justifies it!"

I was passed by a guy in business attire who started from a track-and-field crouch, but Masquerade was still dead ahead—and I needed to at least be tenth to arrive!

"Just you wait, zombie sashimi!"

Then I could see it. Beyond the transparent automatic door, the middle-aged man on the shop floor, grinning in glee at all of us. And if I could sum up the feelings of everyone there:

How could you be so tacky?!

That night:

"Hey, I'm back..."
"Hey there, big bro. What'd you buy?"